HOPE

BY MARIAN FOWLER

The Embroidered Tent: Five Gentlewomen in Early Canada
Redney: A Life of Sara Jeannette Duncan
Below the Peacock Fan: First Ladies of the Raj
Blenheim: Biography of a Palace
In a Gilded Cage: American Heiresses Who Married
British Aristocrats
The Way She Looks Tonight: Five Women of Style
Hope: Adventures of a Diamond

HOPE

ADVENTURES OF A DIAMOND

Marian Fowler

BALLANTINE BOOKS • NEW YORK

A Ballantine Book
Published by The Ballantine Publishing Group
Copyright © 2002 by Marian Fowler

www.ballantinebooks.com

A Library of Congress card number
is available from the publisher upon request.

ISBN 0-345-44486-8

Text design Mary A. Wirth

Manufactured in the United States of America

First Edition: April 2002

10 9 8 7 6 5 4 3 2

For my diamond-wearing friends
Diana, Mary, Norma, and Phyllis,
with a special nod to Leslea and Madeline
whose stones inspire

Intrinsically, material objects have in themselves no power,
but . . . it is our practice to bestow power upon them.

I had realized before now that it is only a clumsy and erroneous form
of perception which places everything in the object, when really everything
is in the mind.

—MARCEL PROUST, *In Search of Lost Time*, vol. VI, *Time Regained*

CONTENTS

CONTENTS

TO THE READER

Here and there in the Diamond's story, biographical details are impossible to come by. Where these small black holes occur, I have either skipped quickly over them or suggested some likely scenarios, but I have always conscientiously kept the reader informed of where historical fact ends and speculation begins. In the well-documented parts of the Diamond's life, I sometimes posit dates, which I believe are the true ones, but which differ slightly from those given by the gem's previous chroniclers, most of whom were geologists or gemologists, who focused more on scientific than biographical accuracy.

The Hope Diamond in its present-day necklace setting.

AUTHOR'S NOTE

In October 2000, I sat on board a plane about to land at Washington's Ronald Reagan National Airport. As I looked below, where blue waters fingered the land, my feelings were contrary and confused. I wanted so much to meet my protagonist face-to-face for the very first time; I wanted just as strongly not to meet the Hope Diamond. At that point, I had almost completed my research for this biography and had already written the first half. I must be prepared, I told myself, to be disappointed when I actually behold this small object. It couldn't possibly live up to the one shining for so many months in my imagination.

Next morning, in crisp autumn air, I mounted the four shallow steps of the Smithsonian's National Museum of Natural History, rose slowly in a decorous brass-bound elevator to the second floor, and entered the Harry Winston Gallery, where the Diamond has a room all to itself. It was so early in the day that I was the only visitor in the room.

With great trepidation I approached the Hope's sealed, glass-sided, bronze-cornered square vault. There it was, rotating slowly, stopping to show itself at each of the four glass sides before moving on: as democratic as its adopted republic, with equal time for all. Round and slowly round it went.

I moved closer and stood transfixed, rooted to the spot. The Hope Diamond draws the eye and mind, holds them rapt and dreaming, and will not let them go. It pulses with the same energy that burst from the great heaving heart of planet Earth more than a billion years ago, when this gem was created. I wanted to stand before it for a week, a month, letting myself be hypnotized by that big, blue, old, wise, un-blinking, all-seeing eye.

The shade of blue rattled my senses. One can try for comparisons: a kingfisher's wing as it flies to its nighttime roost; ocean at its deepest; sky just before night; morning glories, just before dawn. But the color, in the final analysis, is just itself, as unique as everything else about the Diamond. It is the only object in the entire world of this particular blue.

I was in Washington for six days only on that October trip, and I had manifold research tasks in the Library of Congress. Each morning as I opened one eye to see bright sky beyond my hotel window, I had the same compulsion . . . I must arise and go now to the Diamond; I must engage it, eye to eye. I found myself envying every previous owner who could commune with it whenever the siren call was felt. I was bewitched; I was Hope-lessly in love as if, like Shakespeare's Tita-nia in *A Midsummer Night's Dream*, I'd drunk a love potion to the dregs. I who possessed no diamonds and no desire for any—with one exception—adored this little midsummer's night.

Of course, one no longer believes, at the beginning of the twenty-first century, that diamonds possess the human touch ascribed to them in old lapidaries. "They grow together, male and female," wrote the traveler Sir John Mandeville in 1520, "and are nourished by the dew of heaven; and they engender commonly and bring forth small children that multiply and grow all year." Yet gemologists today speak of the "faces" of a diamond, and call the most characteristic arrangement of them into an octahedron the stone's natural "habit." Gem experts say a diamond "plays" with light and call the amount reflected from both surface and interior its "life." Somewhere in our collective uncon-scious, perhaps we still wish the Hope and its fellows were sentient.

They are certainly potent. The Diamond's awesome power had al-ready changed my life, as it had changed so many, sending me on a long, hard quest, searching in archives and libraries, uncovering the adventures described in the chapters that follow. These include perilous ocean crossings—and some brown-paper trips by parcel post; brutal cuts and amputations; strange new settings and rooms and countries; the splendor in the glass of four thousand candles at Versailles dancing in the Hall of Mirrors; many other triumphs and trials.

Some owners suffered astonishingly bad luck; one died a very slow, horribly painful death; another quite literally lost his head; a third lost a young son to a car accident, a daughter to suicide and a husband to an insane asylum. Is some of the power of this jewel, paradoxically called Hope, malevolent? Does the stone embody a curse, as so many people down the years have believed? In the pages beyond, we'll trace the curse's evolution carefully and untangle myth from fact.

Much of the Hope's power is invested in it by humans. "Certain people, whose minds are prone to mystery, like to believe that objects retain something of the eyes that have looked at them," writes Marcel Proust in *Time Regained*, that such objects "appear to us not as they originally were but beneath a perceptible veil woven for them over the centuries by the love and contemplation of millions of admirers." So it is with the Diamond, whose shining orb holds thousands of human aspirations in its depths, for each owner embraced and employed it differently, depending on character and cultural context. They all—at least initially—believed in the gem's ability to improve their lot, to take them from mere fancy to fulfillment, whether their goals were magical, spiritual, financial, political, or social.

There in the Harry Winston Gallery I was still immobilized before the Diamond, but the room was now full of people, all of them peering and pushing, trying for an unobstructed view of this fabled jewel. A quarter turn to strange faces filling the glass; full stop; another quarter turn. Like a different kind of rock star, the Diamond is now captive to its own celebrity. If only it could talk, could tell its own tale, reveal its secrets, solve its many mysteries! The stone takes refuge, as it always has, in proud, self-contained silence. But it can, as it always has, do with consummate brilliance what it does best: it can reflect. . . .

Siva as Nataraja. Bronze sculpture of the eleventh century.

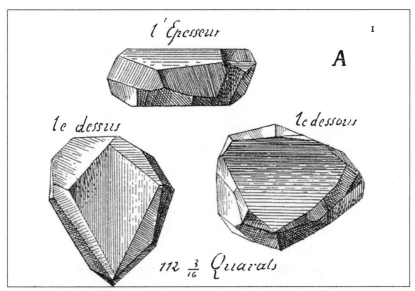

The first extant drawing of the Diamond, c. 1676.

1

NATURE

Framed in the prodigality of nature.
—WILLIAM SHAKESPEARE, *Richard III*, act 1, scene 2

Around the Diamond, as provocative as a woman's perfume, as protective as a force field, there has always been mystery. It was present at the very beginning to hide the jewel's conception and swaddle its birth.

After five hundred years of studying diamonds, geologists can make informed speculations but still can't determine the exact details of their genesis. The one in this story has proved more intractable than most, for it contains none of the inclusions of other mineral crystals that would help to determine its age. Like a great many beauties, our protagonist guards the secret of how old it is—as well it might, since it is far older than those primitive forms of life that first crawled on the ocean's floor. The amazing truth is that the Diamond, much more beautiful now than in its early years and still utterly desirable, is—don't shout it from the rooftops but whisper it discreetly—between one and three billion years old. It was conceived when Earth itself was still a hot young planet, when time had no past tense.

If we can't fix the date of its creation except vaguely, give or take a billion years, we do know the place. The Diamond formed in the southern, peninsular part of India, which is now bounded on both seacoasts by ranges of hills (the Western and Eastern Ghats) and is known as the Deccan plateau. Its four-billion-year-old spine makes it India's oldest part. The gem originated about 120 miles below the Deccan plains, not in the Earth's crust, which is only about 25 miles thick, but in the fiery caldron of the mantle beneath, which goes down 1,750 miles.

The upper mantle was incredibly hot and turbulent, where gases roared and reservoirs of molten rock rippled and heaved. Nothing in the Diamond's future would be half so cataclysmic as its beginnings. Its creation required what geologists call "a special melting event" with a heat between 1300 and 4500 degrees Fahrenheit to liquefy the dark, heavy rock called peridotite, combined with a pressure somewhere between 0.5 and 1.3 million pounds per square inch.

There in that tremendous heat and pressure, in one of the great cosmic coincidences that, thus far in human history, has yielded man only forty tons of diamonds, crystallization began. Like every crystal, be it snowflake or gemstone, this one would be unique, its own self, as different from other diamonds as one human is from another.

The growing process was probably quite gradual, for the larger the crystal, the slower its formation must be. While the Diamond was getting bigger, the great pressure of the carbon dioxide gas below the layer of slowly cooling molten peridotite containing it had to remain equal to the pressure of the layers of rock above. Although it was the rarest prize in nature, it was made of the most ordinary matter, namely, carbon. This exists in our own bodies, in the clothes we wear, the food we eat, the fuels we burn: wood, coal, oil, gasoline. One might say that the Diamond then coming into being was both high class and low, aristocrat and commoner. The magic was in the making.

Eighteen atoms of carbon darted together into a minute cube, an isometric cell, a diamond's basic building block. The cubes in turn multiplied into a regular latticework. The shape evolving basically conformed to the one diamonds prefer, an octahedron, which looks like two pyramids joined base to base. The Diamond's cubic structure was probably taking on the contours to be seen in the first extant drawing we have of it, done in the seventeenth century. This shows a rough stone that, if held with its broader end as base, resembled a giant teardrop; if reversed, it looked like a heart; it could, therefore, depending on a viewer's sensibility, accommodate itself to tragedy or romantic comedy.

While crystallization was still taking place, there were three distinct miracles. The first one involved color. While some diamonds are being created, an atom of another element may take the place of a carbon one. In this Diamond's coalescing atoms, there was an atom of boron for every million of carbon. Once the gem had reached light and received its first polish—and that was a long way off—it was the boron that would make it blue. With the exception of red, blue is the rarest of all colors for a diamond. Depending on the nature of its alien atoms—for a fine stone, there must be no more than one foreign part for every hundred thousand of carbon—a diamond may also be green, yellow, pink (the highly valued hues) or brown, gray, or black. Most blues are light in color and less than 2 carats. The Diamond then forming in that hot, heaving womb would be the biggest dark blue ever found.

The second miracle concerned matter. If the pressures had been lower, carbon atoms might have stacked themselves in flat six-sided sheets, with the bonds between the layers so weak that they could easily slide over each other; the resulting dull mineral would have been graphite, from which pencils are made.

Hardness was the third miracle. It is the strength of a crystal's bonds that determines this, and a diamond's are the strongest in the world, giving it the highest point, 10, on Mohs' scale of hardness now used in mineralogy, where graphite gets 1.5. Diamonds are eighty-five times harder than the next gems on the scale, rubies and sapphires, and can only be scratched by their own kind. However, the Diamond was not invulnerable, as we shall see later.

At last the stone's long gestation came to an end, and its creation was complete. It weighed at least 110.5 metric carats, and was nature's absolute kernel of energy and beauty, of her striving, driving, pounding life force, compressed to firmest, clearest compass. It was

Creation's brightest thought. However, until man came to its rescue and revealed its beauty, it would wear a disfiguring, slightly shiny, greasy gray caul.

Somewhere between one billion and five hundred million years ago, the stone's passage from darkness to light, from womb to world, began. It would be a long and perilous journey, for the Diamond had to pass unharmed up through almost a hundred miles of mantle, then twenty-five miles of crust. While the first stages were probably gentle enough, with the gemstone moving upward an inch or two a year, eventually it accelerated to the speed of a rocket. During this wild, jolting ride, it was in great danger, for it could have shattered at any moment. This was no easy delivery. En route, the pressures of the molten rock around the gem cracked the surrounding rocks, so that bits of other minerals joined the thrust and push; most probably spinel and garnet, bloodred as the magma itself, were among them.

When the mother rock that had held the Diamond for so long hit the Earth's surface, along with trapped gases, it exploded with the force of a volcano, the fizz and roar of a million champagne corks, and a dense shower of ash and rock fragments.

After the shock of this explosion, the Diamond was still imprisoned in its red-hot surrounding rock, which didn't flow out and down like lava but instead, due to the pressure of ascending magma, merely bulged upward on the Earth's surface, then collapsed at the center once the gases had escaped. This mother rock in which all diamonds originate wouldn't acquire a name until 1870, when they were first found in abundance in South Africa near the town of Kimberley: the rock was named kimberlite. It is an altered and broken form of peridotite, blue-green in color due to its iron content, consisting mainly of the minerals pyroxene and olivine. In the crater resulting from the explosion, the kimberlite cooled and hardened into a deposit measuring between a few hundred yards and a mile wide, with the Diamond still somewhere inside it. Beneath the surface, the rock became a vertical "pipe" with kimberlite's typical carrot shape, broad at the top, then narrowing as it goes deeper into the Earth.

Millions of years passed while the big, shiny gray stone waited to be released. The top of the kimberlite cone gradually grew more concave and began to crack and crumble, owing to the then prevailing violent extremes of heat and cold. The north polar ice sheet crept as far south as the Himalayan mountains several times; in these glacial periods, the Deccan area didn't freeze but was flooded with torrential rains.

Being much stronger and harder than the kimberlite around it, the Diamond stood firm, while the mother rock grew pale, turning from blue-green to yellow, cracking and crumbling. Then came the day when the rock released the gemstone and the Diamond was freed into a rushing, muddy torrent of water, yellow rock fragments, and other pebbles.

It began its second journey, and this was not like its dangerous escape from the underworld but rather a vagabond adventure in which the gray rolling stone bumped and tumbled along in mudslides and rivers. Because of its great density, it traveled close to the bottom of streams, just as a big fish swims below the minnows, and rushed ahead unharmed. Diamonds not as lucky, flat ones that were poorly crystallized or contained impurities, broke along the way. It was a kind of natural selection, in which only superior, perfectly formed stones survived.

Then the Diamond rested for a few more million years as it became imprisoned again in a new rock conglomerate. When that in turn eroded after several million more, the gray stone traveled farther before it found itself imbedded and stationary yet again. And so it went from age to age, from the Paleozoic to the Mesozoic, when great dinosaurs swished and heaved their bulk about, to the Cenozoic, which covers the past seventy million years.

When did the first hand close around it, taking it forever from nature's world to man's? Was it around 40,000 B.C. when humans first appeared on the horizon in what is known as the Paleolithic or Old Stone Age? Perhaps, as they kicked stones about, looking for basalt and quartz to point and polish into tools, they discovered the shiny

gray one that was the Diamond. Or maybe the first hand belonged to a
figure in loincloth bent over neat fields of waving green, as nomadic
hunters gave way, around 5000 B.C., to people who lived in huts and
worked the land with iron, not stone, implements. Or it could have
been clasped initially in the slender hand of a Dravidian miner who
knew exactly what it was and how to value it.

The Dravidians, with well-chiseled features and eagle-beak noses,
came by sea or land from southern and eastern Persia to India's
west coast around 2500 B.C. and gradually moved east across the
peninsula. Between 800 and 600 B.C., when they were already busy
searching for gold in India's alluvial deposits, the Dravidians began
to recover rough diamonds as well, although they did so sporadically,
whenever they found a promising pothole in a riverbed. From that
time on, humans would always collect, treasure, and weave legends
around diamonds. Until diamonds were discovered in Borneo in A.D. 600,
India would be the only source of supply, but to this day no one has
ever found the kimberlite pipes where Indian diamonds originated.
The Dravidians sifted and sorted mainly in the Deccan area, later
called the Kingdom of Golconda, near the mighty Krishna River,
which empties into the Bay of Bengal on the east coast. This is the
region where most of the biggest and all of the colored Indian diamonds have been found. It is therefore likely that our gem first saw the
light in this general area, being too heavy to travel far. But whether a
Dravidian may have picked it up sometime after 800 B.C., or whether
a later Indian miner might have, perhaps as late as the 1650s, we do
not know.

On the momentous day when the very first hand, whomever it belonged to, grasped it, the Diamond's life changed forever. At that moment, it made the passage from nature to civilization, from innocence
to experience. From then on, it would be more subject than object,
more symbol than stone, packed as densely with meanings as it was
with carbon atoms. Because all diamonds have a very high thermal
conductivity, when those first fingers cradled the gem, it grew warmer.
That first touch also ushered in the era that would give the Diamond

great supernatural and spiritual power that would last as long as Indians owned it. Paradoxically, when the Diamond's loveliness was least, its magic was greatest.

The public relations campaign launched in the twentieth century by De Beers to sell their diamonds pales in comparison with the fantastic claims made for them in ancient and medieval times in the East. People there would have laughed at the modest assertion that "a diamond is forever." For them, diamonds held mystery, myth, and a hundred kinds of magic.

By 500 B.C. Aryans, who had already been in northern India for a thousand years, reached the Deccan and intermarried with the Dravidians. Both these Hindu groups shared the belief that every soul must pass through many incarnations, in animals, plants—and gemstones, thus endowing the latter with life. Perhaps the Diamond was already among them when Gautama Buddha (556–478 B.C.) sat beneath the spreading branches of his sacred peepul tree preaching the doctrine that rejected the Hindu caste system but kept the idea of reincarnation. Near his tree stood, according to myth, a throne as old as Earth itself, one hundred feet in circumference and made of a single diamond. Upon it the thousand sage buddhas of an ancient age had rested and fallen into a state of reverence and adoration for the gem, known as "the ecstasy of the diamond."

Indian physicians believed the stone could lower fevers if placed on the forehead, cure pains when placed on the stomach, ward off mania when clutched in the right hand, and generally produce a strength of body to match its own. The *Ratnapariska* of Buddhabhatta, a Sanskrit manual on gems dating from about A.D. 500, states that "he who wears a diamond will see dangers recede from him whether he be threatened by serpents, fire, poison, sickness, thieves, flood or evil spirits."

The first mention of diamonds in Indian writings, however, comes some eight hundred years before the *Ratnapariska*. At that time, and for years to come, peasants who worked the land rallied around whatever strong, resourceful (and diamond-wearing?) ruler emerged to lead them, warring constantly with weaker neighboring tribes, cutting them down with swords whose dazzling blades had diamond points aligned to slice through flesh and bone as if they were overripe mangoes. In 321 B.C. a young adventurer of the Mauryan clan named Candragupta conquered the powerful Nanda dynasty and established his capital near modern-day Patna. His chief minister, Kautilya, who had tutored him and guided him to power, wrote a book called *Arthasastra* (The Science of Profit), a Sanskrit document that makes it plain that by the time of Raja Candragupta's reign (321–298 B.C.), diamonds were not only mined and valued but also taxed to augment a raja's revenues and traded with other countries, not because they possessed beauty—the rough, uncut stones had little—but because they had such amazing supernatural powers.

While our Diamond stayed in India, some of its fellows were loaded onto boats and rowed west by galley slaves across the Arabian Sea, then packed onto camels' backs for the long desert trek to the Mediterranean and thence to Europe. More gems went north overland to a trading center at Ormus, before fanning out to Persia, Arabia, and Turkey, entering Europe via a second trade mart at Constantinople.

Some of the traveling diamonds reached the Greeks as early as the fifth century B.C. They called them *adamant*, which means "unconquerable," and which is probably the root of the French *diamant* and English *diamond*. Plato (428–347 B.C.) in his *Timaeus* believed they were formed out of the finest and densest parts of gold. Aristotle's pupil, Theophrastus, writing in 315 B.C., was quite sure that the precious stones were living beings and divided them into male and female.

By 65 B.C. a few bags of diamonds had arrived in Rome. When Mark Antony solemnized the coronation of Cleopatra in 33 B.C., he is said to have worn a gold-embroidered purple robe with diamond buttons. Pliny writes in his *Natural History* in A.D. 77, two years before he died in the Vesuvius eruption that destroyed Herculaneum and Pompeii, that the diamond is "the most valuable not only of precious stones but of all things in the world . . . known only to kings and princes, and even to few of them." It could, he continues, offset the bad effects of poison, drive away "those hallucinations that cause people to go insane," and banish "vain fears that trouble and possess the mind." The Latin poet and astronomer Manilius, in the first century A.D., considered the diamond "only a speck of stone, but more precious than gold," and an anonymous Roman poet, in the second, wrote:

> The evil eye shall have no power to harm
> Him that shall wear the diamond as a charm.
> No monarch shall attempt to thwart his will
> And e'en the gods his wishes shall fulfill.

The diamonds that were being praised and promoted abroad, however, weren't the largest stones; those stayed in India, claimed by its rulers for personal use to ensure victory on the battlefield and a long reign. Did the Diamond flash from a raja's coiling turban or gem-encrusted throne? Perhaps not, for a few Sanskrit texts suggest that blue diamonds carried a potent curse. This raises another question: when did the Diamond lose its disfiguring gray caul and show its true colors?

Indians valued size rather than brilliance, so while stones were polished from the sixth century A.D. on, the only cuts made were to remove or conceal flaws. The *Agastimata*, an early text that can't be precisely dated, proclaims that stones shouldn't be cut but only polished, using other diamonds to do it.

We know that sometime before 1660, the Diamond was perhaps cut and most certainly polished. One day some Indian jeweler held the shiny gray gem firmly in the fingers of his left hand and pressed it against a polishing disk fixed to the left end of a horizontal wooden axle revolving in sockets on two upright pegs driven into the earthen floor of his shop. In his right hand, the jeweler operated a long stick bent into a bow, its taut cord fixed to both ends and looped once around the axle. This was the motor power for making the disk revolve. A small boy stood beside him, frequently scooping up from half a coconut shell spoonfuls of a paste made from diamond powder and oil, which he spread on the polishing disk.

Patiently, expertly, the workman ground and polished each natural face of the Diamond, his strong right arm working the bow back and forth from dawn to dusk, day after scorching day, week after week. Gradually the stone's gray gave way to blue-gray and then to an astonishingly rich shade of blue, like a sky slowly clearing after long, heavy rains.

For the Diamond, blueness had come. True brilliance and "life" were still many years away.

The newly polished gem still held all its magic and was about to add another kind of power. To every famous Indian diamond the same story clings: it once served as an eye in the statue of a Hindu god, before being pried out under very shady circumstances. At least four chroniclers of the Diamond's history mention such a phase, when its light became a prayer. Indians believed it, as a talisman, could vastly improve their present earthly incarnation; as part of a god, it could lead them to Nirvana, beyond time and place.

The statue in question may have been carved from stone or wood, but to be worthy of a big blue diamond eye, it was probably made of bronze. It was the Chola dynasty ruling in south India from about A.D. 850 that, in the eleventh and twelfth centuries, brought bronze sculpture to new heights. The Cholas' best-loved god was Siva, whose most popular pose showed him as Nataraja, Lord of the Dance. Let us do a little imaginative dance of our own and picture the Diamond in this particular sacred guise.

The sculptor would have trained in the workshop of a master, likely his father or grandfather, where he'd learned the formulas spelled out in ancient Sanskrit texts that decreed exact measurements, proportions, and every detail for making a god, such as how many arms, distances between them, which knee should bend, that kind of thing. The artist would be familiar with the Siva stories of the *Puranas*, those thousands of very old Sanskrit verses, difficult to date, whose million myths show Siva as a god of dichotomies, embodying "the coincidence of opposites." He is both darkness and fire, cruel and kind, ascetic and erotic, wild and tranquil, creative and meditative. From the Ocean of Milk, he and other gods once churned and drank the divine nectar that rendered them immortal while spilled drops of nectar turned into diamonds—or so say the *Puranas*.

The sculptor would first model Siva in wax, wrap him in a thick coat of clay kept in place by wires, then melt the wax away in a hot fire, leaving a hollow into which he poured the amalgam of copper, brass, white lead, silver, and gold that made bronze. After it had set and cooled, he removed the clay wrapper.

Then he had to give Siva character by much chiseling and chasing, digging his sharpest tool deeply into the bronze face to make Siva's three eyes, the third one vertical and in the middle of his forehead. When he was almost finished, the sculptor attached the ring of leaping flames that he'd cast separately, inside which Siva as Nataraja always dances, carefully fitting its two peg ends into sockets on the god's pedestal.

There was only one thing left to do. The sculptor unwrapped the polished blue Diamond. Perhaps he held it for a moment in his hand, seeing in its gleaming depths favors from the gods and artistic triumphs still to come. Then he fixed the Diamond in the waiting hollow of Siva's third eye. The god's two ordinary eyes, large and almond shaped, symbolized sun and moon; the third eye was fire, source of all his power, enabling him to create or destroy, to bless or curse, to see in wondrous ways.

The sculptor stepped back from his workbench and looked at his masterpiece. Inside cresting flames, Siva danced in the bliss of creation, in the ecstasy of the universe's primal motion. Strands of plaited hair rayed out from his head; his long sash whipped in the cosmic wind; his legs leapt to the pulse of life. Under an elaborate headdress, high on his forehead, glowed the Diamond, once more part of the tearing energy of nature that had brought it into being millions of years before.

Siva would then be carried in procession to the temple's dark, innermost shrine where priests performed the ceremony of giving him *prana*, the breath of life. At the end of this ritual they touched a golden needle to Siva's two ordinary almond eyes, and to the Diamond in his forehead, to "open" them and bestow sight. Seeing and being seen by the image of a god, called *darsan*, is still the most significant element of Hindu worship; the worshiper sees the deity but the deity also sees him or her. As soon as Siva's blue eye received sight, it became so powerful that it had to fall first on a pleasing object; the priest at once held up a shiny metal mirror showing the god his splendid self. Had Siva been in a black mood, and had his Diamond eye fallen first on a person, he or she might well have died from its awesome power.

On holy days, peasants came from miles around, cleansed themselves in the large tank of water beside the temple, and entered Siva's dark cell. In silent, private meditation, they focused on the huge blue eye, feeling its life force, feeling their own quicken to meet it.

Eventually, since the real always in the end outweighs the ideal, the day came when two of the eyes looking at the Diamond were not reverential but merely greedy and covetous. Perhaps their owner waited to make his move until the crowds and chaos of *Siva-ratri*, the annual festival held to honor the god, were at hand.

For three days and nights, oiled brown bodies chanted loud mantras, whirled and danced in a frenzied, joyous celebration of the life force. In Siva's cell, gifts of flowers and fruit formed a huge carpet for his dancing feet. When the fourth day dawned, and the little oil lamps that had been thick as stars in Siva's shrine had all gone out, the god still danced creation into being inside his ring of fire, but his blue Diamond eye blazed no more. A frantic hand had pried it loose and stuffed it into the blindness of a small purse, thereby depriving it of what is every gemstone's essential *prana*: the gift of light.

If the Diamond was indeed stolen from the statue of an idol, was it because the thief wanted to harness its supernatural powers, or because he planned to sell it to the highest bidder? Was the theft the finale to this stage of the Diamond's existence—or an omen of the next?

When, in our story, we get to the seventeenth century, we are once more on firm ground where facts abound. But the Diamond's golden youth is over. It will never again, in fantasy, fly so high or reach so near to heaven. Soon the marketplace will claim it.

A little dust cloud appears on the Indian horizon and the Western world approaches in a carriage.

*Jean-Baptiste Tavernier in the Robe of Honor
presented to him by the Shah of Persia.*

2

MONEY

Nothing comes amiss, so money comes withal.
—WILLIAM SHAKESPEARE, *The Taming of the Shrew*, act 1, scene 2

Jean-Baptiste Tavernier, a short, plump fifty-four-year-old French-man, was glad to be once more on the move, in search of fresh trade and amazing bargains. He'd been in the busy, commercial west coast Indian port of Surat for six months, both buying and selling. Now, in mid-October 1659, with his usual entourage of servants and armed guards, he was parading along its main street for the last time, en route to Golconda, where India's biggest diamonds awaited.

He'd just passed the Hindu temple, which had a famous banyan tree beside it, into the trunk of which some artist had carved the like-ness of Siva's wife, Parvati, and painted it in bright colors. "Every day a large number of idolaters assemble there to adore this monster" and to leave it gifts of rice, millet, and other grains, according to Tavernier in his book *Les Six Voyages de Jean-Baptiste Tavernier Qu'il a Fait en Turque, en Perse et aux Indes*, published in 1676 and translated into En-glish in an annotated edition in 1889 as *Travels in India*. Jean-Baptiste was a Protestant realist who thought Indian idols "hideous." They never had the proper number of arms or eyes. He was quitting Surat; he wouldn't have to look at this garish, grinning face again.

Once in the famous temple at Puri, on India's east coast, he'd seen the huge sandalwood idol that, he writes, had "two diamonds for his eyes and a pendant from his neck which reaches to the waist and the

smallest of these diamonds weighs about forty carats. It should be re-
marked that jewellers are not now permitted to enter the pagoda, since
one of them intending to steal it, who allowed himself to be shut up
during the night, extracted a diamond from one of the eyes of the
idol." Diamond eyes, indeed! What a waste of marketable stones! No
wonder the jeweler had turned thief. Jean-Baptiste's hand patted the
wide leather girdle at his waist that he wore day and night and that
held a fortune in precious stones. Once he'd caught out idolaters at
their so-called magic. A widow had been in a Hindu temple for three
days, listening to its bronze idol tell her what to do since her husband
had died. Tavernier waited until the temple was almost empty, sent the
priest out of the sanctuary on the pretext of fetching water, nipped behind the idol, and discovered a hole through which the priest himself
had done the talking. He'd cursed Jean-Baptiste roundly when he'd returned with the water "because I had profaned his temple but we soon
became friends by means of two rupees I placed in his hands, and he at
the same time offered me betel." Money, not hocus-pocus magic, was
what served a man best, that and always ingratiating himself with the
natives in the country where he was doing business. Since chewing betel, made from the plant's leaves mixed with foufel nuts and ground
seashells, was the expected prelude to every Indian conversation, Tavernier chewed, swallowing the juice and spitting out the rest. It turned
his mouth and tongue red as rubies, but Jean-Baptiste wasn't a fastidious man. One couldn't be to survive in seventeenth-century India. After he'd spent many years there, the manners and refinement of this
Frenchman had peeled away along with his sunburned skin. Years later,
in France, one acquaintance, Daunou, called him "bizarre" and Nicolas
Boileau (1636–1711), famous poet, satirist, and official historian to
King Louis XIV, thought Tavernier "very coarse in manner and language" and an "oddity." In his *Oeuvres Diverses* (1701), Boileau wrote
in verse that although Tavernier returned to France from the East with
"lavish piles" of "the rarest treasures of the rising sun," he brought back
"nothing as rare as himself," the word *rare* being used ironically, as
Boileau's biographer Claude Brossette assures us.

Tavernier was the perennial voyager and stranger, losing himself in many cultures, at home in none. At his core there was a faint, bleating loneliness that he chose to ignore. "I'm a citizen of the world," he liked to boast, to himself, or to anyone who'd listen, as he swilled the local brew in Constantinople or Isfahan or Goa. He never lost his lust for adventure or his love of freedom from constraining social conventions. But he never found true belonging either.

This man, destined for a key role in the Diamond's story, was born in Paris in 1605, son of Susanne, née Tonnelier, and Gabriel Tavernier, engraver and mapmaker, whose Protestant father had, thirty years earlier, fled religious persecution in Antwerp to settle in Paris. There Gabriel and Susanne married, worked hard, prospered, and produced four sons: Jean-Baptiste; Daniel, who would accompany him on one of his voyages to the East; Gabriel, who became a goldsmith at Uzes in Provence; and Melchoir, a mediocre engraver not up to the standard of his famous uncle Melchoir (1544–1641), who had been printer and engraver to Louis XIII.

Jean-Baptiste declares in *Six Voyages*, "I came into the world with a desire to travel. The interviews which many learned men had daily with my father upon geographical matters to which, young as I was, I listened with pleasure, inspired me at an early age with the desire to go see some of the countries shown to me in the maps, from which I could not take my eyes." He eagerly set about learning foreign languages and devoured such travelogs as *The Book of Ser Marco Polo*, who had explored the East in the thirteenth century, sold sapphires to the great Kublai Khan (1215–1294) for "twice what they were worth," and even visited the Golconda mines in India. "There are certain lofty mountains in those parts," writes Marco Polo of Golconda, where monsoon waters "come roaring down the mountains in great torrents." When the rains are over, "they search the beds of the torrents and find plenty of diamonds." Jean-Baptiste may also have read the Dutchman Jan Huygen Van Linschoten's account of India in the 1580s, which was translated into French in 1610, five years after Tavernier's birth. According to Linschoten, there were diamonds in the Deccan that were "digged like gold out of mines and where they dig one year the length of a man into the ground, within three or four years after, there are

diamonds found again in the same place which grow there." In a corner of his father's shop, young Jean-Baptiste read about the fabulous
East, remembered what he'd read (for his memory was prodigious),
pored over maps, listened to his father's friends, and made his private
vows. Someday he would see all these wonders for himself.

He began his travels at fifteen and went first to England and Germany. At Nuremburg he met the cavalry colonel Hans Brener, son of
the Governor of Vienna, joined his service, and fought in a major battle
at Prague on November 8, 1620, and then in minor skirmishes with
the Turks. Tavernier acted as page for the next four and a half years to
the Viceroy of Hungary. He liked Hungary, mainly because "food is so
cheap that we did not expend at Belgrade for fourteen mouths as much
as two crowns a day." But he grew restless, with a wanderlust that
would be lifelong and insatiable. "At age twenty-two," he boasts, "I
had seen the most beautiful regions of Europe, France, England, the
Low Countries, Germany, Switzerland, Poland, Hungary and Italy and
I spoke fairly well the necessary languages which have greatest use."
His time in Italy was spent in the ordinance company of the Duke of
Mantua. When the city of Mantua was besieged by the Austrian imperial army in 1630, Tavernier would have been shot for sure, according
to his account of the battle, had he not been wearing very strong, thick
armor. In the end, quality always paid for itself. After Mantua fell, he
returned to his Paris home only long enough to muster fresh funds
from his well-heeled father. Jean-Baptiste enlisted briefly in the regiment of a Scot, Colonel Butler, before rushing off to Frankfurt to see
Ferdinand III, Emperor of the Austrian Empire, crowned first as King
of the Romans. It was in Frankfurt that Tavernier, always convivial,
was invited in 1631 by a Catholic priest and a French merchant to accompany them on a voyage to the East. He did so as far as Constantinople, a major trading center, staying for eleven months after his new
friends had moved on, fingering carpets, shaking out silk stuffs, letting
jewels cascade through his stubby fingers. It was precisely then that
Jean-Baptiste Tavernier, age twenty-seven, found his life calling: merchant trader in such exotic goods as Eastern textiles and precious gems.
He joined a caravan going to Persia; there he bought pearls, turquoises,

rugs, embroidered fabrics, with a wild passion he'd never felt before. But he realized that he needed to acquire knowledge of gems, so he stayed in Paris for more than a year as apprentice to a prominent jeweler called Goisse, who passed on his expertise.

Jean-Baptiste listened, remembered, examined, and peered into the depths of hundreds of stones—and met the one true love of his life: the diamond. (Women couldn't compete. He wouldn't marry until he was fifty-seven, and then it would be to Goisse's daughter, for self-serving, sensible reasons.) Tavernier became such an expert on diamonds that his descriptions in *Six Voyages* concerning their value, weight, flaws, mining, and cutting techniques are still the historical base for all Western records of these gems.

On September 13, 1638, Jean-Baptiste set sail from Marseilles on the first of his five trips to India, staying each time for four or five years, moving up and down the country, trading all the way, both buying and selling gemstones, for he soon discovered that he could sell those bought in Europe to Indian potentates, who paid "much better than do people in Europe, not only for pearls, but for all kinds of jewels—when they are out of the common run—excepting only diamonds." For the latter, traffic was one-way: buy cheaply in India; sell profitably in Europe. Diamonds were dropped lovingly into his leather pouch and stayed there; pearls, rubies, topazes, and sapphires came and went on a short-term basis. Tavernier had visited Golconda's mines on that first Indian trip, probably returning to Paris in early 1643. He sold everything at enormous profit; he was one of the few Frenchman then venturing as far afield as India, so his exotic goods and gems were in great demand. On December 6, 1643, he was off to India again, buying some fine diamonds at the Golconda mines and more on his third trip, which lasted from 1651 to 1655.

Now here he was on his fourth venture, having left Paris two years before, in February 1657, making his way out of Surat, lured by the jewel's siren song. "The diamond is the most precious of all stones," enthuses Tavernier, and is "the article of trade to which I am most devoted. In order to acquire a thorough knowledge of it I resolved to visit all the mines, and as the fear of dangers has never restrained me in any of my journeys, the terrible picture that was drawn of these mines, as being in barbarous countries to which one could not travel except by the most dangerous routes, served neither to terrify me nor to turn me from my intention." He didn't visit "all the mines," but only three of them: Kollur in the Kingdom of Golconda, Ramulkota in the Kingdom of Bijapur, and Soumelpour in the Kingdom of Bengal. Jean-Baptiste liked to boast, "I am the first European who has opened the route to these mines which are the only places in the world where the diamond is found." In truth, he wasn't the first European. Gaveia de Orta, a Portuguese physician, had visited the Golconda mines in 1565, the Venetian Caesar Fredericke around 1570, and the Englishman William Methwold circa 1622.

The most important revelation of character here is not, however, to be found in Tavernier's bragging but in the first sentence where he names the diamond as the "article of trade to which I am most devoted." This sums up his attitude to diamonds, including the great blue one that he was soon to meet; they were not—at least not in his conscious mind—magical or spiritual objects inspiring man's imagination and soul as they were for Indians. He told himself they were mere articles of trade, to be hunted down, examined, and eventually sold for very satisfying profits. He didn't desire diamonds for himself. In the two extant portraits of him he wears no jewelry at all, although men of his time decked themselves lavishly in jewels and, if they could afford them, in diamonds. Voltaire once observed that Tavernier "speaks the language of a merchant more than that of a philosopher, and knows nothing except how to recognize the great trade routes and diamonds." Jean-Baptiste's good friend the Abbé of Longuerue agreed: "He knew about gems, and that is all; he had, beyond that, neither wit nor knowledge of any kind whatsoever." His *Six Voyages*, which devotes a whole chapter to a discussion of currencies, custom charges, weights, and measures, is a dry, unemotional account, not the record of a man who, as he professed, was "born to travel" but rather of one born to trade. He had seen the white marble radiance of Agra's Taj Mahal, completed just a few years before, in 1650, the most romantic palace in the world, and commented only that it took twenty thousand workmen twenty-two years to build and that "the cost of it has been enormous." If India's magic and mystery impinged on this Gradgrind of facts, this Babbitt of business, he didn't acknowledge it in print. When a Muslim noble gave Tavernier an unbroken horse as a gift, he returned it, asked for one he could ride, then took the twenty-eight-year-old nag to Golconda, sold it for the tidy sum of five hundred rupees, and congratulated himself on his cleverness. That was the kind of thing that excited him, not the Taj Mahal.

Historically speaking, Tavernier follows on the heels of such intrepid sixteenth-century adventurers as Sir Walter Raleigh, who landed in Virginia, and Sir Francis Drake, who circled the world from 1577 to 1580, men who laid the foundations of world markets and capitalism, looting the globe for economic gain. Such men, who crossed raging seas in frail sailing ships and trekked through inhospitable lands, were driven partly by curiosity and the lure of romantic adventure but mostly by the desire to turn a neat profit. The English novelist Daniel Defoe grasped the nature of such entrepreneurs completely. "When you find yourself sleepy in a morning," says a minor character in *The Dumb Philosopher* (1719), "rouse yourself and consider that you are born to business." The main characters in Defoe's *Robinson Crusoe* (1719) and *Moll Flanders* (1722) embody Tavernier's strenuous voyaging and Protestant economic individualism. "Really stirring about and trading, the profit being so great," says Crusoe, gives "more pleasure and more satisfaction to the mind than sitting still." "With money in the pocket," declares Moll Flanders, "one is at home anywhere." If Tavernier follows men like Raleigh and Drake, and coincides with the first European wave of colonialism and capitalist expansion in the seventeenth century, he also prefigures the modern capitalist "born to business," who is still pillaging the global village but doing it at speeds that would make Jean-Baptiste emerald-green with envy. One feels that Tavernier would have felt completely at home in such a modern metropolis as New York, where the pulse of commercial possibility beats with perennial optimism.

But then Surat, which bustled, which positively bulged with consumerism, was Tavernier's natural habitat. Its harbor was always crowded with Chinese junks bringing tea and porcelain; Arab dhows with red sails loaded with carpets and copper; Dutch and English schooners about to depart, their holds tightly packed with Indian goods: embroidered silks from Ahmadabad; chintzes from Agra; spices from Calicut; pearls from Cape Cormorin; tortoiseshell from Coromandel. The Dutch and English had established trading centers, called factories, in Surat around 1608. The Portuguese had been trading in India the longest, since 1510, but it would be another fifteen years before the French would open three factories, one of them at Surat.

Jean-Baptiste would miss the company of the commander of the Dutch factory, his good friend and business associate, for Tavernier bought diamonds in India on commission for the Dutch, who in turn kept the diamond cutters of Amsterdam and Antwerp, the two main European centers, well supplied. On an earlier stay in Surat Jean-Baptiste had had his brother Daniel for company, but Daniel had died suddenly in 1648 of a "bloody flux" in Batavia, where the Dutch traded. The funeral had cost Jean-Baptiste an exorbitant "1223 *livres* of French money, and after I had paid this sum I resolved, for my own part, not to die in a country where it cost so much to be interred." Seven years earlier, he'd roomed in Surat with a fellow Frenchman and jeweler, Louis du Jardin, but Louis had died there of a fever. Death was never far away in India. Nor was loneliness.

Jean-Baptiste sought company where he could and talked and talked. He'd spent most days on this trip inside the fortress walls of the Dutch and English factories buying from Indian merchants come to sell their wares, while shippers and warehouse supervisors loaded and packed and shouted, and young factors minded their ledgers and minced about, dandies all, in bottle green or black velvet coats. Around their necks, they all wore, as did Jean-Baptiste, "snake-stones," hardened ovals made of the ashes of some plant mixed with charred bone, guaranteed to cure snakebite. If one had the misfortune to be bitten by a poisonous snake—they often came indoors during the rainy season and dropped onto one's neck from doorways—one applied the snake-stone to the bite, and it drew off all the poison. Whenever Tavernier bought a new stone, he always tested it first in his mouth: "If good, it leaps and attaches itself immediately to the palate." These were the stones, rather than gemstones, which held magic for Jean-Baptiste.

At sundown, the great gates to the Dutch and English factories clanged shut, for the men employed there were not allowed out at night to avail themselves of Surat's many prostitutes. Gregarious Tavernier, who liked to tell a good yarn, often stayed at the factory to dine on mutton and chicken, washed down with Shiraz wines from Persia or with *palepuntz* made from brandy, sugar, lime juice, and spices, the drink we call punch, invented by India's European factors.

Tavernier's first two months in Surat, April and May, had been the hottest, with temperatures often above 100 degrees Fahrenheit, when to walk the streets at noon could mean sudden death. The rains began in mid-June, lasted for four months, and brought cholera, leprosy, malaria, and plague, due to all the standing puddles of muck. Tavernier's shoes mildewed; walls crawled with lice; insects ate through his growing piles of copperplate invoices and worst of all, big flying bugs called *barattas* got into the silks he'd bought so carefully, after counting every pure gold thread to make sure they contained the promised number. The cursed *barattas* spotted the fabrics with eggs that stuck as fast as syrup to paper. Tavernier had to keep his storage chests in the middle of the room, away from crawling wall insects, and to place little pots of water under furniture legs so that ants couldn't crawl up and eat their way through everything he owned. Rats as big as piglets ran about; they dug down beneath houses and made them collapse; smaller ones had rusty red hair and smelled of civet. One day every surface in Tavernier's lodging became covered with flying white ants, thousands of them. Later his servants swept up the corpses by the bucketful. India was a land of violent extremes: sudden life and death; splendor and squalor; parched sands and pelting rains. One could make no sense or order from it, although Jean-Baptiste tried.

Surat was left behind now, its fortress and temple towers mere blue specks on the flat plain. Snug inside his custom-built carriage, Jean-Baptiste took out his pocket watch for the hundredth time and began a complex mental calculation of hours and days and leagues to be covered. Corps of figures constantly formed and reformed in his head.

From Surat to Golconda was about 324 leagues (800 miles). In 1645 he'd made the trip in an astonishing twenty-seven days, but he'd been younger then. Six years earlier, in 1653, he'd tried a different route, but that had taken thirty-two days, leaving Surat in March, when the weather had been scorching hot. On that trip he'd traveled only at night, making sure he got beyond a town's gates before they were shut at sundown, camping under a tree until it was cool enough to lumber ahead on the road. He'd learned the hard way to avoid day travel in the hot weather, having done it once across a desert waste and complained in a letter, "I have no sooner taken into my stomach a pint of water than I see it issue out of my limbs like dew. The sun is intolerable. My face and hands are peeled off. I know not in the morning whether I should live until night."

His mode of conveyance in India depended on the condition of the terrain and the roads. On good ones, and there weren't many of those, he could use his custom-built carriage; on rough ones he switched to a bumping, jolting tonga, a small covered wagon with curtains and cushions but no springs and only hand-hewn teak wheels around a bowed axle. Oxen rather than horses or camels drew most of the vehicles and could keep a slow but steady pace of thirty-five miles a day, urged on by balls of flour kneaded with butter and black sugar and fed in evening camp on chickpeas mashed in water. Where roads were nonexistent, Jean-Baptiste used a palanquin, a curtained bed slung on bamboo poles carried by three men before and three behind. To cover thirty-five miles a day, he hired twelve men so that six could carry him while six walked behind.

Tavernier traveled as befitted a man of substance: with a retinue of up to sixty servants, including a corps of men who marched with muskets or bows and arrows to protect his precious goods from robbers. Behind the marching men came a long string of oxen carrying saddlebags full of his trade goods and personal luggage, including plenty of gifts to be presented to all the Indian rulers to whom he hoped to sell jewels: pocket watches from Paris, bronzes from Burgundy, decorative boxes and telescopes from Italy, braces of pearl-handled pistols from England.

The wearisome days on the road to Golconda slowly passed, and the oxen's load of wine bottles lightened. Storks flapped by above tamarind and mango trees, green parrots screamed from their branches, and sleeping fruit bats hung by their claws. The sun set every evening in a blaze of topaz and cabochon rubies, while fish jumped in the large village tanks where water was stored, and peacocks garlanded their edges. Tavernier was careful never to shoot a peacock. He'd heard the tale of the rich European merchant who'd shot one for his dinner. Hindus, who considered every form of life sacred and peacocks good luck, had seized the offender, tied him to a tree, and whipped him so severely for three days that he died. They'd also stolen his bag of 300,000 rupees.

As November arrived and Tavernier got closer to Golconda, there were windstorms originating in the Bay of Bengal, which blew dust from the road into columns and rattled every leaf. The fields he passed were green with waving rice, millet, and the indigo plants that yielded three crops a year to be made into little cakes of bright violet-blue used to dye cloth. There were many streams and rivers to cross, still swollen from the annual rains. Since there were no bridges, crossing each was a tedious business that often took half a day.

Several times Tavernier met a caravan of ten or twelve thousand oxen, all laden with corn, rice, millet, or salt. Then he had to halt for two or three days until the whole train had passed. The men who drove the oxen were nomads, so children and wives traveled with them, the latter's completely naked torsos painted with bright flowers above pieces of white calico twisted into skirts. The caravan's chiefs wore chains of pearls around their necks, and the other men dangled little silver boxes containing some sacred text.

After more than three weeks on the road, Tavernier could see up ahead the jagged blue shapes of the Eastern Ghats, the hills in whose crevices hid panthers—and diamonds. Not far now to Golconda. Its Hindu natives, who spoke Telugu, had concocted the name from *golla* ("shepherd") and *konda* ("hill"), for theirs was a green, boulder-strewn land ideally suited to grazing sheep. Golconda was the name both of the kingdom or province, and of its capital, a town near the present city of Hyderabad.

From about 1350 until 1700, when output would decline sharply, Golconda was the most important of India's three main diamond-producing areas, with twenty-three operating mines in the region bounded by the Godavari River on the north and the Penner on the south, with the Krishna River, where the biggest diamonds were found, in between. From about 1500, when the Bahmani kings were defeated, the kingdom belonged to the Muslim Kutb Shah dynasty, but by 1659, when Tavernier visited, real power was in the hands of the Mogul dynasty, which had swept down from the north, scimitars flashing, in 1636, under Emperor Shah Jehan who, in his more peaceful moments, was then building the Taj Mahal. He let the King of Golconda go on sitting on his throne but made him pay a stiff annual tribute. Aurungzeb, who had succeeded Shah Jehan in 1658, was a cruel, ruthless ruler with a passion for gems and a heel firmly placed on the neck of Kutb Shah (1625–1672), Golconda's king.

Now in the distance loomed Golconda's ancient fortress, high on its hill above the town, once the residence of its proud kings, now only the repository of Kutb Shah's jewels. Soon Jean-Baptiste and entourage were passing through the town's suburb of Aurangabad, where all its artisans and merchants lived. (Only nobles, officials, and foreign visitors were allowed to dwell within the town itself.) Tavernier crossed the stone bridge over the Musi River, glad to be finally arriving. It was November, and the Musi was in full flood from the rains; it had once swept four thousand houses away in its rushing waters.

At the town gates he had to stop for several days while local police searched everything to make sure he wasn't bringing in tobacco or salt, which were heavily taxed to provide Kutb Shah with his main source of revenue. At long last they waved him on his way along the dusty main street, past mansions with cool, fretted marble interiors, where the king's courtiers dwelt, most of them Persian. At the end of the main street stood the palace, with its famous rooftop gardens, its colonnaded quarters for elephants, and a balcony where Kutb Shah gave audience to his subjects, whose written petitions, gathered down in the square, were placed in a bag dangling from a rope and drawn up by a eunuch who stood beside him.

Tavernier settled into lodgings and renewed his friendships with Golconda's jewel merchants. He visited the palace square on Fridays, the day when the town prostitutes danced there for the king, who had his own thousand concubines, as well. On Mondays, Jean-Baptiste watched the spectacle of the changing of the royal guard, which assembled beyond the town and marched the full length of the main street to the palace. The king's nobles took turns providing the troop. A dozen elephants came first, all brightly caparisoned, then forty camels with a long gun across each saddle to which a man in tiger skins held a match. Crimson silk carriages with yellow fringe preceded six thousand horses with jeweled bridles glinting in the sun. The noble who owned all this intimidating splendor paraded with a dozen of his concubines dancing around him. Bringing up the rear was the more earnest contingent: the infantry, wearing only loincloths but armed with broadswords and muskets; the cavalry, carrying bows and arrows, with chain mail hanging from the back of their helmets to preserve their necks from sun and enemies.

The diamond merchants came into town each day from the suburbs, staying from ten in the morning until five in the afternoon and selling to most of the foreign jewelers who, as Tavernier tells us, "are influenced by the false reports that the people at the mines are unsophisticated and almost savages, and that, moreover, the routes from Golconda to the mines are very dangerous." Jean-Baptiste, who might well have contributed to the "false reports," would brave the perils for the sake of the plunder. Buying at source, not only for himself but for the Dutch on commission, he had first choice, little competition, and better prices.

In the cool of the evenings, Tavernier sat beneath a lemon tree whose canopy gave off a heady perfume, drinking tari, a palm wine "as sweet as our new wines," brought into town each morning in leather bottles strapped to horses. One evening several weeks after his arrival, Jean-Baptiste first felt a dream, no bigger than a grain of rice, plant itself in his head. He was a prosaic man who tamped down the poetry in his soul, but somehow in that country where every leaf netted magic in its shadows, he imagined himself at the French court, bowing to King

Louis XIV, trading spectacular gemstones for riches and renown. He took a long drink of tari; it was time to quit Surat and head for the Kollur mine on the Krishna's right bank, where such enormous, fabled diamonds as the Kohinoor (Mountain of Light), 186 carats, had been found.

The story of the Kohinoor is quite as fascinating as that of the Diamond, but more consistently bloody and violent. The Indians believed that whoever owned the Kohinoor could conquer the world, so it was tossed about, in cruel conflicts, among rival brothers or dynasties, for several thousand years. The Raja of Malwa owned it in the early 1300s. The Afghans kept it in Kabul and Kandahar for sixty-six years; the Moguls had it in Delhi for the next 213, during which time three contenders were blinded and one had his scalp ringed with boiling oil. The Moguls finally had to relinquish it to the Lion of the Punjab, Sikh leader Ranjit Singh, who wore it proudly on his arm in Lahore until his death in 1839. When in their galloping conquest of India, the British annexed the Punjab ten years later, they grabbed the Kohinoor, too. Like the Indians, they seemed to believe that whoever owned it would rule the world. The diamond went at once home to Queen Victoria in London, who sent it for safekeeping to the Tower. Since 1937 the gem, recut to 108.93 metric carats, has been casting its mountain of light from the crown made that year for Elizabeth, now Queen Mother. In 1947 the newly autonomous Indian government politely asked Britain for its return, and again in 1953, a little less politely, when Queen Elizabeth II was crowned with the jewel sitting squarely and securely on her young head. In 1976 the prime minister of Pakistan, Zulifikar Ali Bhutto, submitted yet another ignored request to get it back. Britain's empire may have gone missing, but the Kohinoor is still locked up in the Tower of London and adorns its monarchs on special occasions, suggesting a power they no longer possess.

Tavernier knew that the King of Golconda had his appointed deputy at each of the mines in his kingdom to make sure all diamonds over 10 carats came straight to him; Jean-Baptiste was also aware of the severe penalties for circumventing this rule—if one was caught. William Methwold, who had visited the Kollur mine thirty-seven years before, had written that not even the king's "many spies can so watch such as there attend such hazards, but that I have heard diamonds of 40 carats have escaped their guard." Jean-Baptiste Tavernier was not a man to be cowed by rules or risks.

Early next morning he went to the money changer, called a *shroff*, to get the various foreign currencies he'd picked up during his six-month stay in Surat changed into new pagodas, plenty of them, given his new-minted dream. The only coins that merchants selling diamonds at Kollur would accept were new pagodas: small, thick pieces of gold the size of little fingernails, minted either by the Mogul king Aurungzeb, Golconda's Kutb Shah, or, with Aurungzeb's permission, by the Dutch or English factories. Old pagodas, thin, well-worn and generally despised, had been coined by long-ago Hindu princes. As Tavernier and the money changer sat opposite each other at a small table, with neat piles of coins between, Jean-Baptiste examined each pagoda carefully; if it had been minted at an English factory, he handed it back, demanding a Dutch-made one instead, which the miners preferred, asking an extra 1 or even 2 percent for English pagodas. He also looked most carefully at the edge of every coin, for sometimes small holes had been drilled to extract gold dust, which of course decreased the worth. He stowed the shining, perfect pagodas in little bags inside the leather girdle where he kept his gems and returned to his lodging, enjoying the new heaviness around his waist. He left other monies, along with bills of exchange and personal goods, in the care of his good friend Boete, an apothecary, to await his return from the mine—if he did manage to return.

As dawn rose the next day he was on his way, with servants and oxen, tonga and palanquin. The diamond mine was roughly 140 miles distant, and it was an arduous weeklong trip over very rough terrain. There were far too many streams to cross using the usual basket-ferry system. Cassia trees grew in every rock crevice that held an inch of soil. His servants ate the cinnamon-flavored pods as they walked along, then all got violent diarrhea, causing annoying delays. The last forty miles to Kollur were so rough that the tonga had to be taken to pieces and reassembled three times.

As he got closer to the mine, he thought of the stupendous diamond found there only about ten years before, 787 carats in the rough,
the so-called Great Mogul, the biggest diamond in the world, which
had been cut—a botched job by a Venetian—to 296 carats, half a
hen's egg in shape. Aurungzeb kept it at his court at Delhi. Tavernier
had only heard about it; he hadn't yet seen it; someday he would. In
the meantime, who knew what mighty diamonds *he* could carry off?

For the final part of the rocky trail, he had to ride an ox, sitting
well back, beyond reach of its long, sharp horns, which could, with one
toss of its head, gore his well-padded stomach. At last he entered
the town, a makeshift community of 100,000 miners and diamond
merchants that had first sprung up on the Krishna in service of the
diamonds.

The actual mine was three miles away, closer to the jagged granite
peaks of the Eastern Ghats, which loomed just beyond it. Sitting
astride his ox on a hill above the mine site, Jean-Baptiste surveyed the
toiling masses below where sixty thousand men, women, and children
labored in the hot sun, lashed by overseers with whips, for an annual
wage of three pagodas or less. Males wore only scanty loincloths; females
had a rag of cotton draped from knee to waist and over one breast. The
mine was divided into claims, each worked by a rich merchant who
paid a levy to the King of Golconda for the privilege, plus a tax
on each diamond found. (The mine at that time was producing about
12 million carats a year, but by mid-twentieth century yielded a mere
trickle of around 100.) Below black soil washed down by floods lay broken sandstone, quartz, and gravels from dried-up riverbeds, mixed with
Precambrian conglomerate a billion years old. Men were digging large
holes down to about fourteen feet in depth by standing one above another and, without pulleys, handing up, from man to man, buckets of
the reddish clay. Women and children carried these to a flat area enclosed by a two-foot wall with holes; poured water in through the holes
to make a muddy clay; plugged the holes; left the mud to dry for several
days in the sun; shook and winnowed the resulting sand in woven baskets until only heavy particles remained, then raked it level.

The sun bore down on the workers' aching backs, some of them red and welted where the whip's lash had landed. Each merchant owner of an area had placed in it a stone statue of a Hindu god. When the laborers were allowed to break for a meal, each prayed first to this god, no doubt asking for a better life in the next incarnation, before taking a few minutes to squat and eat a handful of cooked rice, using a large leaf as a plate.

Once women and children had readied the earth, men formed a tight line and pounded it with long-handled wooden pestles, marching across it from one end to the other several times. Finally, they walked across very slowly, bending and peering, and if the gods willed it, picking up diamonds.

It was in Kollur town proper, not at the mine site, where Tavernier settled into lodgings and began his diamond buying. When he bought and sold diamonds in Europe, the weight was given in carats, the carat being an ancient unit of measure derived from the small, black, very uniform beans of the carob tree. When John the Baptist, Tavernier's namesake, dwelled in the wilderness eating only "locusts and wild honey," it wasn't the insect he ate, but the fruit of the locust, or carob, tree. Each European diamond center in the seventeenth century had its own prescribed carat weight, so an Amsterdam carat wasn't quite the same as a London one. Not until 1913 (and not until 1923 in South Africa) would weight be standardized at one metric carat = 200 milligrams, or ⅕ of a gram, so there are 142 carats to the ounce.

In most of India, however, diamonds were weighed in *ratis*, a rati being equal to ⅞ of a carat. In Golconda the *mangelin* was the unit used, that being the seed of the red sandalwood tree, equal to 1⅜ of a carat. In his head, Tavernier could, quick as lightning, convert ratis or mangelins to carats—not to mention rupees and pagodas into the French currencies of *livres* and *écus*. Figures darted about his brain as thick as flying white ants on a table.

On his first day in Kollur, Jean-Baptiste went to the town's money changer to do a transaction that would save him time when buying really large, expensive diamonds. He piled his gold pagodas on the table and watched closely while the *shroff* examined each, counted out 2,000, then enclosed that number in a little bag to which he affixed his seal. When many such bags had been sealed, Tavernier paid the money changer his 0.25 percent of the total for his services, stowed the bags carefully in his leather girdle, chewed the requisite betel, and left the shop, spitting exuberantly all the way, purpose in every stride, his smile crimson and broad.

Then one morning, probably in January 1660, Jean-Baptiste dressed with the help of his manservants, breakfasted well, and walked from his lodging to the town square, where all the boys age ten to sixteen who were learning the diamond trade sat cross-legged in a circle under a large tree, each with his diamond weights in a little pouch on one side of his waistband, and a purse containing as much as 600 gold pagodas on the other. When someone with a diamond to sell arrived, "either brought from this or from some other mine," writes Tavernier, the seller gave it to the eldest boy, who passed it to the next, and so on, around the circle, with no one saying a word. The eldest named his price, and bargaining began. At the end of the day, as tree shadows grew long and blue across the square, the boys sorted their newly acquired diamonds, mostly small ones, by color, weight, and "cleanness." They would later sell them to the town's diamond merchants and divide the profits, with the chief boy getting 0.25 percent more. "Young as they are," concludes Jean-Baptiste approvingly, "they know the value of all the stones."

After Tavernier greeted the boys, he entered the nearby shop of a diamond dealer and sat down opposite its owner at a small table. The merchant brought out his parcels of small diamonds first. Since Tavernier adopted Indian ways to facilitate trade, he probably did his buying in the approved native fashion. In complete silence, the merchant and Jean-Baptiste would have stretched their waist sashes across the narrow table to cover what their hands were doing underneath. The price of a diamond was never stated out loud; it was kept secret so the same stone could be sold four or five times with a profit each time and no one the wiser. To reveal his price, the merchant grasped one of Tavernier's short fingers for every 100 pagodas or touched only the knuckle for 50. If he grasped the whole hand, that signified 1,000. Jean-Baptiste then did the finger language for what he was willing to pay; the trader made a counter offer, and so they continued until they reached an agreement.

Toward the end of their session, by which time both Tavernier's square hand and the trader's slim brown one were slippery with sweat, the merchant brought out his great find, his most spectacular stone, his income for months to come, and placed it, his hand trembling, in Tavernier's. It was the Diamond, as big and bright and blue as when we last glimpsed it serving as Siva's omnipotent eye.

As the dealer placed the Diamond in Tavernier's eager hand, his heart raced, excited by its very rare color, its stupendous weight. This was a diamond to bring a man fortune and fame! His hands and eyes both underwent a change, as they did whenever he handled a gemstone. All his crudeness left him. Suddenly he was focused, precise, as expert and graceful in his movements as any virtuoso pianist practicing his art. First, he laid the stone on a small sheet of clean paper, pulled from his waistcoat pocket. Against the white, he could best judge the Diamond's unique hue, which he would later call, in a rare lyrical moment, *"un beau violet"* ("a beautiful violet"; in seventeenth-century France, the terms *violet* and *bleu intense* were interchangeable). He examined it closely, turning it again and again to see each natural face of the huge heart, looking for inclusions and imperfections. He could see none. He took it into the square for a moment and looked at it under the shade of a tree, in natural light. He knew that the buyer he had in mind would want this *pointe naife* cut and polished to European standards; he tried to ascertain how much weight it would lose in the process, how much brilliance it would gain. He peered and pondered.

The Diamond was placed in the scales and weighed in mangelins, which Tavernier quickly converted in his head to an astonishing 112¾₆ carats (110.5 modern metric carats). He had to have it. Tavernier and the merchant raised their sashes across the table and got down to bargaining, the part Jean-Baptiste loved best, for he knew his skills were great. The twenty fingers touched and parted again and again, as if they were weaving invisible threads into a tight little nest.

The only sounds were the buzz of flies and the squawk of a bird from the trees in the square. Finally the two men agreed on a price, which, like so much else, remains a mystery.

Before Tavernier paid for the gem, he and the dealer had to go, as custom decreed, across the square to Kollur's money changer, where Jean-Baptiste produced his sealed bags of pagodas, so that the *shroff* could assure the trader that he had himself sealed them, that they were indeed all good new gold pagodas, all correct, all counted. At last the sale of the Diamond was completed, and Jean-Baptiste tenderly wrapped his new marvel in its own paper and deposited it, with one thumping, triumphant pat, in his leather pouch.

As he stowed it, the Diamond got a new name: for the next eight years, it would be known publicly as the Tavernier Blue—but not privately. Sometimes in the evenings, when loneliness and longing overwhelmed him, Jean-Baptiste liked to talk to his diamonds and give them names: Mélisande . . . Virginie . . . Félicité. He called his blue treasure La Céleste, letting his tongue loll on the *l*'s.

He might have given it a feminine name, but he lived in a time when females were little more than chattels, there to be used, including La Céleste. The Diamond, like the others in the pouch above his groin, provided an excuse to travel, entrée to the sumptuous courts of kings, and, best of all, money, lots of money. He didn't dwell on the blue stone's mystique or terrible beauty or intimations of immortality. It was an item in the marketplace; that was its natural milieu. The squat, determined figure of Jean-Baptiste Tavernier was the villain who invaded the East, kidnaped one of its weighted symbols, and carried it to commerce. From now on, the monetary value of the famous stone will be the first consideration, before its imaginative or historical or aesthetic appeal. And as the years pass and we get to the twenty-first century, the majority of diamonds, not just this one, will be desired and bought for one simple reason: because they are expensive.

Tavernier stayed in Golconda for a total of three or four months, acquiring some other very large, rare diamonds to facilitate his dream. Somehow, with a reliable network of accomplices fed a steady diet of rupees, he managed to smuggle them out past the King of Golconda's corruptible officials and was reunited with his Dutch friends in Surat in the spring of 1660. After further treks across the Indian plains to buy and sell, he sailed back to France in 1662, well satisfied, his bags stuffed to bursting. On all his previous Eastern voyages, he'd returned to France by an overland route through Constantinople, but this time, fearful of all the robbers en route who might steal La Céleste and his other beauties, he went by sea, around the dangerous waters of the Cape of Good Hope.

On that long sea voyage, the Diamond lay inside the scarred old leather girdling Tavernier's ample waist, often on its head from his movements and the ship's. There were many days of darkness, dampness, and creaking timbers.

Shortly after his return to Paris, the fifty-seven-year-old Tavernier married Madeleine Goisse, daughter of the jeweler who had trained him well twenty-six years before and with whom Jean-Baptiste had been dealing over the years. Perhaps he married her for her substantial dowry or out of gratitude to Goisse; perhaps he wanted a reliable, stay-at-home custodian for his treasures or wanted to save himself the cost of a housekeeper. In any case it seems to have been a *mariage de convenance*. He swore to Madeleine that he would stay at her side till death did them part and that his traveling days were over.

In November of the very next year, 1663, before she'd even unpacked her chest of bridal linens, Jean-Baptiste left her in charge of the Tavernier Blue, kissed her perfunctorily on both cheeks, told her to guard his unsold diamonds with her life, and sailed gleefully away on his final trip to India.

He would be gone for five years and took with him his nephew, son of his brother Gabriel, the goldsmith of Uzes, who wanted Uncle Jean-Baptiste to teach him how to grow rich from Eastern trade. Tavernier left his nephew at a Capuchin convent in Tauris, to learn Turkish and Armenian, and pushed on to India but didn't make the taxing trip to Golconda or its mines.

In the autumn of 1665, he got himself invited to the five-day birthday party honoring King Aurungzeb, wanting not only to see his jewel collection, the most fabulous in the world, but also to carry coals to Newcastle, as it were, and sell him more gems. Aurungzeb was a formidable monarch, who had seized power by imprisoning his father, cutting off the heads of his three brothers and inventing a hooked device to be worn as a glove with which he could, with one swipe, disembowel anyone who crossed him.

To gain access to Aurungzeb, Tavernier had to pack his trunks with many expensive gifts to be lavished on king, kin, and court officials, including "a battle axe of crystal set with rubies and emeralds." The presents had cost Jean-Baptiste 23,187 *livres* (about $186,000 in today's currency. Note: Amounts given are all in U.S. dollars). He was therefore justly incensed on arriving at the king's Delhi palace to be refused admittance; he at once drew his sword and threatened a guard. This was, given Aurungzeb's high-handed ways, rather rash and reckless behavior, but somehow the guards let him proceed to the room where the mighty Mogul ruler reclined on his famous bed-shaped Peacock Throne, its every surface ablaze with jewels, which Jean-Baptiste wasn't too goggle-eyed to count: 108 cabochon rubies, all over 100 carats, 116 emeralds. . . . Spread tailed and gem studded above the canopy was the world's biggest, brightest peacock, symbol of the sun for the Moguls. Two of Aurungzeb's eunuchs brought all his gems for Jean-Baptiste to see, carrying them in on two gold-leaf trays, one covered with a red velvet cloth, the other with a green. He was the first European ever to see the Great Mogul, the half-egg 296-carat diamond that he'd long pictured in his mind.

On December 6, 1668, a triumphant Tavernier arrived in Paris with a cargo of furniture, fabrics, and 3 million *livres'* worth of gems ($24 million today). He was relieved to find that Madeleine had kept all his jewels including La Céleste safe from thieves, floods, fire, and all other acts of God. The bride who had languished husbandless for five years was now left to amuse herself in the evenings before flagging hearth flames. Jean-Baptiste was in his jeweler's stronghold, playing with his gems, sorting, weighing, talking to them fondly, lining them up on paper, ready at last to execute the ambitious plan that he'd conceived one evening nine years before, sipping his tari wine beneath

Golconda's lemon tree. The blue Diamond had the place of honor in the exact center of the paper, since of all the gems he'd assembled it had the greatest value.

In just a few more days, the Diamond would quit the depressing company of this profit-minded, middle-class capitalist. It was about to fall into the hands of another man who would exploit it, but for very different, and much grander, reasons. It would never see its homeland again, but in compensation, it was bound for a burst of light as glorious and far-reaching as the sun itself.

The Sun King, Louis XIV, in full complement of diamond buttons.

3

GLORY

Glory is like a circle in the water,
Which never ceaseth to enlarge itself,
Till by broad spreading it disperse to nought.
—WILLIAM SHAKESPEARE, *King Henry VI, Part I*, act 1, scene 2

It was so cold on that iron-gray morning in late December 1668 that the edges of the Seine had frozen into a filigree of Venetian point lace, making the Paris river, full, as always, of floating refuse, look unusually elegant. But its resident swans had trouble finding food. France's current king, Louis XIV, had ordered them imported to add a note of grace and opulence to the river. His minister of finance had protested—but mildly—that swans would prove impractical, one more extravagance. What His Majesty wanted, however, he always got, including decorative birds on the dirty brown Seine.

In a part of Paris not far from the river, Tavernier was getting dressed with the help of his valet. Today Jean-Baptiste would see his dream become reality; he was about to sell gems to France's supreme consumer, his sovereign. Louis XIV insisted that every man who appeared at court, so as not to offend the discriminating royal eye, be attired in full court dress, complete with sword. Jean-Baptiste was therefore putting on a shirt with lace ruffles on its sleeves, a vest richly embroidered, fine woolen knee breeches, and a brand-new frock coat, stylishly cut in brown velvet. Louis XIV had issued a decree six years before, forbidding the middle classes to wear cloth-of-gold (fabric interwoven with real gold threads), which was strictly for king and nobles. When he'd donned all his finery and buckled on his sword,

Jean-Baptiste surveyed himself briefly in the nearest mirror. Where was his precious freedom to be his own man now? There he stood, in ruffled lace and shoulder ribbons, turned into a fop, a dandy, by his king. And he felt naked, bereft, without his habitual gem pouch, which was far too old and worn to appear at court, and vastly constrained inside new shoes that pinched and a starched cravat that chafed his neck if he turned his head. He was sweating already; drops were forming beneath the fat folds of his chin.

He turned his back on the mirror, walked stiffly into his gem office, opened the strongbox where the blue Diamond rested, removed it, wrapped it carefully, and put it, with many fellow gemstones, all very fine, into a velvet pouch. Then, as Madeleine stood smiling and waving in their doorway, Jean-Baptiste climbed into his coach for the ride to the Louvre palace.

Tavernier's carriage and driver made their way along the broad streets where shops catered to gentry and through the narrower, noisier, crowded alleys where vendors hawked their wares, their loud voices rising above the constant clatter of iron wheels on stones: "Rabbit skins!" "Prunes from Tours!" "Soles for boots!" At that time Paris streets were so ill-lit that no one went out after dark, fearing robbers, so that when daylight came, cats slunk home to sleep and everyone else emerged.

As Tavernier's carriage reached the Quai d'Orsay, where he noticed the frustrated swans, gliding and bobbing on the freezing Seine, Louis XIV was still in his gilded bed, putting on his underclothes. By seventeenth-century standards, he was fanatically clean, so he'd already been rubbed down with spirits by his valet, as he was every morning, and would change his linen three times that day. But like his subjects, the king eschewed water as a cleansing agent. When His Majesty had his underwear on, he emerged from the bed to go through the daily morning dressing ceremony known as the *lever*. At this time it was still a work in progress, a kind of out-of-town tryout for the spectacular show to come on the far more splendid stage that Louis would later create. As star performer and producer, he hadn't yet had a long enough run to maximize the ritual involved and perfect every gesture.

The *lever* ceremony, however, was already immensely popular. A member of the court had described it one year earlier as "three rooms full of people of quality, and a crowd and a crush which is unbelievable trying to get into the room of His Majesty, and more than eight hundred carriages outside the Louvre." Louis loved the audience for his dressing, all craning their necks to see him, but hated having to perform in the gloomy, decrepit, drafty old Louvre. This palace skulked, as if feeling its shame, behind high crenellated towers and filthy moats and ditches into which every butcher and fish peddler in the nearby Quartier des Halles threw his garbage, so the palace itself seemed to give off an embarrassing stench. It was a rabbit warren of ill-assorted structures, tottering and unfinished.

The only part of the Louvre that this royal consumer really liked was the row of shops under the Long Gallery running along the edge of the Seine all the way to the Tuileries, where the king would move three years later after a fire made the Louvre uninhabitable. Here at the Louvre, Louis had given space and stipends to the jewelers, painters, engravers, sculptors, tailors, and others who were, at the very moment when their sovereign was going through the dressing ceremony, opening the shutters of their shop fronts to the morning light and beginning the delicious business of making him appear grand and glorious to the world.

When all his outer garments had been duly handed to him, each by a different court noble, and duly donned, he walked with his usual perfect posture to an elaborately carved and gilded mirror and regarded the splendid figure reflected there.

In projecting the image of a king, God had given thirty-year-old Louis a good start, and the rest he was more than capable of doing himself. His light brown hair, thick and luxuriant and wavy, fell to his shoulders. He had not yet begun to wear a long, curly wig; that would come five years later, after some hair loss. His olive skin was tanned from hours on horseback; he had an aquiline nose, sensual mouth, cleft chin, and small but brilliant eyes, which saw everything. He sported a debonair little mustache, recently grown, and "sometimes spent half an hour in front of his mirror arranging it with wax," according to one court diarist. He moved, always, with exquisite grace and was the best-mannered man in Europe. His bearing was so proud, so upright, that although he was only five feet five inches tall, one subject described him as "six feet tall as near as makes no matter."

The king regarded himself with complacency in the mirror but didn't smile, even at himself. His smiles were rare. Under a long coat in gold brocade, he wore an embroidered vest in the bright colors he preferred in the springtime of his life: tulip red, leaf green, and his favorite violet-blue. His woolen knee breeches were snuff brown, as were his hose and buckled shoes, which had high red heels; he knew that he had the shapeliest male legs in the kingdom. On shoulders, sleeves, garters, and shoes, on every possible perch, were scarlet satin ribbon explosions of sheer vanity and exuberance.

Louis turned reluctantly from the mirror. A courtier handed him his sword; another gave him the Cordon Bleu sash, with its diamond-studded cross of the Order of the Holy Ghost at one end. Louis slipped it on diagonally across his manly chest. The grand master of the robes entered, bearing an oval tray on which lay three handkerchiefs, each with a different kind of lace. Louis pondered this important decision; then chose two. The grand master handed him his large plumed hat with diamond buckle, his gloves with wide embroidered cuffs, and his cane. His Majesty, Louis XIV, King of France, was now ready to face the day.

He looked one last time in the mirror and frowned. There were diamonds in all the possible places one could put them: they sat on shoulder knots, sleeve ribbons, on buttons and around buttonholes, on lapels and lace cravat and fingers. The trouble was, diamonds in daylight looked like insipid bits of not-very-good glass. They only came to life and sparkled at night, in candlelight. This posed, for Louis, a major problem. Other gemstones didn't cost as much as diamonds, and so didn't suit the image of a great king. What he needed—*bien sûr!*—was a *colored* diamond, something truly spectacular. Perhaps the jeweler he was seeing today, just back from India—what was his name?—would have something.

As Louis promenaded the length of the very sparsely furnished Long Gallery on his way to Mass in the chapel, the crowds parted before him, and his red heels rang out on the black-and-white-marble floor, the only attractive thing, apart from himself, in the entire Louvre.

He had been conceived there, a conception that was declared by everyone in France, including his surprised parents, as God's miracle. On Christmas Day 1615, his father, King Louis XIII, had married Anne of Austria, a Hapsburg who was actually Spanish. On her wedding day, declaring "I want everything to be French," she proved her allegiance to her new country by wearing fleur-de-lis earrings. Since her husband's sexual preferences ran to young men, Anne, understandably enough, couldn't seem to produce an heir during the following twenty-two years. Then, on the night of December 5, 1637, by which time Anne was thirty-eight and hadn't slept with Louis for years, a violent rainstorm occurring when he was en route to his hunting lodge forced Louis to spend the night in the Louvre. Since his own apartment there was unfurnished, he shared Anne's bed and proved most obliging. Nine months later, on September 5, 1638, Anne gave birth to a healthy son, France's future Louis XIV, who weighed nine pounds and already sported two teeth; he was washed in wine and oil of roses and declared a gift of God. Anne gave birth to a second son, Philip, two years later, who joined Louis in the nursery, hung with white damask, and shared his seventeen servants. In the fashion of the time, Louis as a child wore satin or brocade dresses on which lay the pale blue sash of the Order of the Holy Ghost. His mother's lady-in-waiting, Madame de Motteville, reported "with astonishment" that he "never laughed."

Court ladies fought over his dark blond curls and preserved them in silver lockets. On April 21, 1643, when he was four, he was taken to the bedside of his father, dying of tuberculosis. "Who is it?" asked the expiring king, with gasping breath. "Louis XIV," came the stout reply.

Three weeks later, on May 14, his father died and Louis became King of France, with his mother acting as regent. "The Queen always insisted that he should be obeyed" wrote Madame de Motteville, "and seemed to desire that his power should be respected." Fortunately for France, there was a power behind the throne: Cardinal Jules Mazarin, who became chief minister, gave good advice to the four-year-old monarch and his mother—and according to some historians, shared her bed.

Olive-skinned and pudgy, Mazarin was Italian, son of the butler to a wealthy Roman family. He was gentle and soft-spoken, the best-dressed man of his day, favoring coats in a rich shade soon known as Mazarin blue and perfuming not only himself but also his pet monkey. He was smart, shrewd, and very ambitious. His one vice was greed, for he loved money and the beautiful things it could buy. Like Tavernier, he was a canny merchant adventurer. Mazarin owned part of a whaling company and a number of cargo ships that enabled him to buy and sell grain, spices, sugar, soap, cork, amber, and coral. By 1658 he had an annual income equivalent to $6.5 million today, with which he indulged his chief pleasures: building and furnishing palaces; collecting works of art; buying precious stones, most particularly diamonds of the highest quality. In Louis's youth, Mazarin would be largely responsible for forming his acquisitive tastes, including his passion for diamonds and for the color blue.

At age seven, the boy king was finally taken out of dresses and put into breeches, while his valets stopped telling him fairy tales at bedtime and started on French history, pointing out the good kings and the bad. Three years later the minor royals and nobility of France rebelled against their sovereign's absolute authority in a civil war known as the Fronde, which would rage off and on for five years before Louis subdued them. Ever since the reign of Francis I, the Swiss had supplied France with troops for their wars, but Louis found himself in the embarrassing position of not having enough money in the treasury to pay them. Twice he had to raise funds by pledging the crown jewels and when, in 1652, he still couldn't pay what had long been owing them, the enraged Swiss officers hauled all the gems off to Zurich, while Louis could do nothing but suffer silently from the indignity and shame of it all. (He didn't pay up and retrieve them until 1665.)

Money was so scarce in those growing-up years that the King of France's bedsheets were in holes, his coach upholstery in tatters, and his shabby old green velvet dressing gown lined with rabbit fur came only to his shapely, well-muscled calves. He had first exhibited them in a ballet at age twelve and would dance in forty court ballets before he finally hung up his dancing shoes just a few months before that cold December morning when he looked at himself in his well-gilded mirror and lusted for a colored diamond.

When Louis was fifteen, on a bright June day, he was crowned king in Rheims cathedral, splendidly garbed in a blue velvet royal robe embroidered with gold fleurs-de-lis and lined in ermine. The presiding bishop placed a diamond ring on the king's left hand to symbolize his marriage to France, but since the crown jewels were still in hock, Louis had to borrow the ring from his mother and return it that night.

When, at the end of the ceremony, the bishop cried, "May the king live forever!" five hundred birds were released from their cages in the galleries. For a few minutes they fluttered about, disoriented, and then flew upward, with one great taffeta rush of wings, to sunlight streaming down from stained-glass windows in sapphire and emerald shards.

"The task of a king," Louis would later write, "is great, noble and delectable," for "God wills that whoever is born a subject should obey without question." He believed wholeheartedly in the divine right of kings and not at all in the rights of individuals. There would be no freedom of speech, of press, or of worship in this monarch's reign. God had chosen and anointed Louis on that glorious day in Rheims cathedral to be his earthly representative. In the royal chapel, the king worshiped God; the rest turned their backs on the altar and worshiped the king, who was accountable to no man. Such absolute power was indeed "delectable."

When he was eighteen, Louis fell in love with black-eyed Marie

Mancini, Cardinal Mazarin's niece, advertising his romantic attachment by giving her earrings with three large diamonds forming a fleur-de-lis above pearl drops. It would be the only time in Louis's adult life that he didn't consummate his love for a woman. This was probably because two years before, when he'd lost his virginity to one of his mother's ladies of the bedchamber twenty years his senior, he'd contracted gonorrhea. His doctors, who, like everyone around him, were properly cowed and deferential, assured him that his discomfort could well be the result of "excessive equestrian exercise."

Three years later, in June 1660, Louis married Marie-Thérèse, the Spanish infanta who was his double first cousin, since they had the same four grandparents. She was a colorless little thing with a child's mentality and teeth blackened by eating too much chocolate. She knew she was no beauty; once, arrayed in full court dress, she said to someone holding a candle to see her better, "This is where you should look," pointing to her diamond-laden gown, "and not here," pointing to her face. For the moment, however, the cash-strapped and crown-jewel-deprived Louis could give his bride only a pair of earrings, rather minuscule compared with Marie Mancini's. Marie-Thérèse adored her new husband and so didn't mind at all; she cared not a whit for jewels, preferring to amuse herself with little dogs, dwarfs, and religious devotions. Perhaps Louis, who would always be the one to wear the diamonds in that family, deliberately chose a wife who didn't like them. He was not attracted physically to Marie-Thérèse, but since his royal duty included producing heirs, he closed his eyes and thought of France again and again in the years to come, until the nursery was full of offspring, six in all. Each morning after he'd shared her bed, Marie-Thérèse clapped her hands at the *lever* to advertise the fact.

In the following year, on March 9, 1661, Cardinal Mazarin, age fifty-nine, in his castle filled to bursting with Persian carpets, Renaissance paintings, tapestries, statuary, and objets d'art, died, as one wag put it, "in the arms of fortune." But only after he'd had his chin shaved, mustache curled, lips rouged, cheeks powdered, been carried in his sedan chair one last time around his beautiful garden, played a final game of cards (he lost), and confessed his sins, including avarice.

On hearing of his prime minister's death, twenty-two-year-old Louis, as he tells us "felt my mind and courage soar" and "felt quite another man. Only then did it seem to me," he continues, "that I was king." He would never appoint another chief minister but would hang on to all the power himself. He was determined that never again would he sink into the poverty-stricken state caused by the Fronde uprising. He reduced his nobles to impotence, appointed all government officials from the middle class, and made parliament only a legal instrument for implementing his wishes.

Mazarin left all his treasures to his godson Louis, of which the greatest was Jean-Baptiste Colbert, the cardinal's financial adviser. "I was fundamentally convinced that I had not been placed and preserved on the throne with so great a passion to do well without being provided with the means," writes the king. Now "the means" had appeared, and not a moment too soon. Colbert, age forty-one, son of a wool merchant, dour, reserved, unsmiling, with thick black eyebrows fixed in a perpetual frown, became the king's minister of finance and superintendent of works. Like the other Jean-Baptiste in this story, Colbert cared only for commerce. He was a workaholic who labored at his desk fifteen hours a day, seven days a week. He told Louis that he should keep track of every expenditure, however small. The king meekly carried a little red leather book thereafter in a pocket and was kept very busy writing in it, page after page after page. In the next ten years, the national revenue would double, thanks to Colbert, who was the real power behind the diamonds Louis just couldn't stop buying.

"When kings have tasted money," according to the French novelist Alexander Dumas, "they are like tigers who have tasted flesh; they devour everything." Once Colbert had filled his coffers, so it was with Louis. He launched himself on a wild, lifelong, compulsive spending spree, and even when, after Colbert's death, the coffers were empty and Louis was deeply in debt, he just went on buying.

In addition to Colbert, Mazarin left to king and crown what we can call Louis's first taste of flesh: eighteen spectacular diamonds, worth the equivalent of $10 million, at a time when the entire French crown jewels, still in pawn, were worth only $4.5 million. When

Charles I of England had been executed in 1649, Mazarin had made a deal with Oliver Cromwell, leader of the Puritans responsible for beheading their king, to buy His Majesty's jewels, including the famous 25-carat Mirror of Portugal. When poor Charles put his head on the block, he had nothing left except a pearl in one ear. The Mazarin collection also included the 53¾-carat Grand Sancy, and the 21-carat Grand Mazarin.

In one amazing year, 1661, lucky young Louis XIV acquired not only Colbert and Mazarin's whopping great diamonds but also a son and heir, his first mistress, and the brilliant idea for his magnificent dream palace. His appetites were tremendous: for power, sex, diamonds, palaces, food, everything. At dinner, taken midafternoon in the seventeenth century, he usually ate his way through four bowls of soup, a whole pheasant, a partridge, several thick slices of ham, mutton and gravy, hard-boiled eggs, a large dish of salad, a whole plate of cakes, and fruit.

One spring evening at a lottery party given by his mother, Louis won the main prize: a pair of diamond bracelets. He sat still for a moment, while every woman in the room held her breath, hoping to become mistress to the handsome young king. Then he crossed the room and handed the bracelets to Louise de la Vallière, who had silvery blond hair, skin like porcelain, and a fragile look resulting from her small, slight frame. Being properly modest—Madame de Sévigné, the famous French letter writer, called her "that little violet hidden under the grass"—Louise immediately handed the bracelets back, commenting wistfully on their beauty. "In that case," Louis told her gravely, "they are in hands too fair to resign them."

"Do you see that girl with the diamond earrings?" sighed plain little Queen Marie-Thérèse to her lady-in-waiting a few days later. "It is she whom the King loves." For two weeks in July, while the court was cavorting at Fontainebleau, one of the royal estates, Louis and Louise—even their names matched—rode together in the beech woods, strolled in the gardens, fed the golden carp glinting in the pond. Then Louis danced the lead in a ballet fittingly titled *Impatience*, and the next day he bedded Louise. Queen Marie-Thérèse retired more or less permanently to her chapel to pray, weep, and take what comfort she could from jeweled chalices and crosses.

In that same year, 1661, Louis conceived his greatest coup of imagination: the château of Versailles, designed, in the words of Madame de Motteville, "to show by its adornment what a great king can do when he spares nothing to satisfy his wishes." In those halcyon days of impulse and indulgence at the beginning of his reign, the court flitted at His Majesty's pleasure from one royal abode near Paris to another: from Fontainebleau to Saint-Germain to Versailles, where his father had built a modest hunting lodge. Rather than tear it down and start his own palace on a more scenic site, Louis decided to keep this jewel at the center and to let his golden vision materialize slowly, magically, as an elaborate setting around it. Building began at once on what would be the most famous dwelling in the Western world, created by its best architects, artists, and craftsmen.

In the year after Louis's life exploded into light and love, he fixed on the sun as his personal symbol, a kind of seventeenth-century equivalent to a modern-day logo. He'd already starred in a ballet as the sun, shining in cloth-of-gold and diamonds, clicking castenets and pointing his jeweled fingers into long, thin rays. To enhance his blazing image, Louis began the serious business of diamond buying. From his cousin Marie of Lorraine in 1665, he bought the famous House of Guise diamond, for the equivalent of $3 million. Two years later the king purchased all the jewels of Marie-Louise de Gonzague, the just-deceased Queen of Poland, paying $1.36 million. Colbert's frown grew formidable, but Louis pointed out that historical tradition endorsed his belief that diamonds are a king's best friend.

Throughout the Middle Ages, no one else in Europe had worn them; they were too costly and too hard to come by for anyone but kings. Charlemagne, legendary monarch and Holy Roman Emperor, who died in A.D. 814, used two diamonds, their natural planes partially polished, to clasp his royal cloak. The crown of Hungary's king, around A.D. 1000, was set with uncut diamonds given him by the Byzantine emperor. Circa 1285, France's Philip IV, called Philip the Fair and eager to remain so, passed a law forbidding commoners to wear the stones. England's Henry IV had his portrait painted around 1400 with two blue octahedrons holding up his sleeves. Until 1444 diamonds in Europe were the exclusive property not only of rulers but of males, to be flashed mainly from scepters, swords, and crowns. In that momentous year, brave, bold Agnès Sorel, who had not a drop of blue blood, mistress to France's Charles VII, dared to appear in diamonds, thus striking a blow for women and commoners, who have been wearing them with great relish ever since. Agnès, who liked her silk dresses and shoes lined with sable—medieval castles were full of drafts—ordered the jeweler Jacques Coeur, just back from India with bagfuls of the precious gems, to set some in necklaces, brooches, and a curve-fitting bodice, where they mixed with emeralds and rubies. When Agnès's diamond choker rasped her neck, turning it an unbecoming shade of turkey-wattle red, she sent it back to Jacques and commanded him to keep polishing until she told him to stop.

Not about to let a low-born mistress get ahead of them, queens and princesses began acquiring the stones. Princess Mary of Burgundy became the very first woman to wear a diamond engagement ring, ordered for her by besotted Archduke Maximilian of Germany in 1477. From that day forward, diamonds became the traditional jewels with which to herald marriage. At roughly the same time, Queen Isabella of Spain began to collect them, then pledged them all to raise the necessary funds for Christopher Columbus to cross the Atlantic looking for a short-cut to India so Isabella could cut out the middleman and buy her gems directly from the only known source. What Columbus "discovered," of course, was America, which was bad luck for its native peoples and for Isabella. I suppose one might say that America owes its present existence to diamonds. On this rock . . .

Francis I of France, at whose court Leonardo da Vinci had stayed three years and painted the *Mona Lisa*, had a collar of eleven huge diamonds, some table-cut, some pointed, made in 1530. It was Francis who instituted the crown jewels of France as a permanent collection, and also what we can call the diplomacy of conspicuous luxury, guaranteed to impress foreign leaders and ambassadors, something Louis XIV would master better than any monarch before or since. Ten years before he acquired his stupendous collar, Francis I had ridden across a French field toward a summit conference with Henry VIII of England, mounted on a gold-caparisoned horse and shining for all he was worth in a cloth-of-gold suit positively polka-dotted with diamonds. Louis XIV's grandmother, Marie de Medici, who'd married his grandfather, first Bourbon French king, Henri IV, in 1600, wore them in her hair, on her forehead, at her throat, in her ears, on every finger and both thumbs. Perhaps Louis XIV's passion for the stones resulted partly from the royal tradition endorsed by history and partly from his genes. When his father, Louis XIII, Queen Marie's son, was christened, she outshone everybody with three thousand diamonds, not to mention two thousand pearls, sewn onto her gown.

Apart from impressing their own subjects as well as rival sovereigns and their representatives, there may have been another reason for kings and consorts to pavé themselves in the world's most precious gem. It may have been a clever ploy for blinding all eyes to their physical deformities. Royals in those days always married other royals, ignoring close blood ties, a practice that accentuated genetic defects in their offspring. If enough diamonds dazzled, maybe gawking subjects wouldn't notice hunchbacks, goiters, crossed eyes, withered arms, and clubfeet. If their bodies were more or less symmetrical, the royal skin, like that of the rest of the population, was probably covered with wens, warts, boils, scars, and pockmarks. They needed their diamonds.

It was during his *annus mirabilis* of 1661, just after his twenty-third birthday, on October 15, that Louis installed his own jeweler, Laurent le Texier de Montarsy, in one of the Louvre boutiques under the Long Gallery so he could shop without ever leaving home. No European monarch before Louis XIV, and none after him, used and exploited diamonds so extensively and so successfully for achieving political and national goals, for showing the world that the country he ruled was the richest one in Europe, wealthier than Holland or England or Spain— even when it wasn't. Diamonds signified wealth, and wealth signified power among nations, successful trade abroad, prosperity at home, victory in wars of territorial conquest. In the three years before Louis summoned Tavernier to court, he'd bought the equivalent today of

$18 million worth of the most expensive of all stones until, as the di-arist Saint-Simon notes, his person positively "crackled with diamonds."

"What might be considered as superfluous expenses make a very favorable impression of magnificence, wealth and greatness," writes Louis. His image-making machine of writers, sculptors, painters, and tapestry makers surfeited his subjects with a stream of books focused on his heroic exploits, medals struck for victories on the battlefield, can-vases painted of special court ceremonies, engravings printed after every picnic or hunting party, all geared to give the king *éclat*, a flash of brilliance, a new burst of *gloire*. Glory was a complex term in the sev-enteenth century, denoting fame, honor, and magnaminity. Glory was the trumpet's highest note, the mountain's peak, the brass ring big enough to girdle the globe. "The love of glory assuredly takes prece-dence over all other [passions] in my soul," declared Louis. Diamonds contributed to *éclat*, confirmed *gloire*.

Louis had two complete sets of them for his coat and vest. One set had 123 buttons, 300 buttonhole surrounds, 19 floral sprays, plus 96 more buttonhole designs for his waistcoat. The second set consisted of 216 buttons, 355 buttonhole decorations, plus another 96 for the vest. Louis often wore a necklace of 45 diamonds, some of them the Maza-rins; his cross belt and sword would eventually sparkle with $12 mil-lion worth. One hat ornament contained seven huge diamonds, one of 42 carats, and many more smaller stones adorned his shoe buckles, so that he dazzled top to toe, a Sun King indeed. Earlier kings had been content with the various orders of chivalry made in gold, silver, and colored enamels. In 1663 Louis had ordered a jeweler called Lescot to make a cross for the Order of the Holy Ghost with $308,000 worth of the precious gems. Louis XIV might well have been the only man in the world to own a diamond-studded desk, acquired later in his reign. It was made in silver gilt, enriched with four diamonds at the corners, plus a large one adorning a drawer handle. His Majesty dipped his quill pen into an inkstand formed from a blue enamel globe with diamond fleurs-de-lis, surmounted by a sun, its gold rays sprinkled with dia-monds. One hopes the prose he wrote was as sparkling.

Louis didn't keep all his diamonds for himself; he scattered them so generously in his path that they might well have been seeds of grain, landing on ambassadors, generals, courtesans, mistresses, even servants. He once gave a diamond worth $8,800 to a man who brought him some pretty birds. Louis also encouraged his courtiers to buy diamonds; many of them did so, fell deeply into debt, and when gambling games became popular at court, played recklessly trying to recoup.

When, in May 1665, Louis's mother, Anne, knew she was dying, she summoned her eldest son to her bedside to tell him that his brother Philip, always known at court as Monsieur, would get her jewels. As Anne's lady-in-waiting tells us, "the king showed that he was not content with this." So Anne, who had always indulged him, revised her will, leaving jewels worth $10,510,400 today to be divided equally between Louis and Philip. Shortly after her death on January 20, 1666, her great chest of jewels covered in red morocco leather embossed with gold fleurs-de-lis was carried, its two clasps still locked and sealed, to a room where Louis and Monsieur eagerly awaited it.

Philip was a flaming homosexual who wore a jet black curly wig, painted his lips into a scarlet cupid's bow, and minced about in five-inch heels and clouds of perfume. On the battlefield, however, his courage was legendary. "He's more afraid of sun and dust than of guns," his soldiers liked to say. Monsieur adored jewels quite as much as Louis did— but perhaps had more need of them to soothe his psyche, for royal duty forced him to marry not once but twice and to sire eleven children. His first wife was Henrietta, the witty, thin, enchanting daughter of Charles I of England, who wore the portrait of her pug Mimi, framed in twenty diamonds, on her slender wrist. On his wedding night— so court gossips whispered—Philip hung gold religious medals on his private parts, then simultaneously prayed and performed. Henrietta would die of peritonitis in 1670, whereupon Monsieur felt duty bound to take another wife in the very next year, and we're glad he did, for she proved to be an indefatigable correspondent to friends across Europe, leaving us one of the best records of Louis XIV's reign in letters that are vivid, opinionated, perceptive, sometimes bawdy, and always amusing. Princess Elisabeth Charlotte (1652–1722), daughter of the Elector-Palatine of Bavaria, known to her intimates as Liselotte, describes herself as "square as a dice, my skin is red, tinged with yellow," nose "crooked and pitted with smallpox to boot" and teeth "jagged." She considered herself "so ugly that I have never been tempted to use much ornamentation." She hunted eight hours a day, clumped about in riding habits, and like Louis's wife, Marie-Thérèse, had no interest in jewels. "It was a good thing that I felt like this," she writes, because "Monsieur, who was extremely fond of dressing up, would have had hundreds of quarrels with me as to which of us should wear the most beautiful diamonds." As it was, he got to wear them all. (Liselotte would always be half in love with her brother-in-law, the king.)

On that January day in 1666, Louis and Philip, with great delight and little or no arguing, since the king's divine rights prevailed, opened their mother's red morocco chest and divided the spoils. Louis went for quality and took only six items: Anne's choker of thirty-one enormous pearls and five extremely choice jewels, all in diamonds and pearls, including coronet and earrings, the total worth almost $6 million. Philip, on the other hand, was content with quantity. Dressed in his usual excess of bows, lace, frills, plumes, and ribbons, he scooped up handfuls of colored gems, loading his arms with bracelets of mixed diamonds, sapphires, rubies, and his fingers with lots and lots of rings. Both brothers sighed in frustration at all the outstanding jewels no one would ever get to wear, which glinted from eighty religious objects, from crosses, chalices, and reliquary boxes now in the Louvre.

In October that year, Louise de la Vallière excused herself from a court ball, gave birth to a daughter and, such being "the king's pleasure," returned to the party. Court life was not for the weak. Louis, of course, was the father, but he was growing tired of Louise, and in the following year, 1667, fell madly in love with sparkling, sophisticated, very pretty Athenaïs de Montespan, married to a marquis and mother of two. Louise had been gentle, pious, and passive; Athenaïs was animated, irreverent, and manipulative. She could mimic everyone at court, engage in quicksilver repartee, and make the king laugh, not an easy thing to do. Louise had been a simple country mouse; Athenaïs was a woman of style who knew that the best Paris shop for tiny black beauty spots was À la Perle des Mouches, that the perfect glove had to be made of leather scented with musk prepared in Spain, cut in France, and sewn in England. She liked to live life on the edge and to gamble for enormous stakes. At the moment when she ensnared Louis, her earrings, set with nine diamonds each, were in pawn at a Paris shop in Place Maubert. (Later, when her gambling addiction grew worse, she would lose $30 million in an evening and win it back the next.) In her selfless, gentle way, Louise had loved Louis for himself; Athenaïs loved him because he was rich and powerful, because her liaison with him resulted in a glittering—but not, alas, unending—stream of mansions, furniture to fill them, carriages, clothes, and jewels. Her passion for diamonds equaled the king's. "The diamond is beyond contradiction the most beautiful creation in the hands of God in the order of inanimate things," she enthuses in her memoirs. "This precious stone, as durable as the sun, and far more accessible than that, shines with the same fire, ties all its rays and colors in a single facet and lavishes its charms, by night and day, in every clime, at all seasons." She would later pour her curves into a dress quite as famous in its day as the one in which Marilyn Monroe, in 1962, sang "Happy Birthday" to President Kennedy in Manhattan's Madison Square Garden. Athenaïs's gown, surely "contrived by fairies," according to Madame de Sévigné, was "a robe of gold cloth on a gold ground, with a double gold border embroidered and worked in gold, so that it makes the finest gold stuff ever imagined by the wit of man." You can't get much golder than that.

Louis was feeling euphoric, at the peak of his sovereign and sexual powers. On July 18, 1668, he staged a fête for three thousand guests in the extensive gardens, newly designed by Le Notre, of his partly built château of Versailles. Three hundred years before the elaborate stage effects of Broadway and West End musicals, Louis XIV was masterminding productions quite as spectacular and costly. Two buildings were built for the day: one for the banquet and another for the ball. Silver tables were heaped with food, flower garlands, spun-sugar confections. The head table was set for sixty-four: the king, sixty-two beautiful women including the enchanting Athenaïs—and Monsieur, who was no competition at all when it came to erotic exchanges. Just before dawn, having danced and feasted all night, the Sun King and his guests watched the dark sky fill with fireworks, climaxed by a giant *L* shooting heavenward in a burst of gold. *L* for Louis, the man who, in appearance and manner, was king to his core.

He certainly looked the part, accoutred as he was by a phalanx of valets, hairdressers, tailors, embroiderers, lace makers, cobblers, glove makers, hatters, jewelers. He played the role of monarch with panache, to packed houses, in a smash hit that ran for seventy-two years. He definitely had star quality. But never, not in any painting, engraving, or verbal description that has come down to us, or in any of his letters, do we see him in a private moment, a man called Louis disheveled and impulsive. His iron control allowed none of his feelings to surface. His adamantine will prevailed. He was a hard, self-centered entity, sufficient unto himself, rare, awesome, "framed in the prodigality of nature." Louis, in short, was himself very like a diamond, more symbol than substance, igniting the imagination of others, bearing the weight of their dreams. The diamond was Louis XIV's most consonant emblem, not the sun.

Five months after the grand fête at Versailles, on that cold December morning when we left King Louis tapping his red heels on the Long Gallery's marble squares, en route to Mass in the Louvre chapel, Tavernier's carriage, with a tense Jean-Baptiste inside, was just passing under the impressive new gate built, on the king's command, at the eastern end of the Louvre by the great Italian sculptor-architect Gian Lorenzo Bernini. Over the gate was carved the inscription "World, come see what I see . . . a King worthy of all the Caesars." Modesty had never been one of Louis's virtues.

Tavernier's driver carefully maneuvered the horse-drawn coach into the courtyard where hundreds of others jockeyed for space. Jean-Baptiste, clutching his velvet pouch of gems, descended and made his way through the well-dressed crowd to the shop beneath the Long Gallery of Laurent Montarsy, the court jeweler with whom he had often had business dealings, some of them, according to one historian, a little less than honest. Laurent, who saw the king often, had agreed to stay by Jean-Baptiste's side through the coming ordeal. Together they entered the crowded Long Gallery where, as Louis XIV paraded through it at slow and regal pace after Mass, supplicant citizens would present their petitions.

The crowd was packed solid, all talking in excited voices, all craning their necks to assess each other's finery while they waited for the Sun King to come out of the chapel. Jean-Baptiste and Montarsy took up their posts in a window embrasure.

At last, beginning at the gallery's far end and running along its length, hundreds of voices murmured "the king . . . king . . . king," as if one crystal bead after another were clicking onto a long string.

There he was! Moving slowly, majestically, stopping to receive a petition, to bestow a gracious word, the Sun King drew nearer. Jean-Baptiste was transfixed. He didn't take in the gold brocade coat or gaudy embroidered vest or the fine, tanned features. Tavernier noticed only the diamonds. Never had he seen anyone wear so many! Not even the King of Golconda or the Great Mogul himself had been this laden! Jean-Baptiste experienced a sudden twinge of doubt: did Louis XIV really want to buy yet *more* diamonds? But Montarsy had assured him that the king's appetite was insatiable. Tavernier felt the dazzle first, then the dignity. *This* was a king, indeed, the very archetype made flesh, descended from the pink-gold clouds of some Baroque ceiling painting to move among men and astound them utterly.

As His Majesty promenaded along the gallery, the crowd opened before him, quickly bowing and backing away, so that he walked alone, as if inside a large, clear bubble. He reached, at long last, the window embrasure where Montarsy and Tavernier stood. Both men bowed low, Montarsy with some grace, Jean-Baptiste with none at all. As the king moved on, Colbert, with his usual sober curtness, motioned them to follow in His Majesty's wake and led them into a nearby room where the king seated himself in a high-backed carved chair while all the courtiers in his train stood. (Had his brother Monsieur been present, he would have been allowed a chair; Queen Marie-Thérèse would have gotten only a stool.)

It was all over in a matter of minutes. Tavernier handed his list of prices and descriptions of each stone to Colbert, along with the velvet bag. Inside, the blue Diamond lay waiting, in a kind of limbo.

The king graciously engaged Jean-Baptiste in conversation, saying little himself, drawing Tavernier out. "The rarity and brevity" of Louis XIV's words, according to Saint-Simon, made them "precious," thus enhancing his "majesty." It was all part of the act. God had given Louis, along with so much else, a remarkably pleasant voice, "at once dignified and charming," according to Voltaire, which "won the hearts of those whom his presence intimidated." Jean-Baptiste felt the charm and relaxed into volubility. The two men made a good team: one the quintessential consumer, the other the quintessential merchant. But they also made a dichotomy: one the politest, most polished man in Europe, the other, one of the rudest and roughest, more foreign than French.

Colbert had briefed His Majesty well, explaining to him that the more he did to promote French trade, both import and export, the more his tax revenues would increase, and the more pages of delicious expenditures he could comfortably list in his little red leather book. The people the king mainly mixed with were aristocrats. None of them could soil their hands in trade without forfeiting their titles. Colbert, the wool merchant's son, urged Louis XIV to be less snobbish and more egalitarian, "to receive with special marks of favor and protection all merchants who come to court. Aid them in everything which concerns their commerce."

Louis didn't need much urging to receive Tavernier, who could not only assuage his diamond fever but also tell him details of Eastern life. One of the king's secretary-interpreters, Antoine Galland, had, earlier that year, translated from Arabic into French *The Thousand and One Nights,* so the exotic East had become the latest French fad. It was just four years since Louis had formed his own East India Company with, as yet, not much in settlement or profit but lots of hope for the future. So he drew out Jean-Baptiste with genuine interest in his travels and commerce, shone his light graciously upon him, and then just as graciously dismissed him.

Jean-Baptiste backed himself awkwardly out of the room, ready to regale anyone who'd listen for the rest of his life about the day he'd met his king and to declare in print, eight years later, when he published *Six Voyages*: "His Majesty had the goodness to give me a very favorable reception, which was a glorious conclusion to my long journeys, in which I have always had for my primary object to spare nothing in order to make known to the great monarchs of Asia, that there is one grander than them all, in Europe, and that our King infinitely surpasses them both in power and glory." To this august being, Jean-Baptiste dedicated his book, with many more paragraphs of fulsome flattery. He could afford, as we shall see later, to be generous in his praise.

As soon as Louis was free of duties later that day, he took the velvet pouch into his private apartments, into the room called, in the language of his time, when every rich man had one, the Grand Cabinet, where he kept his favorite possessions: paintings, bronzes, medals, ancient coins, cameos—and jewels. The king sat down at his desk and spread out the gems. There were 45 large, spectacular stones, and 1,122 smaller ones.

When he picked up the blue Diamond, he gasped. It was the exact color of his royal cloak, worn whenever he wanted to appear most regal. Louis cradled the stone in his finely boned hands. It was the very hue of majesty, fit jewel for a Sun King, blue as the sun's surround, blazing as the orb itself, celestial, divine.

As Louis looked into the Diamond's heart, he saw *éclat*, he saw *gloire*. Like the stone's previous owners, he also felt his imagination leap to new visions. He saw Versailles, not as it was with scaffolding, dirt piles, workmen everywhere, but as it would be: as refulgent as this much smaller sphere, radiating light from tall windows, splendid mirrors, gilded walls, marble floors, silver furniture, crystal chandeliers. When its construction was far enough along for him to move in, he would dress his sixty favorite courtiers in gold-embroidered coats this shade of blue. (Eleven times during his reign, Louis would renew the ordinance that decreed that such blue coats were never to be worn by anyone not of noble birth.)

But the Diamond was not yet perfect. Above all, as he'd once written, he prized "greatness, order, and beauty." The gem had greatness and beauty aplenty, but no order. It was still more or less as nature formed it, rough and misshapen. It had to be improved by man; like his formal gardens at Versailles, like the ranks of his army, it had to be schooled to symmetry and geometrical precision. And it had to be made more brilliant, more *éclatant*.

Louis read its description in the long list of stones Tavernier had carefully written in brown ink (still in the Bibliothèque Nationale), and noted its weight: "112³⁄₁₆th carats."

The Diamond had to be cut to the king's pleasure—perhaps not at once, but sometime soon. Cutting would make it irrevocably his, would mark it with his strong, indenting will. Louis put the Diamond to one side on his desktop. He had to have it.

And this one. He picked up an almond-shaped diamond, slightly brown in color, "20¼ carats," according to the list. He had to have it, too. Louis was enjoying himself. And this oval one, and this heart-shaped one. He paid no attention to the prices on Tavernier's list. He had to have them all.

The king ordered Colbert to pay Tavernier for every stone he'd brought. Colbert sighed, shrugged, and paid. When Jean-Baptiste received his bank order from Colbert, he was suddenly richer by 897,751 *livres* (more than $7 million in today's currency). For the blue Diamond he received 220,000 *livres*.

In February of the very next year, 1669, a grateful Louis XIV granted letters to the middle-class merchant Jean-Baptiste Tavernier that would enable him to acquire a title. On August 27, 1670, Tavernier purchased the barony of Aubonne, in Switzerland, near Lake Geneva, from the Marquis of Montpouillan and paid the marquis the equivalent of $1,032,000 for it. All those years of dust and heat in India had paid off handsomely for Jean-Baptiste. He also bought a fine mansion in Paris, which boasted the new baron's name in gold letters on a black marble plaque beside the front door and his arms carved in the center of the overarching porte-cochère.

As for the Diamond, it was put into a shallow drawer in Louis's jewel cabinet and acquired a new name. No longer "the Tavernier Blue," it became "the Blue Diamond of the French Crown." From time to time, when duty weighed too heavily on him, Louis would take it out and recharge himself from its sparkling, royal color; sometimes he showed it proudly to visitors, usually female. But for most of the next five years, the Diamond lay quietly in eclipse and neglect, while pretty entertainments, love affairs, political intrigue, and amusing gossip whirled, like a planet's far-off rings, around it.

Louis was preoccupied with landscaping and building Versailles, his magnum opus, his affront in stone to time, as permanent as his precious gems. Europe had never seen anything like it. The facade stretched for a third of a mile; the gardens, whose plan later became the inspiration for the city layout of Washington, D.C., covered eleven square miles and had full-grown forests transplanted from Normandy and Flanders; fifty thousand bulbs imported from Constantinople; statues behind every second clipped tree of the king's prototype, the sun god Apollo.

In March 1669, his enchanting Athenaïs gave birth to Louis's child, a girl, whereupon her husband informed his friends of "the death of my wife from coquetry and ambition," invited them to a mock funeral, and draped himself and his coach in blackest mourning. Louis was having such a good time with his mistress and his wondrous palace that his euphoria, as always, took the form of manic spending. He summoned the French jewel merchant Bazu, just back from a buying trip to India, and purchased the equivalent of $4 million worth of gems, including fourteen large diamonds including one of 43½ carats, which joined the Blue in one of Louis's shallow cabinet drawers.

The Sun King then decided that his Blue Diamond would be cut to greater brilliance and to a form he could wear. Late in 1672 he summoned to his Grand Cabinet the court jeweler Pitau, who had recently done a fine job of adding 274 diamonds to Louis's sword and another 683 to the cross-belt. His Majesty extracted the blue gem from its dark drawer, and in his pleasant voice, as he handed it to Pitau, explained exactly what he wanted done with it.

Pitau was a highly skilled diamond cutter, one of approximately seventy-five then working in Paris. By the end of the seventeenth century, the art had been mastered in Europe, mainly by Jews and Protestants. Venice, gateway to the East, had been the earliest city to establish an active diamond-cutting industry, circa 1330; by 1636, there would be 186 diamond cutters working there. The art quickly spread to Paris, the principal market at the time for finished diamonds, where a guild of cutters and polishers formed in the late 1300s. A 1360 inventory of the jewels of Louis, Duke of Anjou, lists seven faceted diamonds in his collection; records show that a famous cutter called Herman was working in Paris in 1407. Guillebert de Metz, describing Paris in 1477, refers to the district of La Courarie as home to its gem cutters, with later centers becoming established in Bruges, Antwerp, Amsterdam, and Lisbon.

A breakthrough came in 1476, by which time some of the optical properties of diamonds were understood and scientific cutting for greater brilliance could begin. In that year Louis de Berquem, a Jewish cutter working at Bruges in Belgium, cut into a modest number of facets the three biggest diamonds in the collection of Charles the Bold, Duke of Burgundy. The first, a famous 137 carat yellow diamond now known as the Florentine, he cut, front and back, with triangular facets. De Berquem cut and set the second stone, a long, narrow 14 carat one, into a gold ring given to Pope Sixtus IV; and the third, into a friendship ring of two clasped hands given to Louis XI of France. By the time Louis XIV entrusted Pitau with the cutting of the Blue Diamond, Pitau had a choice of the simple twenty-four-facet rose-cut, perfected in 1520, or the Mazarin cut, named for the diamond-mad cardinal, who had encouraged Paris cutters to experiment. What they came up with, around 1640, was a cut of thirty-four facets, seventeen above the girdle and seventeen below, not unlike today's brilliant cut, although with fewer facets. The Mazarin cut allowed diamonds for the first time to leap ahead of colored stones in beauty and appeal; before then, they were worn because of their value and rarity but for dazzle needed their country cousins around them and were usually set in gold encircled by rubies, emeralds, and sapphires. Now they could dispense with lesser lights and shine proudly on their own.

The Mazarin cut, however, while a great improvement, still made a sleepy stone, for a lot of light dropped through bottom and sides without being refracted. (Refraction refers to the amount of bending and slowing imposed on light by a stone; diamond has a high refractive index of 2.417, which means that light travels 2.417 times as fast in air as it does in the stone.) What diamond cutters such as Pitau and those early experimenters wanted was faceting in accord with the rules of optics concerning reflection, refraction, and dispersion of light, striving for maximum luster, fire, brilliance, and scintillation.

Luster depends not only on the light reflected from a diamond's surface—this is known as adamantine luster—but also on rays that have been partly absorbed before being reflected. In an ideal cut, light enters the stone from the front, is reflected as much as possible from the rear facets, and bounces back through the front. This combination of surface luster and internal reflection is known in the trade as the diamond's "life." Life depends first, of course, on a diamond's cut but also on how much light its surroundings provide. Is it dependent for its shining on the light of day, candles, gas, electric bulbs, or horrid fluorescent ones? All these affect the stone differently.

The fire of a gem is the so-called dispersion of colors caused by white light breaking up into the spectrum before returning to the eye. Isaac Newton had discovered this in 1666—just six years before Pitau was given the Blue Diamond to cut—by aiming a narrow beam of white light into a prism and discovering that it split into all the colors of the rainbow. Like luster, fire is enhanced by moving a diamond. More fire results from more refraction, but some light will be lost to the viewer as fire is increased, so that maximum life and maximum fire cannot be achieved at the same time.

The brilliance of a stone depends on the optimum combination of life and fire. The whiter the stone, the greater its brilliance; with the Blue Diamond, as with all colored gems, some light was lost by absorption.

The scintillation, not as important as the other three optical properties, refers to the number, intensity, and frequency of flashing sparks of white and colored light.

After Pitau received the Diamond from the king in 1672, he studied it carefully, keeping these optical properties in mind. He would not finish his cutting, polishing, and setting until sometime in 1673. While the stone was being radically altered in his well-trained hands, it went through five stages: cleaving, sawing, bruting, grinding, and polishing.

Cleaving, which involves splitting a diamond in accordance with its grain, was for Pitau the most nerve-racking part, and for the Blue, the "unkindest cut of all." Cleaving has not changed, either in technique or tools, since the earliest days it was done. The English physicist Robert Boyle gave a correct explanation of cleaving in relation to a diamond's grain in 1672, the year Pitau received the stone from King Louis, in his *Essay about the Origin and Virtue of Gems*. Even though diamond is the hardest substance known, like wood it has a grain; owing to its atomic structure it is not equally hard in all directions but cleaves perfectly in layers in four directions parallel to its octahedral planes. For the gem cutter, understanding the correct lines of cleavage is essential. Pitau knew that one misplaced blow could shatter the stone, so he studied it carefully, turning and examining it, for weeks, determing the exact direction of the grain before the crucial cleaving.

On the day when he was ready, he made a notch in the Diamond at the point where he gauged it wanted to be cut. Then he fitted a wedge into the notch and raised his mallet above it, above the Blue Diamond so rare, so precious, so beloved by His Majesty. As he did so, Pitau was well aware that he risked his reputation and his livelihood. Then, with silent prayers and sweating brow, he struck one mighty blow—and the stone fell cleanly, perfectly, just as he wished, into two pieces. The Diamond lost more than a third of its mass, reducing its weight from 112³⁄₁₆ carats to 67⅛ when all Pitau's work was done. It probably took him a day or more to recover from the tension of that one irrevocable mallet stroke. When, in 1907, Joseph Asscher of Amsterdam was asked to cleave the Cullinan, an enormous diamond found in a South African mine, which weighed 3,024.75 carats, he took two months to study the stone. On the day of cleaving, he struck the fatal blow with nurse and doctor in attendance, then fell to the floor in a dead faint. The blow was sure; the stone split cleanly into three pieces, cleaved later into nine.

We do not know what became of the rejected piece of the Diamond, weighing some 41 carats. Was it cut into a whole family of small offspring, and if so, where did they go? No doubt unusable bits were crushed to particles by Pitau's assistants, using mortar and hammer-driven pestle, a method that produces powder to be used in grinding and polishing.

The blue stone's trauma most likely continued, for it probably had to submit next to sawing, which removed small parts impossible to remove by cleaving because their angles didn't match the grain. For sawing, Pitau used brass or iron wire stretched taut between the ends of a piece of whalebone, the necessary teeth being formed by particles of diamond powder, which became embedded in the wire as soon as he pressed it onto the sawing line. For Pitau, sawing was a very slow, very laborious process. (It would later take a year to saw in half the 410-carat Regent diamond, also found in Golconda and also added to the French crown jewels.)

Once cleaving and sawing were done, the Diamond, no longer in a natural state, no longer so prepossessing, but well on the way to paramount beauty, underwent bruting. The Italian sculptor and goldsmith Benvenuto Cellini first describes this operation in 1568: "One diamond is rubbed against another until by mutual abrasion both take a form which the skilled polisher wishes to achieve." Pitau began by cementing a diamond called a "sharp" into one end of a stick to make his tool for bruting the Blue, which he set in another stick. He donned leather gloves, plus a leather "stall" on his right thumb, and placed a box strategically to catch the chips. Then he took a stick in each hand, leaned his arms against two upright pieces of iron fastened to the edge of his cutting bench, and rubbed and rubbed, day after day, until a facet was achieved. Rubbing took all his physical strength, and his arm muscles bulged. (Bruting was done by hand until the British patented a machine to do it in 1891.) He stopped frequently, brushing powder from the Diamond with a camel's hair brush, then moistening it with his tongue, to see what progress he'd made. Bruting gave Pitau the general outline of the finished facets. If, say, a cutter today is making the fifty-eight facets of a brilliant cut, bruting gives him only the first eighteen, with the other forty formed in the next two processes, which are grinding and polishing. Pitau's chosen profession was a nerve-racking, backbreaking, invalid-making one. Each night during this stage, when he went home exhausted to his wife and family, his back and arms ached fiercely, and his hands, even though they'd been inside leather gloves, were red and blistered.

Once the really hard work of cleaving, sawing, and bruting was done, Pitau heaved a great sigh of relief. He looked down into the blue depths of the Diamond, beginning, under his expert touch to come to "life" and saw his own there, with himself rewarded and renowned in bounteous measure. Perhaps, like his lucky friend Tavernier, he'd be ennobled by a grateful king for doing such a fine job. If he could make the blue stone really brilliant, who knew what good fortune might follow? Pitau bent again to his task.

Grinding and polishing were slow work, too, but not hard on one's nerves or body. He softened plumber's solder over a flame and used it to fix the Diamond into a "dop"—a little cup on a flexible copper stalk— so that only the part to be polished was exposed. Pitau smoothed the hot solder, which had been heated to 420 degrees Fahrenheit to make it melt, with his thumb, on which the skin was toughened from years of doing so. The copper stalk was then bent to achieve the correct facet angle.

Pitau held the dop with the Diamond in it to the horizontal rotating disk, the scaife, which looked very much like the one the Indian jeweler, many years before, had used for grinding and polishing the Blue, although this one was harder and bigger, and the horsepower necessary for turning it was supplied by an assistant. Pitau ground using coarse diamond powder, then polished with finer, until the Diamond came, at long last, millions of years after its creation, vibrantly alive. Pitau was ecstatic, exultant, his dreams for it fulfilled, as he moved the stone about. Light bent, bounced, and streamed, leapt, flashed, and sparked in and out of every lustrous facet. The Diamond was still shaped like a broad, octahedral heart, but was now symmetrical, as King Louis had decreed. Its cut was very similar to the brilliant one of fifty-eight facets that the Venetian Vincent Peruzzi would first achieve twenty-seven years later, in 1700. We know that the crown (top) had many facets, and that the pavilion (bottom) had them radiating out from a star of seven small facets surrounding the culet (the slightly flattened bottom point). The Diamond embodied sky, star, and rainbow and seemed to hold in its small heart the light of the world. Nature, in creating it aeons ago below the Deccan plateau of India, had been extremely prodigal, but it took man's brain, tools, and talent to release this Sleeping Beauty.

Pitau set the Diamond, as the king had ordered, in a simple pronged setting made of gold and enameled on the back. Modern French gemologists differ about what happened next. Some say that the gold bezel was fixed to a long pin so Louis could stick it through his lace cravat; others maintain that the setting merely had a loop at the top enabling His Majesty to wear the gem on a ribbon. This particular incarnation of the stone is long gone, but perhaps it could be worn either way; we do have documentation for one later appearance on a ribbon.

Pitau delivered the finished Diamond to Louis who, when he tried it on, looked in one of Versailles' six thousand mirrors and smiled. He stowed it in his Grand Cabinet and looked forward to the next ceremony when he could attach himself to all its light. It would be solely, exclusively, for the rest of his life, his to wear. He let his queen and mistresses appear in other crown jewels, but never, ever, in this one.

Louis's pleasure in the Diamond's fine new shining was tempered by one dark little cloud. His enormous expenditures were beginning and would continue to exceed his revenues. The 1673 national deficit was the equivalent of $8 million, causing Colbert's beetle brows to become permanently knotted.

Did the king feel at least a twinge of guilt when, in the following year, Louise de la Vallière, neglected and eclipsed by the scintillating Athenaïs de Montespan, had her portrait painted with one thin hand pointing to a casket of jewels abandoned on the ground, then on a gray winter morning, bade her three illegitimate royal offspring farewell, dropped her final curtsy to the king, and entered her coach? It stopped, in Paris, before the Carmelite convent. Louise got out and without so much as a backward glance, crossed its threshold to become a nun. The heavy gates clanged shut behind her forever. She never saw the king again.

On June 6 that year, Louis penned a note to Colbert: "Madame de Montespan absolutely refuses to let me give her jewels; but so that she will not lack them [a fate, in Louis's estimation, worse than death], I would like you to order a small handsome coffer in which you will put what I will list hereafter so that I can easily lend her whatever she would like. You will put in that coffer a pearl necklace," he continued in peremptory tone, "two pairs of earrings, one in diamonds, which I want to be fine; the other of mixed stones; a box and some links of diamonds; a box and some links of mixed stones which can be taken apart and used with the diamonds as well. We must have stones of every color. We must also have a pair of pearl earrings. We must also have four dozen buttons, of which the stones can be changed in the middle; the outside being of small diamonds that will go with everything. You must spend freely on this; it will please me." This missive shows not only what a detailed interest—with none at all in the deficit—Louis took in jewelry but also what a clever minx his latest mistress was. Louis would never have given her, all at once, this great a haul; but since she'd insisted it be on loan, everything would eventually revert to him. He could therefore afford to be generous.

All was not well, however, between this diamond-obsessed pair of lovers. His Majesty was in a randy mood, and his lustful eye was roving. He indulged himself in a series of quick, hot-blooded affairs. One evening at Versailles, where Louis and the court were spending more time since his Grand Apartment, a suite of seven splendid rooms, had been finished, his restless eye fell on the earlobes of his current flame, Anne, Princess of Soubise. From them hung the emerald earrings he'd given her. He grasped at once their message: they were to let him know that the princess's husband had galloped off to Paris and that later, after

Louis had played his habitual game of billiards, he could, with great relish, bed her.

Athenaïs, meanwhile, twitched her golden gown and clutched *her* earrings, afraid they were about to disappear back into the king's gem drawers. She won him back, however, in 1677, causing Madame de Sévigné to note that she "was covered with diamonds the other day, such a brilliant divinity that one's eyes dazzled." Not to be outdone by their king and his mistress, ladies of the court took to wearing diamond clips holding up their diamond-sprinkled overskirts, with more of the gems above and below lace undersleeves and outlining a gown's seams.

Kings who can instantly indulge their every wish grow ever harder to please, and by the very next year, Athenaïs had palled again. She had borne the king six children and was, understandably enough, getting rather thick around the middle. As Voltaire so crisply put it, the king "reproached himself for his liaison with a married woman, and when he was no longer in love his conscience made itself felt more keenly."

Poor Athenaïs ate and ate to console herself until her legs were the size of a small elephant's. Inside Versailles' Grand Apartment there were Grand Scenes—the king hated scenes—in which Athenaïs reproached him angrily and cried tears bigger than her lend-lease pearls. Louis went more and more to the rooms of the quiet, devout lady who was governess to the half-royal children Athenaïs had produced. Her later name, once the king had made her a marquise, would be Madame de Maintenon.

The king fled from Athenaïs's recriminations to Alvarez, whom he now thought the best jeweler in his kingdom, his taste in jewelers being as fickle as in women. Louis ordered Alvarez to cut 665 diamonds from his latest purchases, of which twelve were large. The king was still riding high—but not for long.

Thus far, his life as king, although he always conscientiously performed his royal duties, had been a midsummer gambol from dwelling to dwelling, woman to woman, a time of pleasure and sensual indulgence. From the moment when Madame de Maintenon began her reign as official mistress and the court moved, in May 1682, when Louis was forty-three, permanently to Versailles, everything changed.

Parties gave way to pieties, youth's fireworks to damp squibs, and the sparkle of Athenaïs's wit and chandelier earrings to Maintenon's pursed lips and rattling rosary. The king's coats of gold brocade ablaze with diamonds were shoved to the back of his wardrobe, to be brought out only for very special occasions. From now on, his daily garb was brown, plain brown. The king shaved off his dashing little mustache, and the next day all the courtiers removed theirs, for they always followed his lead.

Everything at Versailles seemed to grow more rigid: the king's countenance; his body moving like an automaton; etiquette rules; the clockwork getting-up and going-to-bed ceremonies; the promenade to chapel; the promenade from chapel; the afternoon stately progress around the gardens.

"We perish in symmetry," moaned Madame de Maintenon. On the surface, she was as proper and pious as a nun, but underneath lurked hypocrisy. "You wear nothing but wool," observed her spiritual adviser one day, "but when you kneel before me, your dress falls in such graceful folds over your feet that somehow I think it too perfect." She prided herself on not wearing jewels, but the cross that she always wore was set with the finest diamonds in the king's collection and dangled from a rope of huge, perfectly matched pearls. And how sincere could a woman be who'd been born Catholic, turned Protestant, and then switched back again to Catholic? At age seventeen, she'd been married off to a much older man, Paul Scarron, paralyzed and helpless, who died eight years later, leaving her still a virgin.

When Louis had first seen her, attending to the children he'd fathered with Athenaïs, he'd exclaimed, "It would be delightful to be loved by her!" Of course, being self-centered Louis, he said "to be loved by her" rather than "to love her." She was five years his senior; when they were both over seventy, she complained to her confessor that the king still insisted on having intercourse—what she called "those painful moments"—sometimes twice a day. Louis became very dependent on her. One day he told her, "A king is called Your Majesty, the pope Your Holiness and you should be Your Solidity." Liselotte in her letters referred to her as "the king's Old Drab" and thought "such enforced piety goes entirely against his nature. It just makes him bad-tempered."

On the magnificent stage set of Versailles, Louis XIV's long-running play began its daily performances, with a huge cast of extras. The palace was home to between five and ten thousand people: nobles, top middle-class government officials, soldiers, and servants. They all had walk-on parts for the daily ceremonies of the king's rising and dressing, when violins played; Mass with suitable motets; dinner to violin accompaniment; the afternoon hunt with horns or the garden promenade to flutes and oboes; the supper when the Grand Band of twenty-five violins played opera extracts; the king's undressing and going-to-bed, when someone usually sang a few songs. Some of the parts had alternates: one night at the *coucher* Count Curlywig would present the royal nightshirt; the next night, Count Cardshark would do it. The scenes underwent minor changes, too: one afternoon the king might eat formally at a long banquet table (the *grand couvert*) and the next, informally (the *petit couvert*) but always with an audience crowding close while he tucked into a gargantuan meal. Watching the king eat was not a pretty sight after botched dental surgery to his upper jaw had left him with a hole in his palate, so food went up into it, down again through his nose, and exploded, like a tiny fireworks display, onto table and anyone within range.

Etiquette rules, unlike the minor actors' roles, never varied. The king had a dozen different ways of doffing his plumed hat, depending on the social class of the person for whom he removed, or merely touched, it. Nobles had to escort ladies by holding only their fingertips and had to gain admittance to a room by scratching the door with a fingernail rather than by knocking.

Probably any courtier asked to review the Versailles musical extravaganza would have given it a thumbs-down. Everyone got so stale and mechanical in his or her part. Daily routines were so fixed that one could set a clock accurately by knowing what king and courtiers were doing at that moment. "Before being at court," sighed Madame de Maintenon, "I never knew what boredom was, but I have since felt it deeply." Behind the scenes, gambling, malicious gossip, adultery, and heavy drinking were the courtiers' antidotes. Many nobles found the same remedy for dull lives used today: they consumed conspicuously, following the royal prerogative. The Egmonts bought more than $9 million worth of pearls; the Créqui family invested in spectacular diamonds.

The king announced a party at which each lady would receive a valuable present. Some of them at once pumped the merchants supplying the loot to see what they'd get and exactly what it was worth. On the night, so many ladies came that there wasn't room for them all. The king got wind of their greed and consequently, as Liselotte reports, made them "gamble for the brocades, ribbons, and fans and kept the precious stones for himself."

Versailles was a golden cage in which Louis imprisoned princes and nobles so they couldn't tend to their country estates and perhaps raise support there for another Fronde-like uprising against his absolute authority. France was "a country," wrote the social historian Jean de la Bruyère in 1682, "in which joys are visible but false, and sorrows are hidden but real."

Like the nation as a whole, Versailles had its underside. Ladies who'd drunk too much wine often threw up in its corridors, and men urinated freely in dark corners. When smells grew overpowering, Louis's blue-uniformed servants sprinkled oil of rosemary distilled in alcohol from bottles kept handy in all the main rooms.

As for the Diamond, which had inspired the color of the servants' livery, at Versailles it found itself in a fine new home, far superior to the cabinet drawer where it had dwelled in Paris. Its new residence was designed by André Charles Boulle (1642–1732), who had begun his career as cabinetmaker extraordinary in 1664 and been appointed *ébéniste* to the king by Colbert in 1672. Thereafter, with twenty assistants in his workshop, Boulle was kept very busy making furniture for Versailles. The Diamond was consequently put into a drawer in a splendid cabinet decorated in characteristic Boulle style, its wood inlaid with tortoiseshell and brass patterned in tendrils and vines, arabesques and curlicues, all erupting in a jubilation that would have been excessive had it not been schooled to perfect symmetry. Behind all this exuberance, however, the Diamond's life was as dull as the courtiers', its light unseen and unappreciated. What a paradox! To be made so eminently wearable by Pitau, so streamlined and beautiful, ready for its close-up, for candlelit all-night frolics, just when its royal owner had grown staid and stuffy and early-to-bed! The Diamond not yet named Hope bided its time. . . .

On July 30, 1683, Queen Marie-Thérèse, gravely ill, took a ring from her finger and gave it to Madame de Maintenon. "Adieu," she whispered, "to you I confide the happiness of the king." That done, she died, age forty-five. She'd been killed by the ignorant court doctors, according to Liselotte, "as surely as if they had pierced her heart with a sword." Marie-Thérèse had been the right queen for Louis, never upstaging him, never straining treasury funds by compulsive spending. "Poor woman," sighed Louis, "it's the only time she has ever given me any trouble." The Venetian ambassador noted that his wife's death "extracted a few polite sighs" from the king, nothing more. A few months later, he married Madame de Maintenon in a secret ceremony. Within eight years, as a 1691 inventory of the crown jewels shows, almost every diamond in Queen Marie-Thérèse's jewelry had been reset for Louis's use.

In September of that year Colbert died, age sixty-four, having worked to his last breath. "My God," he moaned, as he finally sent away his bookkeepers, "won't they even give me time to die?" His death, again according to the Venetian ambassador, elicited from Louis, ever polished on the surface and adamantine underneath, no reaction at all. "If only God had given me a nature as unfeeling as the Great Man's and his brother's!" exclaims Liselotte. "Truly, it is astonishing to see how hard these people are." When a poor woman whose son had been killed in an accident while building Versailles shouted insults at His Majesty, he didn't investigate her plight, or sympathize, but merely had her whipped.

The morning of May 15, 1685, found the king dressing for a really grand show geared to the politics of display. Louis chose a gold lamé outfit carefully from the rows of costumes kept in a ground-floor room at Versailles, looked after by the grand master of the wardrobe, two subordinate masters, four first valets, sixteen other valets, four odd-job boys and twenty-six tailors, hosiers, bootmakers, embroiderers, and jewelers. There were two laundrymen, plus a cravat starcher whose job it was, on special days, to attach the diamonds and lace ruffles chosen by His Majesty to the wristbands of his shirt.

Louis performed the *grand lever*, with all its due ritual, in the Salon of Mercury, at that time his state bedchamber, whose winter wall hangings and bed curtains of gold-embroidered red velvet had just given way to summer ones of gold and silver brocade. Once he was dressed, Louis chose his curly, past-shoulder-length wig from two brought from their glass cases in his wig room by Quentin, his barber. Finally, the king gave the order to the grand master of the wardrobe to enter his Grand Cabinet and bring him the many jewels he would wear.

Carefully, the grand master maneuvered his way around all the pedestals, bronzes, marble busts, precious blue lapis lazuli vases, opened the drawers of the Boulle cabinet, and extracted the gems, placing them on a velvet-lined tray to be carried back to the king. Last of all, he opened the drawer where the Blue Diamond was awaiting him, held it for a private moment of pleasure in his hand, and placed it, too, on the tray.

As it was being carried to the king and positioned to lie against the creamy cobwebs of his lace cravat, the stone caught the morning light streaming on that bright May morning through Versailles' huge windows, and its rainbows danced. The Blue Diamond of the French Crown was more than ready for its first appearance on the Versailles stage.

Its owner, with an army of 400,000 men and a navy of 250 ships, was still waging wars of territorial aggression and, at this point, was winning them. He'd recently annexed Franche Comté, Strasbourg, and Luxembourg, following which he turned his sights on Genoa, bombarding it until it lay conquered and in ruins. Taking the city-state gave Louis no real commercial or geographical advantage; it was just one more show of power, macho muscle-flexing on the European stage.

Genoa's doge, Lescari, and four senators, ready to be humbled at Versailles, had arrived in Paris on April 18 and cooled their heels for almost a month before the King of France deigned to give them an audience on that sun-filled morning of May 15.

Preceded by twelve pages on horseback and forty guards of honor, the two coaches containing doge and senators rumbled through Versailles' outer gates and along the subtle gradation upward to the palace itself, which stood on higher ground. They descended from their carriages in the final marble courtyard and slowly ascended the thirty-three marble steps of the Ambassador's staircase, lined with Swiss Guards, its railings draped with cloth-of-gold, its walls conjoining marbles in different colors from all the French quarries. In a niche on the landing loomed a white marble Louis XIV to intimidate them before they met the real thing.

Having reached the second floor, the doge's party passed through the rooms of the Grand Apartment, where almost every painted or sculpted detail served the royal propaganda, rooms so stuffed with spectators come to see the greatest show on earth that Doge Lescari could hardly push his way through. The five Italians inched forward through the Salons of Venus, Diana, Mars, Mercury, and Apollo, tried to hurry through the Salon of War, feeling Genoa's defeat, but slowed in wonder when they reached the most splendid room in Europe, the Hall of Mirrors.

To drumroll and trumpet they entered the Salon of Peace beyond, where the king awaited. Across the ceiling galloped France in a chariot, accompanied by Peace and Abundance. Six busts of Caesars on marble pedestals, inherited by Louis from Mazarin, mutely underscored a truth that the Sun King chose to ignore, namely, *sic transit gloria mundi*.

The eight-foot-long solid silver throne on which His Majesty sat, its seat and back covered in crimson velvet, was decorated with four plump silver children offering flower baskets, silver pedestals holding velvet banners, and an eight-foot-high silver candelabrum at each corner. Around the throne clustered the king's brother, Monsieur, in all his bracelets and furbelows; Louis's son, the twenty-four-year-old grand dauphin, heir to the throne, sunk in fat and lethargy; all the Bourbon princes of the blood; and the crown's highest officials.

The doge addressed the king in a speech concerning the peace treaty terms concluded on February 2, with much bowing and hat doffing, to which the royal males removed their hats in varying degrees of doffing, depending on their rank—except for the king who flicked his off for a nanosecond and then replaced it firmly on his well-curled head. (After the ceremony, one of the senators would ask Doge Lescari what had astonished him most, seeing the splendors of Versailles for the first time, to which he replied, "It was to see myself there.")

From the Sun King's lace cravat, the Diamond took in all that light from windows, gilded walls, gleaming throne, royal jewels, and tossed it out again. The palace's silk-and-silver shine was perhaps greater than anything the jewel had, in its long life, reflected. But this event was only the dress rehearsal for an even more brilliant production still twelve years away. The Diamond would refract that spectacle in its generous blue heart, as it did this one, but the sad truth was that it had become a mere stage prop, nothing more.

Later that spring day, the Diamond found itself again confined to darkness in its drawer, symptomatic of a general gloom beyond. With good physical reasons for it, Louis was turning into an old grouch in the arms of his "old drab." He would be forty-seven in September, and his gout was so crippling that he found it hard to walk. "A worm, half a foot long, alive" had been found in his stools, which meant that tapeworms still in his stomach consumed his food, leaving the poor king with gnawing, insatiable hunger. He ate and ate; he no longer had enough teeth to chew properly, so doctors who daily examined the contents of the royal solid silver chamber pot found "truffles that had hardly been digested."

His general peevishness certainly caused suffering on a grand scale to his Protestant subjects. Earlier in his reign, Louis had merely tried, through Colbert, to convert them to Catholicism, not to suppress them. His naval chief, Duquesne, his beloved general, Turenne, and all his favorite jewelers were Protestant. King Louis bore them no grudge.

On October 19, 1685, however, perhaps egged on by the overly pious Madame de Maintenon, he revoked the Edict of Nantes, which had been passed in 1598 by his grandfather Henri IV guaranteeing Protestants the right to worship as they pleased. On a dark October day, as storm clouds gathered, King Louis thundered his decree: all Protestant churches were to be razed to the ground and their clergy were ordered to leave France within two weeks; all children were to be raised as Catholics and their elders forced to convert. Any Protestant caught trying to leave the country would be sent to sea to row the galleys or imprisoned and their property confiscated.

Fifteen hundred Protestants went to the galleys. Estimates differ widely, but between 100,000 and two million secretly left the country, including many of France's best artisans, to seek refuge in England, Switzerland, and Holland. Thirty years later, in a Philadelphia church, a youth named Benjamin Franklin would hear his preacher denouncing "that accursed man, persecutor of God's people, Louis XIV." Foreign opinion against such an autocratic king hardened.

Most of the diamond cutters left France. One of them, Sir John Chardin, became jeweler to Charles II of England. Others fled to Amsterdam or Antwerp, both of which became important diamond-cutting centers, completely usurping the earlier preeminence of Paris. The exodus continued until finally, in 1775, only seven master cutters were left in the city, eking out a meager living.

The Revocation of the Edict of Nantes was bad news for Jean-Baptiste Tavernier, who was having serious money problems as well. He had, it seemed, lived in India too long, seen and coveted too much opulence at the courts of Golconda's king and the Great Mogul and other rajas. Tavernier picked up notions of luxury and conspicuous show beyond his station. For the past fifteen years, he'd been living the life of a grand seigneur in his Paris mansion and Swiss barony and spending far too freely. He got into debt, and, on top of that, suffered the humiliating treachery of his nephew, the same young man who'd accompanied him on his final 1663–68 Indian voyage. Jean-Baptiste had dispatched him to Persia on his own with a cargo of goods worth, in today's currency, $8 million. The nephew sold everything, pocketed the cash, and disappeared forthwith and forever into the back alleys and opium dens of Isfahan.

Hounded by creditors, Tavernier was forced to sell his barony of Aubonne to the Protestant son of Duquesne, King Louis's naval wizard, who had fled to Switzerland when Louis XIV passed his Revocation. Not wanting to be imprisoned in the Bastille, and unwilling to turn Catholic to please a king who had, finally, betrayed him, Jean-Baptiste, in July of 1687, with the help of a guaranty worth $400,000, obtained Swiss passports for himself and his wife, left Paris secretly for Switzerland, and one month later surfaced in Berlin. There the Elector of Brandenburg welcomed him warmly, and at once appointed him director of the East India Company he was forming. Jean-Baptiste was too old a tiger to change his stripes. He'd always been a merchant adventurer and such he would, till death, remain. In 1689, at age eighty-four, he set off on yet another buying trip to India, going via Moscow and the Caucasus. Some historians maintain that he died in Copenhagen, at the house of Henry de Moor, who was trying in vain to convert him to Catholicism. In fact, Tavernier died in Moscow, having arrived there from Copenhagen in February. In that icy, snowbound place, poor Jean-Baptiste caught a severe cold and died alone, with nothing but his free spirit to comfort him. He lies buried in a Protestant cemetery in Moscow, where the exact date of his departure from this life is impossible to read. But one feels sure that death must have surprised him shortly after his arrival in Russia; a wanderer such as Tavernier, forever wanting to push on over the next horizon, would not have stopped there long.

As for the King of France, he was undergoing trials, too. Louis had surgery—without benefit of anaesthetic, which was still to be discovered—for an anal fistula, a suppurating ulcer in his anus, on November 18, 1686. He insisted on holding his council meeting that evening, while sweat poured down his face from the extreme pain, and the next day he received foreign ambassadors, his face so contorted that it was unrecognizable. His physician, Fagon, having botched the initial operation, made further cuts on December 6, 8, and 10.

After that ordeal, Louis for the rest of his life sat in a specially de-signed, but ungilded, invalid's three-wheel chair for his garden prome-nades, up and down those raked, clipped, geometrical, properly subdued flowerbeds and vistas. His face was deeply grooved, his nose pinched and hawklike. The handsome, virile thirty-year-old king whom we first met in 1668, in all the exuberance of buying the Blue Diamond, had become ever more remote and stoic, more icon than man, almost as im-mobile as the marble statues around him.

Louis consoled himself for his diminished vigor and fortunes by buying $16 million worth of jewels in a single year, 1687, and having a new detailed inventory of the crown jewels made to include them. When he'd purchased diamonds from Tavernier nineteen years before, he had plenty of money to pay for them; now he didn't. The national debt, without Colbert to balance the books, was increasing steadily and alarmingly.

By September 1691 Louis had bought so many additional gems that he ordered Pontchartrain, head of his household, to make another inventory, getting jewelers Alvarez and Montarsy to do the valua-tions. It shows that not counting jewels inherited from former kings, Mazarin, his mother, Anne, and deceased wife, Marie-Thérèse, Louis himself had purchased jewels worth today more than $29 million, so that the total value of all the French crown jewels was $59 million, making them by far the finest and richest collection in Europe. Of the diamonds whose weights were given, no less than 109 were of 10 carats or more, and 273 weighed between 4 and 10 carats. Most were white, but in addition to the Blue, there were two rose-colored, two yellow, and one brown. The Diamond was described thus: "A very large violet diamond, very thick, cut in the fashion of facets on both sides, in the form of a short heart with eight sides, of a very brilliant and flawless water," worth 400,000 *livres* (thanks to its 1673 cutting by Pitau, it had almost doubled in value since 1668).

Five years later, in November 1696, a new and engaging character skipped lightly onto the Versailles stage and totally enchanted its aging hero. This was ten-year-old Marie Adelaide of Savoy, who arrived at Versailles as the betrothed of Louis, Duke of Burgundy, the king's grandson (and future father of Louis XV). According to Liselotte, Marie Adelaide was "dainty as a doll" with "fair hair and black eyes with lovely long lashes." "I am delighted with her," the king told Madame de Maintenon. "I find her just as she should be." She certainly livened things up at that staid court. She played blindman's buff and spillikins with the courtiers, cuddled up to the king, addressed him by the intimate *tu*, rumpled his clothes, and mussed his wig. "In the middle of dinner she starts to sing, dances about on her chair," reports Liselotte, "pulls frightful faces, tears dishes of chickens and partridge apart with her hands, sticks her fingers into the sauces; in short, no one could be naughtier." The wedding was fixed for the day of her twelfth birthday, Saturday, December 7, 1697. The king ordered everyone at court to buy new clothes and for himself planned something splendid.

Louis lavished the bride with wedding gifts, including a set of diamonds worth $4 million today and a necklace of twenty-one large pearls that poor, discarded Athenaïs had had to return to her sovereign when she fell from favor. When the wedding day came, Louis threw off his habitual brown garb and arrayed himself in a cloth-of-gold coat studded with more than $20 million worth of gems. Brother Monsieur, in gold-embroidered black velvet, wore, according to wife Liselotte, "all his big diamonds," while she herself, broad-shouldered and fat, looked "so exactly like a pagoda that I have to laugh whenever I happen to pass a mirror." The groom's fine suit, alas, couldn't hide his physical defects. He was humpbacked, with one shoulder so much higher than the other that he limped. Below his upper jaw, his mouth and chin receded so very sharply that in profile he bore an unfortunate resemblance to a shark. Louis had also given the bride a bedspread of Venetian point lace worth 50,000 *livres*. Perhaps he thought that on the wedding night, its beauty might help.

To celebrate the marriage, a party was held in the Hall of Mirrors on Wednesday evening, December 11, described in the broadsheet *Mercure Galant* as "the largest and most magnificent ball that had ever been seen at court." For the Blue Diamond, it was the climax of this royal drama and—to use the word literally—the highlight of its French existence.

All diamonds look their best in candlelight because each flicker of flame calls forth new brilliance and amazing scintillation. Four thousand candles conspired that night to give the Diamond full, glorious life and its most beautiful setting ever. With seventeen huge arched windows on one marble eighty-foot-long wall, and seventeen arched mirrors on the other; with sixteen massive chandeliers, twenty-four crystal candelabra, plus two great silver ones with eight branches each; with sixty-four silver tubs on silver bases holding orange trees; with alabaster and blue lapis vases on silver tables; with gleaming silver benches and chairs lined up against the walls; with dancers of both sexes ablaze in diamonds, there was, on that fairy night, a festival of light and fire beyond imagining. The entire Hall of Mirrors became one enormous diamond suspended on the black velvet night beyond.

As for the stooped, stiff-limbed, inflexible Louis XIV, did he glance upward at the thirty pictures Charles Le Brun had painted on the ceiling, showing the Sun King ascending to his zenith, victorious and in his prime? There he was at twenty-three, in *The King Rules by Himself*, resolute and hopeful, snatching the reins of power from parliament, wearing his violet-blue robe of state. Did he perhaps recall the December morning in 1668 when, living in the decrepit old Louvre, he'd first dreamed this effulgent room and palace into being, seeing its spark deep in the heart of the Blue Diamond, now hanging heavily on his neck? Like many wishes that find fulfillment, the king's had materialized too late, too late, when he was beyond a dancing spirit and almost beyond delight.

After that enchanted evening, the king foreswore diamonds for himself. There would, however, be one last flash before the sun went down.

Monsieur died of a stroke in June of 1701, leaving debts of 7.5 million *livres*. He'd been eating and laughing with his usual gusto, when suddenly he began to speak nonsense and slur his words; "the ladies," reports Liselotte, "thought he was doing it in fun." As soon as Monsieur had expired, she found "all the [violet-scented] letters that his young men had written him" and burned the lot "in case they fell into other hands." The whole court donned black clothes, put away their diamonds, and wore restrained jewelry in black jet.

Eleven months later, in May 1702, the War of the Spanish Succession broke out, in which Austria, most of Germany, Denmark, Holland, and Britain joined against France and Spain to dethrone Philip V of Spain, Louis XIV's grandson, in favor of Archduke Charles, second son of the Austrian emperor. Louis and his soldiers suffered one crushing defeat after another by England's army, commanded by John, 1st Duke of Marlborough, a military genius whose diamonds were modestly confined to one set of coat buttons. The Spanish royal family had to flee their Madrid palace four years later, while at Versailles, Louis XIV sadly provided sanctuary for the casket containing the Spanish crown jewels, brought to him by Philip's faithful valet so that they would not fall into enemy hands.

All was not well at Versailles, where the caged, bored courtiers were drinking, gambling, and fornicating as never before. "Some of them hate women and only love men, others like both men and women, some only like children of ten or eleven," writes Liselotte in disgust. "Then there are those who don't mind what they have, human or animal; they take whatever comes along. I know someone here who brags that he has had relations with everything under the sun except toads."

Louis's gout rendered him increasingly stationary. He abolished the *grand coucher* in 1705 and gradually retreated from public view toward backstage. He left his lifesize portrait, with himself in full-length blue royal robe, painted by Hyacinthe Rigaud in 1702, to take his place in the throne room and made it an offense for subjects to turn their backs on it.

On January 12, 1709, an unbelievable cold spell paralyzed France, freezing all its rivers, even the mighty Seine and the Atlantic Ocean on its western edge. The extreme cold lasted for two months, ruining all crops, killing twenty-four thousand Parisians and thousands of starving peasants who clogged the roads, begging weakly for food. Eleven thousand Frenchmen died that year at Malplaquet, another ignominious defeat by England's army. At Versailles, where all the wine froze in its bottles, Louis kept his legs in a bearskin sack and wondered if God had turned his back on him permanently.

The war and the terrible cold were bankrupting his country. (By the war's end in 1713, the *livre* had declined in value by 25 percent, and the funded and unfunded debt were still rising astronomically.) In that dark year of 1709, King Louis had to pledge the crown jewels to pay his soldiers, just as he'd had to sixty years before; now, as well, he had to sell some gems outright, choosing ones from former kings that he deemed dispensable. The Blue stayed, like all his chosen ones, in its decorated drawer. Louis very regretfully sent his solid-silver tables and chairs to be melted down. Colbert was not there to tell him that this made no economic sense, since furniture for which he'd paid 10 million *livres* fetched only 3 million; Louis would have raised far more cash, everyone agreed, by selling his diamonds, whose value stayed rocklike and stable, but this the Sun King could not bring himself to do.

"God seems to have forgotten all I have done for him," sighed Louis. He sank into a depression, had frequent crying fits—the king crying!—that he couldn't control. "He has no conversation," complained Madame de Maintenon. His gout got so bad that he directed his daily council meetings of ministers from his bed. He developed gallstones and a persistent cough that left ropes of phlegm in his lace handkerchiefs.

Even his jeweler, Pierre de Montarsy, son of Laurent, Tavernier's friend, betrayed him that year. Louis had ordered him to make a set of jewels to be given to the Elector of Bavaria, using some of the diamonds of the crown then in his safe. But Montarsy, like his monarch, had fallen into debt and pledged the required royal diamonds to a pawnbroker. He hurried at once to jeweler Rondé, bought replacements, but never paid for them. Pierre died the next year in disgrace. The original pawned stones were never found.

There was one glimmer of hope in all this gloom. On Saturday, February 15, 1710, the king was wakened at 7 A.M., an hour before his usual time, with the news that his pretty pet, Marie Adelaide, Duchess of Burgundy, was in labor, and at precisely three minutes, three seconds after 8 A.M. she gave birth to a son, to general rejoicing. The new prince was immediately christened, then carried to his own apartments in the lap of his nurse and future governess, the Duchess de Ventadour, as she sat securely—lest she drop the precious bundle—in the king's wheeled chair, accompanied by a detachment of guards and officers. Pomp came early to the baby who would become Louis XV, after death claimed not one but two heirs to the throne.

The king's only son, the dauphin, the only one of his six legitimate children to reach adulthood, died in April of the next year. Louis sat weeping in the dark, without a fire, in Madame de Maintenon's antechamber. "His grief would melt a stone," writes Liselotte. "He is choked with sighs."

Louis's grandson, the physically unimpressive but well-liked and fine-principled Duke of Burgundy, became the new dauphin and heir to the throne. He caught a severe case of measles in 1712 and when, on Tuesday, February 16, he knew he was dying, he gave the order for all his mother's jewels to be sold at auction to aid impoverished, wounded army officers. Two days later, at 8:30 A.M., he died. The king had a severe cold, so his attendants let him sleep on and told him the tragic news when he finally surfaced from his fretful dreams.

But God had not finished with Louis yet. Later that same cruel month, the king's darling, his adorable plaything, Marie Adelaide, the dead Duke of Burgundy's wife, died of measles, too. The king wrote to a relative, "You cannot begin to imagine how deeply her loss afflicts me." He resorted to his last and only comfort. In December, when light was short-lived and night closed in early, Louis commanded his secretary to write to the new royal jeweler Rondé: "I return the two florets that you have made; the king wishes to have them made into two ornaments for sleeves. [I return] also the two square diamonds which you sent some time ago. Please make a hat clip with these diamonds placed side by side, but it must suit the king's taste."

Only his shining rocks remained. Gone, all of them taken from him, were his only son, his grandson, his grandson's beloved wife, his health, youth, wealth, dreams of glory, even the unconditional love of his subjects. "He lost during the last three years of his life," writes the astringent Voltaire, "all the prestige of the great and memorable things he had accomplished." There were no more parties at Versailles, no myriad candle flames dancing in and out of diamonds. Louis spent his evenings quietly in Maintenon's room, spoke seldom, drank lemonade, and went to bed early.

The Blue Diamond of the French Crown, however, had still to play its last scene opposite Louis XIV. It began with the arrival in Paris on February 6, 1715, of an ambassador from Persia to France, of whom, as Liselotte writes, "everyone is talking. He is the oddest-looking being that was ever seen. He has brought a soothsayer with him, whom he consults on all occasions to know if days or hours are lucky or unlucky. If it is proposed to him," she continues, "to do anything and the day does not prove to be a lucky one, he flies into a fury and grinds his teeth." Thus did the mystical Orient, with its reliance on the occult, come to confront the rational, fixed, clockwork world of the French court.

France was exhausted by Louis XIV's wars. Since he had come to power in 1661, he'd been fighting one country or another on and off for a total of thirty years. In spite of high taxes, lotteries, the issue of paper money, sale of titles and official posts, the country's resources were sucked dry. Its population, because of wars, starvation, and expulsion of Protestants, had been reduced by 20 percent. But at Versailles, a luxe island in a sea of misery, the show had to go on; the Persian ambassador, like all previous foreign ones, had to be duly impressed with King Louis's diplomacy of display.

Slowly, painfully, on the morning of Tuesday, February 19—a day to which, apparently, the Persian ambassador's soothsayer had given the nod—the bent, aged king put his arthritic bones into his costume. Europe had never known so long a reign, or France so old a king. He'd survived all his progeny, except the beset Philip of Spain and offspring, and the five-year-old great-grandson who would succeed him. Louis arrayed himself in black velvet embroidered in gold, with diamonds everywhere, more diamonds than he'd ever worn, more, possibly, than *any* man had ever worn. He bent under their weight, feeling as well the weight of defeat, of debts, of so many deaths . . . and of adultery. With death drawing closer, he was preparing to meet his God and knew his carnal sins were legion.

He chose a ringlet-mad wig from his vast store and, at the very last, allowed the Blue Diamond, his prize and joy, right royal in its hue, to be hung from a light blue ribbon around his withered neck. He hardly glanced in his full-length gilded mirror before walking, a little before 11 A.M., to the balcony of his bedchamber to acknowledge the shouts of "*Vive le Roi!*" from the vast crowd assembled in the Avenue de Paris, on the roofs and in the courtyards of Versailles, come to enrich their thin lives, come to see the grand spectacle. They cheered just as loudly for the Persian ambassador as his carriage approached along the avenue, as he alighted, mounted a horse for the final paces, and trotted with his modest entourage into the marble courtyard.

Meanwhile, Louis XIV and nobles paraded into the Hall of Mirrors. There were tiers of benches along both long walls, which held gentlemen and "more than four hundred ladies, magnificently attired." The diarist Saint-Simon was there, and notes that the king looked "worn out, thin and vastly ill-favored." Did he, as he shuffled forward, recall that December ball eighteen years before, when his pert Marie Adelaide, God rest her soul, had just been wedded and bedded, and he'd caught the glory and the gleam in the blue heart and heaven held fast on a ribbon? Suddenly a large pearl dropped, like one great tear, from Louis's coat and rolled across the floor. It stopped near the foot of the Marquis of Lange, who retrieved it. Louis continued to the far end of the hall, climbed the steps of the platform erected there, sat down thankfully on a throne of gilded wood, his silver one long gone, and prepared, as he had so many times before, to shine and astound. But it all seemed somehow unreal, too far away. Had he lived too long?

On his right was the five-year-old dauphin who would succeed him, a pretty little boy with curly hair and big black eyes, "in a dress and cap covered with jewels," his leading strings held securely by his governess, the Duchess of Ventadour. On the king's left was his nephew, Philip, Duke of Orléans, son of Monsieur and Liselotte, in blue velvet with a mosaic pattern of diamonds and pearls, who, according to Saint-Simon, "set no limits on his wild speeches or his debauchery, acting partly from self-indulgence, partly from boredom at the Court." His daughter sat nearby, the fat, blowsy young Duchess of Berry, widow of a grandson of the king's who had died three years before. At almost every meal, she drank herself into unconsciousness, but not before she'd vomited food and wine in all directions. Louis treated her with "icy formality" and did his best to ignore her. Also present was the Duke of Maine, eldest son of Louis XIV and Athenaïs, costumed in "pearls and diamonds lent him by the king," a lame, ugly creature whose nature matched his body.

Liselotte was there, looking more pagodalike than ever, mentally composing a burlesque account of the occasion. And the court painter, Antoine Coypel, brush in hand, inconspicuously positioned off to one side, was preparing to depict every shining shoe buckle of the splendiferous charade.

The Persian ambassador entered the Hall of Mirrors and slowly approached the throne. His entourage, as Saint-Simon notes, "appeared in every way poverty-stricken" and he himself "highly embarrassed and very ill-clad." The gifts he brought the Sun King were "beneath contempt": a few "mediocre" pearls, a few "very ugly" turquoises, and some magical ointment supposed to bestow long life.

King Louis, as always, was courtesy and civility personified, but his diamond-laden coat grew heavier and heavier as the day wore on. After the initial ceremony came a grand dinner for the ambassador, and after that he had another audience with the king in the apartments of the late queen. As the diarist Dangeau tells us, His Majesty, aching in every joint, had to change his stone-covered coat for a lighter one "immediately after dinner." So it was, in the final act, that Louis XIV's diamonds, the eternal rocks on which his whole reign rested, became too much to bear.

As soon as the Persian ambassador departed, Louis took off the Blue Diamond and returned it to its festive-fronted drawer in his Boulle cabinet, where it would lie in oblivion for many years to come. The tired old king, at considerable personal cost had, as always, performed his royal duties to the letter and took comfort from that.

What everyone at court except the king knew, and what no one was prepared to tell him, was that the Persian ambassador was an impostor, completely bogus, not a deputy from the Persian king at all, but a merchant on the make called Mehemet Mira Bey, an individual far more full of pretence and illusion than the ceremony just ended in Versailles' marble halls. Seeing the "ambassador's" raggle-taggle attendants, his inferior garb and gifts, did Louis suspect? And if so, did he nevertheless go through his paces because the iron of royal routines, after seventy-two years on the throne, went right through to his soul?

Six months later, the Sun King began to fail. On Monday, August 12, he felt severe pains in one leg and thigh but went that evening as usual to Madame de Maintenon's apartment for some supper and music. It was the last day he managed to walk.

Next day, King Louis, now very ill, nevertheless granted a farewell audience to the sham Persian ambassador, who had hung around Paris for eight months, trading and filling his purse, milking his connection to France's monarch for all it was worth. This final interface of East with West, of a man come from the same part of the globe as diamonds with the man who loved them best was, aptly, the last public act of Louis XIV's life. "On returning from mass in his chair," writes Saint-Simon, the king "standing without support" met "that dubious ambassador from Persia. His weakness did not allow him to repeat the magnificence of the first audience, and he had to be content to receive him in the throne room, where nothing was out of the ordinary." Louis was in great pain, and the audience was long and tiring. The following day, still totally dedicated to duty, the sick king, sitting up in his white-plumed four-poster bed, with gilded arch above, where figures of fame held trumpets, ordered gifts "including some jewelry," sent to the Persian, who, two days later, "was escorted to the house of a merchant at Chaillot and shortly afterward left for Havre-de-Grace, where he embarked."

There is one farcical footnote to be added to the tale of the fake Persian. According to Liselotte, "There was a married woman who was pregnant through his fault and after making her abjure Christianity, he had her shut up in a trunk. The ambassador forbade anyone to open the box." Fortunately, someone discovered the lady within and released her just before she ran out of air. She was the Marquise d'Espinay, wife of one of King Louis's courtiers.

On Tuesday, August 20, the king was too ill to dress and sat all day in his dressing gown, while rows and rows of his gold brocade coats, his diamond-buckled plumed hats, his violet-blue regal robes reproached him silently. He would never dress again. Next day, he had trouble swallowing bread, which he normally ate ground into crumbs, having lost all his teeth. He sipped a few spoonsful of soup.

On Saturday, August 24, black spots appeared on his leg, the first sign of gangrene. Fagon, his physician, prescribed a bath of burgundy for it, and asses' milk by mouth. The king was in agony day and night as the gangrene spread. It was too late for amputation. Fagon swaddled the leg in feather pillows and advised a diet of icewater, with plenty of overripe figs, melons, and mulberries. (This caused Saint-Simon to note, in those dark ages of medicine, that no doubt it was all that rotten fruit that was turning the king's leg black.)

When he knew he was dying, he sent for the adorable little black-eyed boy who would succeed him. "My dear child," said Louis, with an irony he couldn't know, "you are going to be a great king." Then he kissed him fondly, saying, "I give you my blessing with all my heart."

On Sunday, August 25, Louis XIV whispered that nothing should be changed in the normal day's rituals, so the drum-and-fife band played beneath his window when he awoke, and twenty-four fiddlers played in the anteroom while he tried, but failed, to eat dinner. The gangrene had reached his thigh; he sometimes lost consciousness from the excruciating pain.

"The king showed the greatest firmness right up to the last moment," writes Liselotte. "He said with a smile to Madame de Maintenon, 'I have heard it said that it is hard to die, but I assure you that I am finding it very easy.'" His steel resolve never faltered. He spent his final hours in prayer, speaking to no one, repeating to the God he had served so long as earthly emissary, "O Lord, I am ready to appear before you, why do you not take me, O Lord?"

On September 1, 1715, at 8:15 A.M., Louis XIV died just four days short of his seventy-seventh birthday. Only his Jesuit confessor and the captain of his guard were with him at the end. "He gave up his soul without any effort," writes Philippe, Marquis of Dangeau, author of the period's dullest but most detailed diary, "as a candle that goes out."

A few minutes later, an officer stepped onto the balcony outside the king's bedchamber and removed his large, black-plumed hat. He went inside, then reappeared wearing one with a white plume, doffed it, and cried three times, "Long live King Louis XV!"

The Duke of Orléans, Liselotte's debauched son, who would act as regent while the new king grew up, went with all the princes of the blood to bow to little Louis. "As soon as that child heard himself addressed as Majesty," notes Dangeau, "he began to cry and sob, even before they told him that the king was dead." Stowed in its drawer in another room, the Blue Diamond of the French Crown lay in ignorance of the fact that it had just passed to a new owner who, when he reached adulthood, would have his own ideas about what to do with it.

"The late king contracted many debts," writes Liselotte, ever the realist, "because he would not give up any of his luxury. He also borrowed a great deal of money." When he died, debts exceeded revenues by 200 million *livres* (about $1.6 billion today). Colbert was surely turning in his grave.

If Louis XIV's legacy to his people was a mountain of unpaid bills, his legacy to French kings who succeeded him was a stash of jewels unequaled by any European monarch before or since.

Perhaps therein lies the final irony of Louis XIV's reign. With his death, his personal glory, "like a circle in the water which never ceaseth to enlarge itself," as Shakespeare puts it, soon disappeared to "nought" on the mirrored surface of Versailles. What survived and endured were all those other circles, very small but eternal, "of clearest water," the Sun King's beloved diamonds.

When he ascended the throne in 1643, the diamond was considered an inferior stone to its colored rivals, sapphires, emeralds, and rubies. With some help from advances in optics and gem cutting, Louis XIV pushed the diamond to center stage and left it there to reign forever over all other precious stones as undisputed king.

As for the Blue Diamond, it waited for the next King of France to focus his will and wish on it. In its Indian existence, it had experienced the triumph of human imagination and holy spirit, as believers beheld it moving in mysterious ways its wonders to perform. When it came into Tavernier's grasp, it counted in the triumph of commerce, and when Louis XIV appropriated its power to serve political ends, in the triumph of advertising. In the next stage of its life, there would be no triumph at all for the stone, but only a new setting of ignominy and decadence. Honor was left behind, dipped below the horizon. The shadow of a lesser monarch than Louis XIV would fall full upon it, and a dragon, red as a setting sun, and crouching far too close.

King Louis XV wearing his Golden Fleece decoration.
Portrait by Quentin de la Tour.

Drawing of the Diamond caught between dragon and
ram in the Order of the Golden Fleece.

4

SMALL THINGS

Small things make base men proud.
> —WILLIAM SHAKESPEARE, *King Henry VI, Part II*, act 4, scene 1

In the center of the dressing table in Madame de Pompadour's Versailles boudoir lay a 31¾ carat brilliant-cut, six-sided diamond, some smaller ones, also unmounted, and one huge, lumpish ruby red gemstone. She'd had to clear a space for them amid the many exquisite little objects lying there: scent bottles carved from jade and ivory; porcelain bonbonnières for pastilles and sweetmeats, their tops painted with tiny baskets of flowers suspended from even tinier ribbon bow knots; tortoiseshell boxes with swirling gold piqué work, holding pomade, powder, beauty patches, or rouge; silver thimbles and chased gold étuis, home to needles and small scissors; fans with ivory lace sticks, the paper leaf of one prettily painted with a gentleman and lady forever well-met halfway across a bridge; snuffboxes in porcelain—later Jeanne de Pompadour would acquire a different snuffbox for every day of the year and several in gold, every surface carved into curvaceous leaves and shells.

The rest of the room, its walls brightly lacquered, was crammed with live songbirds in gilded cages and fresh flowers in tall vases; porcelain birds and flowers almost as lifelike; silks and damasks in poufs and rolls; architectural plans and maps; large books of engravings; little leatherbound novels in precarious piles; half-done canvases of embroidery; skeins of rainbow silks and wools; bundles of ribbon-tied letters.

All this beauty assembled in one cozy room, however, didn't result in a confused clutter. Madame de Pompadour had arranged it, with her finely tuned aesthetic sense, to pattern and order. Light streamed in, on that late November morning in 1749, from Versailles' big north windows, so that the whole effect was as merry as a goldfinch. No wonder King Louis XV spent more time there with his mistress than anywhere else.

He was seated close to the dressing table in an armchair whose legs weren't rigidly straight, as in Louis XIV's day, but rounded into lines that suggested some bowlegged maiden stopped short at the beginning of her curtsy. Louis was staring down at the loose diamonds and the big red stone, called the Côte de Bretagne, originally thought to be a ruby but actually an Indian spinel of 206 carats, acquired for the French crown jewels by their founder, Francis I, Leonardo da Vinci's patron, in 1530, the same year that King Francis had bought his collar of eleven huge diamonds. Pompadour was talking with her usual animation, her small beringed hands fluttering over the stones as she described what might be done with them. Thirty-nine-year-old Louis merely bent his handsome head, which unfortunately doubled his chin, and listened. At one point, he picked up the red spinel and held it in his hand, but it turned into a pool of blood; at once he put it back on the table as if it were too slippery to hold. Pompadour was working hard, as always, draining herself of energy she didn't really have, to keep His Majesty focused on the project at hand. Louis's attention seemed forever on the point of dividing, scattering aimlessly, like grains of mercury across a polished floor.

"It's terrible the life I lead," she'd sighed to a friend earlier that year. "I've scarcely a minute to myself." The clear skin of her round face, below chestnut curls already coiffed for evening to save time, was the slightly yellow hue of old ivory, the result of insomnia and chronic fatigue, so that the ovals of rouge on each cheek, exactly two inches across, as fashion decreed, looked like crimson rose petals. She would celebrate her twenty-eighth birthday the next month. Jeanne was exquisitely gowned in flower-strewn silk and had been described seven years earlier by a gentleman acquaintance as "one of the prettiest women ever" with "a fascinating smile, dimples, animation" and eyes that were "the brightest, wittiest, and most sparkling I ever saw."

Born Jeanne Antoinette Poisson in 1721, daughter of a man who supplied food to the army, at age twenty she'd married Seigneur d'Étioles, nephew of a tax collector, and gathered the literary men of the day into her salon, starting with Voltaire, who would later call her "sincere and tender Pompadour." Jeanne, however, having set her sights on the biggest catch in the kingdom, turned up on February 25, 1745, at a masked ball at Versailles, dressed, fittingly enough, as Diana the huntress, and went in search of her prey. This was no easy task, for King Louis, wanting as always to be anonymous and undistinguished, was part of a moving group of eight men, all identically disguised as yew trees clipped into the formal shape Louis XIV had loved of pillar with vase. When Pompadour appeared in the king's line of vision, he removed his vase; she unmasked, and very soon thereafter Louis, who had been married for twenty years, made Jeanne his official mistress and created her Marquise de Pompadour. For her twenty-sixth birthday he'd given her a little box now resting, among so many, on her dressing table, on which her coat of arms, three castles on a bright blue ground, was delineated in diamonds. (Inside had been a bank order for 50,000 *livres*, but that had long since been converted into beautiful objects.)

"You are the most charming woman in France!" exclaimed the besotted Louis, and she was. She acted, sang, and danced in the theatricals that she got up to entertain the king, having been taught by a master of the Comédie Française. She played the clavichord, drew and painted exquisitely, was well versed in botany, art, and literature. Before he met her, Louis had spent his days hunting, but soon, like any man who lacks a firm center, he adopted the interests of the woman he loved. Together they spent happy hours designing new dwellings, some hers, some his, choosing furniture, paintings, statues. Just as Cardinal Mazarin had formed Louis XIV's taste, Pompadour formed that of his great-grandson. In fact, she influenced that of the whole nation and, through her involvement in such enterprises as the royal porcelain factory then at Vincennes but that would move in another seven years to Sèvres, helped to push France to the supremacy in the decorative arts that many agree it still holds.

Seated now at her dressing table, where she often received crafts-men and friends as well as her royal lover, Jeanne, in her pleasing voice, went on talking to the king, trying to determine His Majesty's wish, his pleasure, in the piece they were currently designing from spinel and diamonds. Her questions dangled unanswered in midair, but she pressed on, her beautiful arms and hands carving up the void. "Everything about her," a courtier once observed, "was rounded, in-cluding all her gestures."

This made her consonant with the artistic style of her time, and the examples of it in her boudoir and beyond, where the heavy, mascu-line Baroque with its fearful symmetry and straight lines, popular in Louis XIV's age, had given way to the light, feminine Rococo with as-symetrical informality and free-flowing curves. Versailles' current fur-niture, silver, porcelain, and objets d'art were frivolous with forms borrowed from seashells, rocks, waves, and plants. The shell was a fit-ting emblem, as we shall see, for Louis XV's reign, for it represents the empty form, the debris left on dry land after the great wave has receded and the vital creature that gave the shell direction and purpose has disappeared.

As he sat in his bowlegged armchair, beside his enchanting mis-tress, Louis XV's greatest asset as king was readily apparent: his splendid appearance. No monarch ever graced a coin, medal, marble pedestal, or canvas with a better head or profile. When the rake Casanova, who sported a "carnelian ring on which was engraved the head of Louis XV," turned up at Versailles, he commented that "never did even the most skillful painter succeed in rendering justice to the expression of that beautiful head, when the king turned it to one side to look with kind-ness at anyone."

Of middle stature, with a figure, as he neared forty, growing plump, Louis had black eyes that were molasses pools without much depth or sparkle. And while his features were fine, they lacked the underlying granite definition of Louis XIV's. His face was puttylike; if one pushed a fingertip into his cheek, it might leave a permanent dent. "When he is thoughtful and not disposed to speak," observed an English visitor, "he is apt to fix his eyes upon some one object, let his chin drop, and open his mouth." He was doing that now, as Pompadour talked. His Majesty's gaping mouth was the only rounded form that Jeanne feared: that tiny well of darkness into which she might sink like a stone to oblivion, as earlier mistresses had, unless she could make it disappear.

Louis had been only four, already orphaned, having lost both parents to measles when he was two, when Liselotte first noted his "pretty little mouth which, however, he keeps open too much." When Louis XIV died a horrible death from gangrene in 1715, France's new king was whisked away from Versailles to a drafty old palace at Vincennes while the Tuileries in Paris was readied for his occupancy. Philip, Duke of Orléans, acting as regent until Louis came of age, preferred to keep the court in Paris rather than Versailles. There, at his nightly orgies, according to Saint-Simon, Philip and his cronies "talked filth and outrivalled one another in blasphemy and when they had made sufficient noise and were all dead drunk, they were put to bed, and on the following day began all over again." Philip was also, in the hot-blooded Bourbon tradition, wildly promiscuous—but not very particular in his choice of women. "Provided they are good-tempered, indelicate, great eaters and drinkers, he troubles little about their looks," his indulgent mother remarked. When she complained of their ugliness, Philip replied, "Bah, Maman. In the dark of night, all cats are gray." Court gossip even hinted that the regent had an incestuous liaison with his eldest daughter, the drunken Duchess of Berry. He was not a good role model for an impressionable young king.

Louis brushed up against a better one when he was seven, and Russia's Peter the Great visited the French court. He was a great bear of a man, six feet seven inches tall, with a mahogany complexion and a brown, unpowdered wig, simply dressed in plain jacket with gold, not diamond, buttons. He had a nervous tic that contorted his whole face and gave him, while it lasted, a ferocious stare, so little Louis, a timid, shy boy, was alarmed when the czar picked him up in his arms on meeting. However, he proved to be very kind and gentle. Louis was still asleep when, early on the morning of Monday, May 24, 1717, Peter went to the Tuileries apartment of the Duke of Villeroy, Marshal of France, to see the Blue Diamond and the other crown jewels. The czar barely glanced at them, pronounced them finer and more numerous than he had supposed, but admitted that he knew little of such things. It was the first slight for the Blue. Louis presented Peter the Great with two tapestries from the Gobelins factory and a sword with a diamond hilt, which he politely refused. This king, rare among his kind, was indifferent to diamonds.

It was about this time that Louis began to focus on the outward signs and minutiae of monarchy that, throughout his reign, would give him so much of his sense of self-worth. Liselotte describes how the little king invented "an Order which he gives to the boys who play with him. It consists of a blue-and-white ribbon, from which hangs an oval piece of enameled metal; on it there is a star and the model of a little pavilion which stands on the terrace where he plays."

In addition to Peter the Great's snub, the Blue Diamond of the French Crown suffered further neglect that same year when it found itself pushed aside to make way for a white diamond that would hog the spotlight relentlessly for all of Louis XV's reign. Its story, like the Blue's, begins in the Krishna River area of India when, around 1701, a worker in the Parteal mine found a 410-carat rough stone, smuggled it out in a self-inflicted leg wound, headed at once for the coast and boarded a ship bound for England. Soon after sailing, its British captain, who heard whispers about the valuable diamond, killed the miner one dark night, pocketed the gem, and tossed the body overboard. Returned to India, he sold the stone to a prominent diamond merchant called Jaurchund for £1,000. The captain, however, began to feel pangs of remorse for the murder he'd committed. He spent all the money as fast as he could in Bombay's bars and brothels, then hanged himself. Jaurchund sold the jewel for £20,000 to Thomas Pitt (1653–1726), Governor of Madras and grandfather of William Pitt, a later British prime minister. Thomas sent the stone to a London gem cutter, Joseph Cope, who charged Pitt £5,000 and took two years to cut it into a

cushion-shaped fifty-eight-facet brilliant of 140.5 carats. Owning it
made "Diamond Pitt," as he came to be called, extremely nervous and
paranoid. Fearing its theft, he never slept two nights running under
the same roof and moved about with great secrecy, sometimes wearing
a disguise.

Pitt felt both relieved and rich when, in 1717, he sold the bother-
some diamond to France's interim ruler, the Duke of Orléans, for
2.5 million *livres*. The regent admired it briefly and gave it into Villeroy's
safekeeping to join the other crown jewels. The Duke of Saint-Simon,
who'd helped persuade Philip to buy the gem, soon christened the
Regent, enthuses in his memoirs that it was "the size of a greengage
plum" and "perfectly white, free from all stains and cloudiness, indeed
quite flawless, a diamond of the first water."

The downgraded Blue had less actual brilliance, using that term in
the gemological context, for two reasons. First of all, it was not white
but colored, so it absorbed more light than the Regent without refract-
ing it. Second, the Blue Diamond had slightly fewer facets, for it had
been cut by Pitau in 1673, twenty-seven years before the fifty-eight-
facet cut had been invented by the Venetian Vincent Peruzzi. The Regent was luckier, for its discovery in the Indian mine had coincided
exactly with that of the cut that henceforth would be used on all important diamonds to give them maximum brilliance. The Blue was also
smaller than the Regent and less valuable. When an inventory of the
crown jewels was done in 1791, it would be valued at 2.2 million *livres*
and the Regent at 9 million, more than four times as much.

So it was that in the fateful year of 1717 the Regent assumed its
number-one position among the royal jewels, while the Blue Diamond,
having lost status and rank, found itself neglected, like some pretty
baroness, whose circle of admirers deserts her as soon as a ravishing
duchess sweeps into the room.

Four years later came another blow. On March 21, 1721, France's
eleven-year-old monarch received the Turkish ambassador wearing a
flame-colored velvet coat adorned with one of Louis XIV's two sets of
diamond buttons and buttonhole surrounds. The young king wore the

Regent in a knot of pearls and diamonds on one shoulder and the Sancy in his hat, while the Blue languished morosely in total eclipse in the galling confines of its drawer.

The 53¾ carat, pear-shaped Sancy diamond had a past as full of adventure as the Regent's. The Frenchman Nicholas de Sancy had bought it in Constantinople in 1580 as a gift for his king, Henri III, to adorn the cap he habitually wore to conceal his baldness. While Sancy's servant was en route to France to deliver the jewel to King Henri, he was killed by robbers who threw his body into a ditch. Thinking that his faithful servant might well have swallowed the diamond before capture, Sancy had his body cut open, and sure enough, there it was, sparkling still in his stomach. Sancy became ambassador to England in 1596 and eight years later sold the stone to King James I. It passed to Charles I, and after he lost his head, it was one of the gems purchased by diamond-mad Cardinal Mazarin who left it to diamond-mad Louis XIV.

His great-grandson gave the Blue Diamond another slight in March 1722, when for a Te Deum Mass celebrating an alliance between France and Spain, Louis XV entered the cathedral dressed in lilac velvet with the Sancy in his hat, the Regent on his shoulder, and the blue gem nowhere to be seen.

Seven months later, on October 25, for his coronation in Rheims cathedral, Louis wore the traditional violet-blue robe and a brand-new crown just made in the jeweler Rondé's workshop, in which the Sancy sparkled above a fleur-de-lis at the very top and the Regent at the front of the band. Again, there is no mention in contemporary accounts of the Blue. (After the ceremony, the two big diamonds in the crown were taken out so that they could be worn throughout the reign in other ways and replaced with fake stones; the crown sits today in the Apollo gallery of the Louvre.)

Next year Louis officially came of age on February 15, his thirteenth birthday, and the newly empowered young king moved himself and the court from Paris to Versailles. He was still very timid, modest, ill-at-ease, and unsure of himself. He crept uncomfortably through the grand palace, which never felt like home or natural habitat, as it had for the Sun King. It was more monument than dwelling. Back in Paris, ex-Regent Philip collapsed from a stroke on December 2 at the feet of his mistress and died without a word, worn out by debauchery at age fifty-one.

By age fifteen, with his Bourbon libido already raging, Louis was deemed by the Duke of Bourbon, head of the Condé branch of the family, to be ripe for marriage. He made an astonishing choice, and on September 4, 1725, wed Marie, penniless daughter of Stanislas Leczinski, who had served five years as elected King of Poland before being dethroned. She had not a drop of blue blood, was seven years older than Louis, and never bothered to improve her very plain features with rouge or powder. But she was sweet-natured and healthy, with a pelvis broad enough for plenty of childbearing. The groom gave orders for some of Louis XIV's out-of-fashion jewels to be broken up and the stones reset for Marie's use into clasps and brooches; an eight-inch-high crown to be worn at the wedding, set with 138 diamonds and 40 colored gems; and chokers called *carcanets*, the latest thing in necklaces, in which diamonds were appliquéd to velvet bands. Louis dressed for the wedding in gold brocade and anchored the white plume of his hat with the Regent, while the Blue, which had only once reflected European nuptials, missed out entirely. Not only Louis but also his new queen seemed to prefer the Sancy, which she often commandeered for the center of her *carcanet*, and the Regent, which she liked to wear in her hair.

The blue jewel suffered two other losses of status, albeit indirect ones, when all Indian diamonds suddenly lost value. First of all, in the very year Louis XV married, just as diamond production from Indian mines slowed to a trickle, and consequently prices rose to an all-time high, a brand-new source was discovered in South America. Bernardino de Fonseca Lobo came to Brazil from India, from the Portuguese colony at Goa, to search for gold at Minas Gervais. One day he joined some native miners in a card game and noticed that the pebbles they were using as counters looked just like the rough diamonds he'd seen in India. On inquiry he learned that the miners had picked the stones out of their gold pans near the town of Tejuco, 250 hard-going miles from the coast. Later that year the very productive mines of Tejuco Diamantina began operating. To keep the price of diamonds from falling drastically, gem merchants in Europe claimed that the South American diamonds were too hard to be faceted. But the resourceful Brazilians shipped their stones to Goa and from there sold them to European dealers as Indian mined. When finally the truth got out and the price of diamonds suddenly plummeted, every venerable diamond of the Old Guard, including the Blue, lost esteem and prestige and moved over reluctantly to make way for the stream of Brazilian ones, which had caused their down-market woes. (It does seem a strange coincidence—or one of nature's clever twists of plot—that the Brazilian diamonds surfaced just when the Indian supply dried up; and when, in the 1870s, the Brazilian source dwindled, diamonds would be discovered in great profusion in South Africa.)

The second loss of status for all diamonds occurred when Georges-Frédéric Strass (1701–1773), who was appointed master goldsmith and jeweler to Louis XV in 1734, invented an imitation diamond of great luster and clarity, known thereafter as strass, by mixing red lead with lesser amounts of silica, potash, and calcined borax. These imitations, forerunners of many much later ones such as rhinestones and zircons, were usually rose-cut and sold in the same shops that carried real diamond jewelry.

Diamonds in general found themselves becoming more plebeian and restricted in three other ways that didn't, fortunately, affect the royal Blue. First of all, men in eighteenth-century Europe, apart from kings, virtually stopped wearing them owing to changes in fashion. Second, new social rules for ordinary mortals decreed that diamonds should not be worn in daytime but only at night. Third, the females wearing them were no longer just upper class but far more likely to be married to middle-class bankers, lawyers, and merchants who were getting rich, entering society, showing off their wealth via diamond-laden wives, and who would eventually seize power from monarchy and nobility. Money was becoming the instrument of class division, not birth and inherited privilege. Middle-class French women followed Queen

Marie's lead and put their best diamonds in their hair. The queen re-marked that whereas a man was judged by what lay inside his head, a woman was judged by what lay on it. Hairdos grew ever higher, were powdered white, then stuck with many flowers and feathers and ribbon bows, all of them anchored by diamond brooches and festooned to their neighbors by diamond necklaces. Sometimes there would be a curving diamond aigrette as well, placed on one side, looking like a question mark asking "Is this perhaps too much?"

On the night of his wedding to Marie, according to court gossip, Louis performed his conjugal duties no less than seven times; eleven months later the queen gave birth to twin daughters and proceeded to produce a baby a year until she'd had ten, all girls but one, the dauphin and heir to the throne being born on September 4, 1729. The queen complained that she was "always being bedded, always pregnant, al-ways in labor." She grew desperate for an excuse to keep Louis out of her bedroom and finally hit on the clever ploy of marking the major saints' days with sexual abstinence. As the years passed, the saints for whom Louis was denied entry proliferated to include all minor ones as well as major. When the king was turned away for one so utterly un-known that he'd never heard of him, he flew into a rage—he'd had a quick temper since childhood—and stomped straight off to the em-brace of a housemaid. (The result of that encounter became a future art dealer called Dorigny.)

One night in 1733, Louis lurched into the queen's bedroom, tiddly from too much champagne, and Marie, sitting up amid her usual plethora of shawls, bits of fur, and rumpled bedclothes, rebuked him for being drunk and sent him on his way. The next day the king openly ac-knowledged his first official mistress: Countess Louise de Mailly, mar-ried daughter of the Marquis of Neslé. When, one day, Louise was too absorbed in her tapestry work for Louis's liking, he grabbed a pair of scissors, cut it into four pieces, and being too lazy to conduct a wide search for a new mistress to replace her, merely moved on to Louise's sister, the Duchess of Vintimille. When she died giving birth to a son known thereafter as "the demi-Louis," the full Louis took as mistress yet another Neslé sister, widowed Madame de la Tournelle, wealthy and calculating. "When I heard him scratching at my door," she chortled gleefully to a friend in November 1742, she played hard to get and sent him away. "He must get used to that," she said smugly.

King Louis seemed never in complete control, never enough of an autocrat, either with his women or his kingdom. He was passive and fatalistic; he let events take their own course and put what energies he had into sexual romps and occasional bursts of temper. When his former tutor, Cardinal Fleury, in whose hands Louis had been content to leave the reins of power, died in 1743, everyone hoped that the thirty-three-year-old king would seize them himself, but he did no such thing.

When the twenty-seven-year-old widow Tournelle died in the following year of peritonitis, Louis toyed with the idea of a fourth Neslé sister, but was too inert to act on it, and in the next year the future Marquise de Pompadour neatly captured him and saved him any further bother. Louis's lethargy had been with him since boyhood. Throughout his reign it caused him to let France drift, the deficit to rise, and discontent among his subjects to fester. "He rises at eleven," complains the diarist Marquis d'Argenson, "and leads a useless life. He steals from his frivolous occupations [such as grinding and making his own coffee] one hour of work; the session with the ministers cannot be called work, for he lets them do everything, merely listening or repeating what they say like a parrot." He was "flaccid in all things," "very lazy in thinking and reflecting," and modest to a fault, for no matter how correct and wise his own opinion was in some matter of state, Louis always thought he was wrong. "I often heard him say," wrote the Duke of Croy in his memoirs, " 'I should have thought so and so but the others say the contrary, so I am mistaken. It is not for me to decide.' " "He spoke of affairs," commented the Count of Cheverny, "as if someone else were on the throne."

This king didn't want to strut across a vast stage dazzling his people and foreign ambassadors as Louis XIV had but to tiptoe behind the scenes giving little suppers for people he'd gotten used to. The plain fact was that Louis didn't enjoy being king; he would have been far happier as a private person, where his unassuming and gentle nature would have served him better.

Having grown up without a father and mother to give him intimacy and to foster his self-esteem, Louis was extremely reserved, shy, and easily intimidated, particularly in the presence of clever men. The king saw Cardinal de Bernis in Pompadour's apartments for three years before he could bring himself to speak to him. Such diffidence was a serious handicap for a ruler. Louis felt slightly more relaxed with women, who found his smoldering moodiness a sexual turn-on, but he was most at ease with animals. He took great pleasure in feeding the hens, pigeons, and rabbits he kept on the palace roof, and his enormous white Angora cat routinely lay on a cushion of crimson damask in the center of the mantelpiece in his bedroom at Versailles.

If Louis XIV's character in general was as hard and firm as a diamond, this king's was more like soapstone, soft and opaque, or, as his chief minister, Choiseul, put it, like "soft wax, on which the most dissimilar objects can be temporarily traced." "What is he at bottom?" wondered d'Argenson. "Impenetrable and indefinable."

Louis began spending more and more time living at one of his many smaller, less ostentatious and demanding abodes. When he was at Versailles, he shut himself up in a suite of fifty rooms in the north wing to which no courtier could come without an invitation. Eventually, this wing of the palace would become a labyrinth of secret passages, hidden staircases, and tiny rooms where no one could disturb the king because no one could find him.

It was at Versailles that Louis's only son, the eighteen-year-old dauphin, was married for the second time in 1747, his first wife having died in childbirth. His new bride was Marie-Josèphe, daughter of Augustus III, the King of Poland who had pushed Queen Marie's father off the throne. This wedding would affect the future fate of the neglected blue stone. The bride's father had a passion for diamonds equal to the late Louis XIV's. Augustus's wedding gifts to his daughter included splendid chandelier earrings, a large pendant to match, and even a knot of diamonds and emeralds for her dressing gown. Augustus himself appeared at Versailles for the wedding in a dazzling Order of the Golden Fleece insignia, which he'd had made seven years before.

It wasn't easy to catch, and hold, the wandering attention of King Louis XV, but it caught, and held, on Augustus's order, which had three huge table-cut rubies, one below the other, each set around with dramatic erupting flames in diamonds, with a little golden fleece hanging limply, as it always did in this decoration, at the bottom. It was very showy and very lovely, and King Louis, who was France's prime member of the order, took careful note and kept the image lodged firmly in his head.

The Golden Fleece Order of European knights had been founded on January 10, 1429, at Bruges by Philip the Good, Duke of Burgundy, on the occasion of his marriage to Isabella of Portugal, and the final chapter, the twenty-third, had been established in 1559. Grand mastership of the order, with both Spain and Austria claiming it, remained in dispute until the Congress of Cambrai decreed in 1721 that each ruling European house should have its own independent order and its own grand master. All members had to be titled, and their privileges included exemption from all taxes and precedence before all peers except princes of royal blood.

The insignia varied from country to country but always incorporated a suspended model in gold of the pelt of a ram to suggest the golden fleece of Greek myth. In this story the fleece of a ram with magical powers, guarded in a sacred grove by a fire-breathing dragon, is carried off in triumph by the Greek hero Jason and his Argonaut friends.

It was the image of Augustus III's splendid Golden Fleece decoration that filled Louis XV's head two years later on that clear November morning in 1749 as he sat in Jeanne de Pompadour's enchanting boudoir, gazing down at the ruby red spinel and white diamonds laid out on her dressing table. He'd already explained to his beloved mistress, his shield against the world, that he wanted them made up into something similar to Augustus's treasure, but he was too reserved to confess to her that although there were already several Golden Fleece insignia among the crown jewels, he wanted one that would be distinctly and only his.

Casanova wrote of Louis XV's court that "the gods worshiped here are Novelty and Fashion." The king was not an original man; he conformed rather than led; he took, chameleonlike, the tone of his cultural milieu. Thus his second reason for wanting a brand new Golden Fleece decoration—and this he shared with Pompadour—was that it would be an up-to-the-minute fashion statement: designed in Rococo style, with perhaps a hint of chinoiserie, for mid-eighteenth-century tastes loved all things Chinese.

King Louis was, in his own quiet way, enjoying himself. Even in his youth, unlike his predecessor, he hadn't dreamed of glory to be achieved through conquest and spectacle. Instead he played with things, all decorative and delightful, some to his own designs. He was always content to lose himself in the detail, in the pretty ground cover of life, to ignore tall trees reaching for the sky and the trumpet call of duty and discipline. His restless self seemed as randomly roving and aimless as a windtossed butterfly. "This prince, like so many others," wrote Voltaire to Frederick the Great, "was little suited to his post. He was indifferent to everything except trifles of personal concern."

The trifle of a new Golden Fleece was, at that moment, keeping him from seeing, and coping with, the larger issues. The Peace of Aix-la-Chapelle that ended the War of the Austrian Succession had been signed the year before, but by that time the national debt was so high that even noble landowners had to pay a direct tax. The Marquis d'Argenson confided to his journal from his Touraine estate that he saw nothing but "fearful misery" and "despair" among the peasants. "There is serious talk of the king traveling round his kingdom next year," he'd written two years before; "God grant that he may thus learn to know the misery of his people and apply the remedies." But Louis couldn't even bring himself to enter Paris, let alone the provinces. Just nine months before he and Pompadour played with spinel and diamonds in her boudoir, on March 1, 1749, Argenson noted that "songs, verses, satirical pictures rain against the person of the king" and a prophecy "predicts that his subjects will revolt, and declares that when they gave him their love they did not know his vices."

It was just as he finished telling Pompadour that they had to have a design both Rococo and somehow Chinese that an idea popped into Louis's head, a rare occurrence indeed, almost a miracle! His mind glowed red-hot and was sharply focused. He was so excited by his own ingenuity and cleverness that he jumped up from his armchair and moved about the room, absentmindedly picking up a snuffbox here, an ivory miniature there, then putting them down again, but not precisely, as Pompadour noted fretfully, in the same spot, talking to her in his curiously husky voice, which no one who heard it ever forgot. The Côte de Bretagne spinel acquired by Francis I—now there was a king with taste!—had to be carved, said Louis excitedly, into a *dragon*, a dragon being one of the principals in the Greek myth *and* a favorite Chinese motif *and* of a form—Pompadour had never heard him talk so fast—of a form, with its twisty tail and serpent length, well adapted, no, perfectly, *ideally* adapted to the sinuous curves of the Rococo!

Louis stopped walking about and sat down again with a satisfied thump, his mouth stretching upward into a Rococo curve of its own, into a smile so broad, with lips so tightly compressed, that Jeanne wondered if perhaps the black hole was gone forever.

She smiled, too, and relaxed. Her hands stopped fluttering over the stones like two of her caged birds. The king looked more animated, more engaged, than he'd been for months. She clapped her little hands twice lightly. Yes indeed, a beautiful dragon! What a truly splendid idea! His Majesty was amazing in his inventiveness, really amazing! And clever Jacques Guay would carve it! She extended both wrists toward Louis to make her point. On each was a wide bracelet set with a cameo Guay had carved: on the left wrist was Henri IV and on the right, Louis XV himself, sporting the world's tiniest crown, made of emeralds.

Against one lacquered wall of Jeanne's boudoir stood a glass-fronted cabinet in which she kept the collection of stones Guay had carved for her. Born in Marseilles in 1715, Guay had come to Paris as a youth and apprenticed himself as a design student to François Boucher, who would later paint such charming portraits of Pompadour. When Guay saw in a French collector's cabinet tiny stones on agate, onyx, carnelian, and coral, he vowed that he, too, would master this art of creating cameos and intaglios using diamonds as cutting tools. He went to Italy, studied the ancient Greek and Roman ones in the Medici collection in Florence, copied more stones in Rome, and tried his hand at original creations. He returned to France just after the death of Barrier, court engraver of semiprecious stones to Louis XV, and succeeded him in the post.

The king wanted Guay to carve all the glorious events of his reign, but these turned out to be in short supply, so Jacques got to incise only one stone depicting Louis's 1745 victory at the battle of Fontenoy in the War of the Spanish Succession. Guay found a better patron in Madame de Pompadour, and a pupil as well. She herself engraved sixty-three stones with his designs, and her glass-fronted cabinet would eventually hold seventy more that Guay had carved exquisitely to record in tiniest compass the events she wanted to remember of her life with Louis. Just one year before, on March 30, 1748, it was Pompadour's influence that got Guay admitted to membership, earlier denied, in France's Academy of Art.

Jeanne placed the huge spinel above the diamonds on her dressing table and arranged them in a pleasing pattern below. She cocked her well-coiffed head and looked down at them. Something was missing. Might it not be a good idea, she wondered aloud, to introduce more color to the design? That would give the insignia more drama, more interest, more . . . *panache*! The last word landed on the table like a glove slapped down in challenge.

At once Louis's shoulders drooped and his mouth dropped open as confidence and certainty drained away. He sighed and shrugged. More color? Could he help it if diamonds—and a king had to use them, given their eminence—didn't have any color? That was just the way it was; God had created nature's most valuable gem to be as colorless as water. But wait . . . He frowned with the effort of remembering. It was all so long ago; he'd been only five and the weight of gems sewn on his little coat had made his shoulders ache and the Oriental ambassador had worn such funny pantaloons and—*yes!*—around Great-grandfather's neck had been a colored diamond on a ribbon, a great big blue stone! It was a diamond, wasn't it, and not just a sapphire?

Louis summoned the master of the household and ordered him to fetch it. The Blue Diamond of the French Crown that had been languishing for thirty-four long years in total neglect and obscurity was lifted up and, from inside its simple gold bezel, once more saw the light.

When it arrived in Pompadour's boudoir, perhaps still attached to the pale blue ribbon that had encircled the tough old sinews of the Sun King's neck, it glinted and sparkled for all it was worth. Louis held it in his hand and really looked at it for the first time. It was much smaller than the Regent and the Sancy and its violet-blue color, the same shade as his coronation cloak, was very strong—perhaps too strong? He put it down. At once Jeanne began arranging it with the other stones and commenting on its vibrant beauty, how it was just what was needed, how it would draw every eye to its brilliance and how brilliant it was of His Majesty to think of it. *"Beaucoup de l'éclat, de la gloire!"* Her words dropped a sun-gold aureole over the Diamond, lying on the dressing table with trinkets and trivia all around it. But irony lay there, too.

It took some months for Guay to carve the spinel into a dragon. He consulted frequently as he worked with Pierre-André Jacquemin, another talented craftsman who was jeweler and goldsmith to King Louis. Jacquemin, while Guay was busy with his carving, had been summoned on December 29, 1749, the day of Pompadour's twenty-eighth birthday, from his Paris workshop under the Louvre's Long Gallery to her boudoir at Versailles. There King Louis and the marquise gave him the Blue Diamond; the large hexagonal white one; the smaller stones, which now included some topazes; and the sheaf of sketches for the Golden Fleece Order that the two of them, heads almost touching as they bent over Jeanne's drawing board had, after many happy hours' work, produced. Jacquemin added further ideas and refinements to their design, for he had a fine aesthetic sense.

Finding itself once more back in the Louvre, the Blue Diamond lay on Jacquemin's worktable reflecting its first day in the palace more than eighty years before, when the dull clink of Tavernier's coins, day after day, gave way to a clarion call to glory. What would its new incarnation be?

One day, about a year later, a carriage was sent from Versailles to Paris to fetch the portrait painter Maurice-Quentin de La Tour from his studio and apartment under the Louvre's Long Gallery. Maurice-Quentin was the third of five sons and one daughter born to Reine-Françoise (née Havard) and François de La Tour, who had once served as trumpeter in a rifle regiment commanded by the Duke of Maine, clubfooted son of Louis XIV and Athenaïs de Montespan. Born September 5, 1704, young Maurice-Quentin apprenticed himself to a Paris painter, Jacques-Jean Spoede, studied the work of the Venetian Rosalba Carriera, and soon mastered the art of doing portraits in pastel chalks, which La Tour preferred to oils because they were light to carry, needed no drying time, and could be done quickly without tiring the sitter. Striking out on his own, he worked hard and fast, made money, and grew very skilled at capturing both likeness and character in his simple medium. When he was only twenty-six, he was asked to do Voltaire's wise face, a great honor, and after that he got to choose his subjects among the high and mighty and to be well paid for doing so. There is an immediate, alive yet relaxed and informal quality to his portraits that makes them very modern in an age when most were stiffly posed and often wooden.

La Tour was used to coming and going at Versailles. He'd first turned up there in December 1739 to paint Louise de Mailly, the king's first official mistress plucked from the bouquet of pretty Neslé sisters. Maurice-Quentin had also done pastels of Louis XV's daughters, portraits now lost, the dauphin and his wife, and one of Queen Marie, exhibited in the 1748 Academy Salon show in Paris, in which she looks like a peasant in head scarf and wildly ruched dress without a single jewel, not even earrings, but in which La Tour has caught her essential being. He liked working for King Louis, who always paid promptly and generously. The artist had received 12,000 *livres* for eight royal portraits in 1749. In another four years, he would paint Madame de Pompadour in candid undress and show the portrait in the Salon of 1755.

When the royal carriage bringing him to Versailles drew up in the marble courtyard, he climbed out and entered the palace through the little guards' room, what they called *par les derrières*, by the back door, which is how Louis XV liked to receive his guests. Forty-seven-year-old Maurice-Quentin was small, sprightly, and elfin, as we know from the self-portrait he drew that year. He had a sharp nose, light brown eyes, a mischievous grin, and small ears neatly pinned against his head. For his royal visit, he'd dressed in black velvet suit, lace jabot, and freshly powdered wig. If the rank of his sitter allowed, he liked to throw off the wig and loosen his cravat once he got down to work. Today he'd have to forgo such informality. He informed the guards at the door of his appointment with the king and proceeded up the private staircase, its iron railings twisted into double *L*'s for kings called Louis.

At the door of the king's cabinet, a blue-coated servant announced La Tour, and he entered the richly furnished room. Against one wall stood Louis XIV's diamond-studded desk, hardly ever used by the man sitting in a gilded armchair. La Tour bowed, then looked around and frowned. There were two windows facing different directions. "How can I capture Your Majesty," he asked plaintively, "inside this great lantern? I must have only one source of light."

King Louis replied meekly that he'd chosen the setting so that they wouldn't be disturbed. "I did not know, sire," replied the artist boldly, "that you were not master in your own house."

Louis at once got up and, rather than ordering one of the ushers standing guard at the door to do it, closed the inside shutters to one window. He clunked about stiffly as he did so, for he was inside a cuirass of armor, riveted to the appearance, if not the actuality, of martial might and glory: the man of action about to be captured for posterity. He adjusted the placement of his chair and, with a final clank, sat down again.

Maurice-Quentin readied his block of paper and pastels and got to work, with complete concentration. The king's handsome head gave him no trouble at all, but how best could he simplify the lines of that very complicated decoration hanging around His Majesty's neck?

It was the newly created Order of the Golden Fleece first conceived by Louis and Madame de Pompadour and masterfully executed by Guay and Jacquemin. The red Côte de Bretagne, reduced from 206 to 105 carats but minus its three holes, formed a dragon with diamond-studded wings and a tail that twisted around the hexagonal white 31¾ carat diamond before forming the ring through which the order's ribbon passed. Around the beast were diamond palm trees to suggest the sacred grove of the Greek legend. The dragon coiled head down; topaz and gold flames erupted from its mouth and bound into the midst of the burning fiery furnace was the Blue Diamond.

(This setting of the stone has long since been broken up, but we know exactly what the insignia looked like, not because we have La Tour's sketchy approximation but because it was the practice of jewelers of the crown to make lead castings of their work. Detailed drawings of this casting are still extant. One sketch, not a very good one, appeared in Pouget's *Traité des Pierres Précieuses*, published in Paris in 1762.)

Having been forced into the shadows by the Regent and the Sancy, the Diamond suffered further shame. Now it had to share the limelight with a whole troupe of diamonds, topazes, and a famous ruby look-alike. And beneath its blues-in-the-light hung the most ignominious companion of all: a lifeless, boneless, very limp ram, fitting symbol for the man who had conceived this travesty.

With quick, sure strokes and tiny rasping sounds, La Tour's chalks conjured a paper king. The real one was content to sit in silence without much of anything floating through his mind, but at least his mouth stayed closed. Louis XIV had worn the Diamond cavalierly and simply, on a ribbon, conscious of his divine right to a gem of such spectacular hue and rarity. Louis XV had found his own much more modest way to wear it: as part of a formal emblem that many men wore and that presumed not power but only brotherhood and privilege. This Louis used the Diamond as one more "trifle of personal concern," to keep ennui and national problems at bay, to help pass the time in petty pace and trivial pursuits. Set in its decoration, the blue stone helped to define him and to plump his ego. It signified no higher ideals, as it had for the Sun King, of glory, stately show, stoic endurance, or God-given authority. The Diamond was no longer a political prop for the staged spectacles at Versailles but a personal prop for one man's inadequate psyche.

There is no portrait of the mighty Sun King wearing the Blue. His historical magnificence stood tall without it. Louis XV would have himself painted not once but twice wearing it atop his carapace of armor: in La Tour's pastel and in a full-length oil by Carl Van Loo. There he is, the Fun King, shielded against history's verdict, leaning heavily on his public roles: France's number-one member of the Order of the Golden Fleece, commander-in-chief of the army.

In the same year as La Tour captured the king in chalks, an event occurred that would ultimately affect the Diamond and change France forever. Denis Diderot and the Philosophes published the first volume of the *Encyclopaedia or Critical Dictionary of Sciences, Arts and Trades*, the final volume of which, the thirty-fifth, would appear in 1776. Its Enlightenment ideals were new: peace, tolerance, and prosperity instead of military glory; progress and reason instead of tradition and superstition; the rule of law and civil liberties instead of absolutism and privilege. Nobles and churchmen pondered or ranted; the growing middle class enthused and rallied around; the lower classes rumbled with complaints and protests against their inept monarch. As Argenson noted in his journal, Louis was "cruelly exasperated at the ill-will of the public." Pompadour felt its wrath on the day she went to Paris, was faced with riots, and retreated to Versailles, where the king seemed oblivious to the new dawn breaking and the changing times. He continued to drift through his orchidaceous life.

The ladies of his court took to painting their veins blue to emphasize the color of the blood beneath and wore a different perfume, some subtle blend of lavender, violet, rose, and thyme, each day. Analyzing the scent *du jour* formed each morning's occupation.

The king grew ever more restless, changing dwellings and women at an astonishing rate. He stopped sharing Pompadour's bed (she was vastly relieved), but kept her firmly in the forefront of his life as friend and only

confidant. He set up a private brothel, a row of small houses in the village of Versailles, which became known as the Parc aux Cerfs. "The king
has a little girl of fourteen," wrote Argenson on December 10, 1752. "He
likes young girls as he is afraid of syphilis." The king's doctor warned him
that for a man in his forties, he was having intercourse far too often.
"But you told me I could, as much as I wanted to, so long as I used no
aphrodisiacs," protested Louis. "Ah, sire," replied the physician, "change
is the greatest aphrodisiac of all!"

Versailles' grand marble staircase, up which ambassadors had ascended to a blazing Sun King on his throne, was torn down in 1752,
to make way for private rooms for Adelaide, one of Louis XV's daughters. "So no further ceremonies are practicable at Versailles," lamented
Argenson.

In another set of rooms there, Dauphine Marie-Josèphe was being
delivered of a baby every autumn, a girl first, then a gratifying number
of boys, including France's next king, Louis XVI, who gave his first cry
in 1754.

Louis appointed a new minister of finance, Étienne Silhouette, who
bequeathed his name to outlines dark and plain, after his austerity measures ruled that gowns be made without flounces and trousers without
pockets. One day Monsieur Silhouette went to see the king, spouted
alarming facts and figures of funds diminishing and debts mounting, and
asked for guidance and direction. Such talk always bored Louis. Silence
reigned. Finally, he inquired in his charming manner and husky voice if
the paneling in Silhouette's Versailles office was gilded. The minister of
finance was rendered speechless and, shortly thereafter, jobless.

When the Seven Years War with Britain broke out in 1756, Louis
met reluctantly with ministers in Pompadour's red lacquer room and
used her tiny black beauty spots to mark the places on the wall map
where France was losing battles. Its East India Company, begun almost
a hundred years before by an optimistic Louis XIV, came to an ignominious end in January 1761, when the English, who had been making
inroads for some years, permanently took control of French headquarters at Pondicherry.

Around this time, the royal porcelain factory at Sèvres came up with a color called *"bleu du roi,"* a shade of such concentration that an all-over pattern called "partridge eye" of tiny gilt dots within white rings was quickly superimposed to tone it down. One might well argue that "king's blue" was the strongest component of Louis XV's reign.

In early January 1757, a hopeful assassin stabbed the king between the ribs with a penknife, which everyone feared was poisoned. Louis felt sure he was dying, called daughters and wife to his bedside, and in a weak little voice apologized to Queen Marie for his years of adultery. When the ladies saw him lying in a pool of blood as red as rubies and spreading, they all fainted dead away. The wound, after all that, proved superficial and the king lived to sin another day.

When Louis wasn't admiring partridge eyes on king's blue, applying beauty spots to hot zones, or lifting some adolescent's skirt, he was amusing himself with an adventurer (and con man) whom Casanova pronounced "good-looking and a perfect ladies' man." This was the Count of Saint Germain, just returned from ten years in India where, so he claimed, he'd learned how to remove flaws from diamonds. The king promptly handed him one worth 6,000 *livres* which, if flawless, would be worth 10,000. The wizard pocketed the stone, returned it with no flaws one month later, and utterly hoodwinked His Majesty, who trusted this charlatan from the Orient as Louis XIV had the so-called Persian ambassador. The king later showed a courtier a 12 carat perfect diamond. "I melted down small diamonds weighing 24 carats," explained Louis, who'd found a new trivial pursuit, "and obtained this large one weighing 12." The clever count was given his own suite of rooms at Versailles so this Western parody of Eastern magic could continue.

When the Seven Years War ended in 1763, France celebrated the peace with the opening in Paris of the Place Louis XV, now renamed the Place de la Concorde. To be sure, there wasn't much cause for celebration; by the Treaty of Paris, signed February 10, Britain got North America, and France lost most of her colonial power. Since 1748 King Louis had been considering more than sixty plans for the square to bear his name, and finally, with Pompadour's help, had chosen the architect Jacques-Ange Gabriel to build the two blocks that today

contain the Hotel Crillon and the Ministry of the Marine, the latter
building destined to play a fearful role in the Blue Diamond's life story.
Edmé Bouchardon sculpted a huge, well-armored Louis XV astride his
horse, with four adoring female figures at his feet: Strength, Peace, Prudence, and Justice—to which he had dubious claims. The statue was
slowly dragged from Bouchardon's studio and set upright in the square
one fine June day, while the mob danced in the streets and gorged
themselves on free meat and wine.

Next night, fireworks were watched by King Louis, other royals
and nobles, and a very ill Jeanne de Pompadour, making her last public
appearance, and spitting blood as red as the damask of the nineteen
draped and tented boxes where everyone sat, and which stretched along
the river, their nineteen chandeliers dropping diamond points into the
dark Seine.

One month later, the diarist Edmond Barbier wrote prophetically:
"Sooner or later the revolution will explode in a kingdom where the
sword and the censer clash without ceasing. The crisis is acute."

Pompadour died in her gaily decorated Versailles apartment from
lung and heart disease on April 15, 1764, leaving the king "in great af-
fliction" and with tears streaming down his cheeks as he stood bereft
watching her funeral cortege depart for Paris. She left him in her will
"all my engraved stones by Guay, whether bracelets, rings, seals, etc.,"
all those small but perfect worlds. It took two lawyers working every
day for a year to list the three thousand lots to be sold, each containing
at least a dozen objects, of her possessions: furniture, carpets, china,
statues, pictures, books, fabrics, clothes, jewels, plants, linen, and silver. She was just forty-two when she died.

Louis suffered further bereavements when his son, the heir to the
throne, died in 1765, the dauphin's wife Marie-Josèphe two years later,
and Queen Marie in 1768. At once Louis paraded a new mistress to
whom he presented a bouquet of flowers "tied round with a string of
diamonds," as she tells us with great relish in her memoirs. This was
the infamous Jeanne du Barry, illegitimate daughter of a dressmaker.
She'd left home at fifteen, seduced her first employer, a hairdresser, and
both sons of her second, a wealthy widow, before marrying debauched

Count Jean du Barry. "Her bloom is entirely gone off," wrote the English Duchess of Northumberland, who saw du Barry two years after she was ensconced at Versailles. "Her eyes are of a lively light blue but she has the most wanton look in them that I ever saw," continued the duchess, who thought her manner "vulgar, her voice loud, her language rough and indelicate." Du Barry was formally presented to court and king, wearing virgin-white satin and plenty of common new diamonds in the Hall of Mirrors, where once a more aristocratic and venerable gem, the pride of Louis XIV, had flashed its true-blue brilliance from every silvery glass down the long reach.

A wife for the dauphin, the future Louis XVI, arrived at Versailles on May 14, 1770, was given twelve wedding rings to try on, and found one that fit her tiny hand. She was Marie Antoinette, daughter of Empress Maria Theresa of Austria and Francis of Lorraine, a small-boned girl with reddish blond hair inclined to friz and a pendulous lower lip beloved by later caricaturists.

Two days later, the wedding took place in the Hall of Mirrors, where thousands of uninvited spectators, in dripping clothes and muddy boots, pushed in out of the rain, past all the guards, and joined the five thousand invited guests in a terrific crush. The bodice of Antoinette's wedding dress, as an English duchess reported, left "a broad stripe of lacing and shift quite visible, which had a bad effect between two broader stripes of diamonds." During the ceremony, the groom "trembled excessively and blushed up to his eyes when he gave the ring." He was as shy and gentle as his grandfather the king, lacked his good looks, and spent his days making clocks, fancy locks, and bits of furniture. His sword was a continual trial to him, and he never seemed to know what to do with his hat. On the wedding night, he accompanied Antoinette to her bedroom door, bowed, and wished her good-night. He had a condition called phimosis, a constriction about the prepuce of his penis that made intercourse impossible until, four years later, he had surgery to correct it and could finally bed his virgin bride.

"The king is most kind and I love him dearly," wrote Antoinette in her first letter to her mother, "but his weakness for Madame du Barry—the most stupid and impertinent creature imaginable—is pitiful." When the royal mistress tried to ingratiate herself with Antoinette by means of a pair of valuable diamond earrings, the dauphine snubbed her soundly; she was, thank you very much, perfectly happy with the diamonds she already had, all her own tasteful choice.

The exchequer was empty and debts enormous, as was the king. He'd grown so corpulent that he had to be helped when mounting his horse or climbing into his carriage. When England's most prolific letter writer, Horace Walpole, arrived in Paris in July 1771, he wrote: "The distress here is incredible, especially at Court. The King's tradesmen are all bankrupt" and "his servants starving." The latter resorted to graft. Antoinette's and Madame du Barry's maids charged "four pairs of shoes every week, three yards of ribbon daily to fasten the dressing gown, two yards of taffeta daily to tie the glove box and so through all the list," wrote the Austrian ambassador on February 29, 1772. The maids sold the items and pocketed the cash. Small things had a new role, antithetic and harmful to the king, within his palace.

On April 27, 1774, Louis XV lay ill at Versailles. When little red spots appeared on his face and body, he looked in a mirror and said: "If I hadn't had smallpox, I should think I had it now." He'd caught a particularly virulent strain of that disease. His handsome face, immortalized on gem, coin, and canvas, swelled and grew black. His body became covered with such foul-smelling scabs that all his bedroom windows were flung open to spring's budding trees and birdsong. On May 10, at noon, he began his death agony. On the ledge of the balcony beyond his bedroom stood a lighted candle, put there to signal to crowds below. At half-past three in the afternoon, an officer extinguished it. The king was dead.

The moment after he'd expired, all the courtiers waiting in the royal bedroom's antechamber rushed to prostrate themselves before the startled young dauphin, France's new king. Then everyone fled the highly contagious palace. Louis XV's body was hastily thrown into a coffin and carried to the Cathedral of St. Denis, where French kings were buried, with a very small escort, traveling at a brisk pace through

dead of night. One observer who saw the cortege pass "thought it inde-
cent to see them go so fast; for the guards who followed the coach galloped." And the mob, instead of "showing the least concern, hoop'd
and hollow'd, as if they had been at a horse race instead of a funeral
procession."

In those final years when celebration ceased, money grew scarce,
and Versailles became a gilded slum, diamonds shone but rarely in its
marble halls. The Blue wasn't among them and resigned itself to the
quiet seclusion of a sedentary life. But beyond imagining were the adventures still to come.

King Louis XV had crammed it into an elitist badge whose mythic
connotations were all ironic, with their echo of Jason's race across
wine-dark seas to snatch glory from overwhelming odds. In this Louis's
reign, the Diamond shrank to a small thing with little resonance. But
still imbedded at its core were invisible strands of the ancient Indian
world of wonders. Sorcery and curse lay there, and crystal gazing of
enormous power. The dragon to which it was currently joined in hate-
ful union would, like its legendary prototype, prove unequal to the task
of guarding its treasure.

Around the Diamond, in fire-breathing monster and spreading
flames, danger flared red and gathered strength with time.

*Execution of Louis XVI in the Place de la Révolution
with Garde-meuble in the background.*

5

BURGLARY

Flat burglary as ever was committed.
—William Shakespeare, *Much Ado about Nothing*, act 4, scene 2

On a spring afternoon in 1790, the handsome figure of Louis XV astride his horse still regarded, unseeing and uncomprehending, the square named after him. The real monarch had been dead for sixteen years; his bronze likeness would exist for two more; its end would be extremely violent and its pride of place usurped by an object just as large and far more forbidding.

Beyond the statue, on the north side of the square, marched in neoclassical order the columns of the two fine buildings that Louis XV had commissioned architect Jacques-Ange Gabriel to build. The one that today houses the Ministry of the Marine was, in 1790, the Garde-meuble, a combined storehouse and museum for the royal treasures of France: tapestries, suits of armor, religious objects, and the crown jewels. Under lock and seal in one large box lay the Diamond, still under the sway of a dragon breathing gelid fire, still imprisoned inside the Order of the Golden Fleece. Red beast; white and blue diamonds; prophetic colors all.

If we draw an imaginary circle around that part of Paris, moving clockwise from the Garde-meuble, it will include, with one exception, all the principal persons and places that figure in this chapter of the Diamond's story. Just to the east of the cavernous, silent building housing the royal jewels, on the north side of the Tuileries gardens, stood an old riding academy. Inside, on that spring afternoon, the members of the National Assembly, France's elected governing body, formed one year before, were very busy changing the course of history with fiery rhetoric, much shouting and clapping, and radical decrees.

Flowers and shrubs were blooming as gaily as ever in the Tuileries gardens, but there were far fewer well-dressed strollers to admire them. And in the palace itself the King and Queen of France, Louis XVI and Marie Antoinette, were kept under close and insolent guard, too afraid of the consequences to venture even as far as the garden. Later that year, the queen, in a letter to her brother, Emperor Leopold II of Austria, wrote with a trembling hand that "murder is at our gates. I cannot appear at a window, even with my children, without being insulted by a drunken populace."

A little northeast of the palace was another venerable building, the Palais Royale, growing less royal every day, the buzzing central hive of all the anger alive in France, which had already clapped the monarch into the Tuileries and his jewels into the Garde-meuble. The environs of the Palais Royale had been an arcaded pleasure complex of theaters and kiosks for the past six years, where the people of Paris could buy lemonade poured from tin jugs for two sous a basin; white mice with ruby-red eyes confined in cages; canaries or linnets released from theirs, carried for sale on grubby fingers. One could avail oneself of a prostitute, a letter writer, a mender of ragged garments. A year before, the fresh wind of liberty had begun to blow there, and to the previous noise and bustle were added impassioned soapbox orators, incendiary pamphlets piled high on kiosks, posters tacked to every tree and column, all inciting the mob to grab political power any way they could.

The dense crowds twisting every day through the streets and alleys in that part of Paris, close to the vulnerable occupants of the Garde-meuble and the Tuileries, were mainly unemployed factory workers from the suburbs of Faubourgs Saint Antoine to the east and Saint Marcel to the south. These men and women had roughly cropped hair instead of the curled periwigs of their social superiors; soon they would show their contempt for anyone who wore breeches and silk hose by wearing only straight trousers, thus earning their name *sans-culottes*.

They were hungry, dirty, smelly, noisy, foul-mouthed, and abusive. Their anger was fueled by memories of humiliations, inadequate wages, empty stomachs, beatings, arrogant orders, condescension, and—worst of all—total disregard of their needs.

On the south side of this circle flowed the river Seine, which, like the Diamond, was good at reflecting history's big and little scenes. Twenty-seven years before, when the square named after him had opened, fat Louis XV and thin Madame de Pompadour watched from scarlet boxes while fireworks soared and the Seine was sequined with a thousand white points of light. In another two years, for six terrible days, the river would mirror a very different scene.

On the Seine's Right Bank, continuing round the Place Louis XV, was a ditch full of stinking refuse, and to the immediate west, where today the Champs-Élysées begins, there was nothing but vacant land. One-third of Paris, where more than half a million people lived, had been built in the previous twenty-five years, and sidewalks didn't yet exist. The Champs-Élysées in 1790 was a mere lane through marshy ground, with heaps of stones, tangles of underbrush, and stagnant pools of water giving off an offensive stench and a threat of infection. It was an unsavory place where well-dressed bourgeois never ventured, where every ruffian and scoundrel in Paris hung out, planning burglaries, fencing stolen goods, and even murdering their enemies. Any criminal just arrived from the provinces knew where the action was and headed straight for this wilderness.

One of the habitués of the Champs-Élysées that spring was Paul Miette, squat, thickset, with a lump of blubber for a nose, due either to congenital syphilis or to all the fists that had smashed into it, and a finger missing from his left hand, sliced off in a tavern brawl by a vengeful pocketknife. Born in a Paris slum thirty-three years before, Paul replied to any official who asked that he was a "dealer in silver." He was, indeed; in silver and gold and gems and counterfeit *assignats*, the banknotes of the day—none of it honestly acquired. He'd begun his life in crime modestly enough as a young boy, pickpocketing lace handkerchiefs and watches, and upgraded as he grew. Miette was conducting much of his nightly business in Île de la Cité where, in historic Renaissance

buildings, the jewelers, goldsmiths, and watchmakers of Paris had their
glittering shops. They were suffering from a dearth of aristocratic customers and a surfeit of robberies. Miette had to be vigilant, on daylight
scouting missions, whenever he crossed the Pont Neuf, for there were always plenty of police spies there, moving nonchalantly among the rau-
cous street vendors hawking their wares, keeping a sharp lookout for
known criminals.

Miette was married to Marie-Françoise Brebant, age thirty-two,
who, whenever he went to prison or the provinces, had her trade as
dressmaker to keep her supplied with bread, wine, and shelter. Miette
had been thrown into a Paris prison for a brief term in 1779. In 1781,
convicted again, he was sentenced by the court judge to nine years'
banishment from Paris, where his presence was "considered dangerous," then led away to be flogged, beaten with rods, and branded on
one well-muscled shoulder with V for *voleur* (thief). Perhaps Miette secretly liked that ropey red V forever seared into his flesh since it was as
much the honorable badge of his profession as the Order of the Golden
Fleece had been for Louis XV.

Exiled from Paris, Miette went to ply his trade where he had connections, in Rouen, Normandy's prosperous capital about seventy
miles northwest. As soon as he arrived, he headed for the tavern in rue
Eau-de-Robec, where local thieves drank and plotted. There he met
one of their ringleaders, Cadet Guillot, who sometimes resorted to the
alias Lordonner, a tall man as thin and pale as some bean sprout raised
in a basement and deprived of light, which, given Guillot's domestic
origins and chosen profession, wasn't far from the truth. He could
slither his way into rich homes through apertures impossibly small; this
made him a popular fellow in the Rouen clique of roistering robbers
and very much in demand. He seldom had to buy his own wine.

When his nine years' banishment was up in January 1790, Paul
Miette returned to Paris and showed his papers at one of the white
stone customs posts built into the twelve-foot-high wall that encircled
the city. That winter the fourteen remaining customs sheds that hadn't
been destroyed by angry mobs were piled high with weapons in case of
another attack: pikes and muskets and bayonets. Miette eyed them

warily, then found his way quickly to wife Marie-Françoise, who was bent over her seams in rented rooms in rue Bossu. That very month, Miette stole again, was arrested again, and served a short stay in prison. But by spring 1790 he was a free man once more, up to his old tricks by night and by day skulking about in the mud and mire of the Champs-Élysées.

There was a thread, slight as a spider's, but fatally adhesive, stretching northeast from Miette across Place Louis XV to the room in the Garde-meuble where the Diamond lay. This taut line completes the invisible circle within which we've placed the protagonists of this dramatic segment of the Diamond's life: a motley group of thieves, an earnest body of legislators, a seething mob, and a beleaguered king and queen.

When Louis XV had succumbed to smallpox in 1774 and his grandson found himself King Louis XVI at age nineteen, he'd rushed to his wife's enfolding arms, exclaiming, "What a burden! At my age! And I have been taught nothing." They were "terrified that we are called to the throne so young," wrote Marie Antoinette to her mother. "*Mon Dieu*, what will become of us?" (Better not to ask.) Unfortunately, her royal spouse shared many of the traits that had made his grandfather such an ineffectual ruler. This Louis was quite as shy, as passive, as inclined to let things drift, as indecisive. He was too fat and slack-jawed to be handsome, walked with a waddle, and squinted nearsightedly at the world's passing show of fuzzy, bewildering shapes, too vain to wear glasses. He listened to his wife's political advice, which was always bad. He was happiest buried in his private study, among his telescopes, sextants, nautical charts, and the timepieces and locks he made himself, both paradoxical symbols for a man who couldn't stop the clock or secure his kingdom.

By 1787, invading Versailles, where the royals still lived, were "blackguard figures that were walking uncontrolled about the palace," as the English visitor Arthur Young notes, even into Louis's bedchamber, "men whose rags betrayed them to be in the last stage of poverty." Louis tolerated them silently, did nothing, sank into gloom and stasis. Antoinette, who was neither well-read nor intelligent, assumed a wild, frenetic gaiety. Particularly in the early years of her marriage, she was utterly frivolous, self-centered, and spendthrift. While Louis tried to make his locks turn easily, Antoinette concentrated on building feather headdresses three feet high, which earned her giddy court coterie the name "featherheads"; on embroidering roses on absolutely everything; on filling the nursery (with a daughter born in 1778, the dauphin in 1781, and another son in 1785); and on collecting diamonds. She'd arrived in France as Louis's betrothed in 1770 wearing a ring set with a gray-blue heart-shaped diamond of 5.46 carats, whose color competed with that of the Blue Diamond of the French Crown. Antoinette bought her gems in delicate sprays of petals, leaves, and dewdrops and kept them in a crimson velvet, gold-embroidered casket called her *bijouterie*. She often spent rainy afternoons at Versailles spreading out on her dressing table the too, too old-fashioned, ponderous jewelry amassed by the Sun King and wondering how best to redesign it. In 1788 she asked her husband to give her for her very own a funny old parure of diamonds and rubies (the property of crown and country) so that she could make something really pretty from it, and Louis XVI, who could refuse her nothing, passed the necessary decree and made it hers alone. The king sent the stones off for recutting to Amsterdam and Antwerp, with one stroke turning all the cutters still left in Paris—there weren't many—into implacable enemies, while Antoinette blithely helped herself to a fresh batch of old-fashioned crown jewels and another afternoon's fun.

The Blue Diamond had been a mere plaything for Louis XV's pleasure thirty-nine years before; now many royal stones, rare miracles of nature, turned into game chips for an idle hour's entertainment. At Louis XVI's collapsing court diamonds provided mere hectic glitter. Light had become an adjective, not a solid noun; it didn't illumine; it signified lack of weight.

When she wasn't sorting diamonds or sticking feathers in her frizzy, reddish hair, Antoinette lived life down on the farm. She took over the Petit Trianon, the country house with extensive gardens at Versailles that the besotted Louis XV had got Jacques-Ange Gabriel to build with his usual neoclassical elegance for Madame de Pompadour. Louis XVI had given it to Antoinette in the year of Louis XV's death, and at once she had enclosed it with railings and locked gates to keep out the public, who had always been free to enjoy the Versailles acres. This caused the first hot breath of resentment, but not the last, against this Austrian queen. She built a rustic village, a dairy, even a water mill. There she played with her beribboned cows and her Bo-Peep sheep, following, as with her diamond settings, the fashion of the time, for the philosopher-writer Jean-Jacques Rousseau's popular ideas included a back-to-nature call. Antoinette, in 1782, even made the pilgrimage to Rousseau's grave at Ermenonville, twenty-five miles from Paris. She might not have been so reverential had she known where Rousseau's ideology was to lead and how it would affect her.

Rousseau's *Treatise on the Social Contract*, published in 1762, begins with a clarion call to action in its very first sentence: "Man is born free and everywhere he is in chains" and follows with the words "Liberty, Equality, Fraternity" trumpeted on every second page. The book encapsulated Enlightenment ideals and postulated a social contract in which the individual surrenders his rights to the general will and the common good. Rousseau advocated kicking aside Europe's solid social plinths from the first half of the eighteenth century and setting up new ones. Live the simple life, he said. Prefer feelings to reason, nature to culture, impulse to order, innocence to experience, the noble savage to the sophisticated urbanite, the plain to the grandiose, the domestic hearth to public pomp. On the farm called Versailles, Antoinette churned the royal butter and skimmed the royal cream, while the bourgeoisie of France read their Rousseau and the waterwheel of history turned in slow, sure revolutions.

The so-called Queen's Necklace Affair in 1784–85 speeded things up. Any noble savage could have told enlightened Frenchmen that diamonds are potent catalysts of human events, but that was something the modern world had forgotten—until the Necklace Affair. Napoleon Bonaparte would later consider it one of three main causes of the French Revolution. From its beginning, this historical event was built on certain symbols that gathered weight and resonance as the months and years rolled on. Two such were hats and trousers; another was the diamond. It represented everything that Rousseau's simple citizens came to hate. They themselves wore, above their feeling hearts, cameo lockets with the hair of loved ones in their domestic circle sentimentally enclosed on the reverse side. Diamonds belonged to the *ancien régime*; to kings who bankrupted the country buying them and created unfair laws; to nobles who had no claim beyond birth and privilege for helping themselves to most of the world's goods. If diamonds had always been a king's best friend, they were now a citizen's worst enemy.

The weighty queen's necklace in question, worth 1.6 million *livres*, contained 647 brilliants weighing 2,800 carats. It was a vulgar, showy piece with four tiers: a choker of seventeen diamonds, big as filberts, above a three-wreathed festoon with pendants, above a double row of diamonds with one 11 carat stone, above four knotted tassels. It had been made for Madame du Barry by the jewelers Charles-Auguste Boehmer and Paul Bassenge, but her benefactor Louis XV had succumbed to smallpox before it could be delivered. Boehmer and Bassenge, naturally, were eager to turn this expensive item of inventory into ready cash and, knowing Queen Marie Antoinette's penchant for diamonds, thought first of her. She'd already bought earrings and a featherweight spray from them. But Antoinette's taste, as we have seen in the previous chapter, when she refused Madame du Barry's offer of earrings, didn't run to a flashy, nouveau-riche object that screamed courtesan, not queen. Boehmer and Bassenge took turns beseeching her at court, with much dropping to knees, wringing of hands, hinting of total ruin, and even of stone-weighted suicide drownings in the Seine unless Her Gracious Majesty took pity on them and purchased this spectacular, splendid, one-of-a-kind, show-stopper necklace. Antoinette stood firm: a thousand times no; the horrid thing wasn't at all to her taste.

Then a wicked schemer and con artist called Jeanne de la Motte heard of Boehmer and Bassenge's plight and told them she had a buyer. On August 10, 1784, she dressed a milliner by day/prostitute by night in the simple kind of white muslin gown that Antoinette favored and sent her off to Versailles to impersonate the queen by standing in the dusk with the light behind her in the garden's Grove of Venus, and handing a single rose without speaking to the gullible Cardinal Louis

René de Rohan, who had fallen out with the queen and was ecstatic to think, as he sniffed his rose, that he had just been restored to Her Majesty's good graces. He was a fop who wore ruby and emerald rings on every finger, minced about in a striped-silk coat with sunburst silver and diamond buttons, and never took his beady eye off the main chance.

Jeanne next convinced de Rohan that the queen wished to purchase the necklace using him as go-between. On January 29, 1785, the necklace as big as a chandelier was brought to the cardinal's Paris mansion from Boehmer and Bassenge's shop and quickly transferred to the supposed courier sent by the queen, who was, in fact, Jeanne's current lover, Réteaux, who hurried around at once to his beloved's boudoir and gave it to her. The next day, she slipped it to an underpaid and underhand jeweler in Île de la Cité who broke it up. Then the stones went to Jeanne's husband, who forthwith departed for London, where he sold them with no trouble at all and returned to Jeanne with bagfuls of presents, including ruby brooches and silver asparagus tongs.

Boehmer and Bassenge waited for the first of four payments, due six months later. And waited and waited. Finally, they went to the queen, who rightly denied any involvement whatsoever and the whole unsavory plot was exposed then and there. The mystified Rohan was tried in 1786 from May 22 to 31 and acquitted. The De la Mottes were also tried, sentenced, escaped from prison and fled to London. During the trial, Jeanne claimed that she was the poor, unhappy victim of a greedy, ungrateful queen, and given the temper of the times and growing antipathy to queens in general and this Austrian one in particular, everyone in France believed Jeanne and repudiated Antoinette.

With the Necklace Affair, rising antiroyalist sentiment and all the grievances of an oppressed people against the luxury prevailing at Versailles coalesced and struck with full venom straight at the queen. She became, in Thomas Carlyle's words, "the symbol of the sin and misery of a thousand years," as that ridiculously overblown bosom wrap of diamonds became her noose. Libelous posters and piles of pamphlets were slapped up, or down, around the Palais Royale, asserting that she was a spendthrift slut. They alleged that she'd deliberately tried to destroy

Rohan because he'd spurned her sexual advances, or that she'd persuaded Jeanne de la Motte to bring him down when she and Jeanne were rolling about engaged in lesbian acts. All of this uproar proved, yet again, if any reader of these adventures needs further proof, that one should never underestimate the power of a diamond and that nothing triggers imagination and suppressed desires faster than that particular gem.

Then, on July 13, 1788, an augury, alarming yet also energizing, occurred in France: a widespread hailstorm stretching from Toulouse in the south all the way to Rouen in the north—where Paul Miette, still exiled from Paris, was hanging out in the Eau-de-Robec tavern with stringbean Guillot. Some hailstones were sixteen inches around; they killed birds and rabbits, ripped branches from trees, smashed windows, ruined all the crops: wheat, grape vines, olives, fruit, vegetables, everything. Peasants, struck speechless, looked up at the noon sky, dark blue as night, sending glittering white rocks hurtling down on them. It was as if the queen's necklace had multiplied by millions, every stone aimed at destroying their livelihood, their lives. Surely this was a sign from God. *Le Bon Dieu* was sending them diamonds, symbols of their oppressors, to tell them it was time to act.

Several weeks after the hailstorm, in August, France's controller-general announced that the Treasury was empty and could no longer make interest payments on the huge national debt, which was consuming half of all revenues. One cause was France's support of the American War of Independence, which had been done entirely through loans rather than increased taxes. On the day France declared war on Britain, July 10, 1778, the French fleet had arrived in American waters, followed by the dashing twenty-year-old noble the Marquis de Lafayette, come to help lead Americans to freedom.

In addition to the drain of this war, the royal family's upkeep took 36 million *livres* a year, plus another 28 million in pensions for their friends, almost one-fifth of the total budget. A laborer, on the other hand, earned 30 sous, or 1½ *livres* a day, and by February 1788 inflation was so bad that two four-pound loaves of bread, needed daily for a family of four, took all his wages, with nothing left for shelter or other necessities. Hunger joined anger as fuel for revolution, while Louis XVI tried to calm his subjects by telling them to write down all their grievances. Throughout the country, they did so, in twenty-five thousand *cahiers* and elected deputies to carry them to Paris and show them to the king.

This body of 1,214 deputies, the Estates General, made up of 308 clergy, 285 nobles, and 621 bourgeoisie from the Third Estate, mostly lawyers and merchants, assembled at Versailles at the beginning of May 1789, to determine what sort of nation should succeed absolute monarchy, which clearly wasn't working. They convened for the first time on May 5 in a venue chosen by the king, the Hall of Lesser Pleasures—aptly named if one were a royal in 1789—which was a quarter mile down the Avenue de Paris from the palace itself, to show the deputies that they should keep their distance from God's Anointed One. At one end of the hall, on a canopied throne placed on a purple carpet, sat Louis XVI, in all his pudgy ineptitude, dressed in cloth-of-gold and ermine-lined cloak, with the very costly Regent diamond blazing from the front of his hat.

If Louis gave equal billing that day to the Blue by wearing it displayed in the Order of the Golden Fleece, no diarist present recorded it, having more momentous matters on their minds. Most likely it didn't appear, for Louis didn't seem to favor that badge fashioned by his grandfather. When, in 1777, Antoinette had engaged the sculptor Louis-Simon Boizot (1745–1809) to make a marble bust of her husband so that she could keep him in the Petit Trianon, King Louis chose a different Order of the Golden Fleece decoration from the crown jewels to adorn his well-padded chest. So in all likelihood, in May 1789 the Diamond stayed in its Versailles stronghold, sinking a little further into obscurity and the general opprobrium toward diamonds that currently were its lot.

Seated that historic May day below and to the left of Louis's splendor were the nobles, in black silk coats lavishly gold embroidered over gold vests, with lace cravats and hats jauntily plumed. To the king's right sat the clergy: cardinals in red, bishops in purple. In the middle sat the lowly members of the Third Estate wearing black from head to foot, sober as undertakers, their hats very plain and deliberately unfeathered.

The deputies and the two thousand spectators behind them regarded King Louis balefully, as he made his opening-day speech, referring irritably to the "much exaggerated desire for innovations." He kept his hat on his head, so its diamond cyclops eye fixed on them, blinding them with its flashes, and looking like nothing so much as a giant hailstone. Louis droned on, noting that "the power and authority of a just king are great; they have always given France its brilliance and its glory *(l'éclat et la gloire)*." Did the long-deceased Sun King, looking down at his old prop room from some baroque cloud, roar with laughter when he heard this excuse-for-a-monarch mouth those words? At the end of his speech, Louis doffed his hat; clergy and nobles, quite correctly, removed theirs. According to court etiquette, the Third Estate should have kept theirs on. Some did, but many didn't—in the first tiny act of defiance, and the first of several hat scenes that would, as the Revolution progressed, accurately manifest the mood of a people growing ever more rebellious.

Later, the deputies went to see the Petit Trianon, wanting above all to see the room they'd been told that the queen had encrusted everywhere, walls, ceiling, doorways, mantel, with diamonds. When no such room materialized on their tour, they left in a huff, quite sure it had been deliberately hidden from them. Once again, as in the Necklace Affair, diamonds bred resentment.

The deputies were still in session, giving passionate vent to years of grievances, when they heard on June 4 that the seven-year-old dauphin had just died from tuberculosis. Only the royals felt grief. The feeling hearts of the members of what they'd just named the National Assembly focused full on freedom, passing decrees that grabbed the sovereign's absolute powers and passed them to the people. They decided to keep a king as figurehead and chief civil servant but answerable to elected legislators. It was in the Hall of Lesser Pleasures in those heady June days of 1789 that modern France was born.

On Sunday, July 12, the disgruntled king decided to use his military force against the National Assembly to reassert his absolute power.

The next morning, church bells summoned the citizens of Paris to oppose him. They formed themselves into an army of forty-eight thousand with eight hundred from each of the sixty districts. This National Guard, composed mainly of middle-class merchants, would, as soon as they'd been made, put on uniforms designed by their leader, Lafayette: blue coats faced in white and trimmed in red, with white leggings. In the meantime, they all wore red, white, and blue ribbon cockades, the new badge of liberty. This citizens' militia needed weapons and proceeded to grab swords, muskets, and pistols from gunsmiths' shops and anywhere they could find them, adding kitchen knives and clubs. They rushed to the Garde-meuble in Place Louis XV and commandeered all the ancient royal halberds, pikes, and swords they found there. They also seized a cannon inlaid with silver that had been presented to the Sun King at one of his Versailles spectaculars by an ambassador from the King of Siam. The Diamond wasn't a victim of this particular invasion of the Garde-meuble; it was still resting in pastoral seclusion at Versailles—but not for long.

The newly empowered militia forced the king's troops to retreat from the center of Paris, leaving it vulnerable to impulsive violence. With the roar and might of herds of elephants, the hungry mob destroyed forty of the fifty-four customs posts whose high taxes spelled vexation and starvation, then broke into the Saint Lazare monastery and made off with all its grain and flour.

Very early on Tuesday, July 14, with low clouds massing over Paris, a crowd eighty thousand strong, which included National Guardsmen; defecting royal troops, some of them veterans of the American war; starving unemployed workers; and hungry peasants from the provinces, snaked through the streets to the Invalides garrison and helped themselves to thirty thousand muskets. They needed powder, which was stored elsewhere. On to the Bastille!

This old fortress, a potent symbol of a French king's absolute power, since he could imprison anyone he wished inside its five-foot-thick walls and eight round towers, held only seven prisoners that day: four criminals, two madmen, one of whom thought he was God, and an accomplice of the man who'd tried to kill Louis XV with his penknife. The citizens set up two cannons in the courtyard, one of them the Sun King's pretty, silver-inlaid trophy. It was charged and aimed to tear down everything he stood for. In the confusion of screaming crowds and flashing weapons, no one could see, as blue smoke coiled upward from carts of burning straw. Finally, through the dense smoke, a white flag waved from one of the towers as the Bastille's governor, Marquis de Launay, and his Swiss Guards surrendered. The guns stopped. The triumphant mob rushed inside, freed the seven prisoners, grabbed all the gunpowder, and marched the governor to the Hôtel de Ville, the Parisian city hall, through a spitting, raging mob who wanted to kill him on the spot. When the marquis hit one of his captors, a pastry cook, in the groin, the noble was stabbed instantly with a dozen butchers' knives and bayonets, kicked into the gutter, and finished off with gunshots. The pastry cook sliced off his head with a kitchen knife as if it were just one more piece of dough. The bloody, dripping head was stuck on a pike and paraded through cheering crowds around the Palais Royale.

That evening, Louis XVI, ensconced among his locks and clocks in his private study at Versailles, having failed miserably to make a constitutional monarchy work, scribbled one word, *rien*, in his hunting journal. That day, as he'd galloped through the forests, he'd failed to show a single beast that he was master, that he had Rousseau's nature by the tail. *Rien*. Nothing to be proud of. Nothing to hope for. When the Duke de La Rochefoucauld-Liancourt came to tell him that the Bastille had fallen, Louis asked, with chins trembling, "Is it a revolt?" "No, sire," the duke replied, "it is a revolution."

When the leader of Louis's troops, Baron de Besenval, arrived at Versailles the next morning to tell him that even his Swiss mercenaries were refusing to fight against the people, King Louis XVI knew that from that moment on, he was no longer the hunter, but the hunted, defenseless as a rabbit.

Two days later came the second hat scene. The king went to Paris, where he was met by Lafayette and taken through streets lined with National Guardsmen in proud cockades to the Hôtel de Ville. There, standing under an arch that read "Louis XVI, Father of the French,

King of a Free People," the monarch accepted the red, white, and blue cockade handed him by the mayor of Paris and pinned it to his hat in the exact spot where, two months before, he'd worn the Regent diamond. It was a momentous exchange: a jewel worth 9 million *livres* replaced by a few inches of ribbon worth less than a sou. Not until Louis had the liberty badge well anchored to his hat did the crowd shout, without much conviction, "Long live the king!"

By August 11, the Assembly, still meeting in the Hall of Lesser Pleasures, had passed decrees ending all feudal rights and church tithes and on August 19 passed a Declaration of the Rights of Man, inspired by the American Declaration of Independence, which began "Men are born and remain free and equal," and asserted that sovereign power belongs to the nation, never to one person. However, not even new, just laws could appease the French people's wrath. Anarchy stalked the poverty-stricken land. Citizens stopped paying taxes; soldiers deserted; castles were burned to the ground and their noble owners occasionally massacred. The wives of French artists such as Jacques Louis David and Jean Honoré Fragonard marched on September 7 from Paris to the Assembly at Versailles, wearing white gowns with the tricolor cockade their only ornament, and formally donated a chest containing all their jewels for freedom's cause. Pamphlets accusing the queen of "incest, adultery, shameful lust" blowing in the wind around the Palais Royale outnumbered leaves. "Paris will be burned down, blood will flood its streets, and all those atrocities are the work of this cruel and vindictive woman," read one.

At Versailles that October, falling leaves swirled in chill winds and piled up in dry fountain basins. The pleasure gardens stopped giving pleasure and night closed in early. On October 2, a delegation from the Assembly asked Louis to sign the Declaration of the Rights of Man and the first nineteen articles of France's constitution. The king dithered and delayed. Three days later, in Paris, a crowd of angry, starving women, seven thousand strong, assembled at the Hôtel de Ville and headed for Versailles, a six-hour trudge through pelting rain and worsening mud. Behind them marched fifteen thousand National Guards, followed by the venomous Paris mob, every one of them armed.

Middle and lower classes, united, were determined to impose their will on a useless, spendthrift king and queen. Arriving at midnight, they stormed into the palace, found a startled Louis, Antoinette, and children and forced them to return to Paris, where they were put under armed guard in the Tuileries.

Versailles' great windows, which, for 107 years, had looked down on only splendor, were blinded with boards; huge locks were clamped on all gates to discourage looters, and Louis XIV's astonishing creation shifted silently, unremarked, from home to tourist attraction. It would never be lived in again. The Sun King would continue to ride his triumphant chariot across the ceiling of the Hall of Mirrors, but everything he'd represented and reflected in his diamonds, particularly in one proud royal blue one, dissolved to dust and memory.

Along with king and queen, the crown jewels, including the Diamond caught between dragon and ram, also left Versailles never to return, and journeyed to Paris. They were placed in company with such anachronisms as medieval armor in cabinets in the Garde-meuble, whose director-general was an aristocrat named Thierry de la Ville d'Avray, responsible to the Ministry of the Interior.

The Assembly abandoned Versailles, too, and on October 19 moved into the old riding academy of the Tuileries, where they passed a law giving the king only a usufruct over crown property so that he could have the crown jewels on loan and sufferance for his lifetime but outright ownership belonged to the state and its people. Members of the Assembly were still busy drafting the constitution, but real power in France, having already passed from monarch to legislative body, was now in the hands of the political clubs that had sprung up and whose views, debated and voted on with great passion, were much more radical. The Jacobin Club, named for the monastery where it first met, by July 1790 had 152 branches in the provinces, twelve hundred members in Paris, and the lawyer Maximilien Robespierre, a small man with weak eyes and voice, as its president. The Cordelier Club, also named for its monastery meeting place, resounded to the fiery rants of the former physician Jean Paul Marat, copper skinned and hook nosed, and the burly young lawyer Georges-Jacques Danton, who had a foghorn voice, both of them bent on pushing France beyond liberty for all to a plebeian dictatorship.

It was at this point in our story that Paul Miette returned from banishment in Rouen to Paris and his Champs-Élysées hangout and debated how best to profit from the general chaos. When the first anniversary of the fall of the Bastille came that year on July 14, he and his wife mingled with gleeful, grinning crowds watching the erection, on the spot where the hated fortress had stood for so long, of a kind of maypole with tricolored ribbons cascading from its top, and a banner proclaiming, "*Ici on danse*" (here is dancing).

All over France villagers danced and sang around liberty poles, or in some cases growing trees, festooned with freedom's high-flying red, white, and blue ribbons. The trees, like cockade flowers and diamond stones, became potent symbols blooming, or looming, in people's minds and dreams. The Revolution's leaders and orchestrators knew what the Diamond had held on to in its true-blue heart ever since it had first found itself in the hands of men: things, mere things, can symbolize an awesome power.

The waterwheel turned in faster revolution. The Assembly abolished all hereditary titles: prince, duke, count, marquis, all swept away, along with coats of arms and liveries, and even, by a decree passed March 17, 1791, the Paris guild of goldsmiths, purveyors of useless objects to that upper class on the way to extinction: the idle rich. The most radical Jacobins and Cordeliers began to wonder if perhaps the monarch shouldn't be jettisoned, too. Wouldn't a republic be better than a constitutional monarchy?

The king, meanwhile, in the spring of 1791, was planning an escape from the Tuileries palace—to Montmédy, a small, fortified town about 160 miles northeast of Paris. There he could marshal his forces to retake France and turn the clock back. As the June day for their getaway drew nearer, Marie Antoinette emptied her red-and-gold *bijouterie*, packed all her personal diamonds in wool, and made arrangements to have them carried in a satchel to safe haven in Brussels. She did so with practical thoughts of how they could serve as collateral to raise money abroad for the monarchist cause and dreams of wearing them in triumph on the day she and Louis were securely back on the throne and their subjects returned to their senses.

From Palma of Paris on the rue de Richelieu, she ordered a magnificent traveling case, a *nécessaire* (now in the Louvre). No queen could leave home without one. Hers was trunk-size, fitted with hundreds of necessities, everything from manicure set and perfume bottles to silver tea service and Sèvres china cups. It was sent ahead to Montmédy to await her, being far too large to go in the carriage, given her husband's dimensions. The *nécessaire* not only set the tone for this well-accoutered, cumbersome flight, which Louis, as inept as ever, let his wife organize in ridiculous royal manner, but also illustrates clearly the total inability of France's current king and queen to adapt to changing times.

At midnight on June 20 the royals made their escape from the Tuileries, disguised as a Swedish baroness (the queen) traveling with her majordomo (the king), her children, and her sister (actually Louis's sister Elizabeth), inside a berline, a very big, heavy, slow-moving carriage requiring six horses to draw it, fitted with white taffeta cushions, double window curtains of taffeta and leather, two iron cooking stoves, and two varnished leather chamber pots. In a second coach, which turned flight into a stately progress, were the *nécessaire* servants without which no royal could travel: governess, hairdresser, two maids, three equerries. Of course, if there had to be a second coach, it should have contained some well-armed guards.

Nobody but the king and queen were surprised when they were recognized and captured at Varennes and escorted back to Paris by six thousand National Guardsmen and an angry mob of peasants who shouted obscenities and spat full in Louis's face when he stuck it out a taffeta-frilled window. As the lumbering coach creaked its way back, what was left in the dust cloud behind it was most of the mystique of royalty that had held sway in France since the days of Charlemagne. Two Assembly representatives actually dared, at one stop, to climb inside the royal coach and sit down, without even asking permission, *between and pressing up against* king and queen. And when the two men wished to relieve themselves, the carriage stopped. Along the route, people kept their hats firmly on their heads and shouted "Fat pig!" and "Austrian witch!" at them all the way back to the Tuileries palace, where the royal family were imprisoned under much stricter guard.

In the nearby former riding academy, the Assembly debated what to do about the crown jewels now that their royal users seemed well on the way to obsolescence. Charles de Lameth proposed on June 22 that the first thing to do was make a new inventory. Three members, Bion, Christin, and Delattre, made this list on June 25 in the Garde-meuble, with the help of two jewelers. When they came to the colored Order of the Golden Fleece, after being so long kept in the dark, the Diamond was grasped in hands rough, gentle, big, small, examined under magnification, moved about in the light, and put away again. For a while, quills scratched on paper, then boxes slammed shut, keys turned, voices and footsteps died away. The Assembly was informed that the crown jewels in total were worth 30 million *livres*, and the Order of the Golden Fleece alone, containing the Côte de Bretagne and the Blue Diamond of the French Crown, was worth 3,394,000.

When the Garde-meuble's director-general, Thierry de Ville d'Avray, heard these figures and read the list, he began to worry about security in those turbulent times, so he carried the crown jewels, with the help of his head guard, to safer storage in his own Paris apartment. He placed their containers in an armoire situated in an alcove. No one would find them there. If the jewels had stayed in Thierry's apartment, the Diamond's whole future would have been different—and much more sedate, for it probably never would have left France. It might have had some fun on Napoleon Bonaparte's small but proudly jutting chest and ended by gathering dust motes and tourist stares in the Apollo gallery of the Louvre.

But the jewels stayed in Thierry's apartment for only two months before he put them back in the Garde-meuble. Perhaps the total responsibility for their safety weighed too heavily on his shoulders. More likely, he was ordered to return them by the minister of the interior, the Assembly having decided that the good bourgeoisie and *sans-culottes* of France should be allowed to see the treasures they collectively owned. Every Monday, beginning in August 1791, the crown jewels were put on display in the Garde-meuble so that citizens not busy rioting and rebelling could file past them without showing any feelings of wonder and awe, should they have them, for useless and costly objects that revolutionary leaders told them they must despise.

Above the Blue Diamond, on those Mondays, appeared a diverting passing show, unwinding like an endless ribbon, of faces dirty and clean, ugly and comely; caps and bonnets in every possible shape; a great many strange red, white, and blue circles . . . on and on.

The faces peering down each Monday were French, not foreign, for by the fall of 1791, tourists no longer came to a city where a menacing, threatening mob surged always in its center, where the National Guard had virtually stopped trying to maintain order, and where only ruffians like Paul Miette felt comfortable.

The diamonds on display in the Garde-meuble were the only ones to be seen anywhere in France. To wear one in the streets was to brand oneself an aristocrat and could have fatal consequences. Diamonds went into hiding in drawers and boxes or were taken out of the country sewn into linings and corsets by the nobles fleeing for their lives to safer regions such as England. As soon as they arrived, gems passed down through generations were sold to cover living expenses.

Five months after the Diamond had gone on public display, in January 1792, the same grimy face with flat, misshapen nose came into view every single Monday above it and stayed for a long time with two burning eyes looking directly down at it or shiftily about the room, eyeing locks, guards, exits. Paul Miette had begun his weekly inspection. He dispatched a letter to his pal, Cadet Guillot, in Rouen, telling him that if he cared to come to Paris, there was something really big-time brewing.

Five months later, however, beginning in June, only unfamiliar faces peered down at the Diamond on Mondays; the one with the familiar squashed nose wasn't among them. Miette had robbed again, been caught, tried, and thrown into the prison called La Force on a four-month sentence. There, amid slop buckets and flea-infested straw mattresses, Miette talked about his ambitious plan and bright idea.

Soon he'd recruited some fellow inmates eager to join him: prisoners Tricot, Delors, and Deslandes. As soon as they got out, by God, they'd do it! As easy a heist to pull off, grinned Deslandes, as stealing horse-shit from the street!

In Rouen that summer of 1792, Cadet Guillot, alias Lordonner, had impulsively one evening in the rue Eau-de-Robec tavern dropped a few hints concerning Miette's scheme. He then drank glass after glass of wine, as everyone around the table fought over who should treat him next, and by the time he staggered out the door, he'd revealed all the details of Miette's letter and had four true friends, good men all, who, when the time was ripe, would go with him to Paris to share the wealth.

Beyond the plots hatching inside La Force prison and the Rouen tavern, the people of France that summer moved on from the first stage of the Revolution, where liberty had been the goal, to the second stage, where equality and the need for the staple of life, namely bread, took over. Coins had virtually disappeared from the country's currency, and paper money had depreciated by 40 percent. As all aristocrats except a liberal-minded few, such as the Duke of Orléans, who espoused the revolutionary cause, fled France, the artisans—tailors, hatters, carriage makers—who had supplied the nobility with luxuries were thrown out of work. The streets of Paris filled up with gaunt men whose families were starving to death, each proclaiming his militancy and revolutionary zeal by means of three symbols: straight trousers, a long pike, and a red wool hat, the *bonnet rouge*, whose conical shape with top bent forward derived from the headgear freed slaves wore on ancient Roman coins. The citizens belted out such popular songs as "Ça ira" in the streets: "The aristocrats, we'll hang them, despotism will die, equality will triumph." A battalion sent by the Marseilles Jacobins to Paris that summer brought with them a great, rousing hymn to freedom called "*La Marseillaise*," which two hundred years later still stirs the heart of every Frenchman.

On June 20, a noisy mob armed with pikes, cudgels, axes, and guns twisted its way from the working-class faubourgs through narrow streets and alleys, snaking forward slowly, red hats as closely packed as scales, toward its prey in the center of Paris, where Louis XV still sat in bronze oblivion astride his horse in the square bearing his name, where the Order of the Golden Fleece lay in shadows in the Garde-meuble, where the royal family cowered inside the Tuileries palace, and where the king, seeing that very morning a poster on his door that said, "No more king. A king is an obstacle to the happiness of the people," was afraid to tear it down.

It was three o'clock, the full-furnace hour of a very hot, sultry afternoon, when the mob reached the Tuileries. They smashed doors down with axes, dragged a cannon up the stairs, rushed into the king's apartments, and enacted the third hat scene by clapping a red bonnet on his head, another on Marie Antoinette's sky-high hairdo, and a third on their four-year-old son's soft curls.

When the crowd finally tired of thrashing its tail, it inched its way back to the faubourgs, but left behind the stench of terror filling every corridor of the Tuileries from that day forward, shortening the breath of king and queen.

When the anniversary of the Bastille's fall rolled around on July 14 that year, Louis XVI, or Louis Capet, as the mob called him, appeared at the ceremonies not in the diamond-encrusted garments favored by his predecessors but in a bulletproof vest of thick, wadded cotton, to satisfy his wife's pleading. "They will not murder me," Louis assured her as he put on his bloodred wool hat. "That is no longer their plan. They will kill me some other way."

When king and queen awoke early on Friday, August 10, the sun beyond the Tuileries window rose deep red, for Paris was in the middle of a heat wave. "So rapid a state of putrefaction I never saw," the American commercial agent Gouverneur Morris wrote in his journal about perch he'd bought a few hours before for his dinner. The mob was on the move again that morning, angrier than ever, and this time it wanted blood. By the time *sans-culottes* and National Guardsmen from the poorer districts of Paris reached the palace at 6 A.M., Louis and Antoinette had been imprisoned, safe for the moment, in a stuffy little room in the Assembly hall nearby, leaving their Swiss Guards to defend the palace. The mob rushed inside and killed everyone they found, even kitchen maids, but slaked their thirst mainly on the Swiss mercenaries, who ran for their lives in all directions, tearing off their conspicuous red jackets, trying to escape. None did. All six hundred were stabbed, clubbed, or stoned to death. Some jumped from upper windows, only to land on pikes waiting below. Bodies were stripped of clothes; ears, hands, genitals were hacked off, tossed into the wide-open jaws of dogs—or humans; corpses were piled onto the cobblestones and burned. When part of the palace went up in flames, firemen who arrived to douse them were greeted with musket shots, so the fire raged unchecked for six days and the Seine ran past in bright red flux.

The Tuileries battle was all over in three hours. Later Robespierre would comment, relishing the people's victory, that "a river of blood will now divide France from its enemies." It was an accurate prophecy; from that point on blood became the fuel propelling the French Revolution.

The next day, the mob surged into Place Louis XV to tear down the statue of the handsome king astride his proud steed. Several blacksmiths filed through the iron bars holding the horse's hooves to the pedestal, after which, according to an eyewitness, the *sans-culottes* stormed the king and pulled him down with ropes. Inside the adjacent Garde-meuble, the Diamond was jarred as bronze Louis, with a mighty thud hit the ground. The statue was hacked to pieces, blow after blow, before the mob attacked its attendant maidens, Strength, Peace, Prudence, and Justice, then smashed the pedestal itself and even the white marble balustrade around it all.

After their August 10 victory, the *sans-culottes* knew they'd become an irresistible force that could impose its will with no resistance from National Guard or anyone else. Around the Palais Royale, where drawings of Louis Capet with the body of a hog and Marie Antoinette with that of a tigress were displayed on every kiosk, the mob formed and reformed in menacing groups, with victims' knee breeches attached to the waving ends of their pikes when they had no bloody body part to put there.

The Garde-meuble was no longer open to the public on Mondays as it wasn't safe to let anyone in. Thierry and his assistants put seals on all the cabinets and boxes containing the jewels, while the Diamond lay quiescent in dust and silence.

The royal family was imprisoned on Monday, August 13, in Temple Tower, a medieval fortress not far from the demolished Bastille, a square, turreted building of four floors with a central stair coiling its narrow way to the top, all of it dark and dank with outer walls ten feet thick. Louis, Antoinette, their son and daughter, and a few attendants heard massive doors clang shut and lock behind them as their world constricted to ever smaller compass.

Joseph Cambon, the minister of the interior, mounted the rostrum of the Assembly on August 16 and proposed that the crown jewels be sold and the money raised used as collateral to help arrest the alarming downward slide of France's currency. No immediate action was taken.

In the following week, a strange apparatus was set up in the Tuileries gardens; it would later take up a more permanent stance in Place Louis XV. This machine was called a guillotine, named for its inventor, Dr. Joseph-Ignace Guillotin, a deputy in the Assembly who'd presented it to his fellow members as a quick, efficient, and humane form of capital punishment. One clean slice, swift and well aimed, all over in a second. That was the trouble. In eighteenth-century Europe, lower-class crowds flocked to executions, which formed their free entertainment. They relished the screaming of a person being slowly drawn and quartered, the prolonged twitching of a body on a gibbet, left to swing and rot for weeks in the wind. The guillotine, on the other hand, turned death into a mechanical, repetitive, impersonal act, just a big bore. One blink and you missed it. In the months and years to come, it was paradoxically this neat instrument of death that helped to swell the river of blood beyond it. The people of France may well have indulged in horrible acts of gore and violence partly because they could get no satisfaction from Dr. Guillotin's invention.

The mob proved its need for blood in the following month. On September 2 began the slaughter of at least fourteen hundred people, the so-called enemies of France then confined in Paris prisons: aristocrats, priests, court lackeys, courtesans. The Assembly washed its hands of the situation by announcing that it "no longer has any means of causing the law to be obeyed." Self-appointed tribunals were set up at each prison, and all inmates were brought before them one at a time to be released, brutally murdered, or, in a very few instances, returned to their cells.

At La Force, the tribunal was set up a little after midnight on September 2. One of those "tried" was the queen's loyal friend, Princess de Lamballe, who'd fled from Paris in June 1791, at the same time as the royal family, and had successfully made her way to London, but had returned to serve as mistress of Her Majesty's household. Condemned to death, she was pushed into an alley, hacked to pieces in minutes, her head stuck on a pike to be paraded through the streets to Temple Tower. When Antoinette was called to a window to see the bloody, blond curls of her friend bobbing just beyond, she fell in a dead faint.

Paul Miette and his friends Tricot, Delors, and Deslandes, on the other hand, were instantly released from La Force, along with all the real criminals, highwaymen, cutpurses, burglars, and others then imprisoned. Within a day or two, Miette's usual group, which included Cottet "the little hunter" and Gros-Cul de Bonne Vierge (whose nickname translates as "Good Virgin's Big Bottom" and suggests homosexual preferences) met up with lanky Cadet Guillot and his four chums, just arrived from Rouen. It was time to put their plan into action. In a lowlife tavern they clinked glasses together so hard that wine gushed over the sides. To riches beyond imagining! Other thieves wanted a piece of the action and were allowed in. The more the merrier! The gang got bigger and bigger, friends of friends of friends . . .

The prison massacres continued for four days while streets literally ran with blood. By September 5, only a few murderers were left at La Force, their bare arms still streaked with scarlet but their bodies drooping with fatigue. By the morning of September 6, no one in the Paris mob lusted for anything except sleep, so they all went home and the killing stopped.

On September 2, the conscientious, dedicated director-general of the Garde-meuble, Thierry de la Ville d'Avray, who thus far had kept the crown jewels safe, was killed in the general carnage. He was succeeded by a man called Restout who seemed equally vigilant but whom government authorities ignored. On September 2, 3, 7, 8, and 9, Restout sent frantic letters asking for tighter security to the commander-general of the National Guard, Santerre, and the adjutant-general, Doucet. Restout told them that one night he'd found only one guard in the whole place, and that on another, the main door had been unguarded from 1 A.M. to 6 A.M. when the men supposed to be on duty returned dead drunk. Often the guards were mere boys, the eldest only seventeen. There were two entrances to the Garde-meuble, the main one facing the square and another door opening onto rue Saint-Florentin. Restout wrote to Jean-Marie Roland, successor to Cambon as minister of the interior, requesting twenty National Guards at each door. On September 8, Doucet came himself to inspect the Garde-meuble's security and pronounced it perfectly adequate. When, the next day, Restout found no one at all guarding the main door, he appealed to Laroche, head of the Tuileries division of the National Guard. Citizen Laroche replied rudely that he didn't give a damn; Restout could guard the fucking door himself. Two days later, Laroche complained to his section superior, "Restout has already the tone of a despot; in that place he sucks the milk of the aristocrat who has dominated him for so long."

There was no moon on the night of September 11, 1792, so the environs of Place Louis XV were very dark and deserted. There had been no public lighting system in Paris at all until twenty years before, when eight thousand lanterns were strung about the city, but they gave a dim light and were often blown out by wind, so people seldom ventured out after dark for fear of robbers. A little before 11 P.M., an ill-dressed band of men nonchalantly crossed the blackness of the square and gathered in a tight knot in front of the Garde-meuble building. One of them threw a well-weighted rope over the lantern shining dimly at one corner of its second story. Six of the most agile and eager shinnied up the rope to the second floor: Paul Miette, Francisque, Gallois (alias Matelot), Badarel (who, when he wasn't in the middle of a burglary, made counterfeit money), and two from Rouen: Cadet Guillot and Gobert. Quickly the six climbed over the balustrade onto the external colonnaded gallery. One of them cut a small square in one window, using a window glazer's diamond as a tool. An ironic touch, that diamond turned accomplice against its own kind. Miette put his hand through the square and released the window catch inside. He opened the window and they all slithered in, Guillot without even touching the glass. There were iron bars made for that window and all the others, but that night they weren't in place. Had they been, the robbers never could have gotten in.

Once they were inside, their first priority was to make sure the guards posted one floor below didn't suddenly come up the internal staircase, so they strung official-looking tapes secured with seals across its first-floor door, thinking that would probably be enough to discourage any guard. As an extra precaution, the burglars wedged the door shut on its other side with iron hooks. If anyone did decide to come have a look, by the time he'd removed the hooks, the robbers chortled and whispered, they'd be well away!

That done, they surveyed the second floor's main room while Badarel and Gallois held candles. Royal suits of armor formed a ghostly, helpless army on one side of the room, with a helmet gleaming through the darkness here, a disembodied steel arm there. Farther away stretched a forest of four-poster state beds. From tapestries on all the walls, brave kings and famous heroes seemed mutely to protest their proximity to six dirty pigs snuffling and panting as if about to root for truffles.

All the crown jewels were in that room, but many of them weren't visible, for they were stored inside a marquetry commode that stood against one wall. But in the very middle of the room, in the most vulnerable and exposed place of all, resting on a porphyry table, was a glass-topped walnut casket decorated with thin sheets of copper and provided with a handle. It contained the king's decorations, including the Blue Diamond in the Order of the Golden Fleece. Paul Miette, who had observed the casket closely on all those public days when he'd visited, led Guillot straight to it.

Once again, that familiar face with blubbery nose, its mouth stretched in a macabre gap-toothed grin as a candle lit it from below, loomed above the Diamond. The man's right arm holding an ax came straight toward it; glass smashed with a horrendous crash; splinters flew in all directions. Then another face was inches away, this one long and thin and dead white, and long, thin, clammy fingers closed tight around Diamond, dragon, ram, everything, and plopped it into a big, smelly bag. From the people of France who by legislative act then owned it, the order worth 3.4 million *livres* had just been well and truly fleeced.

Badarel and Gallois continued to merely hold candles while the other four grabbed as many jewels as they could carry. Miette took a diamond Order of the Holy Spirit, a sword, and much more. Guillot, in addition to the Order of the Golden Fleece, stole Louis XVI's diamond sword, two large watches with diamonds chains, the Sun King's splendid shoe buckles and coat buttons, and an enormous pearl inside a gold box inscribed "Queen of Pearls" on its lid. Cadet Guillot threw all this loot into the big bag already holding the Blue Diamond, which was hit more than once, being uncossetted by padding or paper.

When the thieves had as much as they could carry—Guillot's lean length was bent almost double—they climbed out through the window and one by one swished down the rope. When Cadet Guillot grabbed the rope to descend, it gave a mighty swing, causing the blue gem to clank loudly against one of the Sun King's shoe buckles. The men waiting and keeping guard below encircled the six heroes as soon as they landed, dizzy with excitement, drunk with power, and holding much of the jeweled history of France in their scrawny arms.

By 2 A.M., Place Louis XV was dark and deserted once more, and the National Guard fellows supposedly keeping watch over the royal treasures were either asleep on the job, carousing elsewhere, or perhaps just totally indifferent to the fate of the despised monarchist baubles.

The Rouen contingent of robbers returned at first light to Normandy—all but Cadet Guillot. He realized that the items he'd taken, especially the Order of the Golden Fleece, were too recogniz-ably royal to be fenced in France and that he'd have to leave the coun-try. He headed at once for Nantes and then went by fishing boat to Le Havre. He planned to lie low there for a while and then escape across the channel to England when he got the chance. Guillot may have had an ill-nourished body, but he had an agile brain and knew exactly how to keep himself beyond reach of the law.

Back in Paris, the Great Jewel Heist was rapidly turning into farce.

On the evening after their first foray to the Garde-meuble, Miette and the other robbers toasted each other in both their favorite taverns, Chez Retour in rue des Fossés-Saint-Germain-l'Auxerrois and that of the widow Noel in the rue Champ-Fleuri. But they were far from fin-ished with the Garde-meuble caper.

On the night of September 13, an even bigger band of thieves, in-cluding all the originals, turned up in Place Louis XV, shinnied up the rope that still hung conveniently over the lantern, snuck in through the diamond-cut open window, and helped themselves to much of what was stored in eight boxes inside the marquetry commode against one wall, including the famed Regent and Sancy diamonds.

The burglars spent the night of September 14 drinking in their taverns but returned to the scene of their crime yet again on Septem-ber 15. They were so cocky by this time that they all went inside, the largest group yet, women as well as men, leaving no one to keep a lookout in the square below.

They took food and wine and, after helping themselves to more gems, had a party that lasted until ancient kings in colored wools on all the walls approached and receded and the parquet floor was littered with smoked-sausage casings, empty wine bottles, bread crusts, candle ends, and several snoring bodies. Getting out the window and back down the rope that night wasn't easy.

Having made it to the ground, two of the thieves proceeded to fight over their loot with bellows and belches that could be heard blocks away. Several others wove their way to a pile of pebbles at the edge of the Seine and began to divvy up their plunder. Two men called Le Blond and Le Leu who happened to be passing got curious, approached and bought, for 6 *livres*, the contents of one robber's box: three diamonds, two of them yellow, seven large pearls, and several more retrieved from the ground where they'd fallen. Le Blond and Le Leu then took the box of gems to be appraised to a goldsmith called Vittard on the Saint-Michel bridge, who persuaded them to report to the nearest police station, whose chief, Letellier, went back with them to the riverbank and found two red rubies in the mud. Then Le Blond, Le Leu, and Letellier went straight round to the Garde-meuble and told the head guard, Courlesvaux, that they thought the place might have been recently burgled. Courlesvaux checked the intact seals on the door to the second floor and told them there wasn't a thing to worry about; everything was just as it should be.

On the night of September 16, a gang of fifty eager burglars spurned the handy rope and opened a second-floor window. Wearing purloined National Guard uniforms, several volunteered to stand guard at the door opening into the square. The rest, also dressed as National Guards, marched to the Saint-Florentin door singing "*La Carmagnole*," a rousing patriot song, and were instantly admitted. The problem was there wasn't much left to steal. They had to settle for some objets d'art from the marquetry cabinet and Cardinal Richelieu's jeweled cross. What was too big to be slipped into a pocket was heaved out the window to the phony National Guards waiting below. Once all the robbers were back on the ground, their yelling and fighting over the spoils got so loud that some *real* National Guards, patroling the nearby Rue Saint-Honoré, heard the noise, marched forthwith up Rue Saint-Florentin, looked sharp but saw nothing amiss in Place Louis XV—which they reached one second after the last robber had safely scurried into the dark underbrush in the Champs-Élysées.

Ringleader Paul Miette had been hanging around the Champs-Élysées for the past six days busily peddling various treasures of the French crown to his usual fences. Earlier that same day, September 16, he and wife Marie-Françoise had purchased, for 15,000 *livres*, a fine home at 20 Rue de Belleville called—most appropriately, given the times—the Red House.

Cadet Guillot was keeping a low profile in Le Havre, able only to dream of what he'd do with his windfall once he got it. Sometimes, in his shabby little rented room, after carefully locking the door, he would hold in his bony hands the strange object with the beast carved from what had to be a ruby, worth God knows how much, and below it a whopping great sapphire—or maybe even a diamond?—staring straight at him like a giant blue eye. He'd be rich soon, really rich.

On the morning of September 17, the Garde-meuble theft was finally discovered by the bona fide National Guard, who were shocked to find the floor of the gallery littered with "small diamonds, pearls, and burglars' tools" and the remains of the robbers' partying two nights before.

Next morning, the current legislative body, the National Convention, which had convened on September 11 (the same day as the thieves) assembled at ten o'clock. Jean-Marie Roland announced that the Garde-meuble had been forcibly entered and plundered, and at once a four-member committee was formed to investigate. The head of the National Guard, Santerre, rose to say that he would immediately double the number of guards and that the theft was just "the last gasp of an aristocracy that would never rise again." Roland replied that unfortunately there wasn't much left to guard. Of the 30 million *livres'* worth of crown jewels owned by the people of France, he continued solemnly, only 5,500 *livres'* worth remained.

The Paris politicians got very busy assigning blame for the burglary. Roland's wife, a well-read lady who presided over her own leftist salon full of members of the new Girondins group, declared that it was the work of Georges Jacques Danton and his secretary, the wild poet Fabre d'Eglantine, who at once accused the Girondins of masterminding the whole thing. In his newspaper *L'Ami du Peuple* Marat wrote on September 20 that "the aristocrats hired a troop of criminals to rob the Garde-meuble." The public prosecutor of the Revolutionary Tribunal, Lullier, blamed the theft on Marie Antoinette: "You will see, in the robbery of the Garde-meuble," he thundered, "the hand of a proud woman, cruel and lascivious, fanning the flames of fanaticism and discord."

The plain fact was, of course, that the robbery had nothing at all to do with politics or revolutionary ideals but from first to last was the work of a band of criminals who took full advantage of France's state of anarchy. This was further ignominy for the Diamond, which hadn't been swept up in the winds of freedom blowing through the nation but merely stuck in the middle of a sordid little plot hatched by underworld thugs. In its long existence, the Diamond had, in sequence, served the causes of magic, religion, commerce, royal self-promotion, and royal self-worth. In 1792, while politicians tried their best to hijack it for the causes of community and the collective will, it served nothing more elevated than the cause of crime.

In the days and months that followed, some of the stolen gems were recovered and some of the thieves arrested. On September 18, a woman called Citizen Corbin, thief Badarel's apparently disenchanted mistress, went straight to Paris mayor Pétion, hopeful of a reward, and told him where Badarel had buried his share of the jewels. They were found by Pétion and his assistant Sergent-Merceau just where she'd indicated: under a tree in Widow's Alley (now Avenue Montaigne). Others were soon discovered in the rafters of another thief's house. The Regent would eventually surface, in October 1793, hidden in the wooden beam of a Paris attic; the Sancy would turn up three months after that.

Two of the thieves arrested shortly after the crime squealed on their ringleader, Paul Miette. The Revolutionary Tribunal ordered his arrest on September 21, but it took them until October 3 to track him down, nicely ensconced in his Red House at 20 Rue de Belleville. He gave himself up as soon as he heard the officers smashing a window. At his trial, which began on November 20, he was accused of stealing 2 million *livres'* worth of gems, not to mention 98,000 cash from a banker in Rue Saint-Honoré, and was condemned to death by the jury. At once he appealed, was retried by the Tribunal in Beauvais, which, like the Paris one, was only concerned with whether or not Miette was a political agent trying to reinstate a monarchy complete with all its symbols of office. He defended himself against such charges, which wasn't hard, and was acquitted on May 15, 1793. Of the fifty criminals involved in the Garde-meuble theft, seventeen were apprehended and tried, but only five of these were guillotined and the rest acquitted. The thirty-three others were never caught.

Louis XVI wasn't as lucky as Miette. On the morning of January 21, 1793, France's former king awoke early in the dark confines of Temple Tower, asked his valet to give his wedding ring and a little packet of family locks of hair to his wife, and went by carriage through silent crowds to Place Louis XV, which had a new name: Place de la Revolution. There twenty thousand Parisians awaited him. The guillotine's blade sliced down at 10:20 A.M.; some of those near the scaffold dipped their fingers in the spurting blood, and one man pronounced it well salted. By spring, the citizens of France were drinking coffee from Sèvres cups depicting in delicate hues the public executioner, Charles Henri Sanson, holding Louis XVI's head aloft. If freedom had forged ahead in France, commerce was never far behind.

Inside her small cell in the Conciergerie where she'd been moved from Temple Tower, Marie Antoinette waited, sick and depressed, for the end. She had her own river of blood to contend with, for she suffered from frequent menstrual hemorrhages, including a bad one that left her very weak and white on the morning of October 16, 1793. She dressed that day in a simple white cotton dress and bonnet, with brave plum-colored high-heeled shoes, and climbed into the waiting wooden tumbril. There would be no closed carriage for the Austrian "she-wolf" and "arch tigress." At Place de la Revolution, her head rolled at 11:45 A.M.

The Revolution's course grew ever wilder and bloodier. Dissent became a crime warranting death; repression replaced the ideals of liberty, equality, and fraternity. Where once kings had sat on France's throne bedecked in jewels materialized from fairy tales, grim Terror reigned: iron-clad, relentless, vengeful, more absolute than any king. No more waterwheel revolving slowly, only that flashing blade, dropping out of the blue to cut and cleave, like some fiendish, raving mad gem cutter practicing his craft on human flesh. The blade sliced through Danton's thick neck, and through Madame Roland's and Robespierre's thin ones, while Charlotte Corday plunged a knife into an unsuspecting Marat while he was relieving his skin disease with a soothing bath, and eventually Napoleon Bonaparte marched with ego as big as his army across Europe, and England acted to contain him.

Where was the Diamond in all this *sturm und drang*? By the time the very last royals it would ever consort with had lost their heads, the stone and Guillot had left Le Havre for England.

He landed with his small but heavy haversack at Dover and took the public coach to London. There he found a room near the London docks, in a rabbit warren of narrow alleys and twisting streets, full of scurrying rats, the smell of wet, rotting wood, and muddy pools of stagnant water that reminded him of less lonely times fencing hot items in the Champs-Élysées.

The Diamond had been cocooned in luxury ever since it had arrived at the French court in 1668, enjoying a pampered life of scented drawers and bodies, soft, cradling hands, sumptuous surroundings. Its existence with a thief on the run was a distinct shock. It is always harder to move downscale than up.

Cadet Guillot hopefully peddled the Order of the Golden Fleece around London in a morocco leather box. As the weeks passed, there were many openings of the lid, many strange faces peering down at the Diamond, many rough hands touching it, and many words exchanged, but always the lid slammed shut and the whole process would start over again at a different location. It wasn't easy to sell jewels in London at a time when aristocrats were fleeing France in ever greater numbers, giving stiff competition to men like Guillot whose gems were less honestly acquired. Every jeweler in London was being daily besieged by French nobles, whose hands shook as they unwrapped their prizes and who were willing to take much less than they were worth.

Sometime before or during 1796 the Diamond was pried from the Order of the Golden Fleece and found itself freed at last from rampant bloodred beast, rival big white diamond, and lower-class topazes not worth mentioning. It was in 1796 that Cadet Guillot entrusted the dragon-carved Côte de Bretagne spinel, on its own, to an émigré called Lancry de La Loyelle, to be sold either back to the French government or to some European sovereign. Before he left London for the continent, Lancry, who seems to have been no more ethical than Guillot, had his friend put in jail so that he himself could pocket all the money from the proposed sale. Guillot was imprisoned for debt, which means that he probably hadn't yet managed to sell the Blue Diamond. At this point, Cadet Guillot disappears from our history back into the murky underworld whence he came. Lancry meanwhile turned up at Altona, near the German port of Hamburg, and there met a painter called Brard who wrote a detailed report of the Côte de Bretagne incident for the Hamburg police department, thereby endearing himself to any future biographer of the Diamond who, at this point in its story, searches desperately for clues. The Côte de Bretagne did eventually return to the French people and to staid retirement in the Apollo gallery of the Louvre.

We've made our way through the very complex political progress of the French Revolution holding tightly—like Theseus guided by Ariadne's string through the Cretan labyrinth—to colored cords of red, white, and blue: the prophetic colors of the Golden Fleece decoration; National Guards' tricolors all in a row; cockades pinned where diamonds dared not go; thick blue smoke at the Bastille clearing the way for freedom; a solid mass of red bonnets coiling for the kill; flags of flame flying above the Tuileries, streaming in the Seine. On we go, quickly past the Red House of a thief caught red-handed, sadly past a simple white dress become a shroud. And when we near the end, the strings are all dipped in the same stain, as the whole of France sees red.

The Blue Diamond's thread, however, leads us straight into impenetrable fog, into one of those pea-soup smogs that, at that time, settled over London and stayed for days, as if a thick, off-white cover had suddenly been clapped over a birdcage. Fog so dense one couldn't see fingers held three inches from one's face, and gas lamps on the streets stayed lit all day, their yellow cats' eyes too weak to see by, and having ventured half a block from home, one had to stumble back blindly, hanging on to iron palings or tracking ghostly footfalls just ahead.

In 1796 the Diamond disappeared into just such a fog as this. Somewhere, most probably in London, waiting for its next flare-up, its low blue pilot light continued to burn, but we have no hope of penetrating the mystery that covers it. Not until 1812 will the fog begin to clear.

Portrait of Henry Philip Hope, by Voordecker.

6

BEAUTY

Beauty itself doth of itself persuade
The eyes of men without an orator.

—WILLIAM SHAKESPEARE, *The Rape of Lucrece*

The Diamond lay in the middle of a sheet of white paper in a narrow-fronted shop at 26 Norfolk Street, a short artery which joined the Strand, one of the busiest commercial thoroughfares in London, to another, the river Thames. On September 19, 1812, early morning mists near the water had vanished as the sun began to climb, an English sun, hiding shyly, as it always did, behind a drop curtain of thin gray silk.

The left-hand thumb and forefinger of the jeweler who owned the shop, John Françillon, pressed the little blue ice floe firmly into the paper, while a pencil held in his right hand traced round its edges. The gem was bare, exposed, vulnerable; it was also lopped in size and lighter in weight than when we last saw it in Cadet Guillot's slum lodging farther east along the river. For twenty years, the stone had been passing from hand to hand, perhaps even country to country, on the lam, just one step ahead of the law, and along the way someone had radically altered its appearance.

The pencil completed its circular journey, slowing round the Diamond's left side, slightly thinner than its right. (The next hand to trace round it in exactly this way would come 163 years later, in 1975.) Françillon laid down his pencil, carefully set the stone to one side, picked up a small paintbrush, mixed watercolors in a tiny dish: ultra-marine, with one flick of cobalt. It was impossible to achieve the exact color, for this Diamond seemed to be as affected by weather as a human. When blue sky prevailed, it was kingfisher bright; when rain threatened, it turned thundercloud dark. Françillon stirred the little puddle with his brush and stroked on the result. He would have to give the Diamond back to Eliason all too soon, but he would have this drawing as his own private memento. John painted the stone's diminished left side last, with real love.

He sat back, assessed his work, pleased, and let the paint dry. Then he dipped a quill pen in ink and in careful script wrote below:

> The above drawing is the exact size and shape of a very curious su-perfine deep blue diamond. Brilliant cut, and equal to a fine deep blue sapphire. It is beauty full and all perfection without specks or flaws, and the colour even and perfect all over the diamond.
>
> I traced round the diamond with a pencil by leave of Mr. Daniel Eliason and it is as finely cut as I have ever seen a diamond.
>
> The colour of the drawing is as near the colour of the diamond as possible.
>
> dated: 19th Sept. 1812   John Françillon
>   No. 26 Norfolk Street
>   Strand, London

The phrase "by leave of Mr. Daniel Eliason" established him, on paper, as the jewel's legal owner. He was a merchant at 1 Birchin Lane, just off 36 Hatton Garden, the Holborn area of London where one still finds its diamond dealers. Mrs. Orpen asserts in *Famous Precious Stones* (1890) that "the little world of diamond lovers was dazzled by the appearance on the market of a unique stone" that "appeared abruptly in the world without provenance." The fact that Eliason chose not to reveal the Blue Diamond's past suggests that he knew about its theft from the Garde-meuble and might well have bought the stone directly from Cadet Guillot after he got out of debtors' prison.

Françillon's memo is dated precisely twenty years and one day after

Roland reported the theft of the French crown jewels to the National Assembly in Paris. According to French law, the statute of limitations for any crimes committed during wartime (France having declared war on Austria in 1792) was twenty years, a fact that Françillon and friend Eliason were surely aware of.

The mystery surrounding the memo itself surpasses the Diamond's, for it went underground for more than a hundred years. One day in the 1920s, Dr. George Frederick Kunz, a gem dealer who bought stones in Europe for such important American collectors as J. P. Morgan, was rummaging and poking about in Quaritch's secondhand London bookshop when he found a copy of the book that contains a detailed drawing of the Golden Fleece order designed by Louis XV, Pouget's *Traité des Pierres Précieuses* (1762). To find this rare book was exciting enough, but when Dr. Kunz opened it, out fluttered the memo Françillon had written in 1812! (Book and piece of paper rest now in the U.S. Geological Survey's library in Reston, Virginia, not far from the Diamond itself.) "Every event in the biography of a great gem," wrote Dr. Kunz in a 1928 *Saturday Evening Post* article relating his discovery, "is as vital to the gem expert as the episodes in the life of a famous man are to the historian," and his serendipitous find is a crucial clue to the Diamond's past.

There is one phrase in Françillon's note that bears scrutiny. He writes that the altered gemstone "is as finely cut as I have ever seen a diamond." Why this indirect praise of the man who dared to cleave and grind again on the wheel a jewel unique, perfect, prized by kings? Was the swashbuckling hero of this cut-and-slash Françillon himself? We know that he was a gem cutter and perhaps, given his French name, an ancestor in the same trade had been one of the Protestants forced to flee France and settle in England when Louis XIV had revoked the Edict of Nantes in 1685. If John Françillon did in fact recut the Diamond, did he perhaps *enjoy* diminishing the Sun King's treasure?

Someone recut it, that we know. Once it had been pried from the Golden Fleece decoration, the Blue Diamond of the French Crown couldn't be sold intact in any European market. Its fences—Guillot, Eliason, whoever—knew that once war between France and England ended (as it did in 1815), since the jewel was unquestionably French royal property, the legitimate sovereign in exile, Louis XVIII, would try to reclaim it. Drastic measures were therefore required.

The Diamond's unusual shape was far too recognizable, so its point had to go, that triangular piece at one end that, throughout its French royal progress, gave it drama and symbolism. Point down, heart-shaped, the stone had stood for romantic comedy (the Sun King and Athenaïs; Louis XV and Pompadour). Point up, tear-shaped, it suggested the tragedy of the Revolution (heads cut off, lives cut short). Sometime after 1792 and before 1812, the Diamond suffered its own Reign of Terror and was sentenced to be guillotined: slice off its head with one clean, swift cut.

For technical reasons, due to the stone's grain, cleaving was the only course; one couldn't remove the point by sawing. So some intrepid hand, Françillon's or another's, notched the Diamond, fitted a wedge, raised high a hammer, just as the Sun King's jeweler Pitau had in 1672, and struck one mighty blow, severing the stone in two. At that moment, the Diamond lost forever its special presence, its singularity and distinction, its royal provenance and known elitism. The pomp and parade of kings were gone forever; and a common, democratic existence had begun. In shape, it became ordinary, its roundness that of a million other diamonds; only its blueness and its bulk saved it from being a complete nonentity.

Edwin Streeter, a later London jeweler, maintains in *The Great Diamonds of the World* (1882) that two stones known to him were cut from the triangular piece removed by cleaving. The first one, weighing 13¾ carats, Streeter believed to be the blue diamond sold to the Duke of Brunswick in 1849, grandson of the duke who commanded the Prussian armies fighting France in 1792. (Soon we'll meet the latter's daughter, Caroline.) This stone first appeared in public when the duke's gem collection was auctioned in Geneva in 1874. The second one, weighing 1½ carats, Streeter himself bought for £300 from a Paris dealer and set in a brooch "as one of the most conspicuous stones in a butterfly, composed of diamonds in all the known colors" made for a London society hostess.

Recent gemologists, however, such as Robert Gaal, editor of the *Diamond Dictionary* (1977), Herbert Tillander in his paper "The Hope Diamond and its Lineage" presented at the 15th International Gemological Conference (October 1975), and Bernard Morel in *Les Joyaux de la Couronne de France* (1988) claim that these two stones of 13 and 1½ carats, though similar in color tones, could not possibly have been cut from the triangular piece and must have originated from other sources.

After its cleaving, the Diamond had been ground and polished. The rotating disk, or scaife, used to do this would not have been turned by humans, as it had been in Indian and French cuttings, but by horses. They supplied the power from about 1800 to 1850; after that scaifes were driven through shafts and belts by steam engines. The Diamond got what lapidaries call a "cushion-shaped," mixed cut of fifty-eight facets, with two extra facets between the girdle and the top of the main pavilion facets. This would be the stone's final major cut, a rather shallow one, which makes it appear larger but also fails to achieve maximum brilliance. When the work was completed, the gem had shrunk from 67⅛ carats to a reputed 44½ or 44¼, so that it had lost about 23 carats—not to mention a lot of status.

One year after John Françillon traced round the Diamond's new cut and shape with his pencil, another London lapidary, John Mawe, in *A Treatise on Diamonds and Precious Stones* (1813) wrote, "There is at this time a superlatively fine blue diamond of above 44 carats in the possession of an individual in London which may be considered matchless." Mawe noted in the same book that Golconda's diamond mines, where the Diamond first saw the light thousands of years before, "are said to be nearly exhausted" and consequently "are now abandoned." Mutability, even for immortal diamonds, is the law of life.

But there is one more piece of paper that surfaced in French archives, history's flotsam, to be examined while we are marshaling facts around the Diamond's 1812 English debut; it suggests that Daniel Eliason was having a hard time selling the transformed gem that had so suddenly appeared in the marketplace, like a foundling on a doorstep, without name or background. "The subject of the attached drawing," this document states,

> is a brilliant Oriental Diamond, unique and of very great value. It is considered as one of the rarest curiosities of nature in which is displayed the depth, richness and the blue of Sapphire and at the same time all the brilliance and perfection which it is possible for a Diamond to have. It is completely transparent, without speck or flaw and without fading. One can presume that this assemblage of qualities, in the entire universe, can never have had a similar conjunction. It is cut and polished to the best standard, being neither too thick nor too long but perfectly proportioned. This incomparable Diamond weighs 177 grains or 44¼ [old] carats, and finds itself at present in the possession of Mr. Daniel Eliason. The dimensions of the sketch attached are exactly those of the Diamond, and the color is as close to that of the original as the drawing allows.

Written in French, the international language of the time, this appears to be Eliason's advertisement for the stone, no doubt distributed in all the European centers where he hoped to snare a buyer.

He need not have cast so wide a net, for the Diamond's next owner was right there in London. On the morning of September 19, 1812, while Françillon in Norfolk Street was tracing around the Diamond's new shape and Eliason at 1 Birchin Lane was planning his strategy for selling it, a thirty-eight-year-old gentleman sat, alone as usual, for he was a virtual recluse, in the study of his fine mansion, Arklow House. Its generous Georgian windows looked south toward Hyde Park, for the dwelling stood at the eastern end of Connaught Place, at number 1. Down the street, at number 7, lived Caroline, Princess of Wales, daughter of Charles William Ferdinand, Duke of Brunswick. The heir to Britain's throne, George, Prince of Wales, had married her in 1795, but she looked so ugly and unwashed when he saw her—for the very first time—waiting at the altar that he called for brandy and by the time he found himself joined to Caroline—"let no man put asunder"—he was dead drunk. After their daughter Charlotte was born the next year, Prince George—"Prinny" to his friends—left Caroline's bed for good, retrieving the pair of pearl bracelets he'd given her so that he could pass them on to his newest mistress, Lady Jersey. George would rule as regent from 1812 to 1820 while his father, King George III, kept going mad.

Arklow House was a true temple of art. Every silk carpet, Greek vase, Roman bust, Dutch and Flemish painting, every treasure collected by an indefatigable traveler on a lifelong aesthetic quest throughout Europe and Asia, was supremely beautiful. The man who'd chosen them needed their beauty to feed his gentle, retiring, secret soul. He was not English, although he'd had a house in London for almost twenty years, having arrived in 1795, three years after the Diamond. He spoke English with an accent and never quite mastered Society's manners but was instead a true cosmopolitan who corresponded with learned men all over Europe, spoke seven languages, and was, as the *Gentleman's Magazine* would later note, "remarkable for his highly cultivated mind and his just and elegant taste in the Fine Arts."

Everywhere the eye looked in his study, it fell on beauty—with one glaring exception. The gentleman himself was remarkably ugly—and so were his two brothers and most of his relatives. His family had been blessed with bounteous wealth for three generations, but God had been remarkably stingy with physical comeliness. This particular family member had a short, inelegant figure, a low forehead, large ears, too long a nose, and too little a chin. His name was Henry Philip Hope, always called Philip, and he was destined—but not quite yet—to give a very famous Diamond its longest-lasting name.

On that September morning in 1812, Philip was bent over a mahogany chest of glass-topped drawers, which was the holy of holies in this temple of art. There he housed his growing gem collection. Inside fifteen of the drawers lay a few pearls (one weighed 455 carats), sapphires, emeralds, rubies, and some humbler stones, such as turquoise and cat's eye. But his special passion was for colored diamonds; searching for them formed his Holy Grail, and he'd already found some spectacular ones: yellow, pink, green, not so many brown and black. Each gem had its habitual place in a numbered drawer, and beside each was a neat little ivory ticket on which Philip had carefully printed the carat weight in black ink.

As the weak English sun peered in on that September morning, Philip took out his "fancy" diamonds, one at a time, and sat down at a small marquetry table to worship their beauty, cradling them in his palm. These were his babies; he had no wife or children and never would have. One wonders if Philip Hope's self-effacing reserve, his generosity and need to be liked were based on his internalizing a guilty secret: he may have been homosexual in a society where any kind of acknowledgment was taboo. (In 1815 it would take a London jury only ten minutes to sentence a waiter accused of sodomy to execution.)

Gently Philip picked up a gem, spent a few moments with it, and put it down again beside its ivory tag. "It is by studying little things," wrote Dr. Samuel Johnson, whose *Lives of the Poets* lay nearby, bound in softest leather, gilt stamped, "that we attain to the art of having as little misery and as much happiness as possible." The good doctor was a wise man; Philip returned the last jewel to its nest and softly closed the fifteenth drawer. The sixteenth one, the deepest, was empty. He was saving it for the pièce de résistance of his collection, for the wonder of wonders, the finest of fancies . . . for the ultimate beauty that would crown his life. He had not yet found such a diamond, but his faith was strong. Someday he would.

When he did find it, he was so inundated with money—a lava flow that never stopped, no matter how much he gave to charity—that no matter how high the price of his special darling, he could well afford to buy it. Philip shuffled in his velvet slippers to the door, closed it quietly, and went to give cook orders for his simple dinner.

The Hope fortune, which gave Philip a comfortable £60,000 a year, and what brother Thomas called "the burden of complete idleness" and "the labor of having constantly to seek some new amusement," came from a Dutch-based trading and banking business, a global corporation as lucrative as the Rothschilds'. Philip's great-

grandfather Archibald Hope (1664–1741) had been a Rotterdam merchant trading goods with England and America. Two of his eleven
children stayed in Rotterdam and fitted out ships to carry emigrants
to the New World. One son, Henry, left in 1727 to set up trading and
banking in Boston. Two other sons began a similar business in Amsterdam called Thomas and Adrian Hope. They both "worked like
slaves," according to a Swedish manufacturer who met them in 1759.
Between 1756 and 1762, they lent Britain nearly £50 million to pay for
the Seven Years War. In the 1760s, Benjamin Franklin, on a visit to
Amsterdam, wrote that he was "recommended to the Hopes," who
were "ranked among the greatest merchants of Europe" and was both
pleased and proud when "one of them sent his coach to carry us to
see everything curious in the city." On January 1, 1762, Thomas
and Adrian took the former's son, John, age twenty-five, and their
nephew Henry, age twenty-seven, who'd arrived from Boston where
his father had prospered, into the firm and changed its name to Hope
and Company.

In the following year John married Philippina van der Hoeven,
from a Rotterdam family above his own in the social scale, and began
to turn himself into an aristocrat, becoming friendly with the United
Provinces' *stadtholder* himself, William V. John and Philippina had
three sons: Thomas, born August 30, 1769, Adrian Elias, born in 1772,
and Henry Philip, born in 1774. It does seem fitting that in the same
year in which Louis XV died at Versailles from smallpox and the Diamond's last royal French owner, Louis XVI, became king, in another
country not far away, the next owner was born. Real life often proceeds
with far more neat coincidence than fiction.

In the year Philip was born, his father acquired Nederhorst den
Berg Castle, amid the Ankeveen lakes, near Hilversum. He already
owned a house in Amsterdam, an estate at The Hague, and another
called Groenendaal, near Haarlem, to which he would eventually add
the adjoining estate and villa known as Bosbeck. Since France was still
Europe's ideal, culturally speaking, the family spoke only French at
home and lived completely in a Versailles-like manner, moving, as

whim dictated, from mansion to mansion, where long rows of footmen in gold-braided livery lined up to greet them in marble halls. His father bought major paintings and tapestries for all the houses, so Philip's taste and appreciation for art developed early.

While his father, John, still helped run Hope and Company, it was Philip's second cousin Henry, two years older than his father and raised to American standards of initiative, who was mainly responsible for the firm's success. Over the years, the Hopes lent money at 4 or 5 percent to Britain, Sweden, Poland, Russia, Spain, and America. (Later, they bankrolled the youthful United States' Louisiana Purchase.) The company traded throughout Europe as well as in North and Central America, buying and selling almost every known kind of merchandise, including grain, gold, silver, textiles, tobacco, tea, wine, tulip bulbs— and diamonds. The Hopes sold uncut diamonds in Amsterdam as well as polished stones abroad, especially to Russia and Turkey. The earliest surviving balance sheet, from 1763, shows sales to such London Jewish diamond dealers as Salomons, Heyman, and Gompertz. Between 1770 and 1794, Hope and Company sold more than 15,000 carats. They also lent money with diamonds as security. When Portugal borrowed from the firm to finance the Napoleonic wars, it paid interest and some of the principal in diamonds received in regular shipments from Brazil. Between 1802 and 1813, more than 280,000 carats would pour into the Dutch office, keeping Amsterdam's cutters very busy at their craft. As he grew up, Philip heard his dear papa and cousin Henry talking of diamonds with broad smiles on their faces. Perhaps Philip Hope's grown-up passion for the stones sparked when he was very young. When he did begin his collection, he had plenty of connections and contacts ready-made.

After his father died in 1784, when Philip was only ten and his brothers Adrian and Thomas were twelve and fifteen, cousin Henry became Philip's role model and mentor in everything except affairs of business, in which none of the three boys showed the slightest interest. Cousin Henry was a lifelong bachelor of great charm and intellect who was passionate about art and who continued Philip's aesthetic education. Henry filled his Haarlem mansion, Welgelegen, completed in

1788, with paintings by Rembrandt, Titian, Van Dyck, and Rubens. That year, and for the next five, Hope and Company lent the equivalent of more than $21 million to Russia's Empress Catherine II, who was so grateful to Henry that she offered to ennoble him (he refused) and gave him a portrait of herself (which now hangs in Hillwood, the former Washington, D.C., home of the late Marjorie Merriweather Post).

Philip said a tearful good-bye when he was thirteen to Tom, who, having turned eighteen, set off on what was the final stage of every aristocratic gentleman's education: the Grand Tour. "From an infant," Tom writes, "architecture was always my favorite amsuement," so off he went for the next eight years to study and sketch buildings, monuments, and statues in Turkey, Egypt, Syria, Greece, Sicily, Spain, Portugal, France, and Germany. Philip was emotionally deeply attached to Tom and always would be. The fact that both boys were short and ugly, shy and sensitive, made a lifelong bond between them; for both, art was their crutch. As tantalizing letters arrived from Tom describing ancient cultures in full bloom, Philip consoled himself with the thought that in another five years he could join his brother on the Grandest of Grand Tours and see these wonders for himself. Adrian got to join Tom first, being two years older than Philip. He was apparently abnormal in some way, mentally challenged or unbalanced, and would grow ever more unmanageable as he aged.

Philip probably set off, with his two older brothers as chaperons, when he was only seventeen, in April 1791, for we know that Thomas was back in Amsterdam briefly that month and then not again until March 1793. Thomas was sketching all the way, and some of the 525 drawings, bound into five volumes (now lost) were by another hand, probably Philip's. Unfortunately, things began to heat up in France just as Philip began to tour with high hopes and a whopping line of credit, and the Revolution's Reign of Terror would target not just aristocrats but wealthy bankers, too. Shortly after declaring war on the Netherlands and England early in 1793, the Convention in Paris, anticipating victory, declared Stadtholder William V's property forfeit as well as that of "his friends, supporters and willing slaves," categories that clearly included the Hopes. The war also temporarily interrupted Hope and Company's profitable diamond trade; later, they would find new channels that led via London and Hamburg to the Amsterdam diamond merchants Insinger and Company.

On October 17, 1794, cousin Henry Hope and his adored, adopted Cornish son, John Williams Hope, who'd been made a partner in the business, crossed by boat to England. From a distant Scots relative, Lord Hopetoun, Henry bought a London house in Harley Street, off Cavendish Square, added a wing for the 372 fine paintings he'd brought with him from Welgelegen, and opened a London branch of Hope and Company, making Thomas and Philip sleeping partners in the firm, just as they were in the Dutch headquarters.

While Henry was settling in London, the three Hope brothers went on a spending spree to Rome. They may have stayed in a Castel Gandolfo villa with the Englishman who acted as banker and art dealer to his countrymen, the bachelor ex-painter Thomas Jenkins, who made a lot of money buying and selling antiquities, especially once the Hopes arrived on the scene. Jenkins had himself made a fine collection of cameos and gems, and it might have been there, handling and admiring these small but immensely satisfying objects, that twenty-year-old Philip first decided to make a collection of his own.

Barely out of their teens, the Hopes enjoyed playing grand connoisseurs, while dealers fawned and courted them. From Pacetti's shop, Philip bought an erotic statue of Bacchus and Ariadne and another of Hermaphrodite. In sculptor Thorwaldsen's studio, Tom ogled his design for *Jason with the Golden Fleece*, in which the muscular hero stood naked, without even a figleaf; Tom promptly ordered it in marble, the bigger the better. (Thorwaldsen would take twenty-five years to deliver it.) Then Tom and Philip lovingly posed together for a portrait by Guy Head.

French forces entered Amsterdam on January 20, 1795, and proclaimed a revolutionary Batavian Republic, and seven days later, the Hope brothers, encumbered with crates and crates of beautiful possessions, reached England and took a temporary abode at 2 Hanover Square, not far from cousin Henry's house in Harley Street. Thomas instantly began to turn himself into a complete English gentleman. Philip was a hybrid, not really Dutch and not really English, a restless traveler, as lonely an exile as Jean-Baptiste Tavernier had been, completely at home nowhere. Philip had inherited from his father the three-story red brick villa Bosbeck, near Haarlem. He was often in residence there, where nightingales sang in the beech woods and every May acres of tulips, scarlet, yellow, orange, looked like huge Persian carpets flung across the fields.

Like his father, Thomas was socially ambitious; he used his wealth to insinuate himself into the highest level of English Society. When Philip saw British aristocrats snickering behind his beloved brother's back and being cold and haughty to his face, he resolved never to enter Society himself except in the most peripheral way possible. It would have been so much easier if poor Tom had been tall and handsome—beauty counted for so much in the world—but Thomas Hope's face, as one Englishwoman noted, was "very much underhung," dwindling to a weak chin and weaker jawline, so he looked rather like an anxious little lemur. "Mr. Hope has a foolish manner and a very disagreeable voice," declared Henry Fox, later 4th Lord Holland, "and says little silly nothings." Another gentleman thought him "disagreeable, fastidious, and conceited," and Lord Glenbervie described him in his diary as "a little, ill-looking man with a sort of effeminate face and manner, speaking a kind of language which you are in doubt whether to think merely affected or what is called broken English."

Thomas persisted. He got himself elected to the Society of Antiquaries and the Society of Dilettanti, both elitist clubs. Philip quietly gave money to local artists. When William Bond engraved Richard Westall's painting *The Expiation of Orestes* he dedicated the plate to Philip Hope, "who has evinced a laudable disposition to patronize the Fine Arts in England." Thomas began to write and publish: *Household Furniture and Interior Decoration* would appear in 1807, *Costume of the Ancients* in 1809, and *Designs of Modern Costumes* in 1812.

While Philip purchased Arklow House and retreated to its shadows, Tom, in 1799, bought from the dowager Lady Warwick her enormous mansion in Duchess Street, off Portland Place. She was the sister of Sir William Hamilton, whose collection of 750 Greek vases Thomas would soon buy, and whose wife, Emma, had run off with Lord Nelson. Designed by Robert Adam, the house had a forecourt in Duchess Street and a long narrow garden stretching south to Queen Anne Street. Philip hardly saw Tom once his brother got his house, where, obsessively, he began to create a very public temple of art, himself drawing up blueprints for new wings and galleries to be filled with furniture built to his own original neoclassical designs. Thomas kept the first-floor rooms as a museum and place for parties and lived above. Tickets were issued to the nobility for Mondays during the London season, when all its members were in town. Like some wily little spider, Thomas Hope gradually lured them all, even the Royals, into his web.

By 1802 Adrian had become so strange and unpredictable in his behavior that Thomas and Philip conferred with cousin Henry, then regretfully packed him off to the Amsterdam homestead, appointing David Berck there as trustee of his income and Entrop Muller as guardian to watch him closely. Philip wept and promised Adrian he would visit often, a promise he kept until the end of his life.

Thomas's next preoccupation was to find the second requisite for social acceptance and conformity: a wife. He went to look for one in Tunbridge Wells, a popular Society resort, and, as the poet Thomas Moore noted, made "assiduous love" to Susan Beckford, whose half-mad father, William, had built the neo-Gothic folly Fonthill Abbey. (The Beckfords will reappear later, for true tales can be quite as economical as novels when it comes to minor characters.) While her father warmed to Thomas Hope's millions, Susan couldn't bring herself to wed such an ugly man and flatly refused him. (She snared the future Duke of Hamilton five years later.) Thomas proposed to "the beautiful Miss Dashwood" next, but she, too, said an emphatic no. Philip expended much sympathy on his brother's plight and strengthened his vow never, ever, to propose to any female himself.

Tom went hunting next at the fashionable spa of Bath and in April 1806 met Louisa, youngest child of William Beresford, Archbishop of

Tuam and later 1st Baron Decies. She, too, on his first proposal, refused Thomas, being madly in love with her cousin, also called William Beresford, with whom she was "carrying on a pretty lively flirtation," according to the diarist Joseph Farington. Beresford was destined for a hero's role in the Peninsular War, being Wellington's choice of field marshal for British forces in Portugal. He, too, will reappear in our story.

Louisa, who was very pretty, good-natured, full of Irish charm, and, luckily, even shorter than Thomas, was "afterward persuaded by her friends," according to Farington's diary, "not to refuse so splendid a prospect." Tom was all smiles when they became engaged, and Philip, who hadn't been able to compete with a house for Tom's attention, grew even more silent. But he was incapable of disliking anybody, and gradually he came to really love Louisa. She and Tom married in 1806, whereupon he had her loveliness immortalized on canvas three times: by Sir Thomas Lawrence, Martin Shee, and George Dawe, and in the following year Tom acquired the next necessity for a social-climbing gentleman: a country seat. At noon on May 26, 1807, at Garraway's Coffee House, Exchange Alley, Cornhill, Thomas bought at auction for £9,030 Deepdene, near Dorking, a fine Surrey estate whose grounds, as described in the sale catalog included "a park with luxurious forest trees, walks, rural retirements, grottoes, cavern, terrace, pleasure garden, canal of water, two hot-houses, kitchen-garden and melon-ground." Best of all, until 1791, Deepdene had been home to the Dukes of Norfolk. John Aubrey in his *Antiquities of Surrey* had described the late seventeenth-century view from the terrace, with unwitting prophecy, as "a long Hope [archaic word for slope]; the true name of this Hope is Dibden or Deep Dene. . . . The pleasures of the garden, with orange trees, syringas and 21 kinds of thyme were so ravishing that I can never expect any enjoyment beyond it but the Kingdom of Heaven."

With his usual generosity, Philip purchased the estate of Chart Park, adjoining Deepdene to the south, and presented it to Tom, who in turn built a vaguely Etruscan temple on one of his hilltops bearing

the inscription "*Fratri Optimus* [best of brothers] H. P. H.," with another inscription in Arabic, which both brothers understood. Philip
went to Deepdene for house parties, happy to be with Tom and Louisa
but suffering agonies of shyness with the other guests. Instead of fox
hunting and partridge shooting, which were the usual male activities
at country estates, at Deepdene guests went in the barouche to view
the architectural delights of neighboring estates, walked in picture
gallery or hothouse on wet days, and in the evenings looked through
volumes of drawings and engravings. Louisa, whose social ambitions
were even greater than her husband's, made guests write comments
in a specially bound album, where we find the signatures of the novelist Sir Walter Scott, the poet George Crabbe, the great chemist Sir
Humphry Davy, and the American writer Washington Irving, who
enthused in a letter to his sister in June 1822 that Deepdene "is furnished in a style of taste and magnificence of which I can give you no
idea."

A son and heir to the splendors of Duchess Street and Deepdene
arrived in 1808, was christened Henry Thomas, wearing a recently acquired ancestral robe, to be followed by Adrian John in 1811, and
then, after a nine-year interval, by Alexander Beresford in 1820.

Since both cousin Henry and John Williams Hope had died by
1813, on July 17 Thomas and Philip bought out John Williams's
troublesome widow and on September 3 sold all their shares in
Hope and Company to Alexander Baring, head of the London
bankers Baring and Company, for £250,521. Hope coffers, for Tom
and Philip and the next generation of Hope males, were now extremely full.

When the Irish novelist Maria Edgeworth paid a visit to Thomas
and Louisa in Duchess Street in 1819, she wrote to her mother that
"Philip, Hope's brother, has given him his fine collection of Dutch and
Flemish paintings" that "are now piled seven deep in the passage leading to our bedchamber with their faces to the wall. Mr. Hope [Thomas]
has built a gallery on purpose for them." There seemed no end to
Philip's altruism. He'd inherited some paintings, bought others on his

travels—among them were three Rembrandts, three Jan Steens, one Ruysdael, and one Hobbema. They left Arklow House, never to return, and hung in the semipublic space that Tom conceived and created, a gallery forty-eight feet long and twenty-two wide, furnished with carved Grecian-style chairs he'd designed and a large sky blue ottoman.

In the same year, Thomas astounded the literary world with a book that put him forever in the limelight and Philip further into the shade. Using detailed journals he'd kept on his Grand Tour, he published *Anastasius, or The Memoirs of a Greek* in three volumes. It was an instant bestseller, running to thirteen editions and four languages. With the profits, Thomas bought Louisa two rows of splendid pearls, known thereafter to Hope descendants as "the Anastasius pearls." Written first in French, and then in English, the book is a rambling, interminable tale of the continental wanderings of doomed Byronic hero, Anastasius. Almost everyone he encounters dies soon after, including his parents, three wives, two mistresses, two illegitimate sons, and his one true friend. He finally succumbs himself, age thirty-five, but not before many tedious pages of overblown descriptive prose. This novel suited the fashion of the times; the poet Lord Byron himself told Lady Blessington that he "wept bitterly over many pages of it, and for two reasons; the first that he had not written it, and the second that Hope had."

This was heady praise for Thomas, and unexpected, for he'd hedged his bets by publishing the work anonymously. When all Britain and half of Europe lavished praise on the book, Thomas threw modesty aside once and for all and, in a letter to *Blackwood's Magazine* dated October 9, 1821, acknowledged himself proudly as "the sole author of *Anastasius*." His self-esteem was now about the same size as his Deepdene and Chart Park acreage; Philip, while genuinely pleased for his brother's success, spent longer hours in his Arklow House study, now bereft of its best paintings and, even though he no longer had a financial interest in Hope and Company, kept up his contacts with Dutch diamond merchants. He told both

Amsterdam and London dealers that if any spectacular "fancy" diamonds appeared on the market, he wanted to be the first to know. The fifteen drawers in his mahogany cabinet were opened and gently closed many times each day.

Where, all this time, was our Diamond? When, in 1823, John Mawe published the second edition of his book A *Treatise on Diamonds and Precious Stones*, he wrote a new footnote concerning it to replace the one in the 1813 edition:

> A superlatively fine blue Diamond weighing 44 carats and valued at £30,000, formerly the property of Mr. Eliason, an eminent diamond merchant, is now said to be in the possession of our most gracious sovereign. This unrivalled gem is of a deep sapphire blue, and from its rarity and colour, might have been estimated at a higher sum. It has found its most worthy destination in passing into the possession of a monarch, whose refined taste has ever been conspicuous in the highest degree.

He included drawings of both the top and side views of the Diamond, which indicate that it was still unset. But did Prinny, who'd been King George IV for three years, actually buy it? An anonymous article on February 20, 1836, in *Chambers Edinburgh Journal* on "Diamonds and Diamond Mines" may have been merely copying Mawe when it refers to a blue diamond "purchased by his late majesty in 1823, from Mr. Eleason [sic] for £30,000." The article describes Eliason as "an eminent diamond merchant" who "received His Majesty's commands to visit the palace as often as he had any rare gems to dispose of." However, Bernard Morel, in *Les Joyaux de la Couronne de France*, claims that a "secret report" that he unearthed while researching states that George IV refused to purchase stones from Eliason because of his reputation as a bore (*raseur*) and because he was forever pestering people in the royal entourage. Whom are we to believe? There is no solid documentary evidence extant to prove the case for King George's ownership, nothing in the Royal Archives at Windsor, nothing in contemporary memoirs or histories, so above his well-curled head, a question mark remains.

Most chroniclers of the Diamond, around which mystery always swirls, suggest that Philip Hope bought it directly from Eliason. Mawe's footnote indicates that Hope had not yet done so in 1823; Eliason died at the end of 1824, so sometime during 1823–24 Philip may have acquired his *summum bonum*, his precious darling, his greatest prize. On that exciting day when he achieved his secret ambition, he parted with only £18,000 (U.S. $90,000 at that time), which made the rare stone a real bargain. Perhaps Daniel Eliason knew he was going to die soon and needed cash for his widow.

(Of course, instead of this scenario, the Diamond may have found its way from London to Hamburg to Amsterdam, along Hope and Company's channel and thence to Philip. It could even have been recut not by John Françillon in London but by Insinger's in Amsterdam. With each new owner, the stone's mystique grows denser.)

The morning after he'd bought the Diamond, Philip entered his study, jubilant, exulting, closed the door to show his servants he mustn't be disturbed, took the jewel with trembling fingers from its wrapping, and sat down at his marquetry table. He'd read in so many old volumes of Asian and European history, read in whatever language they'd been written in, how down the centuries rajas and royals lusted— yes, it was almost a sexual thing—for diamonds. Philip looked into the blue stone's heart and saw there a beauty so pure that it seemed the highest proof of being. He thought at once of John Keats's "Ode on a Grecian Urn," published in the 1820 leather volume of poems that he often reached for during his solitary evenings. Two of the verses could well have been written for a rare Blue Diamond:

> Thou still unravish'd bride of quietness,
> Thou foster-child of silence and slow time,
> Sylvan historian, who canst thus express
> A flowery tale more sweetly than our rhyme.
> . . . .
> When old age doth this generation waste,
> Thou shalt remain, in midst of other woe
> Than ours, a friend to man, to whom thou say'st

> "Beauty is truth, truth beauty",—that is all
> Ye know on earth, and all ye need to know.

Precisely; Keats said it so much better than he could, but then he wasn't a poet, or even, like clever Tom, a prose writer. Beauty is truth, truth beauty. He'd known that for a long time, all his life, really. And here, in his palm was his "friend to man," his very own adored Fancy, whose supreme authority, certainty, affirmation—he never could find just the right word—made the entire rest of creation turn to clay.

But he couldn't keep this miracle only for his own selfish pleasure; that would be wrong. He would have it suitably mounted into a brooch so that Louisa, who loved jewels, who loved *him*, bless her dear, warm heart, could borrow it for her grandest parties. But not yet. Right now he couldn't part with it even for a day.

After holding it for a long time, Philip went to his mahogany cabinet, opened drawer number sixteen and tenderly placed the Hope Diamond inside. The jewel settled onto softest velvet, while Philip rummaged in his desk for a blank ivory ticket, found a quill pen, dipped it in black ink, and slowly wrote, "44¼ carats." This stone would bear the Hope name and carry his love of beauty into the future. It would be his gauntlet thrown in death's face, his bid for immortality. Philip planted the ivory tag beside his ultimate hope and carefully closed the drawer.

The Diamond had not only left its very public royal life behind and the trauma of the past twenty low-class years, it had found the man who, of all its many owners, would love it most faithfully and intensely, love it for its own essence and grace, not, like Tavernier and the Garde-meuble thieves, for its monetary value; not, like the Sun King, for its political clout; not, like Louis XV, for its entertainment value. It seems fitting and just that the Diamond's long-term name came from its first (and last but one) real lover. The gem had found its way from public platform to private closet. Each day, tête-à-tête, it revealed its intimate charms to Henry Philip Hope, changing mood, as he never failed to note, with every shift of light, its impact clandestine and confidential.

We wish we knew more details of this too-private person. Sometimes when he left his study for other people's drawing rooms, he would, because it seemed to give them pleasure, cut their silhouettes from black paper with a pair of little gold scissors that he kept in a waistcoat pocket. He himself, the man who definitively christened the Hope Diamond, remains for us little more than a silhouette, almost as mysterious as the stone itself. Unfortunately, most Hope family papers were destroyed in a 1941 fire during the bombing of London in World War II. Memoirs of his own time give Philip barely a mention; they have room only for Thomas. *The Diary of Joseph Farington*, a society painter who scribbled daily from July 1793 until he died in December 1821, whose journal in the Yale University Press edition runs to sixteen volumes, contains in its index more than a page of references to Thomas Hope but not a single one to Philip. His self-effacement was far too thorough. He eludes us like a Cheshire cat, leaving only his modest, timid, and truly benevolent smile behind.

After the intimate honeymoon period, Philip, like most lovers, decided to show off his beauty to the world—and make Louisa happy at the same time. Having renounced manly Lord William for the effeminate, lemur-faced Thomas, Louisa had fixed on two goals to console her for her choice. She would become London's greatest Society hostess and she would adorn herself with the greatest jewels. In both these ambitions she seems to have succeeded, for Regency memoirs enthuse for pages about her parties at the Duchess Street mansion; her jewels inspired the poet and wit Henry Luttrell to dash off a couplet: "Of diamond, emerald and topaz/the charming Mrs. Hope has" and one diarist reports Louisa "crushed under the weight of gems and pearls." She may have been trying to outshine Lady Londonderry, her rival for the position of number-one hostess, who was always so covered with jewels at every party that she could barely stand upright and had to be followed around by a chair.

There was also the horrid incident, which kept tongues wagging in the late spring of 1810. When Dubost painted a portrait of Louisa that Thomas didn't like, he refused to pay for it. Dubost retaliated with a painting in which Louisa is being offered jewels by a monster, easily recognizable as her husband, who is saying, "I am sensible that I am a most horrible beast and that you can have no thoughts of me, but if you will accept of me you shall have all these riches at your disposal." *Beauty and the Beast* was exhibited with other Dubost works at a Pall Mall gallery, where absolutely everyone, even the Prince of Wales, came to stare and snigger—until Louisa's brother, Captain John Beresford, stormed in on Wednesday, June 20, and slashed the canvas to pieces with his sword.

Thomas gave Louisa even more spectacular gems after that. But it wasn't until one magical night around 1824 that she was able, at one and the same time, to erase from everyone's mind the ignominy of Dubost's monster and turn Lady Londonderry into a green-eyed one, positively sick with envy.

On that memorable evening, as darkness fell on London, West End streets filled with carriages, each with its torch of flame and its painted coat-of-arms showing fitfully upon its doors. Louisa routinely invited nine hundred to her soirées; all too soon Duchess, Mansfield, and Queen Anne Streets and Portland Place were filled with coaches that couldn't move and stamping horses that wanted to. The last guests to arrive on the scene had to be carried by their footmen in sedan chairs in order to reach the Hopes' front door. Some never made it there at all.

The fashionable slang for such a party was a "crush" and indeed it was, "a glittering sea/Of gems and plumes and pearls and silks," according to Lord Byron's satiric poem *Don Juan*. Until he fled England in disgrace for having an incestuous affair with his half sister, Byron was often a guest at Duchess Street, always wearing a brooch on his cravat, and describes the scene thus:

> Salon, room, hall, o'erflow beyond their brink,
> And long the latest of arrivals halts,
> Midst royal dukes and dames condemn'd to climb,
> And gain an inch of staircase at a time.

At the top of the staircase, flushed and smiling, dropping a curtsy to each guest, stood Louisa, wearing a pale silk gown, column straight in the Regency mode, which Thomas had designed—he created most of her clothes—to match his mansion-cum-museum's decor. On her bosom, just below her rosy cleavage, gleamed the Hope Diamond, making its London society debut. Philip had parted with it long enough to allow a jeweler to place it in the center of a medallion brooch, giving it an inner border, in arabesque designs, of little rose-cut diamonds, and an outer one of twenty 1-carat brilliants. At the bottom of the brooch, rising and falling with every breath Louisa took, hung an enormous pearl. One guest in particular ogled that sensual spot: Field Marshal Lord William Beresford, returned a hero from the Peninsular War, splendid in scarlet coat and face to match.

For Louisa the Diamond symbolized her triumph, but neither Philip nor Thomas enjoyed these parties, although both were there, unnoticed in the crush. Philip had come to follow his Fancy with his eye and to feel Louisa's warm gratitude flow over him. Tom was there as reluctant host. Once he was asked by a guest who someone was. "I really don't know; I don't know half the people here," he sighed, "nor do they know me or Mrs. Hope even by sight. Just now I was behind a lady who was making her *speech*, as she thought, to Mrs. Hope, but she was addressing a stranger." The man-about-town Samuel Rogers records how Tom had been "standing in a very forlorn condition, leaning against the chimneypiece, when a gentleman, coming up to him, said, 'Sir, as neither of us is acquainted with any of the people here, I think we had best go home.' " His beloved rooms, with every architectural motif, every stick of furniture designed by himself, looked better empty. With all these people, one couldn't see the detail.

The detail was highly idiosyncratic, overloaded with symbols of past civilizations; the whole house was a visual foray In Search of Lost Time. Take, for example, the Egyptian room, now packed with bobbing tiaras, perfectly tied white cravats, and footmen holding trays. Mummy cases were painted on the ceiling; panels on a mahogany daybed showed the jackal-headed god Anubis facing hawk-headed Horus, with bronze scarabs crawling around its feet. Square sofas and chairs in black wood and yellow satin upholstery were adorned with gold sphinxes. Having finished her duties at the top of the stairs,

Louisa stood, with one hand absently caressing a bronze scorpion, talking to Lord William, while the blue-fire medallion on her breast moved dangerously close to his rows of medals. The Diamond fitted easily into this setting where everything was more symbol than object.

But who was that fat gentleman in the blue coat, holding court in the painting gallery, not far from *The Glutton* by Jan Steen? No other than Prinny himself, King George IV, a habitué at Louisa's parties, who may or may not have recently snubbed the Diamond. He had the best manners in the kingdom—and the worst morals. He ate too much and drank too much and spent money like water on lavish Carlton House in London and the Pavilion at Brighton, where dinner parties, sometimes attended by the Hopes, ran to 116 dishes served in nine complete "courses," with wines for each. The circumference of George's blue coat at the waist was consequently more whale than wasp and under it was a tightly laced but ineffectual corset. At least he'd got rid of dirty Caroline of Brunswick. She'd swept out of 7 Connaught Place, down the street from Philip, in 1814, flounced off to Europe, carried on a ragged, raffish life there, bedding her servants, and finally died in 1821.

Philip was not in the gallery full of his paintings but rather leaning against the most inconspicuous piece of wall in the dining room and wondering how soon he could make his escape. In the very center of the mantelpiece, Thomas had placed the bust of Philip sculpted by Flaxman in 1803; at both ends, looking ridiculous, far too large for the space, were antique horses' heads—there because Philip in Greek means "horse lover." Their namesake avoided looking at the mantel and fixed his gaze instead on the blue jewel coming toward him attached to Louisa.

She gave him a radiant smile and touched it lightly. Louisa had grown up in a shabby, untidy, drafty Irish house, and often at Duchess Street she longed for just one scruffy old chair that she could fall into, just a simple chair that didn't have snakes or disembodied heads anywhere on it. Ah, Philip was leaving, and dear, brave William, her two favorite men in all the world. They both bowed before her, Philip awkwardly as always, William with a tintinnabulation of medals. Louisa dipped in a quick curtsy, and all the candles in hydra-headed wall sconces caught the Diamond's blue sparks and tossed them around the strange room where iconography ran riot.

If Louisa needed her gems so, too, as the years passed, did Philip, but for different reasons. He felt increasingly lonely. He never got close to his three nephews; Henry and Adrian, in their teens, argued and fought and clumped about with muddy boots and cricket bats when they were home from Eton; Alexander, thoroughly spoiled, threw temper tantrums in the nursery. Philip still missed fireside chats with cousin Henry, and then, in 1830, Tom's health began to fail. Committed to the last to his own self-involved ideal of beauty, Thomas had had his armchair carried onto the roof of the Duchess Street house "and sat to examine and direct what some workmen should do who were repairing the skylight over the picture gallery." "Ruling passion still!" sniffed Maria Edgeworth, quite sure it was that inspection, plus a too-strong dose of James's Powder, that precipitated Thomas Hope's demise.

"I am extinguishing," Thomas sighed to a clergyman friend, in mournful Anastasian tones, "but not so fast as I could wish." Philip was constantly at his brother's bedside, depressed and distraught. Miss Edgeworth visited Thomas a few days before he died, when he'd retreated from his first-floor showplace to the cozy attic at Duchess Street. "I saw a figure sunk in his chair," Maria writes, "in figured silk *robe de chambre* and nightcap; death in his pale, sunk, shrunk face," with "the half-finished picture of his second son [twenty-year-old Adrian] in the corner beside his armchair, as if to cheer his eyes." "By an Irish artist," whispered Thomas, "of great talent."

Tom died on February 3, 1831, and was buried on February 12, in the mausoleum he'd designed and built at Deepdene.

Philip's extreme grief was tempered by all he had to do, beyond comforting Louisa (who didn't seem to need much) and the three fatherless boys, for Philip was co-executor of Tom's will, probated at £180,000. The house and contents of Duchess Street went to Henry, then twenty-three, with Adrian receiving £30,000 and Alexander

£35,000. Louisa got £10,000, a life annuity of £1,000 a year, and during her lifetime use of the Deepdene mansion, contents, and lands. She exited the Duchess Street house with never a backward glance, and on December 29 of the very next year, in a room festooned with mistletoe and not a single ersatz mummy case or scorpion, married Lord William Beresford, on whom her heart had always doted.

Philip's other brother, Adrian, babbling and incoherent in his Amsterdam and Haarlem houses, died two years later, on September 16, 1834. He died without a will, so property worth £500,000 came to Philip, and about £193,000 each to nephews Henry, Adrian, and Alexander. At once, with his usual generosity, Philip gave £37,000 to Louisa, which enabled her to exit Deepdene, with never a backward glance, leaving it for Henry, and move with Lord William to a fine estate she'd bought in Kent, Bedgebury Park. Ten miles from Tunbridge Wells, it had a seventeenth-century house, to which they soon added wings, and two thousand acres, thirty of them kept in grass, which two men and a donkey were never finished cutting. Amid vistas of green growth, Louisa settled into wedded bliss, leaving son Henry to cope with treasure-stuffed Deepdene.

By 1838 Philip was becoming frail, and on April 5, hunched over the desk in his study, wrote a letter to "my dear nephews" to be delivered after his death. He informed them that all his considerable wealth and property would be left to them and implored them "to cherish and cultivate a fraternal regard and affectionate feelings for each other, and not to dishonour or disparage the memory of your parents and uncles by unworthy differences among yourselves, for their memory will be the more respected and revered the more your conduct evinces brotherly love and affection towards each other, and rectitude and benevolence towards your fellow creatures." This excellent advice, as we shall see, fell on deaf ears.

Philip laid down his pen, shuffled to the mahogany cabinet, opened drawer number sixteen, and gazed at his Diamond. None of those three undisciplined young bucks deserved it, but to one of them it would have to go. He decided that his will would say nothing about how his gem collection, now valued at £150,000, should be split up. Instead, partly to escape death duties, he'd dispose of his beloved jewels by deeds executed while he was still alive.

Unfortunately, Philip Hope's mind was growing befuddled, his memory failing; he wrote deed after deed full of contradictory instructions, then promptly forgot where he'd put them. He became most troubled and anxious and at one point wrote a pathetic letter to his solicitor:

> Instead of sending you the deed you expected I am now myself in despair to tell you that I cannot find it and don't know what has become of it, at least I cannot recollect it, for if it is in existence at all it must be deposited somewhere so snugly that I cannot recollect it, another instance, alas, to prove to what my poor memory is reduced, and another prognostic I am afraid that I shall some day or other lose my senses altogether and become crazy. I cannot tell you how this disappointment vexes, as I in vain look for a cause for or a reason to account for it. The only way I can do so is to suppose I left it in some box which is in the hands of a safe person whose name or person I cannot recollect, in short, if ever I were disposed to hang myself it would be now. God bless you, my dear sir, and pray excuse the wanderings of your ever faithful, humble servant.

"I am afraid I shall some day or other lose my senses altogether and become crazy." It had happened to brother Adrian; it could happen to him. This was now Philip's greatest fear. He puttered about Arklow House in a perpetual fog, searching, searching, pulling out papers, putting them back, hands shaking, head throbbing, until he couldn't remember what it was he was searching for.

He still had one clear goal. Before his jewels were thrown to the lions, to three greedy young men who cared not a whit for such marvels, he had to immortalize them in print. He was far too muddled to attempt it himself, but he could hire fellow collector Bram Hertz to put together a handsome leatherbound folio, not too ostentatious, not like the Duke of Devonshire's edition of Camoens that he'd once seen, with *D* and coronet in diamonds on its brown and gold cover.

No, the Hope folio would be something simpler and more modest altogether.

Little is known of Bram Hertz, except that his own collections of art objects were eclectic and extensive. Sotheby's would auction them after his death; sales catalogs list Assyrian, Babylonian, Egyptian, Greek, Etruscan, Roman, Indian, Peruvian, Mexican, and Chinese antiquities, not to mention Italian mosaics, miniature portraits, and Sèvres porcelain.

In August 1839, Philip slowly and proudly turned the thick, creamy pages of A *Catalogue of the Collection/Of Pearls and Precious Stones/formed by Henry Philip Hope, Esq./Systematically arranged and described by B. Hertz,* which had just come from the London printer William Clowes and Sons, in Stamford Street. Written descriptions of each stone, followed by line drawings, included assorted precious gems and pearls, and fifty diamonds, both rough and cut, forty-five of which were colored, with weights ranging from 45 carats to less than 1. In addition, there were four engraved diamonds and a few either cut into unusual shapes or containing rare inclusions. The blue Hope Diamond got pride of place as number one, under the section "Polished Diamonds," and merited the following description, which Philip, proud as a parent, had written with Hertz's help:

A most magnificent and rare brilliant of a deep sapphire blue, of the greatest purity, and most beautifully cut; it is of true proportions, not too thick, nor too spread. This matchless gem combines the beautiful colour of the sapphire with the prismatic fire and brilliancy of the diamond, and, on account of its extraordinary colour, great size and other fine qualities, it certainly may be called unique; as we may presume that there exists no cabinet, not any collection of crown jewels in the world, which can boast of the possession of so curious and fine a gem as the one we are now describing; and we may expect to be borne out in our opinion by our readers, since there are extant and historical records and treatises on precious gems, which give us descriptions of all the extraordinary diamonds in the possession of all the crowned heads of Europe as well as the princes of Eastern countries. But in vain do we search for any record of a gem which can in point of curiosity, beauty, and perfection, be compared with this blue brilliant.

Diamonds are found of almost every colour which is proved by the great variety of coloured diamonds in this collection; but the blue colour is the most rare and most valuable, since there has very seldom been found a diamond of any size of a fine deep sapphire blue, those which are termed blue diamonds being generally of a very light or of a steel-blue colour; it would, therefore, be a difficult task to form a just estimate of the value of this unrivalled gem, there being no precedent, the value cannot be established by comparison. The price which was once asked for this diamond was 30,000 *l*. but we must confess, for the above-stated reasons, that it might have been estimated even at a higher sum. To convey to the reader by a description of the beauty and splendour of this unique production of nature would be a vain attempt.

This beautiful gem is most tastefully mounted as a medallion . . . [a detailed description of the brooch setting follows].

Philip's spectacles slid down his nose as he read these words over and over that autumn, while a few dead leaves fell in slow spirals in Hyde Park, and twilight came too soon. When, one cold day, Philip fell ill, Louisa came for him in her carriage, bundled him into rugs and shawls, and carried him off to the care and comfort of Bedgebury Park.

There he died as he had lived, without fuss or fanfare, on December 5, 1839, age sixty-five, less than four months after he'd given his Diamond its own glowing, heartfelt epitaph. The *Gentleman's Magazine* noted in its obituary that Henry Philip Hope, Esq., had formed "one of the most perfect collections of diamonds and precious stones that has, perhaps, been ever possessed by a private individual." "Although [he was] possessed of an ample fortune," the obituary states, "his habits were of the most simple and unostentatious nature; he seemed to regard wealth only as the means of doing good," for not only was he "a principal contributor to all the public charities of the metropolis," but he "distributed annually in private charity many thousands."

In 1925 the granddaughter of Philip's nephew Alexander would write this concerning the Hope Diamond, "Much has been written of the ill-luck that is supposed to attend the possession of this stone, but there is no family evidence that Henry Philip believed or had even heard of the legend, and he certainly lived a peaceful and prosperous life and died a quiet and natural death." Philip neither believed in the "curse" nor had heard of it, because, as we shall discover in a later chapter, the modern world's version of it had not yet been invented.

On December 14, with an icy wind making a clatter in rhododendron leaves, Philip was laid to rest next to beloved brother Tom in the mausoleum at Deepdene. (Even here he eludes us, for although the mausoleum survived, it was sealed up for all time in 1957.) As the coffin slid into its niche, Louisa sobbed with little hiccups, leaning heavily on Lord William's strong arm, while her three sons, Henry, Adrian, and Alexander, shifted from foot to foot, wondering how much money Uncle Philip had left them and who would get the valuable gem collection and the Diamond.

The stone's rare, romantic pastoral interlude was over, finished, and the more usual mercenary subtext of its existence, initiated 179 years earlier by Tavernier, was about to explode onto the velvet lawns of English country life.

Like most offspring of the rich, who are given everything except the one essential—the drive and passion that generated all that wealth in the first place—Henry, Adrian, and Alexander were quite ordinary, mediocre young men. Nor did they feel for each other the strong bonds of affection that had existed between their father and uncle. They would also prove unfeeling toward their mother. Henry, age thirty-one, had very small eyes that, combined with very bushy eyebrows, gave him the look of some fierce little creature furtively peering out from beneath an overgrown hedgerow. He inherited, alas, his father's body and his mother's brain rather than the reverse, for already when he was thirteen, Maria Edgeworth was calling him "ugly" and "as much a simple good boy as if he had never been to Eton." His father regretted that Henry, at seventeen, was "not more desirous of distinction." He spent one year at Trinity College, Cambridge, before beginning a desultory, undistinguished parliamentary career. From 1829 to 1832 he represented East Looe, a rotten borough his father bought for him, then from 1833 to 1841 and 1847 to 1852 stood for Gloucester. When he joined the Young Tories, the group clustered around the future Prime Minister Benjamin Disraeli, who would become a friend, Disraeli noted Henry's "inflexible will," and that "suspicion embittered his life. It was his sovereign malady. He was an immensely wealthy man, and given his ugliness, he could never believe, and usually with justification, that people loved him for himself alone and not for what they could get from him." Henry was still unmarried in 1839, as he paid his last respects to Uncle Philip, and would remain so for another twelve years. As eldest brother, he felt that the Diamond should, without question, come to him.

Adrian at twenty-eight had no interest in politics or in anything else except food. At age eleven, he'd consumed on Good Friday, as he reported, "eight [hot-] cross buns and was very near losing my dinner." After Eton, he went off to the University of Bonn, and commented en route that he much preferred a good dinner to looking at ruins. He joined the 4th Dragoon Guards as captain but soon resigned his commission; perhaps the mess table wasn't up to his standard. Three years before his uncle Philip's death, Adrian chose, as one could have predicted, a bride from the land of hautest cuisine, Emily Matilda Rapp, whose father, Jean, one of Napoleon's generals, had been made Count of Rapp in 1809. Adrian and his French wife settled into a Paris abode on the Quai d'Orsai and to generous twice-daily helpings of *foie gras*, but the marriage was not a success, and after much bitter litigation, they would finally part for good in 1854. As for the Diamond, mused Adrian, as he shifted his corpulence from foot to foot inside the Deepdene mausoleum as Uncle Philip slid out of sight, it wasn't something a chap could salivate over. But it could be sold soon enough and thus converted into so many tons of caviar of the best Beluga sort.

Alexander, age nineteen, was his mother's favorite. Tutored first at home, he'd finally gone to Harrow and Trinity College, Cambridge, where he walked off with several Latin prizes, and his mother was convinced that he was, without question, the cleverest young man in the

British Empire. Two years later, he'd become a Tory member for Maidstone, a town close enough to Bedgebury that he could go on living there with Louisa to indulge him. Disraeli, at least, had no illusions, and had the pleasure, at a sitting of the House, of watching "the great Mr. Alexander Beresford Hope make a great fool of himself. I never knew such an imbecile," Dizzy told his wife with obvious glee, "no voice and the manner and appearance of a cretin." When Maria Edgeworth, then seventy-six, with a black wig under her lace cap, dined off a gold plate at Bedgebury in 1843, she was disenchanted with the Hope family once and for all, finding Alexander "uglier than sin" and Louisa "grown fat and flaccid in mind and body. There never was much in there and now there's nothing." Alexander would, on July 7, 1842, be married to Lady Mildred Cecil, elder daughter of the Marquess of Salisbury, in the private chapel of her family's great house, Hatfield, by the Primate of Ireland, much the handsomest man there, who was always known as "The Beauty of Holiness." Lady Mildred's grandmother had been consumed in a Hatfield fire so hot that it burned the entire west wing to cinders, melted the pearls around her neck and the gold around her fingers, so that nothing remained of old Lady Salisbury but one tiny heap of ashes and one enormous diamond. Alexander grew pasty and sedentary as he aged until he resembled a suet pudding. "Doing the polite to the queen is a great bore," he sighed from Hatfield, and once fell asleep in Her Majesty's presence, leaning against a cabinet. Queen Victoria wouldn't let him be wakened, for fear he should break the china it contained. "Religion was his absorbing interest," according to his granddaughter, the "be-all and end-all of his life." He wrote hymn verses that didn't rhyme and long-winded tomes with such arresting titles as *Two Years of Church Progress* and *The Social Influence of the Prayer Book*. He even dared to publish two novels, the second one greeted by a most unfeeling review that stated that it was "even duller than its predecessor, which seemed to realize a rounded ideal of dullness." When his stepfather Lord William Beresford died in 1854, Alexander received £30,000 and Bedgebury, with the stipulation that he add another Beresford to his name, so he became Alexander James Beresford Beresford-Hope, ever after sounding like a comic character from a Gilbert and Sullivan opera. Like Adrian, Alexander planned to convert the Diamond, should it become his, into cash to be spent on some church scheme that the Almighty would approve of.

Philip's will was duly unsealed and read. Each nephew got £30,000. Henry got his uncle's extensive library; Adrian got the Dutch estate of Bosbeck; Alexander got Arklow House in Connaught Place. That seemed straightforward enough. But the gems and the Hope Diamond were not mentioned in the will and were up for grabs. The battle lines were drawn. Whereas the preoccupation of their father and uncle had been beauty, Henry's was Henry; Adrian's was his next delicious meal, and Alexander's was God. The prospects for the Hope Diamond, after halcyon years of truly belonging, were grim indeed.

Disraeli summed up the War of the Diamonds thus: "The three brothers Hope, though the wealth of the whole family had become concentrated in them, were always at war. There were some famous jewels, which had belonged to their uncle Philip Hope, which were a fruitful subject of litigation. There was a blue diamond that all the brothers wanted. They hated each other."

The feud began when three deeds came to light among Philip's papers. The first of these, dated May 19, 1821, gave the gem collection to a nephew whom, unfortunately, Philip forgot to name but whom Henry, as eldest, insisted could only be himself and no other. But deeds dated 1832 and 1838 left the gems to Alexander. Oh, what a hornet's nest of litigation and acrimony followed! Notaries' acts, stamped papers, angry personal letters, thinly veiled insults, outright accusations, cries of innocence outraged, pride insulted, an uncle's memory besmirched! The three main points of dispute centered on who was entitled to the gems, especially the Hope Diamond; whether a will filed in Holland by which Bosbeck was left to some Dutch relatives was revoked by a later English will leaving it to Adrian; and whether Louisa's sons could compel her to return to them the £37,000 that Philip had given her in his lifetime. Lawsuits dragged on for ten long years while lawyers grew rich, transcripts swelled to 250 dense folio pages, and the Diamond languished in a bank vault.

Henry and Adrian were so intent on keeping the jewels out of

Alexander's clutches that they even suggested selling the lot and using the money to found "some institution for the benefit of mankind." Alexander replied that since it was his "invariable rule" to carry out his most beloved uncle's requests to the absolute letter, he would therefore renounce all claims to Bosbeck and take the gems instead. Henry shot back that Alexander's great generosity of spirit would thereupon result in his renouncing foreign property worth £2,000 and gaining jewels worth £150,000, concluding that his brother's "means of observation have been more than commonly circumscribed." Louisa then joined the fray, firing off a letter of thirty-four salvos, the thirty-fourth of which assured Henry that not only were Alexander's means of observation *not* circumscribed but that he was "particularly well-informed for his age." In a later letter, Louisa wrote tearfully, "The unfortunate mother who pens this is obliged to declare that her two elder sons have been remarkable for nothing but the illiberality of their proceedings since the death of their uncle and benefactor."

In the end a compromise was reached whereby Henry got eight of the principal gems, including the Diamond, while Alexander got the famous Hope pearl, two inches long and four and a half around, plus seven hundred smaller stones; Adrian got Bosbeck, on making provision for the Dutch relatives, and Louisa retained her £37,000 absolutely.

Of course, Henry couldn't wear a woman's brooch with a great useless Diamond the size of a plum on his finely tailored worsteds, but at least he'd made his brothers fume. He might well let his lady love wear it, if she behaved herself. Unwilling to accommodate himself to the demands of wife and menagerie of screaming children, Henry had indulged himself instead with a very pretty French mistress whom he could visit in Paris when he felt the urge and leave when he didn't. Her name was Anne Adèle Bichat, and she'd cunningly secured his continued support by presenting him with a daughter, christened Henrietta Adela, born around 1840. (Since she was illegitimate, her exact birthdate was never revealed.) She grew to be as pretty as her mother, thank God, and didn't look like a Hope. Henry was too busy in England to see her often, turning Deepdene into what Disraeli called on an autumn visit there "a perfect Italian palace, full of balconies adorned with busts." Dizzy's political novel *Coningsby* (1844) was "conceived and partly executed amid the glades and galleries of Deepdene." Being of such a suspicious nature himself, Henry, in a letter to friend Dizzy of May 18, 1844, applauded the book's "terrible power of wit and sarcasm" and "the spirit of daring" in "attacking people who have always been deemed bugbears."

When Louisa died at Bedgebury on July 21, 1851, having grown, under son Alexander's influence, ever more pious, her last exhortation to her husband, Lord William, distraught at her bedside, was "for the rest of his days to care for nothing but his soul, and to relieve distressed persons." When she died Henry got the Anastasian pearls, which he lent to Anne Adèle, with many provisos, and since his mother was no longer alive to disapprove, he at long last married Adèle and legitimized his daughter, who had already reached the age of ten or more.

Once he'd buried his mother, Henry swung into action. He brought his new bride and daughter across the channel to London, demolished the Duchess Street temple of art carefully created by his father, having already sold off most of its collection of antique vases, built himself a new house at 116 Piccadilly, at the corner of Down Street, just east of Park Lane, to designs by the French architect P. C. Dusillion, with lavish decorative detailing, all done by French craftsmen, costing £18,000. Here Adèle and little Henrietta happily installed themselves, while the latter's governess took her for daily walks in Green Park.

Henry was very busy doing his civic duty, feeling himself to be at the very hub of power, helping to plan London's Great Exhibition of 1851, acting as deputy chairman of Jury Number 23, shouldering the task of including—or better yet, excluding—objects to be exhibited in Section 23: "Work in Precious Metals and Jewelry."

The idea for the Great Exhibition came from Queen Victoria's beloved consort, Prince Albert, and between September 1850 and January 1851 an awesome structure, the Crystal Palace, rose in Hyde Park, its cast-iron girders and 900,000 square feet of glass erected by twenty-one hundred workmen.

On the cloudy morning of May 1, 1851, twenty-five thousand members of the public who had purchased season tickets (three guineas for gentlemen, but only two for ladies, although their wide, bell-shaped skirts took up far more room) entered from 9 to 11 A.M. and were marshaled behind barriers. Then a discharge of artillery signaled that the Royal Party was approaching across the park. At noon, just as they were entering the building, the sun broke through, and four hundred tons of glass overhead turned into one huge, sparkling diamond.

The thirty-two-year-old queen, only five feet tall, with Prince Albert beside her in field marshal's uniform and about fifty assorted Royals and committee members, including Henry Hope, gimlet-eyed as ever, progressed slowly to the north end of the main floor and mounted a platform. The queen wore pink satin embroidered in gold. At this point in her reign, she filled in low necklines with necklaces of old rose-cut diamonds. In private, she favored such sentimental jewelry as a bracelet set with the first teeth of her children and lockets containing a beloved's hair. Prince Albert spoke first; the Archbishop of Canterbury prayed; a choir belted out Handel's Hallelujah Chorus and the National Anthem; the Marquess of Breadalbane announced that the queen (who, being female, was not expected to speak) declared the exhibition open; barriers were removed and the public rushed in to admire exhibits spread over sixteen acres and two floors, more than half from foreign countries and the rest from the very flourishing British Empire.

The Great Exhibition of the Works of Industry of All Nations, to give it its official title, included machinery, scientific and musical instruments, weapons, raw and processed materials of all kinds, engineering models, every known craft including embroidery, waxwork, shellwork, mosaics, enamels, and jewelry, all of it, since Victorians had very orderly, tidy minds, divided into categories, subcategories, and subsub. After the twenty-second day, admission shrank to one shilling and everyone in Britain, not to mention fifty-eight thousand foreigners, flocked to see the marvels, to buy the one shilling catalog, and partake of sandwiches, jellies, ices, tea, coffee, ginger beer, savory pies for six-pence, and boxed ginger, all provided by Messrs. Schweppe, who got the refreshment contract.

Henry came often with wife or friends but never both at once, and little Henrietta came with her governess, since it was all so educational. Henry always made his way first to the southwest side of the second-floor gallery, to Class 23 of the British Division: Working in Precious Metals and Their Imitations; Jewelry and All Articles of Virtu and Luxury Not Included in the Other Juries, subdivided into ten sections of which number 1 was "Communion Service" and Number 10 was "Articles of Use or Curiosity Not Included in the Previous Enumeration." Section number 7 was Jewelry and there, lying on a satin surround under a sheet of glass, was the Hope Diamond brooch, graciously lent to Section 23 by its generous deputy chairman and cavalier owner—who perhaps was hoping someone would steal it so he could collect the insurance.

Between May 1 and October 18, when the exhibition closed, more than twelve million staring eyes and six million awestruck faces filed slowly past the Diamond. Given its mystique, its subtle and symbolic emanations, it was not at home in such pigeonholed precision. But the Great Exhibition, in turn, served as rehearsal and foretaste of a much later, and much longer, public exposure.

In a nearby case was another famous diamond with which the Hope had to share the limelight, a much bigger one, a brute of 186 carats, the famous Kohinoor, the British Empire's sun that would never set, presented to Queen Victoria only the year before. After Britain had squashed the rebelling Sikhs in India's Punjab, on March 29, 1849, Maharaja Dulip Singh, age twelve, sat on the golden throne of his father, mighty Ranjit Singh who'd wrested the Kohinoor from the Moguls, and signed away his kingdom. The British grabbed not only the stone but the golden throne, too (today in London's Victoria and Albert Museum). The diamond was entrusted to John Lawrence, Britain's top man in the Punjab, who absently put it in his waistcoat pocket. When Lord Dalhousie, India's governor general, decided to take it himself from Lahore to Bombay, Lawrence couldn't find it until a servant noticed it next to his bathroom shaving mirror. Dalhousie then had the gem double-sewn into a belt fastened to a chain around his neck. At Bombay, it waited two months for a ship, sailed to England in a dispatch box guarded around the clock by two officers, and was presented to Queen Victoria at a June 3 reception marking the 250th anniversary of the founding of the British East India Company.

After its very hectic summer under the crystal dome, the Hope Diamond was returned to a bank vault to rest in the dark, and the Kohinoor went off to London's Garrard and Company to be recut. On the afternoon of Friday, July 17, 1852, the Duke of Wellington rode up on his favorite gray charger to Garrard's shop in Panton Street, off the Haymarket, to watch the first cleaving. The cutting took thirty-eight days, and the stone lost almost 43 percent of its weight, emerging as an oval brilliant of 108.93 metric carats.

Having done his civic duty, Henry decided to indulge himself by buying a country estate in Ireland where he and Adèle—and, of course, his little namesake, Henrietta—could go when the spirit moved him to live a freer, less scrutinized life. He bought a twelve-hundred-acre domain called Castle Blayney in County Monaghan, remodeled its Georgian house, stuck his coat of arms on the garden-front pediment, encouraged the Castle Blayney villagers to call it Hope Castle rather than Blayney, and hunted snipe in his bogs, where he always waited until he saw the white of their breasts before he fired.

Four years later the Diamond did go home again—not to India but to France. It was packed off to the Paris Exposition Universelle, held from May to November, with industrial exhibits in a building in the Champs-Élysées and artistic ones nearby in Avenue Montaigne. Emperor Napoleon III and Empress Eugénie opened the exposition on May 15. She was a beautiful Spanish count's daughter, with auburn hair and magnolia skin, who'd married France's emperor two years before. As with Thomas Hope and Louisa, it was a case of "Beauty and the Beast," for Napoleon III had tobacco-stained teeth, very short bow legs, a spreading paunch, and a halting gait that always looked as if he had one foot in a ditch. Eugénie loved diamonds, was enchanted with the Hope set in its medallion brooch, and persuaded her husband to have a copy made, which has since disappeared.

For the Diamond, the Paris exposition, coming so soon after the British show, was a bit déjà vu, as ten million staring eyes and five million awestruck faces (one million less than in London) filed slowly past. Instead of the Kohinoor, rivals were old-time contenders from Garde-meuble days, the Regent and the Sancy. They were some distance away, the Hope being part of the British exhibit and the other stunners part of the display of French imperial jewels.

Six years later, on February 11, 1861, another event occurred in Paris that the Diamond may or may not have been witness to. At the British embassy, at a very small but suitably elegant ceremony, Henry Hope, with his wife, Adèle, beaming beside him, gave his pretty daughter in marriage to the Earl of Lincoln, heir to a British dukedom, son of the 5th Duke of Newcastle. Both Adèle and Henrietta wore expensive Paris couture, but whether Adèle also wore the Diamond, or whether for the bride it was the "something borrowed, something blue," we do not know. Given his daughter's stain of illegitimacy, it looked on the surface as if Henry Hope's millions had enabled him to buy his daughter a real prize, since dukes stood at the very pinnacle of British peerage, right below the royal princes, and above all such lesser nobles as mere marquesses, earls, viscounts, barons, and knights. Only twenty-seven dukes in the entire kingdom, exulted Henry, as he stood very straight in morning coat and striped trousers. Someday, soon he hoped, for he'd heard rumours that the 5th Duke's health was failing, he'd be father-in-law to a duke, father to a duchess; he'd have not just money but a higher social status, too, in a society where peers were at the top.

The dazzle of very old heirloom diamonds and lineage, however, can blind one to a number of serious flaws, and this noble family had plenty. At Henrietta's side, swearing in suitably solemn tones "with all my worldly goods I thee endow," stood twenty-seven-year-old Henry Pelham Alexander Pelham-Clinton, always known to family and friends as "Linky." Born January 25, 1834, educated at Eton and Christ Church, Oxford, declared "very worthless" by Queen Victoria, notorious for huge horseracing debts, he was a man who "could not show his face but for his marriage," as Lady Londonderry would soon note, "and has not one sixpence but Mr. Hope's money."

By the summer of 1860 Linky had run up racing debts of £230,000 and fled England after paying only £28,000, unable to meet the rest. He met Henrietta in Naples, heard rumors that she'd someday have £50,000 a year, and went straight to Henry Hope to ask for her hand in marriage. After a few seconds dwelling on her loveliness and his smitten heart, Linky asked Mr. Hope bluntly what it was worth to him to have his daughter become a duchess. Henry agreed to pay all the earl's present debts, to give him £35,000 cash as well, to provide the couple with £12,000 a year now with "four times as much to follow" annually after Henry died.

Linky's father, the 5th Duke of Newcastle, a dour man with no sense of humor and a permanent black cloud over his head, causing Queen Victoria to comment, "Trials like the duke's seldom fall to the lot of man!," was not present that February day at the Paris wedding of his no-good firstborn to the born-out-of-wedlock daughter of a commoner and his French trollop. The duke, in fact, hadn't spoken to Linky for two years.

Linky's mother, Suzie, however, was there and had encouraged the marriage. She was the unstable, half-mad, opium-addicted granddaughter of eccentric William Beckford of Fonthill Abbey, whose daughter had in 1805 refused the hand of Thomas Hope. Suzie had married Linky's father in 1834, fled from husband and offspring to the Isle of Wight in 1848, and been divorced by the 5th Duke in 1850. At the same time that Linky, fleeing his English creditors, turned up in Naples and found solvency through Henrietta, his mother, also in Naples, married her Belgian travel guide, Jean Alexis Opdebeck.

Linky's sister, Susan, as unstable as their mother, and so addicted to opium that she "hardly knows what she does or says," was also at the wedding. One year before, on April 23, 1860, Susan had left her father's house in Portman Square, driven in a cab paid for with borrowed coins to St. Mary's Church, and secretly married Lord Adolphus Vane-

Tempest ("Dolly" to his intimates), favorite spoiled son of Frances Anne, second wife of the Marquess of Londonderry. Dolly was a complete rogue who had gambled away all his money and was currently going insane, probably from tertiary syphilis. Only Susan's brother Linky and one other person witnessed that marriage, and the poor 5th Duke, her father, had one more reason to hold his head in his hands and moan. As she watched her brother joined to Henrietta Hope, Susan was holding tightly on to Dolly's arm so that she could remain upright and unswaying until the ceremony ended.

The last member of the Newcastle clan present on the day that would disastrously affect both the Hope family and their famous Diamond was Linky and Susan's brother Arthur, in a wasp-waisted frock coat, huge boutonnière, and cloud of cologne. Arty was a secret transvestite who wrote, as Linky complained, on "mauve scented paper" and ran up bills "of 130 francs to a coiffeur!" Later, Arty would be charged in a murky case of "Men in Women's Attire" at London's Central Criminal Court.

Of course, on that ominous February day in 1861 when Henry Hope stood smiling proudly, he didn't know the unsavory background of the family that he couldn't wait to ally himself to. He saw only the strawberry leaves on the ducal coronet, the ermine on the ducal robes, heard only the golden tones of "your daughter, the duchess." He wasn't far enough down history's road to perceive, as we can, that by mid-Victorian years, the British peerage was suffering the same fate as some thoroughbred dogs: too much inbreeding was leading to some weird results.

On the evening of the wedding, Henry and Adèle celebrated their *coup* by giving a dinner for the nuptial party, and Henry got the first hint of what was in store for him. The groom's sister, Susan, had hysterics and her husband, Lord Adolphus, got roaring drunk and had to be escorted back to their hotel. Somehow he got out again, staggered into various low dives, and ended up at the Café Anglais, where he hit a French gentleman and an American one, both of whom behaved impeccably and merely handed him over to the police. At some ungodly

hour, when he was snug and smug in his bed, Henry was rudely wakened by the déclassé duchess, Suzie Opdebeck, and forced to go with
her to the police station to get Lord Adolphus released. Dolly's antics
were repeated on the following two nights, by the third of which it
took three men to control him, and even then he succeeded in breaking a bed.

Back in England Henry reluctantly paid all Linky's debts, made
him promise to stop betting, and in order to save on household costs,
made the newlyweds move into Henry's own Piccadilly and Deepdene
houses. In the following month, Henrietta met Linky's father, the formidable, unlucky 5th Duke of Newcastle for the first time, but he still
refused to see his son. She gradually won the duke over with her Gallic
charm, and in October that year the couple were invited to Clumber,
the Newcastle estate carved from Sherwood Forest, famous for its
beech woods and long avenue of limes, with a white eighteenth-
century house—said to have the finest marble hall in England—
showing itself upside-down in a two-hundred-acre lake. The highlight
of the October visit was a banquet in honor of twenty-year-old Edward,
Prince of Wales (later King Edward VII), and one wonders if Henrietta
was allowed by Papa to wear the Hope Diamond pinned to her décol-
leté. Perhaps she witnessed the funny scene recorded by another guest.
A mayor from a neighboring town mistook the ice placed on the
table—it had just come into fashion—for an entrée, got it onto his
plate, and was trying in vain to cut it when a servant mercifully
whisked it away.

Next summer Henry's blood pressure mounted as Linky handed
him a list of debts amounting to £3,000, "which he said he had *overlooked* after having sworn that he had given in everything," as Lord
Clarendon, who loved gossip, gleefully told the Duchess of Manchester. Just before Henrietta's marriage, her father had settled Castle
Blayney on her, worth £25,000 a year in rent-roll income, but he angrily tore up the agreement when he learned that Linky had broken his
promise not to gamble, returned to the racetrack, and was betting
heavily again.

Henry took to his bed at 116 Piccadilly, seriously ill, and society speculated wildly on who would inherit his vast wealth. "I have a suspicion," wrote Frances, Lady Waldegrave, longtime mistress of the 5th Duke of Newcastle, "that Mr. Hope will leave nearly the whole of his property to his widow; she is clever, he is devoted to her and [she] would like to improve her position in society and at the same time he is wary as to giving too much into Lincoln's foolish hands." Brothers Adrian and Alexander, one grown very portly and the other very pious, seemed to know that nothing would come to them, for neither came to their brother's bedside "though he was dying, and long dying," as Disraeli pointed out in critical tone. (Adrian himself would die a year later.)

Henry Hope expired, only fifty-four, at 8 A.M. on December 4, 1862, and as predicted by Lady Waldegrave, left £300,000 to Adèle, as well as a life interest in Deepdene and Castle Blayney. The Hope Diamond also became Adèle's. "The income left absolutely at the disposal of Mrs. Hope is nearer a hundred than 80,000 a year," scribbled Lord Clarendon to the Duchess of Manchester the instant he heard the news, "not a shilling to [the Earl of] Lincoln. Mr. Harris, the clergyman who managed Hope's affairs and is a great friend of Mrs. Hope's," continued his lordship, "is trying to make her do what is right, and I believe she has intimated that she will give them the house in Piccadilly and the wherewithal to live in it as it was time that her daughter took up a proper position in society. They say she [Mrs. Hope] is still wonderfully good-looking and is known to a good many people, most of whom will I daresay now come forward with the most *honourable* intentions."

Unfortunately Anne Adèle (née Bichat) Hope is even more of a shadowy owner of the Diamond than Philip Hope was. Since most extant English memoirs and correspondence of the time are scribbled by aristocrats, the only people with enough time on their hands to write them, and since Adèle, former mistress and foreigner as well, was always outside their tight circle, there is barely a mention of her. We can perhaps presume that because in mid-Victorian England jewels conferred status, she wore the famous blue gem and lived in hope of eventual acceptance.

Henrietta and Linky went to Clumber in August 1864, where she gave birth on September 28 to a son, destined to become the 7th Duke of Newcastle after his father's death. Linky's father, the 5th Duke, lay very ill at Clumber that autumn, with not only Henrietta and Linky at the bedside but also his daughter, Susan, whose husband, the mad Dolly, had died in June—but not before trying to kill her in a fit of dementia. At 6:25 P.M. on October 18, age fifty-three, the 5th Duke had his last piece of bad luck in the form of a massive stroke and died seven minutes later. The day of his funeral, October 27, brought, as one could have predicted, "a deluge of rain" as Linky, now 6th Duke, and Henrietta, now duchess, followed a coffin draped in crimson Genoa velvet to the family mausoleum and prepared to take up residence and responsibilities at Clumber.

While their circumstances changed, so, two years later, did the Hope brilliant's, in two ways, one direct and one peripheral. First, Henrietta's second son, Lord Henry Francis Hope Pelham-Clinton, was born on February 3, 1866—bad news for the Diamond, as we'll see in the next chapter. And later that year diamonds suddenly moved down-market. The output from both Indian and Brazilian mines had been small enough to keep prices so high that only the very rich could afford them. Then, on a December day in 1866, Erasmus Jacobs, a fifteen-year-old working on his father's farm in South Africa, picked up a pebble shining in the sun. It was a 21-carat diamond, and in the next ten years South Africa's new mines would yield more diamonds than the 16 million carats taken from Brazil's riverbeds in the previous 150. Twenty years after Jacob's find, South African mines would be disgorging 3 million carats annually, so many more people could afford to own at least one stone. The first mechanically made culet setting appeared in 1869, so both stone and setting cost less. Diamonds may have become common, but fortunately for the Hope, it was still a blue-blood aristocrat, at the very top of any gemologist's grading, kept there by its color.

Much to the chagrin of Henrietta and Adèle, Linky was declared bankrupt on February 11, 1870, but they succeeded in getting an annulment to the bankruptcy on the last day of January. His brother, Arthur, was arrested for debt but got himself into male attire long enough to marry a rich widow (who would divorce him seven years later). Linky died in a London hotel at 10 Park Place, St. James, of unknown causes, on February 22, 1879, age forty-five, and the title of duke, along with a mountain of debts, passed to his son, Henry Pelham Archibald Douglas Pelham-Clinton, only fourteen years old.

In the very next year, on April 7, 1880, having married for rank and lived to regret it, Henrietta married for love, a nobody called Thomas Theobald Hohler, son of the Reverend F. W. Hohler, rector of Winstone, Gloucester county.

We catch a glimpse of Henrietta three years later in a memoir by Walpurga, Lady Paget. She was "still a most attractive woman" and after the Duke of Newcastle died "hastened to rectify the only *faux pas* she ever was supposed to have made by marrying a handsome Mr. Hohler, chiefly known for his fine voice. This act of tender conscience was not forgiven her by a critical and heartless world, and she never quite settled down again into London society." Henrietta spent much time in Europe, where Emily, one of her three daughters, married Prince Alfonso Doria Pamphili, Duke d'Avigliano, in 1882 and moved among the first families of Europe. Henrietta left the Anglican faith and embraced the Roman Catholic Church.

Of Henrietta's two sons, the little 7th Duke of Newcastle seems to have had some physical deformity, so his mentor Prime Minister Gladstone calls him "weakly" in 1882, when he was seventeen and at Eton, and the next year, Gladstone's daughter Mary refers to him in her diary as "poor little fellow—such a mite with his wooden leg and large head—uncanny in look and manners." Henrietta's other son, Francis, worried her for different reasons, but his tragicomic tale belongs in the next chapter.

On March 31, 1884, Anne Adèle, twenty-year owner of the Hope Diamond, of Deepdene and Castle Blayney, died at her residence in

Belgrave Square. The obituary in the *Times* was extremely brief and chary of birthdates both for Mrs. Hope and her daughter Henrietta.

When Adèle's will was read, Henrietta's younger son, Lord Francis, then eighteen, found to his delight and surprise that his grandmother had left to his worthy self, not to his puny brother: a life interest in Deepdene in Surrey, with all its riches of goods and lands; a life interest in Castle Blayney in Ireland, where girls were apple-cheeked and shooting was capital; and certain heirlooms, including the spectacular, world-famous, bluer-than-blue Hope Diamond. The only catch was that he had to wait until he turned twenty-one to get his hands on all this property, and he also had to change his name to Hope. In another three years, when he reached his majority, he would be (raise the baton on Gilbert and Sullivan) the very rich Lord Henry Francis Hope Pelham-Clinton Hope.

Lord Francis waited impatiently for the blue stone resting in a London bank vault to become his. Every morning for three interminably long years, he smiled at his handsome young face in his shaving mirror. He had plans for that Diamond; he who would soon have a double-Hope name knew exactly what he was going to do with it.

Lord Francis Hope's madcap wife, May Yohe.

7

WANING HOPES

... whose large style / Agrees not with the leanness of his purse.
—WILLIAM SHAKESPEARE, *King Henry VI, Part II*, act 1, scene 1

Lord Francis Hope, twenty-seven years old, long-limbed and debonair, sauntered to the Lyric theater's best box, flipped up the tails of his exquisitely cut coat, bespoke from the best tailor, and sat down. He tossed his pearl gray top hat, his custom-made pearl gray gloves, onto the empty seat beside him, and nodded to some of his own set in neighboring boxes. In his buttonhole was the largest, freshest boutonnière anywhere in sight. Everything Lord Francis ate, drank, wore, owned, used, everything that was allowed inside the charmed circle of his presence, had to be the very best quality. The tradesmen who supplied it waited for years—or forever—to be paid. Lord Francis felt a keen sense of entitlement to all this swank. It was significant that planted squarely in the middle of that word *entitlement* was *title*. He was a lord, and someday, when his sickly elder brother died—an event bound to happen soon, Lord Francis always assured his moneylenders—he would be a rich duke. He belonged to the last generation of playboy peers who gambled heavily at their exclusive clubs, bet on the horses, caroused at home and abroad, using money that they neither possessed nor had earned. After World War I, steep succession duties and income tax would permanently shackle their self-centered largesse. In the Gay Nineties, however, Lord Francis and his fellow nobles truly felt lords of all they surveyed and entitled to as much of it as they chose to take—and hang the consequences.

Six years before, his lordship had helped himself, according to the terms of grandmother Adèle Hope's will, to Deepdene, Castle Blayney, two lesser estates, manifold art treasures and furnishings, and the Hope Diamond, when on April 7, 1887, having turned twenty-one the previous February, he had by Royal Licence added Hope to the end of his already long-winded name. He'd given a bang-up party for all the tenants at Castle Blayney, no expense spared, with roasted sides of beef, free-flowing ale and wine, and fireworks shooting their golden coins up into velvet black sky.

Now he noticed smugly, and congratulated himself, how quickly the theater was filling up. His mother, Henrietta, whose second husband, the straitlaced Thomas Theobald Hohler, had died one year before, in 1892, had declined Lord Francis's invitation to attend, saying that she was still in mourning, but he knew by the grim, thin-lipped set of her mouth that she disapproved of his theatrical ventures. Lately she'd become so enmeshed in Catholic ritual and charity that she might as well have been a nun. Where the Hope Diamond had sometimes glittered, she now wore nothing but a large, plain cross.

Lord Francis was in his element. He loved opening nights and was looking forward to the songs of the light opera's leading lady—well, perhaps *lady* wasn't quite the right word—to a tête-à-tête with her afterward, and to the final thunder of applause for a production that he'd generously underwritten (with borrowed money). In the fall of 1892 Lord Francis had given forty-year-old Horace Sedger, leesee and manager of the Lyric theater, £21,600 ($108,000) on the understanding (no contract, just a gentleman's handshake) that Lord Francis would get all the show's box-office profits until this amount had been repaid. After that he'd share the bounty equally with Sedger. His lordship prided himself on knowing a thing or two about theater, and he was quite sure that this show was bound for a very long run and very large profits. He adjusted his monocle, not yet paid for, and opened the thick, creamy program. On that evening of January 19, 1893, it stated,

Miss May Yohe was playing Martina in a brand-new light opera, *The Magic Opal*, with libretto by Arthur Law, music by Señor Albeniz (his first attempt at anything more ambitious than playing the piano), the whole directed by Sedger. Good old Hoary, clever as they come, wise in the ways of the world of greasepaint.

Sedger had first leased the Prince of Wales theater in 1886, and become partner with Henry Leslie in the hit comic opera *Dorothy*, which they'd transferred to the new Lyric two years later, having used the £100,000 profit they'd cleared on *Dorothy* to build it. The Lyric's Renaissance-style red brick and Portland stone had gone up in only ten months, on empty Shaftesbury Avenue, where the only other theater, the Shaftesbury, had opened four months before. The Lyric had 944 seats, a proscenium framed in brown and white alabaster, and stalls and pit lined with walnut and sycamore paneling, all very grand. Its central chandelier featured an "inverted bouquet of corn, barley and poppies in prodigal profusion," according to *Theatre* magazine for February 1889. Beneath this harvest plenty, patrons of stalls and boxes were hurrying into their seats, the ladies sparkling with diamonds everywhere on their décolletages, already overladen with draped chiffon, beading, ribbon rosettes, and lace medallions.

Lord Francis leaned forward eagerly as the curtain rose, and soon Miss Yohe made her entrance to a mere flutter of applause, most of it coming from his lordship's box, for he'd already seen her triumph on America's stage. London didn't yet know her; this was her debut—but just wait. Audiences were going to love her. In another three years, George Bernard Shaw in a review would commend May's "personal charm and gay grace of movement, with the suggestion of suppressed wildness beneath." Lord Francis was a conventional, reserved, rather shy upper-class Englishman. It was May's "suppressed wildness" that drew him.

Miss Yohe pranced about the stage, with just a hint of panther, as the plot, as silly as that of most light operas, unfolded. A spinster, bent on marrying the chief of a band of brigands, steals a magic opal ring from the mayor of a Greek town. Whoever wears this jewel can win their chosen lover. It does seem paradoxical that the new owner of the Hope Diamond, currently being ignored and neglected in the dark confines of a safe-deposit box in Parr's bank in Cavendish Square, had invested money in a light opera centered on a gem with supernatural powers, for Lord Francis put no stock in such nonsense. As far as he was concerned, jewels were good for only one thing—no, make that two. To light up a lady love's eyes when you presented them to her; and, if they were as valuable as the Hope, to be converted into cash, the sooner the better. The trouble with that damn Diamond was that it was entailed; he had only a life interest and was expected to pass it on once he died to his heir, along with the other treasures his grand-mother had left him. If he died without a son, the Hope would go to Beatrice, eldest of his three sisters and thence to her eldest son; if she died without issue, it would pass to Emily and her sons; and so on to Florence, his youngest sister, with an ultimate remainder in fee to his brother the duke. What possible use to him, Lord Francis often asked himself, was a bloody great blue stone stuck away in a vault waiting for him to die? There had to be a way around the entail. Great-Uncle Alexander's offspring had been lucky. The instant he'd died at Bedge-bury in October 1887, they'd taken the huge pearl and the other seven hundred gems he'd gotten from Philip Hope's collection and sold them forthwith. (All those dearly beloved fancies are now scattered around the world. Some were bought for American collectors by Dr. George Kunz, who'd found Françillon's crucial 1812 memo and drawing. Some found a home in London's Victoria and Albert Museum, and the great Hope pearl will surface briefly in our next chapter.)

As the second act began, Lord Francis reached for his mother-of-pearl opera glasses, not yet paid for, and focused them on Miss Yohe's bosom, rising and falling as she belted out another song in a rich con-tralto voice, whose four justly famous low notes made him positively mad with desire.

Born in Bethlehem, Pennsylvania, on April 6, 1869, Mary Au-gusta Yohe was the daughter of a saloon keeper of Dutch ancestry and a seamstress, whose family tree included a Narraganset native Indian. Little Mary Augusta began performing onstage at age ten and never looked back. Later, Bethlehem's miners were so impressed by her singing and acting that they took up a subscription to send her to Paris for operatic training. But the first thing she did when she returned to America was to join a Pittsburgh burlesque show as a chorus girl. Soon, however, she moved up-market to opera and made her debut at Philadelphia's Temple theater. May Yohe, as she billed herself, had real star quality and triumphed at the Chicago Opera House in 1887 in *The Crystal Slipper*. One evening, just as the curtain was about to rise, the manager, David Henderson, grew apoplectic when he discovered that May was nowhere to be found; she'd run off to Buffalo with Ely B. Shaw, son of a wealthy Chicagoan—*and* a married man. "Madcap May," as she soon became known, was always a creature of impulse, ruled by her emotions, blindly optimistic, making grand, romantic gestures, ignoring responsibility and reality. She eventually returned to Chicago and got back into *The Crystal Slipper* but only after a deluge of telegrams from Henderson, which escalated from polite pleading to dire threats. May went on to many more rash liaisons with rich men who filled her head with promises and, occasionally, her jewelbox with gems.

She made her New York debut, fittingly, on May 1, 1888, in a farcical comedy called *Natural Gas* and followed that with another, *Hoss and Hoss*, which ran for a year beginning in November 1890.

May met Lord Francis Hope in New York, at a dinner party at Delmonico's in November 1892, after which they both went on to the Horse Show at Madison Square Garden, always a brilliant social event. She thought Mr. Hope—she didn't know then that he was a lord—extremely charming, well-informed, and courteous.

By the time he'd persuaded her to leave New York and try her luck with *The Magic Opal* in London, May was far gone in fantasy, fed over the years on trashy novels and silly opera plots, in which beautiful young women—and she knew she was lovely—captured rich husbands and lifelong rainbows. May, however, was not totally a misty-eyed romantic. There was quite a lot of the 1890s "New Woman"—so called by the first wave of British and American feminists—in Madcap May, who was independent and career driven. There was even more in her of a twentieth-century female who knows exactly how to work the media to advance her career. It would be this very modern May who would, more than anyone who ever came close to it, profoundly and permanently affect the destiny of the Hope Diamond. However, as she sang that night on the Lyric stage about the powers of a magical gem, May, at twenty-three, was still more dreaming than scheming, and it would be another twenty-eight years before she would debase the Diamond.

She really was amazing; never mind opals, it was darling May who possessed magic! Lord Francis smiled into the darkness as the final curtain dropped and librettist, composer, and good old Hoary joined the cast for curtain calls. Lord Francis clapped and clapped; he'd make thousands from this show! Then he picked up his pearl gray topper, his pearl gray gloves, and strolled around the corner to the stage-door entrance in Great Windmill Street to claim May, where the doorman recognized him at once, touched his cap, and let him in. Lord Francis beamed down at him; he'd buy May whatever her little heart desired, perhaps take her on a trip around the world.

Reviews the next morning were less than enthusiastic. Miss Yohe, whose voice resonated to the back of any theater, which soon earned her the English sobriquet "the girl with the foghorn voice," had, according to the *Times* reviewer, sung "with more emphasis than beauty of tone." *The Magic Opal* closed on April 3, after only a month and a half, and his lordship lost a lot of money.

By June he was desperate for funds. Even though his estates produced an income of £16,000 ($80,000) a year, it was never enough, never as big as his sense of entitlement. As Lord Francis drank his hundred-year-old brandy one night at Deepdene, he squinted at the Dutch and Flemish masterpieces on its walls, in which he had only a life interest, the paintings Philip Hope had lent to brother Thomas for the Duchess Street gallery and that Thomas's son Henry, after he'd demolished that house, had hung at Deepdene. Now what might they be worth, Lord Francis wondered, swirling his brandy in its antique crystal glass. That same month he petitioned the court for permission to sell

them, but his brother, the duke, and his three sisters protested vehe-
mently, since these valuable paintings might someday come to them,
and the petition was denied.

Financially, it was May who was prospering. She'd starred in *Mademoiselle Nitouche* from May 6 to August 18 at the Trafalgar Square theater, and then opened, on October 10, at the Lyric, in *Little Christopher
Columbus*, whose plot, involving a cabin boy who turns out to be heir
to a dukedom "only serves the purpose," as the London *Times* noted,
"of presenting Miss May Yohe in a variety of costumes." When she
sang "What Can a Poor Girl Do?" and "Honey, Mah Honey," the audience went wild, so the show ran for more than a year while Horace
Sedger, but not the real heir to a dukedom, got rich on the profits.

It was still running, and Lord Francis was still mad about May,
when, on September 29, 1893, his debts having grown to £405,277
($2,026,385), creditors presented their unpaid bills to London's High
Court of Justice, and bankruptcy proceedings began. And all the while
that great blue useless stone smirked in its safe-deposit box and Parr's
added their unpaid invoices for monthly rental to the ever-mounting
pile. His lordship was really beginning to hate that Diamond. Still,
May was a fine diversion from his financial woes. He might well take
the damn thing out of Parr's someday and let her wear it. After all, his
elder brother's wife was sporting some spectacular stones. Henry Pelham Archibald Douglas, 7th Duke of Newcastle, physically inferior
but master of Clumber and all its lucrative rent-rolls, had in 1889 married Kathleen Florence May, daughter of Maj. Henry Augustus Candy,
formerly of the 9th Lancers, and the Honorable Mrs. Candy, daughter
of 3rd Baron Rossmore. Kathleen habitually wore two anchor brooches
pavé-set with diamonds, originally given to France's Empress Eugénie
when she'd opened the Suez Canal in 1869, fourteen years after she'd
admired the Hope Diamond in the Paris Exposition Universelle and
had a copy made.

Lord Francis's mother, Henrietta, who approved of Kathleen and
her genteel origins, pursed her lips even harder when she heard Francis
had taken up with some vulgar Yankee actress and been hauled into

bankruptcy court. Henrietta, that same year, "took the Cross" of the new Crusade of the Catholic Social Union (later known as the Ladies of Charity of St. Vincent de Paul) and became head worker at the Girls' Club at Tower Hill Settlement. Two years later, according to Walpurga, Lady Paget, she'd moved into a modest house in Whitechapel, where "she lives with two other ladies" and is "completely given up to good works."

Meanwhile, the bankruptcy proceedings went on, with Lord Francis appealing, and losing, and lawyers representing him leaving the case as soon as they realized that they would never be paid, to be replaced by others more sanguine. Lord Francis moved into modest quarters at 161a Piccadilly and rented out Deepdene on a twenty-one-year-lease to Lily, widow of the 8th Duke of Marlborough, another dedicated spendthrift who'd indulged himself from her immense American fortune. In the following spring, Lily would marry yet another William Beresford in our story, this one brother of the 5th Marquess of Waterford and just back from many years of army service in India.

One day, according to May's account of the event (in a book we'll discuss later), Lord Francis turned up at her suburban dwelling just outside London, entered her memento-cluttered sitting room with his hat still on his head, and asked her to remove it. When she did so, she found a red leather case containing a pearl necklace worth £70,000 ($350,000). It is precisely at this point that we begin to grow skeptical of Madcap May's veracity. Where on earth would this bankrupt lord get money for such a gift? Moreover, she describes it as a perfectly matched string of all pear-shaped pearls, itself an impossibility.

In any case, May and Lord Francis began living together—she was gainfully employed in *The Lady Slavey* at the Avenue—and much to the disapproval of his family, with none of them present, he married her in the Hampstead Registry Office on November 27, 1894. According to one newspaper report, the Duke of Newcastle had offered his brother money not to be so foolish. While many young nobles of the time took actresses as mistresses, they were careful to wed blue-blooded ladies of their own class. To *marry* an actress simply wasn't done.

The new bride made her society debut at a London dinner party given shortly after the wedding by Lord Alfred Rothschild at his elegant house in Seamore Place. May contends that she wore the Hope Diamond that evening, one of only two occasions, according to her, when it escaped from Parr's bank to a little excitement. But Lord Francis, in a *New York Times* article dated February 5, 1911, declared, "I became the owner of the stone in 1887 and from that year until I sold it it was never worn by anyone." Whom are we to believe? If indeed the Diamond was imprisoned at Parr's nonstop for all the years of Lord Francis's ownership, with no chance to shine its light anywhere, it does seem a great waste of beauty and charisma.

It could have helped bolster May's ego that evening and fortified her for a painful entry into society. Rothschild's white drawing room was already full of guests when May and Lord Francis arrived. Their bachelor host, who welcomed them warmly, was blond, slender, with blue eyes and exquisite side whiskers, the first Jew to be appointed a director of the Bank of England; this financial distinction may explain part of his appeal for Lord Francis. Like those earlier bankers, Thomas and Philip Hope, Rothschild was a keen patron of art. Unlike them, however, Lord Alfred did put in a daily appearance at the family banking firm—except on Fridays, when a bank employee turned up at Seamore Place with his weekend spending money, £1,000 in clean, crisp bills. Alfred acquired a French mistress, Marie, wife of a Mr. Wombwell, and produced an illegitimate daughter, Almina, whose wealth would persuade the Earl of Carnarvon to marry her. "A connoisseur in the art of living," Alfred placed a mink foot warmer in the auto he would acquire as soon as such appeared on the scene and was always followed by a second car and chauffeur in case the first one broke down. At his country house, Halton, he conducted his own orchestra with an ivory baton banded in diamonds. He loved the theater, took over the Gaiety when it got into trouble, and liked to arrange what he called "adoration dinners" for four or five gentleman friends and one beautiful actress.

A clandestine "adoration dinner" was one thing, but to boldly invite Lord Francis Hope's vulgar actress wife to Seamore Place was another! When May entered the drawing room, every lady present turned her back and kept it resolutely turned for the entire evening. They took their cue from Marie, daughter of Alexander II, Czar of Russia, wearing her spectacular Romanov diamonds, who'd married Queen Victoria's son Alfred, Duke of Edinburgh, now portly, middle-aged, short-tempered, long-winded, and chronically inebriated. Most of the other men present, taking an unspoken but understood directive from their wives, ignored May, too. But the highest-ranking noble there, His Royal Highness Edward, Prince of Wales, made a beeline for her, laughed uproariously at all her little jokes, and stayed faithfully by her side until the butler announced dinner. The prince's outsize head, ears, and nose inspired the populace to christen him "Spuds," while his aristocratic friends, eyeing his forty-eight-inch waist and chest, called him—behind his back, of course—"Tum-Tum." Prince Edward was fifty-three, and since his mother, Queen Victoria, gave him nothing to do in the way of ruling, he'd got very good at amusing himself while he waited for her to die so he could become King Edward VII. He spent time at the track with his racehorses; played endless games of bridge; tucked into gargantuan meals; escaped often to the raunchy delights of Paris, and bedded pretty women, especially actresses such as Lily Langtry and Sarah Bernhardt and American women who were already married and so considered fair game. "A few fair Stars and Stripes," he called them, who brought "a little fresh air into Society." Now here before him—what luck!—was an actress and American wife rolled into one delicious morsel!

After his guests had consumed dinner, during which host Alfred, who suffered from chronic indigestion, sat at the head of the table eating and drinking nothing, the ladies repaired to the drawing room, with May sitting silent in humiliating isolation from the group. But as soon as the gentlemen left their port and walnuts to rejoin them, Prince Edward eased his girth into a gilt chair next to May's and stayed for most of the evening, while the ladies seethed and Lord Francis beamed.

For the rest of her life, May would embroider that one evening into a tale whereby she and the prince became fast friends, meeting frequently and calling each other Maysie and Eddie. Like most of May's colorful creations, it is the embroidery around one thread of truth that gives her away. No one ever called Prince Albert Edward Eddie; he was Bertie to his family, Sir to close friends, and Your Highness to everyone else.

By early 1895, in spite of the fact that May claims in her memoir that her husband had an annual income of $600,000, Lord Francis's gross liabilities, as the bankruptcy court proceedings dragged on, had mounted to an astonishing £657,942 ($3,289,710), while his latest gullible lawyer, Mr. Burgin of Denton, Burgin, and Hall, assured the court that arrangements to satisfy his lordship's creditors were proceeding apace. "The debtor's failure," chided the Times on January 18, "would appear to be attributable to extravagance in living, combined with betting and gambling and with theatrical speculation."

His lordship's life interest in his four estates became vested in the prudent trusteeship of the Gresham Life Assurance Society who paid him only £2,000 ($10,000) a year, with the rest of the income held in trust until a "sinking" or residue fund of £210,000 had accumulated. Mr. Burgin soon yielded to Mr. Stewart Smith for the privilege of representing Lord Francis Hope. His mother in her little Whitechapel house, each morning when she opened the Times to "Sittings in Bankruptcy," read the latest humiliating chapter in the parable of an unpenitent prodigal son, while his wife appeared in Dandy Dick Whittington at the Avenue from March 2 to July 13, bringing home about £125 a week, which put food on the table and paid the Piccadilly rent. At the end of the year, on December 19, Lord Francis applied to bankruptcy court for an order of discharge but the official receiver opposed the application, owing to the "insufficiency of the assets to yield 10 shillings in the pound and on the further grounds that the debtor had contracted debts without having at the time any reasonable expectation of being able to pay them."

Not until May 1896 did creditors get their 10 shillings per pound. Since a pound equaled 20 shillings, this was half of what they were owed, and Lord Francis Hope, his bankruptcy finally discharged, found himself free to start piling up debts again. May opened on June 1 at the Royal Court theater in a revival of one of her earlier hits, *Mademoiselle Nitouche*, so desperate for more income than £125 a week that she herself produced it. It was panned by George Bernard Shaw in the *Saturday Review* on June 20, in words so ironic that she must have laughed bitterly when she read them. "I take it that Miss Yohe is not now living by her profession," wrote GBS. "She is, is she not, in an independent position, gained by an alliance with the British aristocracy," and should therefore conform by "plastering herself with diamonds and sitting in an opera-box like a wax figure in a jeweller's shop window. Miss Yohe's own extraordinary artificial contralto," he continued blithely, "had so little tone on the first night that it was largely mistaken for an attack of hoarseness." He noted that "her sustaining power seems gone; she breathes after every little phrase and cannot handle a melody in her old, broad, rich manner" and "will only waste her time and money if she turns back to cast-off favourites." May did indeed, whenever she looked at her slack-jawed husband lounging about with the *Racing Daily* in one limp hand, feel her "sustaining power" almost gone. She played *The Belle of Cairo* at the Royal Court from October to December that year, and Lord Francis went on nonchalantly betting and gambling.

He was delighted when, in July 1898, he finally received permission from the court and his siblings, with solicitors Farwell and Martinelli acting for him, to sell eighty-three of Philip Hope's Dutch and Flemish paintings for £121,500 to the art dealer Asher Wertheimer. This would generate an additional income of £3,000 per annum, which would go not to Lord Francis but straight into the sinking fund, less £600 a year with which he'd bribed his sister Beatrice in order to get her consent to the sale, and which would go "toward the education and maintenance" of her six-year-old son. Beatrice had married Cecil Lister-Kaye, brother and heir presumptive of Sir John Lister-Kaye, who had replenished the empty family coffers by marrying a very rich American, Natica Yznaga. The fortune of her sister Consuelo, in turn, had been quickly consumed by the gambling, betting, playboy 8th Duke of Manchester.

Once the paintings went, the handwriting was on the wall; the Diamond's days with this less-than-devoted owner were numbered. As it languished in a subterranean bank vault, it seemed an eternity since Philip Hope had lavished endless care and concern on it. Less than a year later, on Tuesday, May 16, 1899, Lord Francis ambled into the Chancery Division of the High Court of Justice, accompanied by his clever and still faithful counsel, Farwell and Martinelli. Beatrice, gloved and tight-lipped, was already there, sitting next to her barristers, Mulligan and Terrell. Her ladyship was wearing a most intimidating hat, both high crowned and far-reaching. Skewered at an unnatural angle at the front was an entire bird, with beady eyes and sharpened beak. She avoided catching her brother's eye. His other sisters, Emily, Princess d'Avigliano, who had one son of fifteen, and Florence, still unmarried, weren't present. The Duke of Newcastle may or may not have been, but Mr. Benn, his barrister, was there. According to legal jargon, Beatrice, Emily, Florence, and the duke were the "remaindermen" who successively stood to inherit the Diamond if Lord Francis died without issue.

On that May morning, the second war over the Hope Diamond began, and it would be as acrimonious as that conducted by Henry, Adrian, and Alexander Hope after Uncle Philip's death. The only differences in the two wars would be that the first raged for ten years while this one would last for only two, and its pitched battles would be kept courteous and impersonal by the calm, rational language of the law.

The proceedings began. For the Diamond, they were full of slights, misinformation, and disrespect. May 16, 1899, was not a happy day for the stone. Mr. Farwell informed Mr. Justice Byrne that his client, Lord Francis Hope, under the Settled Land Act of 1882, Section 37, requested the court to approve a provisional contract made in December 1898 between his client and L. M. Lowenstein and Company, gem merchants, "for the sale of the blue Indian diamond, known as the Tavernier blue or Hope diamond." The contract price was not specified, but was "closely approximate to the sum of £18,115" ($90,575), the value given in his affidavit submitted to the court by the Bond Street gem merchant Edwin Streeter (the same Streeter who wrote *The Great*

Diamonds of the World mentioned in the previous chapter). He had arrived at the modest estimate of £18,115 because recently a blue diamond twice the size of the Hope had come into the market "which
naturally reduced its value." This was the stone's first belittlement.

"The diamond was said to have formerly been one of the crown
jewels of Louis XIV," continued Farwell, addressing the bench, "and
was purchased by the applicant's grandfather." A second blow to the
Diamond! Its present owner was so uncaring, so utterly ignorant of its
past, that he thought his grandfather, Henry Hope, had acquired it.
With this mistake, the jewel's most loving, if shadowy, owner, Philip
Hope, is erased not just from this particular record but from almost all
future histories, particularly newspaper accounts, which copy this one
and routinely list Henry Thomas Hope as the man who not only
bought the famous gem but bestowed his name on it.

As Farwell droned on in his uninflected legal jargon, it became apparent that Lord Francis had put a third slight on the stone, for he'd
told his lawyers that in its present medallion brooch setting, there were
twenty-two large white brilliants around it, when in fact there were
only twenty. Had he *ever* really looked into its blue heart, focused his
eye squarely on its awesome, eternal one? Probably not; his lordship
routinely looked for pleasure in far more ordinary, conventional places.

Farwell argued, while Lady Beatrice frowned and fidgeted and Lord
Francis smiled and nodded emphatically at every point made, that "a
sale of the diamond was a course an ordinarily prudent person would
adopt." One wonders if anyone in the court that day sniggered when
they heard Lord Francis Hope referred to as an "ordinarily prudent person." "A jewel of this kind," Farwell continued smoothly, "was absolutely
useless to the tenant for life, and a *damnosa hereditas* [destructive inheri-
tance]." What a blessing the Diamond was in Cavendish Square, far
away from such language!

Messrs. Mulligan and Terrell, acting for Lady Beatrice, and Benn,
acting for the Duke of Newcastle, then informed Justice Byrne that
their clients were "united in their wishes" that the Hope Diamond not
be sold and "all agreed that there was no necessity for its sale." They

argued that "the pecuniary position of the estate was not the real test." Lady Beatrice glared at her brother, the chronic bankrupt. "The applicant was himself responsible," her lawyer said, while she nodded vigorously and the bird on her hat made pecking motions, "for the reduction of his income"; moreover, "the feelings and sentimental objections of the remaindermen were to be considered," for "the diamond was in fact a unique possession and highly valued as such by the family." Then the lawyers quoted the *Encyclopedia Brittanica* on the subject: "Some [diamonds] are valued for other properties, as the Hope diamond, of a rare colour, a fine blue and high brilliancy, estimated at £25,000 [$125,000] though only 44½ carats."

After all the barristers in the courtroom had presented their arguments, tossing both calumny and compliments at the absent Diamond, Mr. Justice Byrne pronounced his verdict, showing that his passions centered not on persons with titles or on famous jewels but on language liberally studded with negatives. The case differed from the earlier one whereby family members had given assent to Lord Francis's selling off the Hope heirloom paintings, he noted, in that it was his own fault that he'd made the pictures homeless by being so spendthrift that he couldn't afford to live where they hung, namely at Deepdene. But, continued the judge solemnly, this was not the case with the Diamond. For it would probably be exactly where it now was, at Parr's bank, even if the applicant hadn't squandered all his money.

Second, in regard to Lord Francis Hope's pleading that he had great need of ready cash, Mr. Justice Byrne wished to point out that he "did not desire to use any harsh term but that was a circumstance which had been brought about by the applicant's own extravagance" and "the fact of a tenant for life having got himself into difficulties was not a circumstance which ought to have weight in deciding in favour of a sale."

Third, the judge had to consider the strong opposition of all the members of the family to the sale. Fourth, it was a question of the possession "of a jewel which was acknowledged to be unique—unique as being the first known, and until recently the only known, blue diamond, and one which had taken its name from the family and which was known to all the world as the 'Hope diamond.' There was evidence to show that it was no longer unique in the sense of being the only known blue diamond in the world," but—the negatives came thick and fast now—"he could not from that circumstance say on the evidence that the diamond itself did not stand out as a jewel unique from its size, from the circumstances connected with its history, and from its being a worldwide known diamond." In conclusion, "giving the best consideration he could to the facts of the case and to the arguments that had been adressed to him"—Lord Francis, Lady Beatrice, and all the assembled lawyers held their breath—"he did not think he ought to say that it had been made out to his satisfaction that this was a proper case in which to sanction the sale"—Lord Francis scowled— "as being to the interests of all parties." Lady Beatrice beamed beneath her ornithological hat, looking smug and triumphant. Justice Byrne thought, therefore—rolling out his final negative—"there was nothing for him to do but to refuse the application."

Lord Francis stumped quickly out of the courtroom with not even a nod to his sister and with none of his usual slow, careless grace. By God, he would appeal and appeal and appeal—his face grew redder and redder—he would employ every lawyer in England if he had to but somehow he would rid himself once and for all of that *damnosa hereditas*.

He launched his first appeal two months later, and upgraded his barrister by hiring the eminent Sir Edward Clarke, Q.C., who four years earlier had figured in Oscar Wilde's trial for sodomy. The Master of the Rolls and Lord Justice Romer, the two men who heard the Hope appeal on July 14 and 15, said that this was not a case in which they ought to differ from the learned judge in the court below. Lord Justice Romer got in one more compliment for the beleaguered Hope, when he said that "this is a unique diamond of a color the like of which had not been seen until quite recently, and he was satisfied upon the evidence that there was no reasonable probability of the value of the diamond being diminished." The appeal was dismissed with costs, so Sir Edward Clarke was no more successful here than he'd been in defending Oscar Wilde, who'd been hauled off to Reading jail to serve time for his "crime." Whether Sir Edward got paid by Lord Francis, we do not know, but we have our suspicions.

Sometime during 1900, May, tired out from all those London matinee and evening performances and feeling the need of a change, persuaded her husband to take her to the United States, where she could see old friends—and make new ones. In New York she met the handsome, twenty-seven-year-old Capt. Putnam Bradlee Strong, son of William Lafayette Strong, former New York mayor. Bradlee's father had come from Ohio to New York City at age twenty-six with only one goal: to become a millionaire, which he did by prospering in his own wholesale drygoods business. Bored with helping run his father's firm, Bradlee became a captain in the 69th Regiment in 1898, served with distinction in the Philippines, and was made a major seven months later. He was honorably discharged in 1899, and was then commissioned a captain in the regular army. "I never have known a woman," May would say years later, "who, after being thrown in Captain Strong's company for a while did not fall in love with him," and she was no exception. She never was a good judge of men; romantic longings always obscured her vision, for Strong would turn out to be a complete rogue and rascal, just as hopeless with money as her titled husband and without his good manners.

Although the Hopes sailed back to England with enamored Captain Strong also on board the ship, Lord Francis seems to have been quite as insouciant about love affairs being conducted under his nose as he was about money. When May and his lordship landed, the Duke of Newcastle and his diamond anchor–adorned duchess entertained them at a dinner party at London's Carlton Hotel, and—if May can be believed—her cuckolded husband actually got the *damnosa hereditas* out of Parr's bank and allowed her to wear it for the second, and last, time.

May returned to New York before her husband. She fell ill, an indisposition perhaps triggered by the fact that in October 1900 theatrical manager Harry Chamberlyn sued her for $50,000, since she had "wrongfully, whimsically and capriciously, broken her contract with him, after he'd arranged a U.S. tour and booked a supporting company."

Putnam Bradlee Strong rushed back across the Atlantic to May's bedside, while Lord Francis, according to her, in response to a cable from her physicians reporting her "dangerous condition" dispatched one saying, "Sorry, can't come now. Midst of fishing season. Advise of developments." "That instant," claims our histrionic heroine, hand to heart, "I became the property, body, soul, and mind, of Putnam Bradlee Strong."

When Lord Francis did arrive back in New York in November, he and May rented an apartment at 215 West Thirty-Fourth Street, while Strong nipped in and out of May's bed at opportune moments and lingered for much longer stays once his lordship had gone shooting in Florida with his brother the duke, then back to England in February 1901 on pressing financial matters. By the end of March Lord Francis was back in the Thirty-fourth Street apartment, finally aware that his wife had taken a lover. It was on April 18 that May left his lordship for good, headed with Bradlee for San Francisco, and sailed under a false name to Japan. When money there ran out, as it soon did, Bradlee took a diamond necklace from her jewel case, which May valued at $50,000, given her by an English admirer, Captain Holford, told her he would pawn it, and sold it outright for $9,000.

In the fall of 1901, while his estranged wife was having her own jewel problems, Lord Francis launched an appeal against the court's 1899 decisions of May and July forbidding the sale of the Hope Diamond. This time, the amazingly clever Messrs. Maddisons, his newest and best law firm, seem to have presented so piteous a case of his lordship's financial woes that by order of a Master in Chancery, permission was given to ignore the feelings of the remaindermen, his sisters and brother, to turn a blind eye to the entail and—Lord Francis was jubilant—to finally sell the damn millstone, which had been, ever since Grandmother's death in 1884, the focus for his frustration with his life in general and his fortune in particular. He opened a bottle of the very best champagne and drank deeply, ecstatically, drank until the Diamond was no more than a tiny, colorless bubble inside his glass and then—pouf!—it was gone.

On November 13, the London *Times* in its usual understated, dignified way, reported that "we are informed by Messrs. Maddisons, solicitors to Lord Francis Hope, that he has sold to Mr. Adolf Weil of 25 Hatton Garden the famous Hope blue diamond. We understand that a large diamond merchant of New York is also interested in the purchase and that the destination of the stone is America." A later *Times* article of April 16, 1910, gave "upward of £29,000" ($145,000) as the amount Lord Francis was paid for the famous gem.

He took no leave of it, felt not a single pang at parting, tossed the money it had brought him into the quicksand sinking fund, where so much money had disappeared before, and, according to information given years later by his son, never, ever, mentioned the Hope Diamond again. It was a case of good riddance and vast relief.

After more than a decade's incarceration in Parr's bank, the Diamond found itself briefly in Weil's Hatton Garden jewel shop among many lesser lights of its own kind, being handled with proper reverence and respect, and sold soon after to Simon Frankel, of Joseph Frankel's Sons, New York, who had come to Weil's to admire and acquire it.

A few days later the Hope was carried by a proud but nervous Frankel on board the *Kronprinz Wilhelm* of the North German Lloyd steamship line and locked into the ship's strongbox for what was, in a long existence, only its fifth sea voyage.

While the Diamond was still somewhere on the heaving Atlantic, the *New York Times* on November 14 heralded its imminent arrival with the headline HOPE DIAMOND COMING HERE and stated below that "it is in the possession of a member of a New York firm now on his way to America from London." The article explained the Hope's claim to fame: "It is not the size of the stone which gives it its value, but the fact that it is the only very large blue diamond known." A brief but erroneous history of the gem followed, repeating the misinformation that had originated with Lord Francis in his May 1899 court case attempting to sell the heirloom, namely, that its first Hope owner had been Philip's nephew Henry. With many repetitions, in no time at all this myth attached itself securely to the story of a famous Diamond.

The *Kronprinz Wilhelm* docked on November 26, and the next day the *New York Times* trumpeted GREAT HOPE DIAMOND HERE. The article stated that it had arrived the day before, that it had cost Simon Frankel $250,000 "according to reports," but that he was being very close-mouthed about it, saying only that he'd bought it "for business purposes," had no immediate buyer in mind, and refused to divulge its price. Before the *Kronprinz* had even docked, Emanuel Gattle, a Fifth Avenue jeweler, had raced out in the revenue cutter to where the steamer was anchored at quarantine headquarters and told Frankel that he'd give him $300,000 for the stone, not a penny more. When the ship berthed four hours later, Mr. Gattle, whose first offer was refused, had, with typical American enterprise, raised it to $350,000, but Frankel stood firm and refused to sell.

The deputy collector of customs duties, a man named Quackenbush, refused a request that the Diamond be sent at once by special messenger to the Public Stores, such treatment being accorded only to live animals and "highly perishable" goods. The least "perishable" object in the universe was, therefore, in proper democratic fashion, sent up for appraisal in the ordinary manner, given a value of $141,032, on which Frankel paid the 10 percent duty required. Was the sterling equivalent of $141,032, namely £28,206, what Frankel had actually paid Weil? It seems unlikely, since this was less than Weil had given Lord Francis.

Simon Frankel deposited his treasure in a safe inside the family firm at 68 Nassau Street in New York's Maiden Lane district, and the Hope began yet another residence in yet another country and culture. But its European travels were not yet over; there would be many more brief stays there in the next fifty-odd years.

From 1901 to 1908, just as from 1792, when Cadet Guillot carried it from France, until 1812, when it surfaced in England, the Diamond disappears into obscuring mists. Most of the rumors, legends, and wild speculations of where the Hope was for those seven years are patently false. And once planted they would prove impossible to eradicate.

By the spring of 1908 facts again stand tall, rooted in documentary evidence. Simon Frankel finally succeeded in selling the Diamond for $400,000 to a resident of Rue Lafitte, Paris, a shadowy figure called Salomon (or Selim) Habib, who was either a private collector or "a dia-

mond dealer with offices in Paris and Bangkok" and who has been
called Armenian, Turkish, Syrian, and Spanish. He may have been as
dedicated a gem collector as Philip Hope but apparently had far less
money. Was he seduced by the Hope's beauty? He seems to have
bought it with more passion than prudence, for he was forced to sell it
for financial reasons only one year later. On June 24, 1909, it was one
of eight spectacular diamonds belonging to Habib put up for sale at
a Paris auction at Hôtel Drouot. The illustrated catalog (now in the
Bibliothèque d'Art et Archéologie in Paris) lists Eugène Bailly and
M. Appart as auctioneers, and Louis Aucoc as gem expert. The Hope
jewel was in excellent company; the other seven diamonds included
four white: one had belonged to Princess Mathilde, cousin of Emperor
Napoleon III; two weighed in at 23 and 24 carats; the fourth was a
slender pear-shaped diamond of 58 carats known as the Half-Regent.
The three fancies included a rosy blue oval of almost 6 carats, an
aquamarine-tinted one of more than 70 carats known as the Idol's
Eye, and a rose-colored stone of 31½. All eight diamonds had been on
public view in London at Garrard's elegant silver and jewel shop from
June 7 to 11 to arouse desire in potential buyers.

The blue Hope apparently had been removed from its Victorian medallion setting to be sold unset and was described in the catalog thus:

> This diamond, of an inestimable value from a mineralogical point of
> view, shows a peculiarity unique in the world, of possessing the ap-
> pearance, color and reflection of a very beautiful sapphire, combined
> with an infinite purity. It was part of the famous collection of
> M. Hope, on whose death it was sold at auction under the name
> "Hope Diamond" [this is a slightly garbled provenance] and became
> the property of an American broker who transferred it to M. Habib
> in 1908.

It was valued by Louis Aucoc at $300,000, $100,000 less than
Habib had paid for it. The bidding on June 24, however, stayed many
thousands below this estimate because all the dealers present knew
that Habib had great need of cash and conspired to keep it low. In *Bi-*

joux et Pierres Précieuses, H. D. Fromanger claims that Habib protested that same day that since the auction house had deceived him as to how much he could get for his outstanding diamonds, all the actual bids being far below the estimates, he'd decided not to sell them after all. With mixed feelings he took back all eight stones. (Had he not fallen on hard times, Habib had dreamed of donating his collection to the Musée de la Légion d'Honneur, in which case the Hope would have found itself permanently back in France.)

Right after the aborted auction, Habib pledged the other seven diamonds to a municipal bank in return for a loan and sold the Hope to a Paris jewel merchant named Rosenau of 9 Rue Chauchat, who represented a French syndicate. On June 25, the *New York Times* headlined the news on page one: HOPE DIAMOND GOES CHEAP; FAMOUS STONE, WHICH COST $400,000, BRINGS ONLY $80,000. The brief article stated that it had been sold to "Louis Aucoc, the leading expert of France, presumably for a customer." It may be that Aucoc, who was the auction house consultant, was also a member of the syndicate headed by Rosenau.

Habib divested himself that year only of the Hope, finally retrieving the other seven diamonds pledged to the bank. Perhaps his regard for the great blue gem was, after all, closer to Tavernier's and Lord Francis's mercenary one than to Philip Hope's faithful adoration.

On a fateful day in June 1909 a brand-new attitude to the Diamond entered its story. Up to that point, apart from the dim and distant beliefs in ancient India that blue brilliants could be unlucky, there was no mention anywhere that this particular one had an evil influence on lives. The myth of its curse began in a newspaper, and in the very one where sensational reporting was least expected: in the sober, staid London *Times*. On June 25, on page five, headed SALE OF THE HOPE DIAMOND, with "From Our Own Correspondent" beneath, datelined Paris, June 24, appeared the first of many libelous biographies of the innocent Diamond.

The chief Paris correspondent for the London *Times* in 1909 was George Saunders, who had come from Berlin to succeed William Lavino in 1908. Saunders's assistant in the Paris office was the American-born William Morton Fullerton (1865–1952), whose greatest claim to fame is that from 1908 to 1910 he was the object of the novelist Edith Wharton's only passionate, adulterous love affair. From June 5, 1909, however, Fullerton was on five weeks' holiday in the United States, so he probably didn't initiate these lies about the Diamond. Perhaps the *Times'* account was merely copied from a French-language newspaper; perhaps Rosenau and the syndicate had planted it, hoping a sensational provenance would enhance the Diamond's sales potential. Whoever he was, the writer of this 1909 article strode boldly and deliberately, with no regard for historical accuracy, into the mists where the Diamond was hidden from 1792 to 1812 and again from 1901 to 1908. He reported rumors and myths to his readers as if they were facts. He also played fast and loose with the other years of the stone's existence.

After briefly reporting the sale of the Diamond by Habib to Rosenau, the journalist declared that "its possession is the story of a long series of tragedies—murder, suicide, madness and various other misfortunes." Tavernier's death "attacked by fever" was the first one attributable to the Hope—even though in reality he died at the ripe age of eighty-four. Once Louis XIV had acquired the stone, he apparently let Athenaïs de Montespan wear it; by "a curious coincidence" her influence over His Majesty declined at once. Louis also let it adorn Nicolas Fouquet, his first finance minister, which is why Fouquet was subsequently imprisoned by Louis and why he died some years later of apoplexy, age sixty-five. Totally ignoring the fact that the Diamond was set from 1749 to 1792 in the Order of the Golden Fleece, a strictly male decoration, the writer claimed that it hung from Marie Antoinette's neck, so its bad vibes led her straight to the guillotine. But not before she'd let Princess de Lamballe wear it, which is why the poor princess was torn to pieces by a mob at La Force prison. This brings us to 1792 and the twenty-year gap in the stone's existence; here invention becomes total. An Amsterdam diamond cutter, Wilhelm Fals, cut the jewel to its present size, but his dissolute son Hendrik stole it and ruined his father. Hendrik killed himself after he'd unloaded the Diamond on François Beaulieu, a native of Marseilles, who came to London and, "in the last stages of destitution and ill-health," sent for Daniel Eliason, who paid the price asked and took the stone. "The next day Beaulieu died of starvation. There can be no doubt," continued the Paris correspondent, repeating the old error, that the diamond was purchased next "by the late Henry Thomas Hope of Deepdene."

Once the malevolent gem had passed from the Hopes to Simon Frankel, imagination runs riot again for the years 1901 to 1908. Frankel "could not find a purchaser and fell into financial difficulties." In 1908 Jacques Colot, a French broker, bought it for $300,000 and committed suicide a few days after he sold it to Russian Prince Kanitovski. The prince promptly lent it to Lorens Ladue, a beautiful actress at the Folies Bergère, then shot her from a box the first night she wore it, grabbed the stone from the cooling corpse, and "was stabbed two days afterwards by revolutionists." The next owner, a Greek called Simon Montharides, was "thrown over a precipice and killed with his wife and two children," after he sold the Diamond to the Turkish Sultan Abdul Hamid. "There is no possible doubt," claimed the *Times* journalist, "that it was in Constantinople until comparatively recently and very little that it was in the Sultan's possession."

There isn't a shred of evidence to suggest that Wilhelm and Hendrik Fals, François Beaulieu, Prince Kanitovski, Lorens Ladue, or Simon Montharides ever existed. Certainly a murder onstage at the Folies Bergère could never have gone unnoticed. There was a jeweler in Paris at the time called Colot, but that is a common French name.

That Sultan Abdul Hamid II of Turkey owned the Hope is the most persistent and widely believed of all these wild tales. But the cruel, despotic ruler of the Ottoman Empire had more pressing matters on his mind than acquiring more gems, for he was then beset by the revolutionary Young Turks, who in 1909 forced him to abdicate, replacing him, as head of the newly formed constitutional government, with his gentle brother Mohammed V. Abdul Hamid, a white-faced, tottering old man, fled Constantinople's Yildiz palace on April 28, while his possessions were hastily loaded into carriages and his eunuchs walked out with richly bound copies of the Koran around their necks, each of which concealed some of the sultan's jewels. So precipitate had been his departure that other diamonds and rubies lay loose on tables and floors in the deserted rooms where cries of "Long live the sultan!" came from the cages of well-trained but hungry parrots. When the deposed leader's gems were auctioned in Paris in December 1911, the Hope wasn't among them for the simple reason that he'd never owned it. It most likely passed from Frankel to Habib to Rosenau.

According to the Paris correspondent who dreamed up the 1909 *Times* article, before the Diamond left the Turkish court of Abdul Hamid, it suffered an unprecedented paroxysm of rage and revenge, for Abu Sabir, a lapidary who polished it, was tortured and imprisoned in a dungeon; Kulub Bey, the eunuch who guarded it, was killed in the street by an angry mob; the keeper of its vault was strangled, and the sultan's favorite in the harem, Salma Zubaya, was shot dead by the sultan himself, "the bullet striking close" to the noxious Diamond, which adorned her breast. All this is errant nonsense.

Less than five months later, on the other side of the Atlantic, American newspapers began to spread the myth of the unfortunate Diamond's curse. The *New York Times* reported on November 17 that Salomon Habib, "a wealthy Turkish diamond collector and merchant, who formerly owned the famous Hope blue diamond" was among the passengers drowned in the shark-infested waters off Singapore aboard the wrecked French mail steamer *Seyne*. This much was true. But the anonymous writer continued, "Because certain of its owners have met with misfortune, a baleful influence has been ascribed" to the famous gem. As proof, the article cited Louis XVI's beheading, unspecified "financial difficulties" of Joseph Frankel's Sons in 1907, as well as those of the just-drowned Habib. While the intriguing idea of the Diamond's magical powers was born in Europe, it subsequently grew and spread faster in the capitalist, materialist United States, where consumerism was just then beginning to control the culture. America's Gilded Age (1880–1914) ushered in the first great wave of machine-run industrial wealth and conspicuous consumption. New millionaires became obsessed with acquiring objects: clothes, antiques, yachts, houses, but their souls longed for something more: for fantasy and the supernatural.

It was in those years, too, that "yellow" or sensational journalism proliferated in the U.S., where the newspaper baron William Randolph Hearst discovered that he could sell more papers if they were filled with disaster, crime, and sin reported in highly emotional terms. An ancient object worth thousands that left a trail of violent death and calamity wherever its powerful rays struck was prime copy, guaranteed to greatly increase circulation. Thus it was that in the first two decades of the twentieth century a famous blue Diamond became infamous, one more victim among many of a materialist age and of the newspapers' yellow peril.

Three days after the report of Habib's drowning, on November 20, the *New York Times* admitted that "the famous Hope diamond did not go down in the wreck of the *Seyne* at Singapore." Habib's nephew, believing that his uncle had it with him, had instructed two divers to go down and search for a leather handbag in the ship's safe. This they found, but it contained no Diamond because, as the *Times* reported sheepishly, it was safe and sound at 9 Rue Chauchat in Paris, in the hands of jeweler Rosenau who "confessed rather ruefully tonight that it was still in his possession." He and the French syndicate kept it for nine months; the story of where it went after that belongs in the next chapter.

In this one, we need to complete the life stories of Lord Francis Hope and May Yohe. Certainly his lordship seems to have suffered the slings and arrows of fate far more severely after he sold the Diamond than when he owned it. By March 1902 he was bankrupt yet again, with liabilities of £21,826, which did not include the £9,000 that May claimed he owed her. Only seven days after the bankruptcy hearings began, Lord Francis appeared in a different court, the divorce division, with a different lawyer, Mr. Barnard, and proceeded to divorce May Yohe Hope on the grounds of her adultery with Putnam Bradlee Strong. Mr. Barnard asked that his client "be allowed to give his evidence seated in the well of the Court, as he has recently met with a gun accident which necessitated amputation of his foot." On January 15, 1903, the court forced Lord Francis, his bankruptcy by then discharged, to pay May £1,000 of the £9,000 she was demanding.

His lordship then married a divorcée, Olive Muriel Owen, daughter of George Horatio Thompson, a Melbourne banker, which seemed to augur well, on February 27, 1904. She presented him with two daughters, then the longed-for son and heir on April 8, 1907. But Olive Muriel died just eight years after marriage, leaving her less than surefooted husband with three small children and an estate valued at only £1,447. She was buried in the mausoleum at Deepdene; Henrietta, Lord Francis's long-suffering mother, now in her seventies, sent a wreath but didn't attend the funeral.

When Henrietta opened her *Times* on the morning of January 19, 1913, she learned that son Francis, who had inherited all the worst traits of her first husband, Linky, was being sued by a commission agent for having borrowed £200,000 (a cool $1 million) at 5 percent interest and then repaying him only 2.5. His lordship lost the case and was ordered to pay the claim, with costs. Henrietta died of a stroke, perhaps precipitated by her profligate son, that same year, on May 8, at her residence The Oaks, at Woodford in Essex. One year later, Lord Francis auctioned off all the furniture from Edgecumbe, a Berkshire estate inherited from grandmother Adèle, and retreated to the bogs of Castle Blayney. Three years later he sold for a mere £134,918 all remaining Hope heirlooms at a Christie's auction, including thirty tons of sculpture collected on their Grand Tour by Thomas and Philip Hope, and nine tons of books from the latter's library. Lord Francis had to sell Castle Blayney in 1926. When his brother died on May 30, 1928, he became, at long last, 8th Duke of Newcastle and proceeded to run through the resources and rent-rolls of Clumber. He lived to be seventy-five, dying on April 20, 1941, and was succeeded by his son, Henry Edward Hugh, the 9th Duke. (On Henry's death the title would become extinct.)

Lord Francis would have hated his London *Times* obituary headed with DUKE OF NEWCASTLE. FORMER OWNER OF THE HOPE BLUE DIAMOND. The stone he'd never loved and, once he'd divested himself of it, never mentioned, was, in the final accounting, his greatest claim to fame. The notorious gem, the *Times* explained, "has provided romancers with many a tale and novelists with many a plot," and then repeated the error Lord Francis had invented in his 1899 attempt to sell it, namely, that it "had been purchased by Mr. H. T. Hope, Lord Francis Hope's grandfather."

As for May Yohe, her romance-to-rags life story was also a tragicomedy. Living with Strong first in Japan, then England, she saw the pattern of life with Lord Francis repeat itself: her partner gambled heavily and lost a lot of money, while May supported them, not by acting but by selling off some of the jewels male admirers had given her over the years. Eventually, she and Strong sailed home to New York, where she stashed the rest of her jewelry in a safe-deposit box at the Knickerbocker Trust Company, on Fifth Avenue at Twenty-seventh Street, including a turquoise-and-diamond arrow, worth $8,000, given her by the London banker Alfred Rothschild.

In July 1902 Strong broke into the box, helped himself to its contents, and fled with his newest lady love. May saw at once how she could profit from this loss of gems and lover and achieve the celebrity that would revive her acting career. She kept *New York Times* journalists well supplied with days and days of sensational copy. With reporters crowding round, pencils poised, on Monday, July 22, May and her lawyer, the well-named Manny Friend, arrived at the Knickerbocker Trust Company to find nothing left in safe-deposit box number thirty-five except a $2 fan, a small watch that bore the inscription "The world is broken but Hope is not," and an imitation pearl necklace worth $4, from which hung a cheap copy of the Hope Diamond, "used by Miss Yohe only when she was on the stage." This marks the first mention of May's ongoing theatrical exploitation of the celebrated blue gem, which she'd worn either twice or not at all, and which was far more famous than she was. When she saw the denuded box, May "fell backward in a fainting condition and uttered a cry." Manny led the distraught heroine to the Sturtevant House restaurant on Broadway where, in simple white shirtwaist and navy skirt, May sat where the great crowd of people peering in at her through a large window could get a clear, unobstructed view.

After this fine free publicity, May not only withdrew her grand larceny charge against Strong but began seeing him again, and Manny Friend admitted that the stolen jewels had been worth a mere $150,000, not $300,000 as first reported. One month later May and Bradlee, happily reunited and cooing like turtledoves, sailed for Spain as "Mr. and Mrs. Atkinson" and from there to Buenos Aires, where, on October 3, May's divorce from Lord Francis having become final, she and Bradlee were married in a simple civil ceremony.

On December 7 they landed back in New York, greeted by the reporters May had informed of her arrival. Madcap May disembarked with "a monkey, twenty-two pieces of baggage, two wicker steamer chairs, a Japanese poodle dog, and a barrel of pineapples." She did an American vaudeville tour in 1904 and divorced Strong in Oregon City in 1910. Two years later she appeared in a London revival of *Little Christopher Columbus*, where the recently widowed Lord Francis Hope listened to his first wife belt out "What Can a Poor Girl Do?" while, sitting as usual in the very best box, he noted with chagrin that she wore around her neck a copy of the Hope Diamond. May would, for the rest of her life, never appear on stage without it. A justly renowned Diamond worn by three French kings, housed in the splendors of Versailles, owned by a rich Dutch art connoisseur, and an indigent but blue-blooded English lord and future duke—such a famous jewel as this didn't deserve the humiliating and tawdry associations a Yankee actress, until she died, would heap upon it.

Acting on tour in South Africa in 1914, still flashing her fake Hope, May found herself a third husband, Capt. John Smuts, a cousin of the famous Boer War hero, Gen. Jan Smuts, but the captain proved no better at providing an income than her first two partners. Invalided out of the army with a "hammertoe" and a small pension, Captain Smuts subjected May to three hard years on a Singapore rubber planta-tion before settling in Seattle, where for $18 a week his actress wife scrubbed office floors. The next unsuccessful venture was a chicken farm in Los Angeles. It is precisely at this point, while May was liv-ing there on next to nothing in 1920 and 1921, that she tried desper-ately to revive her acting career and increase her income, using her very tenuous connection to the Hope as means to this end. Like the journalists in the 1909 London and *New York Times* articles, May in-vented fictional episodes in the Diamond's life story to prove its evil powers.

She had several willing accomplices. The first one was George Kleine (1864–1931), a silent movie producer and importer. A na-tive New Yorker of German background, Kleine got into the film business in 1896 when he placed his first ad for a moving picture in the *New York Clipper* on September 19. By 1903 he was importing European movies to the U.S. and three years later set up film rental and selling branches there and in Canada. One of the European films he brought in was the very popular 1913 nine-reel Italian film *Quo Vadis*, but for six years after 1914, George didn't actively pursue his career in films.

In early February 1920, having turned her back on unprofitable chickens, May somehow persuaded Kleine to produce a fifteen-episode serial titled *The Hope Diamond Mystery*, which she'd be author and star of. As early as May 10, 1920, a promotional letter appeared in *Motion Picture News*, on the notepaper of Kosmik Films Incorporated, which Kleine was president of, with an office at 110 West Fortieth Street in New York and another in Chicago. The letter was written and signed by Kosmik's treasurer, Jack Wheeler, stating that he'd been in Los An-geles for three months and had already spent $60,000 making the first six episodes of this serial. "Say! My sets alone will cost one hundred thousand dollars," boasted Jack. "Stuart Paton is directing; May Yohe, formerly Lady Francis Hope, wrote the plot and acts in it." Other ac-tors included Boris Karloff, who played Dakar, an Indian; Grace Charmond as Bibi, the fairest virgin in Burma; and William Marion as James Marcon, the totally fictitious owner of the Diamond.

Madcap May gave her imagination complete license to invent for the beleaguered, defenseless Hope fifteen episodes of a story that never happened, a cast of characters who, with the one exception of Tavernier, never existed, and a melodramatic plot whose episodes bore such titles as A Virgin's Love, Flames of Despair, The Evil Eye, The Cup of Fear, The Ring of Death, The Lash of Hate, Primitive Passions.

The completed movie ran to 10,027 feet of 16 mm black-and-white film, copyrighted by Kosmik Films on February 19, 1921. Unfortunately, movie audiences were no longer interested in serials, and The Hope Diamond Mystery didn't make money for either George Kleine or May Yohe.

She wasn't yet finished, however, with the Diamond and moved on later that year to a related project. May contacted a hack writer called Henry Leyford Gates (1880–1937) and persuaded him to help her write a nonfiction book titled The Mystery of the Hope Diamond, illustrated with stills from the movie Kleine had produced. It was published in New York at 2 Duane Street, by a press called International Copyright Bureau, which seems to have been a fly-by-night operation, for it is mentioned in Publishers Weekly annual Directory of Publishers, Printers and Authors Issuing Books During 1921 but not listed for 1920 or 1922. H. L. Gates had previously co-authored—or "interpreted" as the blurb puts it—Auction of Souls by Aurora Mardiganian, "the frank story of the Christian girl who suffered unmentionable torments from the Turks and Kurds," another movie tie-in, illustrated with stills from the silent film that preceded it. The title page of The Mystery of the Hope Diamond ($1.75 cloth; 75 cents paper) reads, "As set down by H. L. Gates from the Personal Narrative of Lady Francis Hope (May Yohe)." The blurb on a back page makes the book's focus clear: it is the malignant power of the Diamond, "that sinister crystal which has wrecked so many lives and still deals death and destruction to all who come beneath its influence."

The story bears only a slight resemblance here and there to the

movie *The Hope Diamond Mystery*, even though it's illustrated with
stills from the film showing such characters as Nang Fu, Mary Hilton,
and John Gregg, none of whom ever appear in the text. The book must
indeed have been a "mystery" to its readers!

Book One weaves a completely fictional construct around the fact
that the blue Diamond may once have been stolen from an idol in
ancient India. We meet a "noble cavalier," not a jewel merchant,
from French King Louis's court called only "Jean-Baptiste" until later
King Louis turns him into "Baron de Tavernier." From the breast, not
eye, of a jade statue of goddess Sita in a temple at Pagan, in Burma,
he steals the "Great Blue Stone, the largest diamond the eyes of man
have ever coveted," in 1588. The trouble with this, apart from a lot
of phony detail, is that the real Tavernier wasn't born until seventeen
years later, in 1605. Jean-Baptiste is given actual dialogue, falls for
a Burmese maiden called Khema, and becomes the first victim of the
stone's curse, dying a horrible death, camped outside Moscow, torn
"into countless shreds" by a pack of wild dogs. (This incident will later
be alluded to by some reputable historians and gemologists who turn
the wild dogs into wolves.)

Book Two contains "What Came After, as Told by May Yohe." "I
have followed the story of this jewel," declares May, "and in its path
lies only sorrow, disaster, tragedy." She blames the stone for all her misfortunes, and with Gates's help, pushes on stage the same cast of phony
curse victims invented by the *Times'* Paris correspondent in 1909—
Wilhelm and Hendrik Fals, François Beaulieu, Jacques Colot, Prince
Kanitovski, Lorens Ladue, and Simon Montharides—and propels them
through events even more sensational and more specific as to time
and place.

Wildly embellishing historical events in the Diamond's story, Yohe
and Gates relate that Nicolas Fouquet was executed by Louis after
wearing the gem at the very opulent ball given at his château (an
event that actually took place seven years before King Louis XIV even
acquired the stone) and that Marat, the Revolutionary leader who died
horribly, assassinated in his bath by Charlotte Corday, was the person
who stole the blue brilliant from the Garde-meuble in 1792. Yohe and

Gates also claim that it hung as pendant from the diamond necklace made by Boehmer and Bassenge that figures in Jeanne de la Motte's scam perpetrated on Marie Antoinette just before she lost her head. To the scene of carnage at Abdul Hamid's Turkish court, the two authors add one more corpse: that of palace official Jehver Agha, who tried to steal the evil stone and was consequently hanged.

The Mystery of the Hope Diamond continues in this ridiculous vein until the book gets to the stone's owner in the 1920s, whom we'll meet in the next chapter and who was then wearing the Hope almost daily, even though Gates and Yohe conclude that it "must be guarded by the strongest locks, seldom if ever worn, and hidden from the gaze of men." "It requires no belief in esoteric power of pagan curse to give credence to the power of evil in the stone," they conclude, "and no chemical analysis will push aside the startling array of facts [*facts?*] which form its history." The final paragraph poses a series of questions concerning the baleful Blue: "Does it retain its pagan curse? Does it sparkle only with reflected evil? Does it bring death, dishonor, disgrace? When will the world know the answer to the MYSTERY OF THE HOPE DIAMOND?"

The biggest mystery here is how May Yohe and Henry Gates found the audacity to pass off on a gullible public this trashy, pulp-fiction thriller disguised as historical fact. After the book appeared in 1921, newspapermen, themselves co-conspirators in manufacturing the myth of the curse, had a handy, hardcover source always at their fingertips. They repeated its tall tales down the years as if they were gospel whenever they mentioned the Hope, as did some historians and gemologists. Minds, to be sure, abhor a vacuum; imaginations never stop working, and if fools rush in where scholars fear to tread, the latter may soon follow.

May Yohe's slight connection to the Diamond helped her to generate some good publicity for herself, but paradoxically, for the Hope the exposure appears—at first glance—to be negative, both uncomplimentary and unfair. It is difficult, at this distance of time, to determine how well the potboiler she'd dictated to Gates sold, or how much money it brought May, but it was the illustrious jewel that ultimately paid the price.

May was not yet done with exploiting it. On July 7, 1923, the *New York Times* announced that the actress and her husband Smuts "have opened a tea room" in Marlow, New Hampshire, on the highway to the White Mountains, called the Blue Diamond, "designed to furnish automobile travelers with a bite of luncheon," prepared by Captain John from South African recipes. "It's going to be a success!" exclaimed May, with her unflagging optimism, but it wasn't, and soon the Blue Diamond Inn suffered the same failure as the rubber plantation, the chicken farm, the Hope-inspired movie, and, possibly, the Hope-inspired book.

One year later, on November 20, according to the *New York Times*, May's husband suffered a gunshot wound to his chest at their Boston lodgings at 129 West Concord Street. The shooting occurred at 2 P.M. but wasn't reported until seven hours later, by which time a suicide note stating that he'd shot himself because he'd been unkind to his wife had materialized in handwriting not his. Since the police affirmed that given its angle, Smuts couldn't possibly have fired the bullet, and since May was the only other person present, we could speculate wildly and jump to melodramatic conclusions, just as she did in *The Mystery of the Hope Diamond*, but we refuse to stoop so low. The police never charged her and the long accounts of the incident in the *Times* over several days noted that "Madcap May's most famous marriage was her romantic union with Lord Francis Hope," whereby "she became the possessor of the noted Hope Diamond," whose ownership invariably "led to exciting adventures or dire mishaps."

When in July 1935 May became ill and was admitted to the Boston State Hospital, the *Times* reiterated that she was the "possessor of the famous Hope Diamond." When May Yohe Hope Strong Smuts died in Boston three years later of heart disease, on August 28, age sixty-nine, the *New York Times'* obituary was headlined: NOTED ACTRESS OF GENERATION AGO ONCE POSSESSED THE FAMOUS HOPE DIAMOND. Considering that she had, by her own account, worn it only twice and by Lord Francis's, not at all, May had done a fine job of attaching herself to the Diamond publicly and permanently.

While for Lord Francis the Diamond was merely an object to be sold, for May it was an object that could promote other objects, causes, and people. She demeaned the Hope Diamond to the level of hype and hard sell, but she also did it a favor. She planted it so deeply into America's imagination and subconscious that there, with luxuriant new growth springing up continuously, it would firmly and triumphantly remain.

Evalyn Walsh McLean in glamorous pose,
with diamonds galore, including the Hope.

8

ADDICTION

Thus ornament is but the guilèd shore
To a most dangerous sea.
—WILLIAM SHAKESPEARE, *The Merchant of Venice*, act 2, scene 2

We left the Diamond in Paris residing in a safe at Rosenau's Rue Bichat establishment after he and the French syndicate bought it from Habib in June 1909. It was literally and figuratively kept in the dark there, except for a few unsuccessful showings to potential buyers, for a year and two months. In August 1910 Cartier's Paris firm purchased it for around 550,000 francs ($110,000). The Hope then moved to Cartier's much more elegant and exclusive shop at 13 Rue de la Paix, with green marble facade and royal coats of arms above its doors to indicate the patronage of the ruling monarchs of England, Portugal, Norway, Russia, Greece, and Siam, with many more to follow in years to come.

All the best jewelers in Paris had their shops in Rue de la Paix. Jules Debut was at number 1; Louis Aucoc, the gem expert who had evaluated the Hope Diamond for Habib's auction sale, was at number 6; Fontana shared premises with top couturier Worth at number 7; Vever was at 14; Edgar Morgan at 17; and Charles Marret at 19. But by far the best shop was Cartier's; if the Diamond had to be confined in one, that was the place to be.

The firm had been founded by Louis François Cartier (1819–1904) in 1847, reviving the business begun by his grandfather at Louis XV's court nearly a century before. Louis François was joined by son

Alfred and in 1898 by grandsons Louis-Joseph (1875–1942), Pierre (1878–1965), and Jacques (1884–1942). After two previous locations, Cartier's moved to Rue de la Paix in 1899, where the three brothers would soon divide and rule: Louis-Joseph in the Paris store, Pierre in the New York branch after it opened on November 1, 1909, Jacques in London.

The Cartier brothers were thrilled to have the prestigious Hope Diamond in their grasp, but for the stone itself, unlucky number 13 Rue de la Paix was just one more confined space, one more ho-hum vault. By now it had been in so many safes: in Paris, in London, on board ship, in New York, on board ship again, back in Paris at rue Laffitte, rue Bichat, rue de la Paix. A diamond needed light and life, warm bodies, adoring eyes, and, above all, action. One diamond in motion was worth a hundred in stasis. Moreover, lodged at Cartier's, the Diamond had to share the limelight with another blue one, not as big a stone, or as distinguished a tone. Pierre Cartier had that same year purchased a heart-shaped blue diamond of 30.62 carats. Soon, however, it was sold to a Mrs. Unzue and went off to Argentina. It would share the Hope's ultimate fate, for the two blues would come together forty-nine years later, ending their days sedately in the same Washington institution, the Smithsonian.

At Cartier's, the Hope had one or two inconclusive sallies from safe to clients seated in the special room darkened with heavy curtains and lit artificially, where diamonds looked their best. Then, on a crisp fall morning, only a month after its arrival at Rue de la Paix, the Diamond was taken by Pierre Cartier through Paris streets, alive with clip-clopping horses and a few automobiles and ladies with hats big as pudding basins, to the luxurious Hotel Bristol.

Pierre descended from his carriage and walked purposefully into the well-gilded lobby. He was an elegant, neatly made man who always looked as if he'd been thoroughly polished. Even his fingernails gleamed like tiny shells. He was dressed, as usual, in silk hat, morning coat, knife-pleated trousers, and oyster-toned spats. He entered the elevator, ascended to an upper floor, knocked on the door of a suite, entered, and bowed to the young American couple who occupied it, Evalyn and Ned McLean.

Twenty-four-year-old Evalyn, small and scrawny, had an instantly forgettable face that was a long way from beauty, with no patrician bones, with eyebrows too heavy, nose too long, chin too receding. She was dressed to kill—to kill all competition and draw all eyes. It was the way she always dressed, taking the latest fashion one step beyond good taste, insisting at Worth's or Lucile's that the collar be made wider, the waist tighter, the trim showier. Over her, as he rose to greet Cartier, towered Ned, six feet two inches, 220 pounds, with features that were handsome except for the weak, fat-blurred chin, which spoiled the strong statement of his dapper mustache. He was only twenty-four, but his puffy skin and bleary eyes were those of an alcoholic, which he'd been since his teens. Sometimes he tied a sling around his elbow so that his arm would be steady enough to get the next drink to his mouth. Evalyn's drinking was intermittent, but she was hooked on laudanum, the black liquid form of opium. The young McLeans were members of what later would be dubbed the Lost Generation, but they didn't yet know that they were lost.

Evalyn looked at Cartier, pink cheeked and shining, perfectly groomed, and compared this sartorial vision with Ned's gray stubble of day-old beard, his skin sallow against a peacock silk dressing gown, his congealing breakfast pushed aside, untasted. She turned back to Cartier and grew curious. He was holding in one well-manicured hand a tantalizing, small, fat parcel tightly closed with wax seals. Inside lay Evalyn's future, her fame and hallmark, not yet recognized. Inside lay the Hope Diamond.

Pierre held the package in his hand while he gave Madame McLean his sales pitch, which was masterful. He began by reminding her that when she'd bought the huge, pear-shaped diamond known as the Star of the East from him two years before, on her honeymoon trip to Europe, she'd described her visit to Sultan Abdul Hamid in Constantinople, where she'd been allowed into the harem. "It seems to me you told me then you had seen a jewel in the harem," prompted Pierre, "a great blue stone that rested against the throat of the sultan's favorite." Evalyn frowned. "I guess I did," she replied without conviction. It was too early in the morning to argue. She didn't really remember. The sultan had an emerald that had made her fingers itch. But a blue diamond? She shrugged. She had a vile taste in her mouth and her temples were pounding.

Pierre kept on talking. Either from Rosenau and the French syndicate or from the tales of the Hope's curse floating around Paris when, a year before, a journalist there had netted them and dispatched them to the London *Times*, Pierre Cartier had become familiar with some of the sensational details relating to the Diamond's malevolent powers. He remembered that Madame McLean had told him that for her bad-luck objects were actually lucky, so into the gilt splendors of the Hotel Bristol suite he let loose Tavernier stealing the Diamond from a Hindu idol and being "torn and eaten by wild dogs"; Marie Antoinette with the guillotine slicing through her slender neck; Lord Francis Hope and May Yohe driven to desperate straits by financial woes; the sad spectacle of poor, flailing Habib going down for the last time in the shark-filled waters near Singapore. Pierre talked on, while the innocuous-looking little paper-wrapped bundle lay in one hand. Finally, Evalyn, in her harsh voice, broke in: "Let me see the thing."

Cartier very slowly took off its covering and revealed the Hope. Evalyn looked at it unmoved. With cold detachment she tried to pinpoint its strange color. Peking blue she considered too dark; West Point blue was too gray; was it that of a hussar's coat, or a piece of Delft china? Oh, what did it matter? What did anything matter? She didn't want it. She rejected it without even asking the price.

Cartier was crushed and silenced. The Diamond went back into its wrappings, back into homeless limbo. Pierre picked up his hat, bowed abruptly, and departed. The time for Evalyn Walsh McLean and the fabled Hope Diamond to come together, to lock into an embrace and dance step closer and quicker than anything the stone had yet experienced, hadn't yet come. When it did, it would be a case of Diamond in perpetual motion. But it certainly wasn't a case of love at first sight.

This was surprising, for Evalyn had been addicted to diamonds since she was thirteen. Her life, however, hadn't always been silk lined and luxe. Evalyn Lucille Walsh was born at 4:30 P.M. on August 1, 1886, in Denver, Colorado, a "puny, bluish little creature" whom no one expected to live. Her father, Thomas Walsh, tall and handsome, with piercing blue eyes and generous, red-fox-colored mustache, had been born in County Tipperary, Ireland, on April 2, 1850. He'd learned the trade of millwright, immigrated to the United States at age nineteen, worked as carpenter in the East, and gone west to Colorado in 1872, when gold fever struck. For the next twenty-four years, Tom Walsh searched for a rich deposit, often penniless, always hopeful. By 1878 he had enough money to open a hotel for miners in booming Leadville, high in the Rockies, where men slept on grubby sheets in three eight-hour shifts. Attending a local church one Sunday, Tom was entranced by the crystal-clear voice of the choir member and school-teacher Carrie Bell Reed, whom he married in 1879.

Whereas Tom was gregarious, chatty and charming, a typical Irish-man, Carrie was introverted, quiet, and shy. Baby Evalyn arrived after seven years of marriage, and a son, Vinson, two years later, on April 9, 1888. While Tom Walsh chased his American dream, the family lived a vagabond existence in shacks, log cabins, and fleabag hotels, so high in the mountains, as Evalyn tells us in her autobiography *Father Struck It Rich* (1936), that "I could suck a wisp of cloud fleece right into my mouth." In personality she took after her father, whom she adored and to whom she was always much closer than to her mother.

According to Evalyn, her "Papa" studied hard in those years to dis-cover all he could of "Nature's customs, of her whims in depositing precious minerals in the earth." This was Evalyn's first lesson: romance lay underground; somewhere way down beneath her little feet were great treasures that could make one happy, treasures to be had for the taking.

One day in 1896, when Evalyn was ten, Tom Walsh discovered a vast true fissure of tellurium gold in an abandoned silver mine near Ouray, Colorado, and life changed forever. That evening, his blue eyes sparking, he whispered to Evalyn in a voice full of excitement, "Daugh-ter, I've struck it rich!" He swore her to secrecy; if she told, there'd be a rush of other men to the site. She felt "proud that I kept my word" and that her father had confided only in her. "What a sound when that mill started!" she remembers of the Camp Bird Mine. "I'll never forget the day it came through the crushing machine, pure gold sand!" The gold sparkled and shone in the sun, a magic mountain. What other riches lay close to the world's heart? Within a year, the mine was yielding $5,000 a day clear profit and the Walshes found themselves incredibly rich.

At that point in her life, the cold cloud mist of a curse descended on Evalyn. By giving her lifelong wealth, her father had snatched away all unfulfilled desire, all reach and longing. His gold strike didn't so much provide as take away. If the Earth's minerals were a blessing, they could also be a malignant force. Her father gave her every material possession she could possibly want the instant she wanted it. There was nothing left to earn by her own efforts, to wait for, to dream of having. From age ten, Evalyn Lucille Walsh McLean was well and truly jinxed.

The Walshes moved to Washington, D.C., one year later, in 1897, where Tom became instantly popular and mixed easily in society; people thought Carrie stiff and cold. When he was with the family, her father showered Evalyn with love, attention, and presents; she liked that. But he was often away seeing to the mine in Colorado. Her mother retreated to a darkened room with yet another headache; Evalyn ran wild and grew into a real hellion. She swiped crème de menthe from her father's liquor closet and downed it secretly and liberally in her room. She ruined the dressmaker's sewing machine with chewing gum. She and brother Vinson together thought up ingenious ways to cause trouble. When an adult dinner party was in progress, they cut a hole in a valuable painted canvas screen and hit guests such as future president William Howard Taft in the face with a peashooter. Evalyn was well on the way to becoming the shock-'em showoff who married Ned McLean.

She met him when she was eleven, the year she arrived in Washington, at a dinner party. He was a tall, gawky eleven-year-old with a

sulky look who "turned around and stuck his tongue out at me." Evalyn
at once recognized a fellow hellion, as spoiled and bored as she was;
they became fast friends.

Ned's grandfather, Washington McLean, had started as boiler-
maker in Ohio and bought the *Cincinnati Enquirer* in 1857. His son,
John Roll, born in 1848, went to Washington, D.C., ambitious to
amass his own fortune, and purchased a local utility, a railroad line
(with a stop in Virginia that he named McLean), and in 1905 the
Washington Post. John raised his social status by marrying Emily
Beale, daughter of Gen. Edward Beale, whose lineage was more distinguished. Their only child, christened Edward Beale, but called Ned or
Neddie, was rumored to be in line for $100 million. Educated by tutors,
with winter frolics in Palm Beach and summer ones in Newport, Ned
grew up two blocks from the White House, at 1500 I Street, in a huge
Florentine villa designed by John Russell Pope, best known for the Jefferson Memorial and the National Gallery of Art. Weekends were
spent at Friendship, a yellow Georgian palazzo in northwest Washington, with seventy-five acres of landscaped grounds.

John Roll McLean was a hard man with an acid heart to match his
acid stomach. Ned, who was neither ambitious nor very intelligent,
felt he could never please Pop. Ned's mother, Emily, embodied the
qualities Evalyn knew she herself lacked, being "a gentlewoman in
every fiber," as Evalyn put it. Emily Beale McLean had pretty patrician
features, slim, elegant diamond-adorned hands, and a great deal
of grace and poise. Enthroned on a high-backed Italian chair in her
tapestry-filled gallery at I Street, she knew she was Washington's top-
ranking and most regal hostess.

She spoiled her only child as thoroughly as Tom Walsh did Evalyn,
giving him everything he wanted but none of the discipline he needed.
She secretly paid his little friends 10 cents to let Neddie win at games—
something he probably couldn't have managed on his own. No wonder
he stuck his tongue out at Evalyn; life was unfair from the start.

The year after she met Ned, Evalyn asked her papa for a horse-
drawn carriage and coachman to drive her to school. This created a

sensation among her classmates—which was exactly what she wanted. "The yearnings to be seen and heard, which I felt in my adolescence, were ten times more bedeviling than anything else that gave me irk," she recalls in her autobiography.

In the spring of 1899, when Evalyn was not quite thirteen, she sailed with her family on the White Star liner *Majestic* for an extended visit to Europe, stretching into 1900, her very first trip abroad. Her mother's sister Lucy Lee went with them; Evalyn loved and admired her popular, vivacious aunt, "the prettiest woman I had ever seen." Aunt Lucy had "extravagant enthusiasms for clothes, jewelry, and fine show horses," and when everyone told her she "ought to be on the stage, why then I knew again," writes Evalyn, "just why I wanted to be an actress: I'd be like my Aunt Lucy."

Tom Walsh had been appointed commissioner from Colorado to the 1900 Paris Exposition, an important world fair. In Paris the Walshes occupied almost an entire floor of the Élysée Palace Hotel, where Tom became friendly with King Leopold of Belgium, who wanted the American millionaire to supply money and expertise for exploring the Belgian Congo's mineral resources.

It was during her Paris stay that Evalyn found her second important role model after Aunt Lucy: Chicago's bejeweled queen, Mrs. Potter Palmer, who was one of the twenty American commissioners to the exposition. Bertha Honoré, nicknamed Cissy, a beautiful Kentucky girl, had married a millionaire twice her age, Potter Palmer, who'd drained Chicago's lakeside marsh, turned it into a Gold Coast of wealth and opulence, and opened the Palmer House Hotel. He built Cissy a Rococo palace and garlanded her with diamonds as big as Tokay grapes. Evalyn was entranced with Mrs. Potter Palmer's platinum hair and porcelain skin. "She let me finger to my heart's content her necklace of emeralds and diamonds," writes Evalyn. "I was allowed to touch her stomacher and exclaimed aloud when I saw into the green of the emerald drop that was suspended there." Right then, in the blinding flash of an epiphany, thirteen-year-old Evalyn was hooked on jewels, hooked for life. When Tom Walsh gave a sumptuous banquet at the Élysée Palace,

Evalyn walked down the golden staircase holding Cissy Palmer's hand, "feeling her large diamonds set in rings sharp against my fingers, catching the glitter of her bracelets in my eyes." Evalyn had found not only her main passion but her ideal self-image as well. Like Cissy Palmer she would aggrandize herself with diamonds as she strutted across life's stage. On that memorable day when she met Mrs. Palmer and her gems, Evalyn also found one form of desire that might not be instantly gratified, for she had to wait another eight years before she acquired her first big stone, the Star of the East, when she was back in Paris on her honeymoon.

Shortly after Evalyn's craving for diamonds began, her papa gave his darling daughter her very first; Evalyn's unconscious subsequently equated diamonds with love. She had copied the hairstyle of actress Edna May, star of the hit musical *The Belle of New York*. On a young girl just into her teens it looked ridiculous. Her father told her, "If you will wear your hair back off your ears as other nice girls do, I'll give you such a diamond ring as will make you quite the envy of all your friends." So Evalyn brushed back her frizzy earmuffs, and the diamond promptly appeared. Her first proposal came soon after, when she sneaked out of her Washington schoolroom to ride with "gawky Ned McLean in his back-firing motor car," flashing her diamond, pretending it came from some rival beau. "I think you ought to marry me," stuttered Ned. Diamonds did indeed spell love and approval.

Her mother hired a French governess, hoping to turn Evalyn into a decorous lady. But Evalyn was far too wild and uninhibited, with a harsh, unmodulated voice that made well-bred people shudder. She liked to declare, "I ain't no lady." She wasn't and never would be.

When pretty, fun-loving Aunt Lucy was killed in 1901, fifteen-year-old Evalyn learned another important lesson. Her aunt's carriage horses had bolted. Trying to jump to safety, Lucy landed instead on her back on the hard street, "wearing a jeweled comb which was driven deep into her skull." If jewels could give pleasure, they could also cause pain, even death. From that point in her life, Evalyn's view of them became ambivalent. When she came to compose *Father Struck It Rich* in the 1930s, she looked back at these years and her crucial meeting with Cissy Palmer. "I sometimes wonder," she muses, "if from my strong admiration for the sure social grace and beauty of that great lady I did not catch an infection that has made me, like her, the slave of jewels." By using such words as *infection* and *slave*, Evalyn reveals that in her maturity she well understood that gems were ambiguous in their power, both good and bad. They could give her self-confidence, a sense of identity, and an audience. But like a drug, they could also destroy.

Nevertheless, when, two years after Aunt Lucy's bizarre death, her father rescued Evalyn from the boarding school where she was desperately homesick to take her for a day's shopping in New York and asked her what she wanted, she replied at once, "Jewels." Off they went to the nearest store. The Camp Bird Mine was still producing and had netted Tom Walsh about $5 million, but he'd decided that he wanted time to enjoy and spend his money, so he sold the mine to a syndicate of British investors for $5.2 million, including cash, stock holdings, and a share of future profits. After looking about the jewel shop, Evalyn chose a showy turquoise-and-pearl dog collar. When she returned to school wearing it, looking like a prostitute with painted cheeks and lips, the headmistress hissed, "You disgrace this school." Jewels could signify love and approval, or death and disaster, or defiance of convention and notoriety.

In the fall of 1903 Tom Walsh, Carrie, Vinson, Evalyn, and twenty-three servants moved into a sixty-room four-story golden palace at 2020 Massachusetts Avenue (now the Indonesian Embassy), which he'd built for $835,000 with another $2 million spent on furnishings. The great hall, the full height of the house, with stained-glass dome, led through doorways with green marble columns into a Louis XIV salon. An elevator ascended to the top-floor ballroom, which had gold brocade walls. Those in Evalyn's suite of bedroom, sitting room, and enormous bathroom were covered in pink satin. Her many-piece dresser set had tops and handles in heavy gold, but "getting new things was less and less exciting." She covered every flat surface with photos of her parents and brother, Vinson; her love for them was fierce and faithful.

There in her pink satin bower Evalyn scribbled a letter to her absent father that hints at an Electra complex: "If you *even look at* any horrid little country girl I will simply come and pull her hair out! Now my own precious darling you must take the very best care of yourself." It was signed "with millions of love and kisses from your own little girl." (She was eighteen at the time.)

Later that year, to further her secret scheme of becoming an actress, Evalyn asked Papa to let her study music in Paris. Off she went with a woefully inadequate chaperon, a $10,000 letter of credit, and, by her own later admission, "about ten cents' worth of judgment." She rented a huge apartment, took one singing lesson from a teacher who winced and dismissed her, rouged her cheeks by licking crimson dye off books, bought a yellow velvet gown sprinkled with diamond stars and a lot of black lace underwear, and returned to America three months later with her dark hair dyed red. (In those days only "loose women" had red hair; those born with it were advised to use a lead comb to darken it.)

So that Evalyn could make her social debut in summer 1905, the Walshes rented Beaulieu from Cornelius Vanderbilt, a "cottage" at Newport, where Gilded Age barons were lining the rustic Atlantic coast with huge, incongruous mansions. Her papa gave Evalyn an $18,000 red Mercedes to tool around in. Brother Vinson was at the wheel on August 19 as they returned from lunching at the Clambake Club. Coming down Honeyman's Hill, the car accelerated; a rear tire blew; the auto swayed, skidded, and slammed through the railing of a bridge across a creek. Vinson was thrown out and killed instantly. Evalyn records that she was pinned beneath the Mercedes, flattened "into a dreadful darkness," which psychologically would last for months and months. As she slowly recovered from the pain of her beloved brother's death and from a compound fracture of the right thigh, she acquired her second addiction, after diamonds: to drugs, in this case, to morphine. Her ego, never very large, had also been crushed; for the rest of her life, her right leg was one and a half inches shorter than the other, necessitating a lift in her shoe, making her limp when she was tired and inept at sports.

During Evalyn's recovery Ned visited her often but "drank so much that he was on the verge of seeing things. We had broken our engagement over and over," but in 1907 she broke with him completely, didn't speak to him for many months, and became half engaged to several other men. On July 4, 1908, however, while she and Ned, reunited yet again, were staying at the Walshes' summer home in Denver, Colorado, they announced—for about the fiftieth time—that they were engaged. It was while driving in the environs of Denver on July 22 in Evalyn's newest present from Papa, a $15,000 yellow Fiat with pigskin seats, that they yelled, "Let's get married!" one minute and did it the next, speeding with maid and chauffeur to St. Mark's Episcopal Church nearby, where they talked the minister into marrying them.

Twenty-two-year-old Evalyn was determined to reform Ned. A rather pathetic card from St. Leo's Church, Denver, dated eight days later, shows that they both signed a total abstinence pledge in which the newlyweds solemnly promised God "to abstain from all intoxicating drink for the course of our lives." All too soon, however, they were both drinking again.

They put off their honeymoon trip until September, then sailed from New York on the *Rotterdam* with their stateroom filled with silver ice buckets holding champagne bottles at tipsy angles. "My own darlings," Evalyn scrawled in a letter to her parents, "dear Ned gets nicer every day" and "is getting to be just like my other darling sweetheart, Papa!"

Each of their fathers had given them $100,000 to spend ($200,000 would today be worth $1 million). As soon as they landed, the honeymooners bought a Mercedes roadster the color of rich, clotted cream in Amsterdam and crossed Europe and the Mideast on a madcap shopping spree, with their chauffeur Platt, maid Maggie, luggage, and purchases following in a Packard. The young McLeans felt like well-mated wizards, aroused by whim, wish, and each other, euphoric, erotic, pointing wands at this and this and this. Dresden, Cologne, Constantinople, Cairo, Paris . . . Evalyn bought a $40,000 chinchilla coat; Ned bought a second Mercedes. They ran out of money and wired home for more.

On December 15, 1908, they turned up at Cartier's Paris shop on Rue de la Paix, because Evalyn remembered that darling Papa had told her to buy herself a wedding present; since it was almost Christmas, she could make one stupendous gift do double duty.

She describes what followed in her autobiography. Suave Pierre Cartier greeted the McLeans, murmured, "We have just the thing for you" to Evalyn, and placed on a velvet cushion a diamond-link necklace from which hung an "entrancing" pearl that was "but the supporting slave of another thing I craved on sight," a huge, hexagonal emerald, bigger than Cissy Palmer's, above the 94.80-carat white Star of the East diamond. Evalyn was "hypnotized" by this "ornament that made bright spots before my eyes." With shaking fingers she put it around her thin throat and gazed at herself in the mirror.

The necklace gave her presence and a married woman's dignity. It made her look like somebody really important; the Star of the East was whopping; wearing a diamond that big would focus all eyes on her; *she* would be the star. "It is only when the thing I buy creates a show for those around me that I get my money's worth," she admits in her book.

"Ned, it's got me!" she cried. "I'll never get away from the spell of this." Never mind that it cost 600,000 francs ($120,000). She had to have it, "so we signed a receipt and Cartier allowed us children to walk out with the Star of the East." It made Evalyn feel "half-drunk" with excitement every time she wore it.

Notice how she describes buying her first really big diamond. She "craved," felt "hypnotized," "half-drunk," fell under a "spell." It was in Cartier's Paris shop on December 15, 1908 that Evalyn McLean's need of special, eye-catching diamonds first seized her and was gratified—which makes her initial rejection of the Hope two years later even more surprising.

She and Ned were kids on a mad caper, buying every toy in sight, looking forward to a bright future together. It was typical that they used Tom Walsh's check for $120,000 for other goods, didn't pay for the Star of the East necklace until four months later, and then only because Cartier threatened to sue. Evalyn and Ned were still too immature to realize that for every self-indulgence one ultimately paid.

If Evalyn's need of huge diamonds like the Star of the East was personal, it was also in accord with social convention for married women of her class and time. Since the 1880s, America's new millionaires, men like Potter Palmer and Tom Walsh, had been draping wives and daughters in spectacular diamonds because they were potent symbols of a self-made man's success in that industrial age, whether he'd made his pile in railroads, oil, steel, manufacturing, or gold. Diamonds conferred status, just as they always had for European aristocrats, the only difference being that New World plutocrats had to go out and buy what Old World blue-bloods inherited from their ancestors.

Harper's Magazine in February 1866 noted that "it is doubtful whether there is any diamond in the U.S. of more than 12 carats." Just under $3 million worth of the cut stones entered the country in 1873; by 1902 that figure had risen to almost $13 million. Diamonds always seem to gravitate to whatever nation holds greatest world power, whether it be France under the Sun King, Britain under Queen Victoria in the days of empire, or the United States in the twentieth century. Since America is still supreme, diamonds sold there account for almost half of worldwide sales.

One notable shift of diamond power from Europe to America came in 1887, when the French government auctioned off jewels that had once belonged to Empress Eugénie. Tiffany and Company, the jewelry firm founded in New York by Charles Louis Tiffany in 1837, bought twenty-four of the sixty-nine items on the block, including all those with the biggest and finest stones. The most spectacular piece, a necklace with four rows of 222 large diamonds, four of which had once been Cardinal Mazarin's, soon graced the neck of Mrs. Joseph Pulitzer, wife of the newspaper baron.

In the Gilded Age, Mrs. John Jacob Astor, Mrs. Clarence McKay, and Mrs. Leland Stanford were said to own more jewels than anyone in Europe except Queen Victoria and the Czarina of Russia, and when the new Metropolitan Opera house opened in New York in 1883, the first tier came to be known as "the Diamond Horseshoe," due to the flash and fire from every female seated there. Even a few of the self-made millionaires got into the act. "Diamond Jim" Brady had thirty-one different sets of diamond cufflinks, shirt studs, belt buckle, tie pin, and watch fob; one set contained 2,548 diamonds. Even

Louis XIV couldn't have topped that! Whereas Europe's aristocrats, whose heirloom diamonds weren't necessarily to their taste, wore them because it was the done thing, Americans such as Jim Brady and Evalyn McLean wore them because it was the fun thing. They got enormous pleasure from their stones. A fellow called Ned Green even put some on his chamber pot. Alva, wife of William K. Vanderbilt, flaunted a diamond chain that fell to her knees once owned by Catherine the Great, and Grace, wife of Cornelius Vanderbilt III, sported a diamond peony as big as a plate. If the sight of twenty-two-year-old nouveau riche Evalyn McLean wearing the huge Star of the East made titled Europeans sneer and murmur "vulgar," Americans understood the tradition she followed and were much more likely to approve—and covet.

When she and Ned returned to Washington, Evalyn smuggled in her giant diamond to avoid paying duty, and the newlyweds moved in with her parents at 2020 Massachusetts Avenue. Ned went, when he remembered to do so, to the *Washington Post*'s offices for desultory meetings and spent his days betting at the racetrack, gambling, drinking, and, all too soon, womanizing. He also continued as always to run through more money than he ever actually had, in a spendthrift pattern similar to Lord Francis Hope's, except that Ned had a generous father-in-law to pay his bills, his own being very tightfisted. Evalyn would later claim that her papa paid all their expenses; once she saw him hand Ned a check for $50,000.

Evalyn gave birth to a son, portentously christened Vinson after her dead brother, on December 18, 1909. The press called him "the Hundred Million Dollar Baby." King Leopold of Belgium sent a golden crib; President Taft came to pay his respects. Little Vinson was as spoiled and indulged in childhood as his parents had been, with an ermine carriage robe and all his clothes ordered from Paris; with birthday parties costing $15,000 or more; with an entire circus hired to perform just for him. Evalyn's anxiety level had been growing ever since her brother's death; she worried nonstop about everything, but especially kidnappers. Around Vinson she kept a tight circle of nurses, servants, guards, and detectives.

Four months after Vinson's birth, from which physically Evalyn had not yet fully recovered, Tom Walsh lay dying of lung cancer at 2020 Massachusetts Avenue. He was paying the price for all those years mining at high altitude. Evalyn was totally distraught and sat by his bed kissing and soothing him. On the evening of April 8, 1910, he gasped, "Take care of Mother, darling," touched her hand, became unconscious, and died at eleven-thirty that night.

Evalyn fell into a black hole that enveloped her for more than a year. Her father had always handled her finances; now there was his estate, worth almost $9 million, for her to deal with; Ned was drinking heavily, well-meaning but useless; her mother seemed to have lost her will to live and took no interest in anything. Evalyn had never felt so lost or so alone. She'd been careful while pregnant not to touch drugs or alcohol; now she needed both. She faked prescriptions for laudanum, went from drugstore to drugstore filling them, used her diamonds as accomplice, as power tool to get her what she wanted. "In those days a woman, diamond laden," she notes in her autobiography, "could buy laudanum by the quart, if she would simply pay the druggist what he asked." She grew pale and scarecrow thin from loss of appetite. Dazed and drugged, Evalyn drove aimlessly in her newest auto, speeding along dirt roads until her writhing black snakes of worries turned into chiffon scarves above her head and then just floated away.

Another trip to Europe might help. She and Ned left Vinson with his nurse and sailed on the *Mauretania* at the end of August 1910. Evalyn remembered how Ned had filled their entire stateroom on their honeymoon trip two years before with orchids; this time, instead, there were vicious fights between them, after which Ned sometimes blacked out and Evalyn poured her black liquid with a shaking hand, its diamond rings mocking with their clarity and sparkle.

When Pierre Cartier had come to the Hotel Bristol in Paris on a crisp autumn day, bringing the Hope in plain brown wrapper, Evalyn was too depressed, too sunk in lethargy, to be aroused even by her first and strongest addiction, diamonds. She was feeling blue enough without a damn diamond that matched her mood.

The disenchanted McLeans returned to Washington in October onboard the *Rotterdam*, and the Hope Diamond followed them across the Atlantic one month later, in Pierre Cartier's pocket. According to the *Jewelers' Circular Weekly* for December 21, 1910, he landed in New York on November 23. Customs officials valued the Diamond at $110,000 and charged 10 percent duty—which means it was unset, for duty on mounted stones was 30 percent. Pierre took the gem straight to Cartier's new store, opened almost exactly a year before, on the fourth floor of 712 Fifth Avenue, where the antique dealer Alavoine had provided wood paneling that closely matched the decor at 13 Rue de la Paix in Paris.

According to Evalyn's autobiography, Cartier dispatched a letter to Ned at once:

> We have the pleasure to inform you that Mr. Pierre Cartier has arrived from Europe this morning on the *Lusitania*. He has brought with him the documents concerning the Hope Diamond. He has a book written by Tavernier himself, who, if you remember, sold the stone to King Louis XIV.
>
> Besides, he has a book written by the great French expert of all the jewels of the crown of France [probably Germain Bapst's *Histoire des Joyaux de la Couronne de France* (1889)] and you will have there all details you require.
>
> Mr. Pierre Cartier will be glad to be honored with an appointment, so as to be able to give you all further details you may require.
>
> > Awaiting your kind answer,
> > We beg to remain, dear sir,
> > Yours respectfully,
> > Cartier

Supersalesman Pierre wasn't about to give up on the McLeans, even though madame had rejected the Hope in Paris. He'd seen how she'd reacted when he'd shown her the Star of the East; clever Pierre could spot an addiction to jewels when he saw one. However, before he presented it to Madame McLean again, the Diamond had to be made irresistible by a stunning setting that would flatter and enhance it.

Either in Paris or New York, the Hope's girdle was cut with many tiny additional facets to give it more "life." This was the stone's fourth treatment on the scaife, now powered by electric motor rather than horses or steam.

When Cartier's New York gem workers had put the newly faceted Diamond into a platinum setting and placed it on a bed of white silk in the Fifth Avenue shop, it had never looked so beautiful. Sixteen diamonds of alternating cushion and pear shape encircled it, handmaidens to a queen, but at a respectful distance, so that the deep indigo jewel had air and space around it. Later Pierre would tell the *New York Times* that soon after the gem was set, several people wanted to buy it, including a "Western capitalist" who wished to surprise his wife, but Cartier had other plans for the stone.

He told the McLeans that he wanted to bring the historic Diamond just given a new lease on life to Washington and leave it with Madame McLean for a weekend. Pierre never underestimated the power of a diamond to conduct a slow but successful seduction. So it happened that one Friday he walked into the imposing hall at 2020 with the Diamond and shortly thereafter walked out again without the Diamond but with a satisfied smile.

Evalyn tossed the Hope onto her dressing table, where it lay amid ropes of pearls, spilled face powder, yellowing invitations, and the gold dresser set given her by her darling papa when they'd moved into the house. She still missed him terribly, every day. In one drawer of her dressing table she kept, and often reread, the card he'd written on her seventeenth birthday:

> To my Little Mountain Maid. One half (½) Steinway special piano decorated to suit room for the Little Mountain Maid's birthday. . . . Get on good terms with Santa Claus and he might "lift" the other half at Christmas.

As she applied makeup with a heavy hand to the face that rarely gave her pleasure or pride when she looked in a mirror, she cleared a bigger space for the Hope. Its piercing blue was exactly like a big, round eye. Darker blue than Papa's, which had always been so full of light and love.

Evalyn picked up the Diamond and held it in her hand. Papa had given her the first one she'd ever owned, and the whopping Star of the East, and many others. Would he want her to have this one? "For hours that jewel stared at me," Evalyn remembers, its blue enlightened eye unblinking, as if it were trying to tell her something. Saturday passed, then Sunday, while she came and went from her dressing table, applying more rouge, letting her maid do her hair and fasten jewel clasps around her neck. On Sunday night Evalyn creamed her face before bed while the Diamond fixed her with a bold look.

She lay in bed unable to sleep, as she often did. "At some time during the night I began to want the thing," she recalls. She was bored with her life; she needed a thrill, something new. She'd long since realized that she could never change Ned's liking for booze and blondes. Hell, she couldn't even change her own life, in spite of all her attempts to cut back on the whiskey, the laudanum. She knew her "pointless, pampered life of spending" was all wrong, but she'd been so unhappy recently that she'd gone out and blown $60,000 on a sable coat. Cartier wanted plenty for the Hope; she was really strapped at the moment, and Ned wasn't much help when it came to money. Or anything else, for that matter. But maybe this time . . .

White diamonds were a dime a dozen; even ones as big as the Star of the East were seen on plenty of bosoms, usually on some old dowager's that looked like a pair of deflating tires, but nobody had a *blue* diamond, and Cartier said this was the biggest blue ever; none of the Vanderbilts or Astors, none of those Old Money snobs who snubbed her and sneered behind her back, had one. She could top them all; she could be the one woman in the world who owned what was probably the most famous diamond in the entire universe. The Hope . . . she liked its name. But what about the curse? Cartier had talked a lot about that. All those owners who'd died in weird ways. She'd flipped through the two French books Cartier had brought, but they were hard going. Still, all that business about the curse made a damn good story. She could hold any dinner table spellbound going on about it, maybe adding a few details of her own, poetic license and all that. There was something about that blue eye. Once you looked at it, really looked, you couldn't look away. The Star of the East wasn't like that, but then who ever heard of a colorless eye, clear as crystal? The Hope was different; it had depth.

She had to have it. It would really put her on the map socially. Evalyn curled her small body inside an imaginary shell and without even one gulp of laudanum went instantly to sleep. "It is no use for anyone to chide me for loving jewels. I cannot help it," she would later write. "They make me feel comfortable, and even happy."

By Monday morning, however, she'd changed her mind and returned the Hope to Cartier, angry that he wouldn't lower the price, so, as Evalyn tells us, "the deal hung fire for several months."

Not until Saturday, January 28, 1911, did Pierre mount the stone steps of 2020 Massachusetts Avenue again, this time with the Hope, a forty-five-diamond necklace, and a diamond bandeau, so that milady could wear the gem around her neck or in her hair. The three pieces nestled in a Cartier leather case custom-made to fit the jewelry's contours. Monsieur McLean told him that there was no way they were going to pay his asking price of $180,000; it was far too much. Cartier dolefully went back down the steps, but he'd seen the way Madame McLean had looked at the Diamond. He wasn't about to give up. He left the Hope residing at 2020.

That evening, realizing that it was Monsieur McLean that he had to convince, since the man of the house paid the bills, persistent Pierre went to see him at the *Washington Post* office and talked numbers, not, as to madame, tales of the stone's exotic past. The McLeans would subsequently claim—and who knows where the truth lay?—that Cartier told Ned that night that the Hope was actually worth $250,000; that to sell it now for a mere $180,000 was to leave Cartier no profit. Why, the diamond bandeau alone was worth $10,000 and there was the necklace as well. He was willing to take, as Madame McLean had suggested, her emerald-and-pearl pendant as part payment, worth $26,000. That left $154,000—$40,000 cash to be paid on signing the deal and the remaining $114,000 in bimonthly installments over three years.

According to Cartier's version of these events, Ned McLean then agreed to buy the Hope and summoned his lawyer, Wilton J. Lambert, who quickly drew up a contract. McLean and Cartier both signed it. Then the three men opened a bottle of champagne and celebrated the deal. Cartier claimed that since it was a Saturday and banks were closed, McLean told him he'd have to wait until Monday for his $40,000 cash; Pierre took the train back to New York that night.

On Sunday he received a telegram from a *Washington Post* employee. It seems that Madame McLean wanted some slight change made to the setting. He was to come at once with a gem setter so she could astound Washington society by wearing the Hope at a White House reception on Monday. Early Monday morning Pierre and his top workman went to Washington, mounted the stone steps at 2020, were told by the butler that Mrs. McLean was ill and couldn't see them and that they should go to her husband at the *Washington Post* office. There they were informed that he'd gone to Baltimore in search of money.

On Sunday, January 29, the *New York Times* had printed the exciting news that J.R. MCLEAN'S SON BUYS HOPE DIAMOND for "over $300,000." The *Times* described the fabled stone in terms almost as insulting as those voiced at the 1899 trial in London when Lord Francis Hope first tried to sell it and his lawyer referred to it as a *damnosa hereditas*. The *Times* reporter wrote that it was as large "as a good-sized horse chestnut" or "a walnut," as if it were something very common, as if there were millions of large blue diamonds! The article noted that William Schindele, a former Secret Service man, had been hired by the McLeans to guard the stone, and he, in turn, would be guarded by Leo Costello and Simeon Blake, private detectives. Of course, the *Times* wasn't going to miss an opportunity of entertaining readers with details of the Diamond's curse, and the whole cast of fictitious victims was mentioned.

After Pierre Cartier had signed the agreement on January 28 for the McLeans to buy the Hope, he went back to New York well pleased with himself and sent a telegram to inform brother Louis in Paris of his coup. Louis enthusiastically congratulated Pierre on the sale and announced it in the international press, since, as he told him, "It is a marvellous advertisement for Cartier's." The firm would soon buy another Hope gem: a 52.17-carat spinel from the London dealer Peake's, an impressive ruby red rectangular stone that had once resided near the Diamond in one of the glass-topped mahogany cabinet drawers where seventy years before Philip Hope had kept his jewel collection.

The Hope blue stone, having moved into 2020 Massachusetts Avenue, began its American life with its new owner, but all was not well in the McLean mansion. The Diamond, it seems, was not wanted; it was treated like an unwelcome houseguest.

Ned had apparently learned, perhaps from newspaper files in the *Washington Post* office, that Rosenau had, in June 1909, bought the Hope from Salomon Habib for the equivalent of $80,000. There was no way, Ned roared at Evalyn and at anyone else who'd listen, that they were going to pay $180,000 for that damn bauble. Cartier had tricked him. And to hell with the signed agreement.

Evalyn, for her part, was having second thoughts about owning a gem that might well bring nothing but doom and disaster to its owner. She thought of Aunt Lucy. She believed in extrasensory forces; she went regularly to an astrologer and often to fortune-tellers. What if the curse was real? Then too, her mother-in-law, "Mummie McLean," whom Evalyn admired and respected because she was a lady right down to her ribbon-threaded, lavender-scented underwear, pleaded with her, begged her, not to attach herself, darling Neddie, and dear little Vinson to such an ill-disposed stone. Either then or later, even May Yohe got into the act. Having seen the January 29 announcement in the *New York Times* of the Hope's new owners, she wrote to Evalyn detailing her own disasters and urging her not to keep it.

While this controversy raged around it, the Diamond lay unworn and unloved in its leather case, seemingly spurned for the second time by Evalyn Walsh McLean. Not knowing how to resolve her quandary, Evalyn increased her laudanum dose, while Ned ranted and raved and downed his whiskey.

The McLeans then told Pierre Cartier that they'd taken the Diamond only on approval and had now decided not to keep it. Cartier later claimed that they gave no reason for wanting to return it "barring some irresponsible 'old woman's talk' about the 'dreaded hoodoo.' "

Pierre stood firm. The stone was irrevocably theirs and he had the signed agreement to prove it.

He may well have wondered to himself at that point whether he should ever have mentioned to Madame McLean the jewel's supposed curse and the long string of victims it had claimed. She did appear, now that he knew her better, to be a rather nervous and neurotic woman and sometimes seemed to be living on some other planet.

During February Cartier sent his New York lawyer, John S. Wise, of 20 Broad Street, to Washington several times to try to collect the initial payment of $40,000 cash. Wise was told that Ned wasn't in Washington; he was in Palm Beach; he was in Havana. Five weeks went by after the signing of the agreement. The McLeans had the Diamond, not to mention the accompanying necklace, bandeau, and custom leather case, but had not yet paid a penny, nor had Evalyn turned over the emerald-and-pearl pendant, the part payment. On the morning of March 9, Louis and Pierre Cartier filed a suit in the Supreme Court of the District of Columbia against Edward McLean, demanding that they be paid. The *New York Times* gleefully pointed out that day that the unlucky new owners of the Hope "have not escaped the ill fortune supposed to follow it," being already in trouble after they'd had it only a few weeks.

Ned hired the lawyer A. S. Worthington to act for him; the final bill would be $5,000. On March 25, both Ned and Evalyn signed affidavits denying that they, the defendants, had ever "received or accepted from the plaintiffs a certain diamond and its accessories known as the Hope diamond and neckless [sic] on the 28th day of January, 1911 or at any other time." Evalyn swore on her affidavit that the Diamond was left at the McLean residence on January 28 "for inspection" and that if there were any subsequent negotiations for its purchase by her husband, she was not a party to them. Both affidavits were filed with the court on April 2, three days before the stipulated deadline.

On May 6, Justice Barnard of the Supreme Court of the District of Columbia declined to grant the motion of the plaintiffs for summary judgment and declared that since the McLeans were entitled to have a jury pass on the matter, the case would be placed on the trial calendar. The Diamond, however, during this stressful and uncertain period, exerted its charms on a woman who was passionate about jewels and who, deep down, in spite of the price, in spite of the curse, wanted to own this one and astound the world ever after. The *Washington Post* announced on February 1, and the *New York Times* the next day, that the McLeans had decided to keep the Hope Diamond, had agreed to Cartier's terms, and had signed a new contract.

For Evalyn, the thrill of being able to grab the limelight at last by wearing the Diamond triumphed over her anxieties concerning the curse—for the moment. After all, the new agreement with Cartier contained the following clause: "Should any fatality occur to the family of Edward B. McLean within six months, the said Hope diamond is agreed to be exchanged for jewelry of equal value." She wasted no time. The Hope would astound Washington society on the night of February 2, and again on the 5th, when she gave two parties as spectacular as her new Diamond, parties the like of which Washington had never seen and which, she hoped, would make Evalyn as great a hostess as her admired mother-in-law. To be crowned by Washington society as Emily Beale McLean's successor had been Evalyn's fierce and secret ambition for some time. Now she had the Hope to help her achieve it. She planned dinner for forty-eight, with another fifteen hundred guests coming later for music in the library and music room, where Madame Gluck and a tenor would sing. Both parties honored the new Russian ambassador to the U.S., George Bakhmeteff, who had a face deeply pitted by smallpox and a monocle in one eye, and who was married to Ned's aunt Mamie, his mother's sister, a sharp-nosed little woman with dyed red hair shading to pink.

The party decor, fittingly, was gold. Four thousand yellow calla lilies imported from London at $2 each decorated the rooms. Dinner guests dined off Tom Walsh's gold plates made from Camp Bird nuggets at a long table lit by his gold candelabra and festooned with yellow orchids. In the middle a fountain splashed mere silver, not gold, drops into a gold, orchid-swathed basin.

Evalyn played hostess in a Worth gown of silver net over white charmeuse, complete with train. The Hope's blue eye took it all in from the center of her diamond bandeau, and the Star of the East hung from a platinum chain around her neck. Of course, everyone admired her newest, bluest-ever Diamond and gushed over the goldest-ever decorations. Evalyn was almost happy that night.

There was, however, one unimpressed guest at both parties: Maj. Archibald Willingham Butt, military aide at the White House for the past four years and a gifted letter writer with a satiric wit. Archie scribbled a long letter to his sister Clara on February 8 telling her all about the parties "in the handsome home of poor old Tom Walsh, who died just when life became worth living to him." The gold table ornaments, according to Archie, "stood so high that no one could see the person opposite." "These are the only entertainments the Ned McLeans have given since their marriage," he continued, "and I think they have been sitting up at night planning to eclipse anything ever given in Washington. They succeeded." He tells Clara that "on direct authority" he knows that the first party cost $30,000. "But as wonderful as the dinners were," scrawled Archie, "nothing created half as much interest as the Hope Diamond. It's a hideous thing too. It looks like a piece of light blue coal. It was set in a bandeau and worn just above the forehead. Around her neck as a pendant she [Evalyn] wore the 'Carafe Stopper,' as most people call it." "A hideous thing . . . a piece of light-blue coal." This is worse than horse chestnuts and walnuts! (If one believed in the Hope's powers to curse, one could well make a causal connection between Archie's critical, negative comments and the fact that two months after he penned this letter, on April 14, he was one of the brave young men who went down with the *Titanic*, selflessly leaving lifeboats for women and children, while he drowned in a cold, coal-colored sea.)

When Archie saw the young McLeans on February 13 at a Republican Club banquet, he reported to his sister Clara that "Mrs. McLean did not wear the Hope diamond last evening at dinner, much to the disappointment of everyone there." He did, however, have an interesting conversation with Evalyn:

She sat next to me at the table and gave much of the history of the diamond. She says the grandparents have made them promise never to allow the diamond to go near the grandchild. She told me that the jewel had cost Ned just $250,000, and when they offered to give it back to Cartier for something of much less value, the jeweler refused to receive it, for he feared it would bring to his firm some fearful catastrophe. He frankly told Ned and his wife that there were no two such fools as they to be found in the world, who would not only possess the jewel but who would actually pay for its possession. It was this jest which infuriated the McLeans and caused them to try to force it back on Cartier.

Here is yet another explanation why the McLeans tried to return the gem. In mentioning Cartier's fear and a purchase price of $250,000, Evalyn was already manufacturing her own mystique around the stone, not letting truth stand in her way, and she would continue to do so for as long as she owned it. After all, its notoriety increased hers.

Seven months later, in September, "Mummie McLean," the person who had no doubts at all concerning the Diamond's evil powers, lay very ill at 1500 I Street with pneumonia, trying "with frightful wheezings to get air into her lungs." Her husband, John, reacted by asking Evalyn to wire Tiffany's or Cartier's in New York to send a superb string of pearls; poor Emily had always wanted one.

Her death a few days later caused Evalyn many sleepless nights while she stared into the black well of the curse. "I did believe that blue Diamond was a talisman of evil," she writes. May Yohe was still sending "letter after letter," trying herself "to recoup some bit of happiness from the ruin of her life." She blamed the Diamond; "as one woman to another," Evalyn tells the reader in *Father Struck It Rich*, "she begged me to throw it away and break its spell." But the six-month period Cartier had allowed for its return had passed.

Evalyn decided to have the Hope blessed by a priest. She and her maid, Maggie, took it to Monsignor Russell, who donned his robes and put the stone-in-league-with-the-Devil on a velvet cushion. Just as he blessed it, according to Evalyn, without any wind or rain, there was sudden darkness, thunder, and lightning that struck a tree in the street. By the time she and Maggie got home, the sun was shining. Evalyn claims that Monsignor Russell's words "gave me strange comfort. Ever since that day I've worn my diamond as a charm. I kid myself, of course—but I like to pretend the thing brings good luck." Her attitude to the stone is forever cleft in two: she both loves and hates it; her rational mind rejects the curse; her psyche accepts it.

She and Ned kept on living their privileged existence, its satin luxe unrolling over the blackness underneath. Their butler brought Evalyn each morning's mail on a silver salver. Holt Renfrew and Company wrote from Quebec to say they had some fine black fox skins at $2,000 each, suitable for muff and stole. Meyer Davis wrote to say his orchestra would be happy to furnish "music for Mrs. McLean at various times when she may require it." Tiffany's wrote to say they'd received her order for menu and place cards and would "give it prompt attention." Charlotte Burby wrote from New York to say she'd sent "by last night's express some very beautiful French hats, which we can duplicate in any color, should you care for them." Garrard and Company Crown Jewellers wrote from 24 Albemarle Street, London, England, in 1913 to offer the Hope pearl "so called because it formed a part of the collection of pearls and precious stones formed by Henry Philip Hope, Esq.," which "it is safe to say is the largest pearl ever found." But Evalyn had enough to cope with owning one jewel from the Hope collection; she didn't want another.

Evalyn and Ned's second son, christened John Roll after his formidable grandfather but always called Jock, was born on January 31, 1916. The baby's namesake died of cancer that year, on June 9, surrounded by nine physicians, at his weekend home, Friendship, after an illness of two months, during which he couldn't stop hiccupping. He left an estate of $7 million, but his will infuriated Ned, for it stipulated that he was to get only interest income, the principal to be kept intact until twenty years after the death of the last survivor of Ned's lineal descendents then living, namely Vinson and Jock. The American Security and Trust Company thereafter doled out something between

$500,000 and $880,000 annually to Ned—not nearly enough for his usual lifestyle.

There was also another mouth to feed, for a third son, Edward, was born on July 26, 1918. On August 1 that year an unsettling invoice arrived one morning on Evalyn's silver salver, bearing the letterhead of Cartier's New York firm. Pierre had for some time been looking for a bigger and better location than 712 Fifth Avenue, and when the splendid six-story Renaissance palace of banker Morton F. Plant came on the market, Cartier negotiated a clever deal whereby part of his payment was a two-strand necklace of fifty-two and seventy-three perfectly matched pearls, worth $1 million, which Mrs. Plant simply had to have. Below Cartier's new address of 653 Fifth Avenue, the invoice sent to the McLeans showed that even though the contract signed February 1, 1912, agreed that all payments for the Hope Diamond were to be made within three years, there was still, six years later, $58,500.25 owing, and that 6 percent interest charges, begun by a patient Pierre only in 1917, amounted to $3,500.23. Ned McLean had been paying only $1,000 a month, with two payments in 1915 of only $25.03 and $974.97. The invoice is still extant, but how its charges were finally resolved remains a mystery.

The McLeans now had two more houses to staff and maintain, having inherited 1500 I Street and Friendship after Ned's father died. The latter had been occupied during World War I by wounded veterans, so it wasn't until the spring of 1919 that Evalyn, Ned, and their three little boys moved in. Still fearful of kidnappers, Evalyn had a high stone wall built around the property, with a locked and guarded black iron gate. Ned built a private golf course; Evalyn indulged herself with a newly landscaped garden and acquired a huge white poodle called Sarto, a llama for the lawn, one monkey, assorted donkeys, goats, geese, and ponies, ostensibly to amuse the children but just as necessary for their mother. "Of all things in the world I hate boredom most," she admitted. Hummingbirds, good-luck symbols according to the Chinese, wove their tiny lichen nests that spring into the screens of the second-floor veranda that overlooked reflecting pools and topiaries. Friendship was a halcyon place; the children, at least, were happy there.

Only a month after they'd moved in, however, on a bright Sunday in May 1919, tragedy struck. Evalyn had packed her diamonds, fondly kissed nine-year-old Vinson, three-year-old Jock, and baby Neddie good-bye, and gone off to Louisville to watch the Kentucky Derby with Ned. She felt utterly depressed and anxious but didn't know why. On that May morning while hummingbirds whirred in iridescence high above the garden, Vinson walked out of the wrought-iron gate holding the hand of Meggett, Ned's valet. A gardener Vinson knew called Goebel went by with a cartful of ferns, so Vinson ran across the road to talk to him. Then, mischievously, he grabbed some ferns, started back across the street, and was knocked down, quite gently, by a Ford going no more than eight miles an hour. He got up, was brushed off, and was comforted by Meggett, by his bodyguard, always in attendance, and by Grand-mother Walsh. But his small head had hit the hard surface of the road; later in the day he became paralyzed from a subdural hematoma, and at six o'clock he died. Evalyn never recovered from this horrendous loss.

Had the Hope been responsible for killing Vinson? Fears, like huge bats, settled into corners of her mind and stayed. The Diamond's blue eye grew baleful. Her friends all told her to get rid of it, the sooner the better. But she had grown ever more dependant on the Hope, which gave her social clout and charisma, confidence, and even a strange kind of comfort. She couldn't live without it; she shouldn't live with it; she was caught in a real bind.

"Perhaps when people do think about it," she would later decide in *Father Struck It Rich*, referring to her blue jewel, "their first thought is 'It is evil'; and with a stone so well known, and with so many people keeping that thought in their minds, that might be the reason for its power and the cause of so much unhappiness always following the stone." She had to try to have nothing but positive thoughts about it.

But positive thinking wasn't part of Evalyn Walsh McLean's personality. The Hope stayed; her anxiety level rose.

In the fall of 1920 Evalyn and Ned's private railroad car, *The*

Enquirer, was attached to Warren and Florence Harding's *Superb* and off they went whistle-stopping through southern and midwestern states as Warren campaigned for the presidency. Wearing a smart fur coat, a hat with two big diamond hatpins, the Hope Diamond always at her throat, and at least one detective in attendance, Evalyn paced each station platform and drew all eyes. It wasn't easy to upstage a handsome presidential candidate, but with the help of the Hope, Evalyn managed it.

The Hardings and McLeans had been close friends ever since 1916, when Warren arrived in Washington as senator from Ohio. With his silver hair, black winged eyebrows, and features that begged to be carved on Mount Rushmore, Evalyn thought him "a stunning man with a powerfully masculine quality to charm a woman." For Ned, he was a hard-drinking, tobacco-chewing, poker-and-golf-playing buddy. His wife Florence, whom Harding always called "Duchess," had kidney problems, swollen ankles, and a tendency to fret and nag. Although Evalyn was only thirty and Florence fifty-five when they met, they soon became intimate; they both loved clothes, jewels, and astrologers, being clients of Madame Marcia. "I look upon you as one of my very tried and true friends," Florence scribbled on one of the many cards protesting deep love and devotion that accompanied huge bouquets of roses sent to Evalyn.

At parties Florence kept her eye on her husband, a chronic womanizer. Each time he vanished from sight, she would look around anxiously. "Where's Wu-rrr-en?" she would ask plaintively. At one party, when she'd gone in search of him once too often, the president muttered, "For God's sake, Duchess, play the game."

For him, the game included frequent moves from bed to bed, or on and off the floor. One mistress, Nan Britton, described a White House closet "no more than five feet square" where she and Harding routinely copulated. Another was sent off to a sanitorium when she got pregnant and a third woman in upstate New York committed suicide because Harding wouldn't leave Florence. The president, Ned, and cronies met their women at "the Love Nest," an H Street dwelling Ned owned, conveniently back-to-back with his I Street mansion and near the

White House. It had a parlor lined in beige satin with a big bay window you could look out of, but not in, a bedroom swathed in pink taffeta. One night things got so rowdy that a man threw a bottle, hit a blonde dancing on a tabletop, and killed her. Florence Harding, like her friend Evalyn, had reason to fret.

The two women took the train to New York on January 31, 1921, to shop for Florence's White House wardrobe. They chose dresses in a dark delphinium shade soon christened "Harding blue," which complemented the First Lady's azure eyes and white hair. Only on their last evening did Florence permit her dear friend to eclipse her by wearing the Hope Diamond while they watched a performance of *Green Goddess* at the Booth theater.

It was during 1921 that May Yohe and H. L. Gates published *The Mystery of the Hope Diamond*, which Evalyn, since she was mentioned in it as current owner, read with great interest. The book gave the idea of the stone's curse much wider currency than before, so the Diamond's fame, and consequently Evalyn's, increased greatly.

On November 16 that year, Evalyn gave birth to a daughter, who was christened Emily after her grandmother but who, at age eleven, would change her name to Evalyn and thereafter be called Evie. Her mother had a new hobby. While at one of the McLean residences, Briarcliffe Manor at Bar Harbor, Maine, in the summer of 1922, Evalyn produced a seven-reel silent film, *Tangled Hearts,* with helpful hints from D. W. Griffith, who'd become a friend, and direction by George Freisinger of Griffith's Hollywood studio. One wonders if Evalyn was inspired by George Kleine's *Hope Diamond Mystery* released one year before, for the plot of *Tangled Hearts* involved a beautiful adventuress, played by the daughter of the musician and radio personality Walter Damrosch, intent on stealing a famous gem who instead steals the heart of its handsome owner. The famous gem, of course, was played by the Hope. One scene necessitated the heroine's diving into the Atlantic from the deck of the McLean yacht with the indigo jewel wedged in her cheek. Evalyn never would tell her whether it was the real stone or a fake. The Diamond these days was finding itself more and more out and about, sometimes in strange places.

One morning it went off to Cartier's and returned with a hook appended to the bottom of its platinum setting, so sometimes when it reposed on Evalyn's chest it had to suffer the rival Star of the East grabbing attention by hanging on below, like some stuntman to a flying machine.

Evalyn and Ned's *Great Gatsby* kind of life continued through the twenties. Long processions of yellow-eyed autos appeared in Friendship's circular drive for wild weekend parties, where young men with patent-leather hair and too much gin inside them fell into the shrubbery, and young women with newly shingled hair and armloads of jade and ivory bangles pulled them out again. The McLeans always hosted a big New Year's Eve bash. At one, Evalyn appeared like a sprite on her stairway's top step, peered down at arriving guests, then darted away almost at once, wearing the Hope Diamond. And nothing else.

Ned's alcoholism got steadily worse—along with his party manners. He urinated on the leg of the Belgian ambassador and into a White House fireplace. He was so "fiendish" to Evalyn that she was drinking heavily, too. They fought constantly. Once, when he bellowed, "I'll knock your head off," Evalyn bit his finger to the bone, at which he hit her so hard that she keeled over. They lived hard and fast, and Evalyn swung the Diamond along for the ride. They drove recklessly on whim from one fully staffed house to another: from Black Point farm at Newport, where Evalyn wore the Hope on her bathing suit when she swam at Bailey's Beach; to twenty-six-hundred-acre Belmont Farm in Leesburg, Virginia, where Ned kept a stableful of racehorses; to Briarcliffe Manor in Bar Harbor; to I Street and 2020 Massachusetts Avenue and Friendship in Washington, where Evalyn gave balls for a thousand, luncheons for a hundred at Thanksgiving and Easter, Sunday night winter dinners for forty, where she often screened a brand-new film. She liked the world to come to her; she hardly ever went to other people's parties. There she couldn't be the star, as she could at her own.

Evalyn was at Bar Harbor when word came in August 1923 that Warren Harding had died in San Francisco. She raced back to Washington to be there when a distraught Florence stepped down slowly from the cross-country coffin-laden train. Underneath the insecurity, the craziness, the showing-off, Evalyn had a pure gold streak of kindness, compassion, and endearing candor. She was faithful to friends and attentive to the poor and needy.

One day when she looked in the mirror, Evalyn noticed "a faintly bulging line just above the place where my blue diamond touches me." It was a goiter, an enlargement of her thyroid gland, requiring surgery to remove it. Had the Hope caused it? Evalyn was by this time so dependant on it as identity badge, beauty mark, Band-Aid for her ego, and dramatic prop that she planned to wear it during the operation until the surgeon said no.

Her life was turning into a smashed martini glass at her feet. Ned was going through money at an alarming rate. One day Evalyn had to send his secretary to New York to pawn, for $70,000, a string of pearls her darling papa had given her. She left Ned; came back when he begged and pleaded and promised reform; left, returned, over and over, until 1928, when she left him for good. The last straw came when he started loading his shapely sweetheart, Rose Douras, the sister of William Randolph Hearst's mistress, the actress Marion Davies, with expensive jewels, while some of Evalyn's were sitting in pawnshops. She and the children stayed on at Friendship; Ned moved about with his rambling Rose from Palm Beach to Atlantic City to New York, where he kept a luxurious suite at the Ritz-Carlton Hotel. (When his unpaid bill there reached $35,000, the hotel sued.)

Whereas Evalyn was permanently addicted to diamonds and intermittently to drink and drugs, since their marriage Ned had been dependent on alcohol and on Evalyn, who'd been more mother than wife, telling him what to do and getting him out of scrapes. When, finally, she withdrew, he fell apart.

When the stock market crashed in October of the following year, Evalyn lost about a third of her capital and scrambled frantically to pay her bills. On November 7, 1930, she sued Ned for nonsupport; in January 1931 the court awarded her 40 percent of Ned's monthly income, with a maximum of $7,500, but Ned refused to pay and tried to divorce her in Mexico. His alcoholism by this time had damaged brain as well as body. In October 1931 Evalyn sued for a limited divorce and for Ned's removal as co-trustee of his father's estate, charging him with "marital unfaithfulness," with neglecting *Washington Post* affairs, with appropriating *Post* funds for his own use, and with refusing to pay personal debts.

The McLeans' party and free ride, begun with their madcap marriage and honeymoon twenty-three years before, was over; now they were paying the price.

When Ned, who had fled to Latvia with Rose to escape creditors, sent Evalyn a Christmas package in 1931 decorated with holly and reindeer, she found inside a summons to appear in a Latvian divorce court. She countered by obtaining a permanent injunction in the District of Columbia Supreme Court restraining Ned from divorcing her. She was so depressed by all this pain and turmoil that she had to go to Cartier's Fifth Avenue store and spend $135,000 on a bracelet with a 16-carat diamond known as the Star of the South surrounded by sixteen rubies and sixteen other diamonds. When she offered Pierre Cartier $50,000 cash and the balance to be paid monthly over two years, Pierre accepted, even though it had taken the McLeans so long to pay for the Hope Diamond. He needed all the business he could get in those lean Depression years, when a woman stepped out of a Rolls-Royce on Madison Avenue and sold it on the spot for $150, when well-dressed businessmen peddled apples on Fifth Avenue, and well-dressed male bodies, bent on suicide, occasionally came hurtling down from high window ledges.

Evalyn's mother died of lung cancer, as her father had, on February 25, 1932, and by the fall of that year Ned was in the American Hospital in Paris suffering from an enlarged liver, a stomach ulcer, high blood pressure, and a brain lesion. Evalyn desperately wanted to hold on to the *Washington Post* for teenage sons Jock and Neddie, after their father had been forced to relinquish control and resign as publisher, but creditors forced the *Post* into receivership in 1932 and left her no choice but to sell.

An auction took place outside the *Post* building on E Street on Thursday, June 1, 1933. From an upstairs window, Evalyn, her hair tinted red, wearing the Hope and a black dress, looked down on a shifting mass of straw boaters and panama hats as the *Post* was sold for $825,000 to Eugene Meyer, whose daughter Katharine Graham would run it for thirty years, and whose grandson Donald Graham is still publisher.

Evalyn's life now was a soap opera of ongoing catastrophe. In the next crisis her bank threatened to foreclose the mortgage on real estate she owned because she was behind in payments. Her eye fell on the Hope, lying so calmly on her dressing table: that two-faced, double-crossing gem, which kept her hurtling between hope and despair, love and fear, giving her daily comfort but also, for all she knew, causing all her woes. The time had come to pawn it. But she wouldn't just let it go quietly; for more than twenty years it had been partner and co-star. Together they'd stage an unforgettable scene.

Evalyn called a top New York pawnbroker, William Simpson, who had a shop at 91 Park Row, and invited him to Friendship. He arrived with wife and secretary, was ushered into an impressive drawing room. While he waited and waited for Mrs. McLean to appear, her friend Elizabeth Poe, women's page editor at the *Washington Post*, regaled him with lurid tales of the Hope's alleged curse. At last Evalyn made her entrance. Simpson saw "a small, very thin, middle-aged woman." He told her how much he was looking forward to seeing the Hope. Evalyn frowned and looked blank. "What *did* I do with that necklace?" she drawled. She sent her maid to search her bedroom, and after the right amount of time had passed, Evalyn exclaimed in a loud voice, "I know. Mike has it!" She walked—slowly, with all eyes on her—the full length of the drawing room to French doors at the far end, opened one, whistled, shouted, "Mike! Here, Mike!" A Great Dane bounded into the room. Twisted tight around his neck on its diamond chain was . . . the Hope!

In later years Simpson would repeat that story to anyone who'd listen, and when he wrote his memoir *Hockshop*, he gave the incident full coverage. On that memorable day, he held the famous stone reverently, thought it resembled "in color, sunlight reflected on the bluish gun-metal barrel of a shotgun" and that "if gazed at steadily for more than two or three moments" it had "a hypnotic effect." He gave Evalyn $36,500 for it (she says $37,500 in her autobiography), and some months later she retrieved it.

Evalyn stopped her divorce proceedings when she had to have Ned committed to the Sheppard and Enoch Pratt Hospital in Towson, Maryland, in the fall of 1933, after a sheriff's jury affirmed psychiatrists' testimony that he was "of unsound mind, a lunatic, without lucid intervals" suffering from "Korsakoff's psychosis and brain atrophy from alcohol saturation." Ned wandered about in pajamas, danced the hokey-pokey with the writer Scott Fitzgerald's wife, Zelda, who was also a patient at the hospital, and soon couldn't recognize Evalyn, who was a faithful and compassionate visitor.

By now she looked older than her years, her bulging blue-gray eyes covered by blue-tinted glasses, her dyed red or pink hair very sparse. For parties, she usually wore a wig but removed it if she wanted to scratch her head. She was drinking heavily and taking cocaine. A friend sent her to Dr. Alvin Barach, physician turned analyst, who noted that Mrs. McLean "would weave instead of walk." As part of her therapy, he went with her to rough waterfront saloons in her chauffeured car, where Evalyn would sit, without a drink, supported by Dr. Barach, her Hope Diamond, and her own courage.

For the rest of her life, sometimes sober, sometimes not, she mainlined on the Hope, which was never far from her person and usually on it. When she sailed with sixteen-year-old daughter Evie on the S.S. *Corinthia* for Russia at the end of June 1934, Evalyn took enough diamonds with her to almost sink the ship, set in eight bracelets, two clips, two pairs of earrings, a long chain, a cigarette case, not to mention two chains of sapphires and emeralds, one of turquoises, a few other pieces and, of course, the Hope. She loved it when one of the *Corinthia*'s daily newsletters slipped under passengers' doors each morning reported, in jest, that the world-famous Hope Diamond had been stolen from Mrs. McLean's cabin. Evalyn told everyone on board that Catherine the Great of Russia had worn it on the day she died.

When Evalyn landed back in New York on the *Berengaria* on August 31, a gratifyingly large group of reporters crowded around, snapped her picture, and interviewed her. The *New York Times* headline next day would read, MRS. MCLEAN BACK/A STUDY IN GEMS/SPARKLES WITH HOPE DIAMOND, BIG/SOLITAIRES AND EIGHT JEWELED BRACELETS. This was in the middle of the day. There was also a starburst of diamonds in her hat and more forming the chain for her diamond-studded purse. By this time Evalyn's diamond wearing had gone from drama to burlesque; the actress had unwittingly become the clown. She told reporters that although Soviet police had warned her not to wear jewels, being an intrepid heroine she'd defied them as she made her nightly round of nightclubs (knocking back the vodka) accompanied by two special Soviet police and conscripted staff from the U.S. Consulate. "I have a passion for jewelry. Everyone knows it. I make no defense of it," Evalyn admitted. "I was interested in wearing the Hope diamond because it had formerly been in the possession of Catherine the Great, and this was the first time it had been in Russia since her reign. Frankly, I think I am the only person in ten years who has given poor, dismal Russia a thrill." It was Evalyn McLean who, in 1934, first added Catherine the Great to the Hope's bogus owners and thereafter most newspapers did, too.

Wanting to spread her diamond-based fame even farther, Evalyn decided that year to write her autobiography and engaged as ghostwriter Boyden Sparkes, a journalist living in Wilmington, North Carolina, who'd written for New York and Washington newspapers before switching in the Depression years to the more lucrative field of ghostwriting. His clients included Walter P. Chrysler, founder of the Chrysler Corporation, and Alfred Sloan Jr., head of General Motors. After his initial meeting with Evalyn in New York at the end of November, Sparkes sent her a telegram that she carefully preserved: "I am so enthusiastic. I am sure we will take the curse off the Hope Diamond. You are simply grand."

On January 3, 1935, Evalyn and Sparkes began their collaboration; she talked and he transcribed, sitting in a sunny room at Friendship, where Evalyn was now ensconced most of the time, since both 2020

Massachusetts Avenue and 1500 I Street, after being closed for years, were about to be leased to the government to house New Deal projects personnel.

Father Struck It Rich, for which Boyden received $10,000 initially, plus half of all royalties, was serialized, for another $25,000 of which he got $6,500, in the *Saturday Evening Post* beginning on November 16, 1935. While Faber and Faber published the book in the United Kingdom and Australia, Little, Brown of Boston released its $3 hardcover U.S. edition on March 9, 1936. Their press release noted that "disregarding the warnings of her Irish father's blood, Mrs. McLean plans to make her first public appearance in New York following the publication of her book, in Brentano's bookshop on Friday, March 13th, wearing the Hope Diamond, to which tradition has ascribed a legend of ill-luck which dogged the footsteps of such famous owners as Marie Antoinette, who was guillotined; Lord Francis Hope; and actress May Yohe." In the land of hype and sell, no one ever missed a chance to exploit the world's most famous diamond for material gain.

Evalyn's arrival in New York and book signing at Brentano's Forty-ninth Street shop was recorded by Pathé News film company, to be shown in movie houses all across America. Ablaze with diamonds and the Hope, which she put on fondly, gratefully, for it had brought her to this pinnacle, Evalyn preened before the cameras, more ham than writer.

Some of the reviews of the book hurt, particularly the word *vulgarity* hurled at her by Robert Van Gelder in the *New York Times*: "Coming out of a mining camp into the inheritance of a big, brand-new fortune," he wrote, meant that Mrs. McLean knew nothing of "good taste" or good manners. Evalyn soothed her chafed ego by planning a grand party at Friendship for New Year's Eve, in honor of her son Jock's twenty-first birthday, a party that cost her $50,000, almost half her annual income, which was then only about $126,000. She enlarged the house to make a dance floor big enough for three orchestras, and invited 325 guests for a sit-down dinner, with another 325 for dancing, all-night buffet, and breakfast. Evalyn took her plaudits in a circle of fifteen private detectives, wearing the Hope, the Star of the East, and diamond bracelets from wrists to elbows.

The blue Diamond never had a moment's rest. When, in July 1937, Central City in Colorado staged their annual Play Festival, the dramas on stage got "strong competition for attention," according to the local newspaper, "from a wholly unexpected source, the storied Hope diamond," which Evalyn wore every day as she strolled about the narrow sidewalks in a flowered dress and every night as she watched a play, sitting in an old red hickory chair in the opera house built by miners. Newspaper accounts of the Colorado visit that called the Hope "the most talked-of diamond in the world" proceeded to focus more on it than on her. The Hope was beginning to upstage her; sometimes Evalyn felt like a mere train bearer to the damn thing.

Later that year, in need of money, Evalyn began writing a column titled "My Say" for the *Washington Herald* (which became the *Times-Herald* in 1939), owned by her friend Cissy Patterson, a clever, rich, red-haired woman, who also owned a spectacular rope of black pearls, a Dupont Circle mansion, and an insatiable sexual appetite. Once someone had turned on the lights in Alice Roosevelt Longworth's bathroom to find Cissy and Alice's husband, Nick, rolling about the floor, locked in drunken and amorous embrace.

Evalyn's columns appeared for the next five years under a photo of her wearing a diamond tiara and the Hope, which she mentioned in one of them:

> If you put it directly under any light, and keep it there, you can see it change, sometimes getting darker and sometimes getting a greenish color. I personally am not afraid of the Hope diamond, but I always warn my friends not to touch it. It is a strange and fearful thing how many people who have touched it have had unnatural and a great many times horrible deaths soon afterwards.

In spite of a lot of fan mail generated by her columns, Evalyn was increasingly lonely at Friendship. Both sons married in 1938 and moved to other states, Jock to Texas and Neddie to Colorado. In the following year, daughter Evie moved to New York to study dress designing. Even the Hope left—temporarily. From April 29 to May 17, 1941, it was part of a special exhibit of famous gems at Cartier's New York store and found itself reunited with some other alumni of the French crown jewels, including a 24-carat oval diamond willed to the Sun King by Cardinal Mazarin, stolen from the Garde-meuble in 1792, repossessed by Emperors Napoleon I and III, and bought eventually by John Astor.

Ned died that year, on July 27, after eight years of insanity and hospitalization, leaving debts of more than $1.5 million and nothing for Evalyn. His obituary in the *New York Times*, predictably, was headlined, E. B. MCLEAN DIES, EX-PUBLISHER, 58, GAVE WIFE HOPE DIAMOND. Evalyn arranged a small private funeral service at Friendship and drank to his memory.

Less than a month later nineteen-year-old Evie, who had an annual income of $80,000 from Grandfather McLean's estate, announced her engagement to her mother's buddy, fifty-seven-year-old Robert Rice Reynolds, who'd been married four times and advanced himself along the way from wrestler, sideshow barker, and lawyer to U.S. senator for North Carolina. Reporters asked Evie if she would wear the Hope Diamond at her wedding. "You mean that thing of Mother's?" she asked ingenuously. No, she told them; it wasn't suitable for wedding jewelry.

Evie and Bob were married at Friendship on October 9 at noon, with only a few relatives and servants present. Evie wore a simple brown wool dress and carried a horse chestnut for good luck; her mother, even though she was in her own home, wore a silver fox jacket over a printed black-and-blue-silk dress, a black felt hat with blue feather, the Hope at her throat, and a modest clutch of only four diamond bracelets.

When the United States entered World War II in December, Evalyn sold Friendship to the Defense Home Corporation to help house war workers and bought Friendship II on Wisconsin Avenue at R Street. She stuffed her last and smallest home with furnishings from former establishments relinquished one by one and set up around the swimming pool statues from gardens foregone, including one of French king Louis XIV, that kindred spirit who wrote the book on diamond power.

She did her bit for the war effort. Every Wednesday Evalyn visited disabled veterans at Walter Reed Hospital, taking them books, soft drinks, and the Hope Diamond on its chain to play with, so that it found itself airborne from wheelchair to bed, or up against some hairy chest. Evalyn also gave biweekly parties at Friendship where a busload of fifty wounded G.I.'s and their girlfriends arrived to drink beer, roll back Oriental rugs, and dance on stiff new artificial limbs. Evalyn was in her element signing autographs, passing around the Hope, and posing at evening's end in a group photo.

In spite of her earlier cautions that other people should eschew close encounters with the dastardly Diamond, it was now practically public property—anybody who wanted to touch or try it on could, as Evalyn's exhibitionism won out over her scruples. When a former WAVE married an amputee veteran in 1945, the Hope adorned her wedding gown, as it did the neck, just for one magic moment, of a little girl who attended a McLean party with her parents.

Evalyn also gave frequent parties for Washington's political and social elite in those tense wartime years, often banging on her dinner table to get everyone's attention, before croaking, "Now, you listen to Old Lady McLean!" Sometimes she gave a dinner and never bothered to appear, preferring to drink whiskey with some politician in her cozy study, oblivious to the fact that the caterers hadn't delivered the main course because she hadn't paid her last bill.

She was growing more frail, eccentric, and addicted to cocaine. "Getting old is a tragic and sad business," she sighed in a "My Say" column. In early September 1942 she fell, broke three ribs, and lost eight pounds while recuperating. When Jock's wife, Agnes, asked her to visit, Evalyn replied on September 28:

> I do honestly think it is better living here alone just to have my dear little nurse and Miss Chase [Nannie Chase, secretary and companion] with me. Take care of yourself, dear girl, and remember any day or night you may see sweep out of the heavens your awful old

Mother-in-law with her hooked beak of a nose and I will fool you because while you will say "that is just another American Eagle going
by" it will be me.

From habit and need, the Hope stayed close. When Evalyn retired,
it rested on the nighttable, whose drawer held a gun in case of burglars,
for in a suitcase beneath the bed lay all her less cherished jewels. When
she stayed in bed all day, the Hope hid under a pillow.

Evalyn was sick in bed on the night of Friday, September 20, 1946;
a physician came to see her. Daughter Evie and Evalyn's adorable little
granddaughter, Mamie Spears Reynolds, not quite four, had arrived
some days before for a visit. When the butler heard Evie's little dog
frantically barking outside her locked door, he broke it down, found
her stretched out, blue and unconscious, on the bed, rushed down the
hall to fetch the doctor, but it was too late; he could do nothing. Evie,
age twenty-four, who, according to news media, had been ill for some
time, was dead, accidentally or not, of a lethal combination of sleeping
pills and alcohol.

Fears of the Hope's curse beset Evalyn through that terrible night.
Surely that wicked blue Diamond was slowly destroying her, blow by
blow; it had taken her father and her darling little Vinson; it had taken
all of Ned's sanity and half of hers; now it had taken Evie. Yet she
couldn't give it up. The Hope was her; she was the Hope. They were
joined till death did them part. . . .

It came soon enough, only seven months later. In April, as the
Japanese cherry trees blossomed around Washington's Tidal Basin,
Evalyn lay dying of pneumonia at Friendship II. She would, however,
leave this world with all the drama she could muster. As she gasped for
breath inside an oxygen tent in her bedroom, on Saturday, April 26,
1947, Evalyn staged her last party. In addition to Dr. Barnard J. Walsh,
her physician, those attending it, in a circle round her, were Father Ed-
mund Walsh, vice president of Georgetown University; Supreme
Court Justice Frank Murphy with his secretary, Eleanor Baumgartner;
Judge Thurman Arnold and Mrs. Arnold; Frank C. Waldrop, *Times-
Herald* editorial writer; son-in-law Bob Reynolds; and Evalyn's secre-

tary Nannie Chase. Sixty-year-old Evalyn Walsh McLean died as she had lived: with a bang, not a whimper.

As soon as Dr. Walsh pronounced her dead, at 6:15 P.M., Thurman Arnold, executor of her estate, and Frank Waldrop went carefully round the room collecting all the jewelry scattered in drawers, vases, and slippers. After much searching, they found the Hope in the back of a tabletop radio, where it had been bombarded with jazz and news bulletins. They dumped all the jewelry, worth a cool million or two, into a shoe box and tied it with string. The two men got Evalyn's butler to drive them to her bank so they could put the shoe box in a safe-deposit box, but it was Saturday night; the time locks were on in every Washington bank vault; no one could get access until Monday. Finally, Frank Waldrop had a good idea. He and Arnold took the very ordinary box with its billion-year-old occupant up to the office of J. Edgar Hoover, head of the Federal Bureau of Investigation and a good friend of Evalyn's, got his approval by phone to deposit the box, and left with a receipt.

But legends, as always, were still growing as fast as fireweed around the Diamond. Justice Murphy soon claimed that after his friend Evalyn died, he put her jewels into a paper bag and cruised around Washington all night in a taxicab before placing them Sunday morning in a safe-deposit box at Riggs National Bank.

Time magazine reported Evalyn's death in their May 5 issue as that of "Washington's most famed and lavish hostess, owner of the reputedly unlucky 44½-carat Hope diamond." *Time* estimated its worth at $2 million and named some of the stone's famous victims, including the fictional Prince Kanitovski and his murdered mistress, Lorens Ladue. In its obituary the *New York Times* added Catherine the Great to the Diamond's list of owners; Evalyn had done her work well.

Evalyn was buried beside her daughter, Evie, in the family vault at Rock Creek Cemetery, while all of America waited breathlessly to learn the disposition of the Hope. The country's newspapers announced on May 1 that the principal of Mrs. McLean's estate, probated at $919,550, and all her jewels were left to her seven grandchildren, to be held untouched in the care of four trustees until the five eldest grandchildren

reached twenty-five years of age. Mamie Spears Reynolds, the fifth eldest, wouldn't be twenty-five until October 15, 1967. When that day
came, the young heirs could decide the Hope Diamond's fate. But that
was twenty years away! Was the world's most notorious jewel to be out
of the news for twenty long years, a complete blackout? All of America
sighed in frustration. They needn't have, for the Hope would be missing
from headlines for only twenty-three months.

Harry Winston, photographed by Alfred Eisenstaedt.

9

WIZARDRY

... expressing,
Although they want the use of tongue, a kind
Of excellent dumb discourse.

—WILLIAM SHAKESPEARE, *The Tempest*, act 3, scene 3

The Diamond had been crisscrossing countries and cultures for more than two thousand years; packed within it now, as tightly as its carbon atoms, was rich and varied reflection. One might have thought, particularly after its roller-coaster existence with Evalyn Walsh McLean, that by 1949 the jaded jewel had been everywhere, done everything. But on Monday, April 4, the Hope underwent an experience quite unlike anything that had ever happened to it.

The brand-new adventure began in a familiar way, for the Diamond was wrapped in brown paper, just as it had been in 1910 when Pierre Cartier carried it through Paris streets to the young McLeans honeymooning at the Hotel Bristol. On that spring day thirty-nine years later, however, there were no class-conscious red wax seals put onto its paper wrapping, only a surfeit of little bitty stamps, for the Hope found itself being launched into the anonymity and jostle of the United States Postal Service. The Hope was handed across a counter, registered, insured, and stamped, which cost $159.87, and with person-to-person handling guaranteed and guards to dance attendance along the way, traveled by train from Washington to New York, where its new owner, who regularly shipped gems to himself by parcel post, and who often said, "If you can't trust the United States mails, who can you trust?" eagerly awaited it.

It was almost exactly two years since Evalyn McLean had died and her executors Thurman Arnold and Frank Murphy had deposited the shoe box containing seventy-four gem-studded items in the FBI's vault. The Diamond remained there until after the will had been probated and it had been appraised, on December 30, 1947, at $176,920. Then Thurman Arnold reappeared at the FBI clutching his receipt, retrieved the shoe box, and clapped it straightaway into another Washington vault. Evalyn had wanted her jewels to stay incognito for twenty years, out of the limelight, so as not to tarnish her posthumous image by adorning some other female. But her extravagant lifestyle had left a mountain of debts. The court therefore granted a petition from executors, trustees, and family, allowing them to sell the entire gem collection to the highest bidder. Millie Considine and Ruth Pool in *Wills: A Dead Giveaway* claim that all seventy-four McLean pieces were sold together for a mere $611,500. However, in his autobiography *Fair Fights and Foul*, Thurman Arnold claims—and as executor he should know—that the collection fetched "roughly one million dollars," a figure later reported by *Time* magazine as $1,100,000.

On the morning of Tuesday, April 5, the day after it was mailed in Washington, an armored post office truck picked up the package containing the Hope and companions at New York City's General Post Office on Thirty-third Street. In addition to the armed driver, the vehicle contained a regular mail carrier, an armed guard, and William J. Brady, senior assistant superintendent of the Division of Registered Mails. The truck drove north and east through the usual heavy midtown traffic and drew up before a six-story graystone mansion at 7 East Fifty-first Street, which bore the sign "Harry Winston Inc." Patrolmen were stationed at the imposing entrance of a town house, which, fittingly enough, formerly belonged to Mrs. Marius Brabant, daughter of a mining millionaire whose wealth, like eminent jeweler Harry Winston's, originated underground.

The guard stepped down from the postal truck with brown paper parcel in hand and nodded to the receptionist, Miss Shaw, whom he could see through a window sitting at a Louis XVI desk on the left side of the massive steel door that could only be electrically opened from inside; she pushed a button to admit him. (Winston's alarm system could simultaneously alert a private security firm and police patrol cars.)

As the heavy door closed behind him, the armed guard was greeted by the proud, excited new owner of the Hope Diamond, the Star of the East, and the lesser lights of Evalyn's collection: fifty-three-year-old Harry Winston. Only five feet four inches tall, with a handsome, boyish face, thick, graying hair, and eyes that normally sparkled with an intense joie de vivre but that could turn in an instant to cold steel, Harry wore a dark, impeccably tailored double-breasted suit and, as always, no jewelry.

Like Jean-Baptiste Tavernier, having learned his trade informally from other jewelers, Harry Winston earned his living by moving diamonds in and out of the marketplace. Like Philip Hope, he loved them for themselves and was deeply in awe of their beauty. Like Evalyn Walsh McLean, he centered his image and built his fame on diamonds. Harry ran his empire like "a little Napoleon," according to New York's Diamond District dealers, and had decreed strict rules for all gemstones entering his sanctum for the first time; today correct procedures would have to wait. Harry had a "genius"—that was the word which rested like an invisible crown on his head whenever jewelers and diamantaires talked about him—a positive genius for publicity. He'd been the very first jeweler to hire a full-time public relations person, Jill Ceraldo. She stood near him now, having just welcomed a group of journalists and photographers to the main salon, an elegant room furnished with antique chairs and tables. The press group hushed, cameras and pencils poised, as Harry ceremoniously unwrapped the paper parcel and spread its gems out on a large black velvet pad atop a Louis XVI gilded table not unlike those the Hope had reflected in its final traumatic days at Versailles 160 years before.

While the press were there, Harry was everywhere at once, talking to them in his charming, vivacious way, concentrating on them, not on the jewels, whose time would come later, when he could be alone with them in his office, up one flight of the spiral marble staircase behind him. After the last camera flashed, the last notebook closed, and the media departed, the gems were taken up to the third floor. They passed through a series of locked doors to the comptroller's office, where the Hope, the Star of the East, and the other pieces were weighed, given numbers, and registered in a loose-leaf notebook. Then they went farther aloft to the sixth floor where, in addition to a big room where all grades of diamonds, including those destined for industrial use, were sorted at long tables placed under north windows, stood a huge, electrically controlled walk-in safe. In it the tissue-wrapped Hope was laid to rest among thousands of its kind hiding in waxed paper pockets inside brown envelopes, which had been carefully filed into thousands of categories by weight, form, brilliance, and color.

Four stories below, after Harry had consumed his usual lunch of tea and graham crackers at his desk, he conducted business around the globe by phone, saw several important clients, dictated letters to his secretary, and raced upstairs several times to examine a diamond in the big sixth-floor north windows. He was a man of brooding quiet, tense, tamped down, ready to explode into rapture over a diamond or rage at some employee's action that didn't meet his perfectionist standards. He had great imagination and intuition and a keen aesthetic sense. His office was tastefully decorated with matching loveseats facing each other before a fireplace, with Louis XVI chests, tables, and chairs. On a small desk in one corner stood photos of his dark-haired, attractive wife, Edna, and his two sons, Ron, age nine, and Bruce, age five. Harry loved life, his family, and most of all diamonds. His relationship with the latter went far beyond a business concern whose profits over the years would yield enough for a Fifth Avenue apartment, a country house in Westchester, Connecticut, and a villa on France's Côte d'Azur.

At the moment Harry Winston Inc. was grossing about $20 million a year. Tavernier, that earlier gem merchant who, 281 years before, used the Hope to get himself a barony and the lucrative custom of a king and court, would have stared in wonder at what Harry Winston had achieved in the gem business. He had interests in South American mines; employed four hundred cutters and polishers in New York, Amsterdam, and Puerto Rico; sold diamonds both wholesale and retail, every grade from world famous down to those in Montgomery Ward's $37.50 engagement rings (the latter not connected to his name); sent salesmen around the world; would open jewel salons, in 1955 and 1957, in Geneva and Paris; designed and manufactured jewelry for the superrich. Inspired by a holly Christmas wreath, Harry got the idea of using diamonds as if they were leaves, setting them in fine platinum or iridium wire—he hated gold—giving them a new three-dimensional lightness. He sold to kings and maharajas, billionaire sheikhs and shipping magnates.

Born March 1, 1896, on the third floor of a five-story walk-up apartment building on New York's West 106th Street, Harry was the third son of Ukrainian immigrants. His father, Jacob (whose surname may have been Weinstein or Weinberg originally), owned a modest retail and repair jewelry store on Columbus Avenue, opened by him in 1888. Unfortunately Harry's mother died when he was only seven, leaving him with a yearning never appeased. One day when he was twelve, he saw in a pawnshop window a green stone in a ring, sitting on a tray below a sign: "Take your pick—25 cents." At that moment, the first of a lifetime of jewels enchanted Harry; he entered the shop and bought the green gem. His father was astonished to find, after cleaning it, that he was holding a 2-carat emerald, which he was able to sell for $800. How had Harry known? "I think I must have been born with some knowledge of them [gemstones]" was his adult claim. Without ever formally studying gemology, "by the time I was thirteen or fourteen," he said, "my judgment of the quality of a gem was so sure, so instinctive, that my father counted on me to advise him." While young Harry's intuition reached to the soul of a jewel, his imagination began creating his personal mythology. For the rest of his life, he loved to tell the story of that green stone; as an adult he was a skilled fabulist who mesmerized listeners with tales of famous rulers and screen goddesses and diamonds he had known. "I love the diamond business," enthused Harry. "It's a Cinderella world. It has everything! People! Drama! Romance! Excitement!" Like Jay Gatsby in Fitzgerald's *Great Gatsby*, Harry Winston possessed "an extraordinary gift for hope, a romantic readiness."

When he was fourteen, he moved to Los Angeles with his father and younger sister, leaving older brothers Charles and Stanley selling antiques and crystal in a Manhattan shop. (Later they would open their own store on Madison Avenue.) The next year Harry left school and went to work full time in his father's jewelry store on Figueroa Street. He learned his trade there and from visits to other jewelers. "Each gem they showed me was like a friend," recalled Harry, "unique and unforgettable." If he met it years later, he recognized it instantly. From then on, Harry anthropomorphized jewels, especially the fairest among them, diamonds. They weren't objects for him; he turned them, with one wand-flash of fancy, into persons.

While working for his father, he often packed a satchel of jewelry, clapped a visor cap on his head, and hit the road, peddling his wares to oil prospectors in southwest California's boomtown saloons. In 1920 the three West Coast Winstons moved back to New York and Jacob opened a shop on St. Nicholas Avenue, which he would run until his death nine years later. Harry, however, struck out on his own, diamond dealing on the Lower East Side, which contained New York's Diamond District until 1926, when it moved uptown to West Forty-seventh Street between Fifth Avenue and Sixth. Harry hustled among the Hasidic Jews in black coats and hats who gathered on the sidewalk, holding little folds of paper full of diamonds, looking at them in the preferred light, which was natural, northern, out of direct sun, and best around 11 A.M. Other diamond dealers hurried in and out of buildings where signs painted on windows above proclaimed "Mr. Diamond," "Diamond-Rama," "Futura Diamonds," and where the elevator operator was often a detective. Harry worked in this wholesale market for long hours each day, looking and accurately reading the diamonds he bought at a bargain and sold at a profit, each deal concluded with a handshake and *"Mazel un brucha"* (luck and blessing).

In four years Harry saved $2,000, rented an office at 535 Fifth

Avenue for $100 a month, and opened his own firm, the Premier
Diamond Company. In need of a loan, he put on his visored cap and
approached the board of directors of the New Netherlands Bank of
New York. They mistook the small, youthful twenty-eight-year-old for a
messenger boy and told him to send his boss. Harry charmed them and
got his loan, but he also hired a tall, white-haired frontman for future
negotiations.

Many of the diamonds with which the new millionaires of the
Gilded Age had adorned their wives were now reappearing in the
marketplace as their original owners died: stones set in massive stom-
achers, tiaras, corsage ornaments, and dog collars, all of them out
of fashion. Harry bought them up, looked into the heart of each diamond, divined its true potential hiding under some old, imperfect cut
and within a cumbersome, heavy setting. Harry became a Prospero figure, enchanter and magician, who communicated with diamonds via
an "excellent dumb discourse," who commanded them to reveal themselves in full and perfect shining. He thought of himself as nature's
helper, as apprentice to the planet's greatest sorcerer who'd wrought
these miracles underground millennia ago. But it was Harry who got to
perform the curtain closer, the last and neatest trick of all!

He made his first major estate purchase in 1925, when he acquired
the jewel collection of Rebecca Darlington Stoddard, a New Haven,
Connecticut, matron from a wealthy Pittsburgh family, whose husband, Louis, had been a famous polo player. Harry beat out all rival
jewelers by the simple ploy of offering more money—which became
his usual practice. He told Stoddard he'd give him $1 million on the
spot, or $1,200,000 if Stoddard would wait six months. The widower
agreed to wait, which gave Harry time to pry out the diamonds and
have them recut for greatest brilliance, reset in simple but sophisticated art deco designs he'd created, and sold on the wholesale market
for $1,250,000, which gave him $125,000 in commissions at 10 percent, plus part of the $50,000 he'd cleared as profit. (Multiply by ten
for today's equivalent amounts.) Diamond District dealers gasped at
Harry's daring—they were a conservative crowd—and prophesied early
bankruptcy. But Harry had the confidence of ten men; he knew what

he was doing, and he loved doing it. His eyes shone with a deep euphoria.

He mailed flyers to names he got from social registers, assuring America's wealthy that he'd give them the best possible price for their jewelry. He persuaded judges and attorneys to let him know when an important gem collection turned up in estates about to be probated. One year after his Stoddard coup, Harry paid $2 million for the entire collection of Arabella Huntington, wife of the railroad magnate Collis P. Huntington and, after he died, of his nephew Henry. Acquiring it became one of Harry's oft-told stories. "Mrs. Huntington had a sixty-inch necklace with 161 pearls," he would chuckle. "It reached from my neck to my toes" and cost her more than $1 million to put together. "Poor old Mrs. Huntington! By the time her rope of pearls was assembled, she was blind and couldn't see them," Harry would sigh. He made necklaces for "at least two dozen women" from Arabella's pearls.

Harry beat out rival jewelers not only by higher bids but also by ex-amining a collection faster. Other dealers took three or four days to as-sess the seventy-nine pieces of Mrs. Emma T. Gary, which included a spectacular necklace of 166 diamonds; Harry did it in three hours. "Al-ways buy the stones, never the mounts" was his creed. Occasionally he blundered—incidents that never figured in Harry's fables; in one such he bought $90,000 worth of gems that turned out to be hot, stolen from the socialite Mrs. Isaac Emerson, married to the Bromo-Seltzer king. Harry had to return the lot.

When the stock market crashed in 1929, Harry was in his element as whole galaxies of diamonds, former property of those among the rich who'd turned paupers overnight, passed through his small Fifth Ave-nue office. By 1932 he was able to move to more luxurious quarters in the British Empire building in Rockefeller Center, where the Premier Diamond Company became incorporated under the new name Harry Winston Inc., still selling only at the wholesale level.

He was taking diamonds to sell in Atlantic City when, on the train, Harry met pretty young Edna Fleishman, who, with her physi-

cian father, was going there to recuperate from a tonsillectomy. In
the following year, 1933, when Harry was peddling gems in Palm
Beach, not having seen Edna in the interim, he telephoned her at
home in New York; she told him she was getting married in two days.
"Why don't you marry me instead?" asked Harry. She said she would;
he came back to New York next day, married her, returned with his
bride at once to Palm Beach, went straight back to selling diamonds,
and spent much of their honeymoon telling her all about the important stones he'd already encountered and those he'd like to have
and hold.

He bought his first world-famous diamond in 1935. Diamantaires
stayed away from the largest stones; the market for a 50-carater or
bigger was too small; better to cut a mighty rock into dozens of
2- to 5-caraters that the well-heeled would readily buy. "If a man
thinks big, he'll be big," Harry told Edna. He went all the way to
London's I. Hennig and Company, from whom he'd bought it sight
unseen for £150,000 (about $730,000) to fetch home his newest love:
the 726-carat rough Jonker diamond, discovered in South Africa in
January 1934, by Jacobus Jonker, employee of an elderly farmer miner.
Harry lost no time telling the press of his feat. The New York Times announced on May 16 that the Jonker's "arrival in New York will be the
first known occasion on which one of the great diamonds of the world
has come into the U.S." This was a terrible slight to the Hope, which
had preceded it by no less than thirty-four years.

Using the Jonker as magic carpet, the thirty-nine-year-old New
York jeweler flew round the globe. "Until a few days ago Harry Winston was just a dealer in precious stones," commented the New York
Times on June 2; "today his name is known all over the world." He
commissioned Lazare Kaplan, who'd learned his art in Antwerp, to first
cut the Jonker into twelve stones, the largest being 140 carats; Harry
invited the press to come see them in his office when Kaplan got that
done in 1937, pointing out to them, with some hyperbole, that Jonker
number one was "nearly four times as large as the Hope diamond
owned by Mrs. Evalyn Walsh McLean" and so should be compared to a

flawless one in its own heavyweight class, such as the 140.5-carat Regent in the Louvre (the Hope's old rival.) Jonker number one underwent more cutting; its final weight dropped to 125.35 carats. Harry didn't know in 1937 that one day he would own the Hope and would harness it with the smaller Jonkers to lead him to even greater fame. He could intuit diamonds, not the future.

"Someday your jewels will possess you and master you," his father had warned Harry, and he himself had to admit that his dad was right. "Harry just can't forget about a diamond once he's made up his mind he wants it," Edna sighed. She knew he loved her; she was his confidant, trusted adviser, and model for his jewels; their marriage was a good one. Yet his incurable romanticism focused on his diamonds; he fell in love with one beau ideal at a time, as if each were a mistress, and when passions cooled moved on to the next. He often kept a priceless stone in his pocket, the world's most expensive worry bead and amulet, so he could caress it all day long. He became obsessed with owning all the world's largest, most famous diamonds, and before he was done, one-third of them would have joined him for a brief liaison, or a longer affair.

Exactly eight years before he acquired the Hope and the Star of the East, both diamonds he'd long lusted after, Harry paid $700,000, in April 1941 for the world's third-biggest rough diamond, the Vargas, named for the president of Brazil where it was found; at 726.60 carats it surpassed the fourth-largest rough, also Harry's, the 726-carat Jonker. Harry waved his wand over the Vargas's dull gray form and twenty-nine glorious offspring, in slow motion, languorously emerged.

When, on the morning of April 27, 1947, he'd read Evalyn Walsh McLean's obituary in the *New York Times*, Harry's spirits rose, Hopeful; they plummeted in early May, when he learned that the McLean jewels were locked away out of his reach for twenty years, and soared to the stars in jubilation when he finally made them his.

In the late afternoon of the spring day when they'd arrived, as shadows on St. Patrick's Cathedral beyond his office window deepened to violet, Harry picked up the phone on his desk and called his head cutter. "Before you go home," Winston told him, "bring me down my new babies, the Hope and the Star of the East; I want to play with them for a while."

A few minutes later the two famous stones that had been together for thirty-eight years sat on the large square of black velvet on Harry's desk. The only other objects there, neatly placed, in addition to the telephone, were a gauge for estimating the weight of gems in settings, a pair of tweezers for picking up small stones, several yellow pencils with sharp points, a pad of white paper, a jeweler's loupe, and a silver pillbox full of saccharine tablets for his tea.

Harry picked up the Hope in its circlet of white diamonds and looked at it through his loupe. He was so happy to have it; earlier in the year he'd had to part with the 125 carat Jonker, which had been his constant companion for fourteen years. King Farouk of Egypt bought it for $1 million; Harry always felt bereft, really miserable, after he'd said good-bye to a favorite. He missed the Jonker, but never mind; here in his hand was this dense, deep violet-blue miracle, still a little cold to the touch. "A great diamond should live, it should talk to you," Harry liked to say, and he felt sure that the Hope would be no exception.

"Ah, Harry, darling," he murmured to himself, "what a blue! What a presence!" Twilight sky, mood indigo, a poignant sense of day's ending, life's ending, regrets, losses, missed opportunities. . . . Why was the Hope making *him* blue? He put down the loupe and rubbed the stone lightly and slowly, cradled it in his hand, rocked it back and forth in the light, talking to it and to himself by turns. "No two diamonds are alike," he once told a reporter. "Each has a different nature, different problems, and each must be handled as you handle a person." All at once he knew why he was feeling sad rather than euphoric. The Hope had suffered in its cutting after the 1792 robbery. Man, not nature, had botched it. The world's greatest blue and most fabled diamond was lopsided; one long side of its oval was thinner than the other, so it lacked full symmetry and refraction. Its cut was also a little too shallow for maximum brilliance. Harry always reached for perfection, for the Platonic ideal. If only he could recut the Hope—but that would be sacrilegious, since, as he would soon explain to the press, its historical value was more important "than any minor improvement anyone could make."

Harry Houdini of the diamond trade, Winston the Wizard, who routinely transformed wallflower diamonds into raving beauties, could do nothing for the Hope. That caused him real pain. He could, however, love it, and he did, with all the passion of his nature. "Diamonds are like your children," he told a journalist. "No matter how bad they are, if they're yours, you can't help being fond of them."

He picked up his loupe again, locked his eye to the Diamond's bigger one. For a long time, Harry and the Hope communed. Finally he laid it very gently down onto its black velvet bed. It would never *sing*. He was close to tears.

He quickly picked up the 94.80 carat Star of the East, and his loupe. Now there was a stunner! He wanted to dive straight into its heart! Cut three times and well nigh perfect! Harry grinned from ear to ear and felt the sudden blood rush, the spine tingle, which his favorites gave him. "A pear shape of great beauty, of the finest color and the finest quality," he would later reminisce to a fellow diamantaire. "I loved it dearly." Just for him, on a high, clear note, the Star began to sing. . . .

What time was it? Harry looked at his watch. Had he really been with his babies that long? He quickly put the Hope and Star into the small safe in one corner of his office, donned his black cashmere overcoat and black homburg, got his usual crisp dollar bill from his secretary waiting patiently in her office—Harry Winston, like royalty, never carried money—and left the building. As he climbed into a yellow cab, the other side of Harry Winston, not the dreaming, romantic one, came into play: the hardheaded business side, which was the dominant one. Eventually, of course, he'd sell the Hope—in spite of its comet tail of bad-luck stories that might put some people off. Harry had full confidence, rightly so, in his selling powers. William Simpson, the New York pawnshop owner who had stared dumbfounded at Evalyn McLean's Great Dane wearing the Hope, pronounced Harry "the greatest jewelery salesman of them all." "Watching him sell," agreed a

British diamantaire, "was the best theater you could want. It was beautiful, like a great actor at work." "You could feel Harry Winston's presence from the other side of a crowded room," claimed a friend. It was partly this charisma that made him a masterful salesman. The King of Saudi Arabia once called Harry from Geneva, asking him to bring eight diamond bracelets for him to choose from early next morning, before he flew back to the desert. Harry chartered planes from New York and Paris, arrived at dawn with thirty-five bracelets, sold them all to the king, and went home with an order for twenty-five more.

His taxi was weaving its way north on Fifth Avenue, past the trees in Central Park putting on their pale green spring veils. Selling the Hope would come later. First he'd make it jump through plenty of hoops, advertising his name, and attracting new clients. Harry looked out the window to where the park was coming to life after cold winter stasis and began to plan the details of the Diamond's future in the media spotlight and in the service of Harry Winston Inc.

First May Yohe and H. L. Gates, then Evalyn Walsh McLean had pushed the Hope into public prominence in America. Harry would propel it much further into celebrity status, using his "genius" for promotion. He'd launched his first publicity campaign in 1940, revolutionizing the ad world with full-page spreads in glossy fashion magazines like *Vogue*, sparked by such original and novel ideas as a close-up of his black cat, Kashmire, furry brow adorned with a pear-shaped diamond above her gleaming eyes. Not until eight years after the Winston initiative would De Beers launch their own campaign with the slogan "A Diamond Is Forever," in order to plant in every American head the idea that betrothal demanded a diamond, knowing that Americans tended to buy the stones more for sentimental reasons than Europeans did, who bought them for investment. Two years before, in 1947, Harry had begun the ongoing tradition of lending Winston jewels to Hollywood movie stars for the annual Academy Awards ceremony. Now it was time to turn his public relations wizardry full on the Hope.

The first rewards came the morning after the world's most illustrious and supposedly cursed diamond had arrived for its press conference at East Fifty-first Street. On Wednesday, April 6, all the big-city U.S. newspapers gave its debut at Harry Winston Inc. many columns of type. The next day, further write-ups and photos appeared. The picture in the *New York Times* showed the former McLean cache laid out like Ali Baba's loot, with the Hope on its necklace around a velvet jeweler's bust, being admired by Jill Ceraldo and another pretty Winston employee.

Time magazine's April 18 issue compared the size of the Hope to a robin's egg—although any robin laying an egg that big would have exploded on the spot in a burst of feathers. "Though Winston laughed at the legend that the Hope diamond had brought only trouble and tragedy to its owners and wearers," wrote the *Time* journalist, "he soon had his press agents grinding out new embellishments of the tale." Of course he did; the curse was as effective a promotion tool as a Hollywood actress; privately, Harry thought it complete nonsense.

On May 7, the *New Yorker*'s "On the Town" reporter noted that thus far diamonds had brought Winston "nothing but good fortune" and that he'd received two legitimate offers to buy the Hope and many crackpot ones. "I got a check for $5 million in the mail," he boasted, "and one for $3 million and both parties requested that I ship them the stone. Several other people wrote and asked me to send it COD, a majority of them not bothering to mention a price." He did plan to sell it privately, he told the journalist, but not before it had been exhibited "throughout the country for the benefit of local charities." Harry was much more enthusiastic about the Star of the East, which he called "one of the four greatest diamonds in the world," the others being, in his opinion, the Jonker, the Regent, and a diamond once belonging to the Hapsburgs currently in a private Swiss collection.

Seven months after Harry acquired it, the Hope held its own in the ballroom of Manhattan's Ritz-Carlton Hotel, amid the glamour and glitter of the Bal de Tête, helping to raise money for the Veterans Music Service, geared to rehabilitation projects for World War II veterans still in government hospitals. A spectacular tableau featured society matrons wearing headdresses quite as high and artificial, as full of flowers, feathers and jewels, as those the Diamond had reflected at Versailles on Marie Antoinette and her ladies. Under a ceiling covered by silver-white balloons, the Hope nestled in the towering hair of the socialite Mrs. Thomas Phipps.

Always the showman, Harry soon marshaled his troupe of beloved gems into a circus act called the Court of Jewels, which would open in New York, tour the country, educate the public in the charming ways of precious stones, raise a lot of money for charity—and indirectly for Harry Winston Inc. by planting in the well-coiffed heads of the wealthy socialites involved in the various charitable causes the clear signal of where to go for beautiful jewelry.

New York's grand opening of the Court of Jewels, a gala affair, with America's "King of Diamonds" (which is what the press routinely called Harry Winston) presiding, took place on Tuesday evening, November 22, 1949, at the Rockefeller Center Forum, in aid of the United Hospital Fund. Next day the *New York Times* ran a banner headline: $10,000,000 GEMS AID HOSPITAL FUND, HOPE, JONKER AND STAR OF THE EAST DIAMONDS AMONG JEWELS ON DISPLAY AT BENEFIT, gratifying the Blue with pride of place, even though it wasn't Harry's best-loved baby.

For the next six weeks, adults paid 50 cents and children 25 to meet the jewels and learn about them, stepping down a staircase, around a fountain encircled by greenery, and into a tentlike arrangement of gray fiberglass walls. In front of the Hope, eight red-bordered cases detailed, as the *New York Times* noted, "the bad luck that befell the men and women who owned it since it was stolen from an Indian temple more than 300 years ago." Near the Diamond, far too close for comfort, was all the wherewithal for diamond cutting, but fortunately the cutters demonstrating their craft used small stones and ignored the Hope.

At the end of a very successful six-week run of his Court of Jewels in Manhattan, Harry had a private hail-and-farewell session with each favorite: the Hope, the Star of the East, the junior Jonkers, Catherine the Great's 337-carat sapphire, and several other prestigious diamonds, then bundled them all up and sent them on their way to astonish the rest of America. Sometimes the Hope found itself back in the U.S. postal system; sometimes it was rolled inside a sock and packed into the luggage of the Winston employee Julius Cohen, an award-winning designer who would open his own business in 1955, and who often served as ringmaster and coordinator as the show toured for the next four years.

San Antonio, Texas . . . Oklahoma City, Oklahoma . . . if it's Tuesday, it must be Chicago, Illinois. In the Diamond's blue depths the cities melted into one gray, skyscraper blur.

By 1953 the touring costs of the Court of Jewels became prohibitive and it ended, but Harry continued generously to lend the Hope, for which he hadn't yet found a private buyer, to various charity events for another five years. Sometimes the Diamond lay quietly in a glass case; often it lay next to the soft, pampered skin of some rich socialite, dancing the night away in a hotel ballroom under sparkling chandeliers. None of these parties could hold a candle to long-ago balls in the Hall of Mirrors at Versailles.

On Friday, August 8, 1958, the Hope left the country, boarding a plane at New York's La Guardia airport for the short flight to Toronto, Canada. When it arrived, it was quickly cleared through customs and, escorted by four detectives, two American, two Canadian, driven through the evening rush-hour traffic to be deposited in the Imperial Bank's maximum security vault at King and Bay Streets in the heart of Toronto's financial district. There it bided its time until Tuesday, August 19, when it was transported to the grounds, bordering sea-size Lake Ontario, of the Canadian National Exhibition, an annual trade, agricultural, and amusement fair, held every year since 1879. The next day the Ex, as Canadians fondly called it, was opened by Prime Minister John Diefenbaker. For the next sixteen days, close to three million people passed through the high-arching gates of the exhibition, many of whom went to see the Hope.

The Diamond underwent a shock shortly after its return to East Fifty-first Street. Harry Winston had tried not to yield to temptation, but finally he could resist no longer. He simply had to exercise his magician's skills to put his mark on the Hope and improve, if only slightly, its beauty. What followed, given the gem's age and history, was a bold move on Harry's part, daring, decisive and self-confident, but that was how he had always conducted his business. The Diamond was wrenched from its setting and its sixteen attendant white brilliants, put into a traditional molten-metal type of dop, wrapped in a wet rag to keep its temperature down while it was being cut, and placed upon a revolving iron disk impregnated with oil and diamond dust for the fifth and final time in its long existence, just long enough to slightly close in the culet (bottom) facet. Doing that, Harry knew, would increase its "life" and brilliance. A colored photo of the Hope during this operation would appear thirty years later in the *Lapidary Journal* (March 1988) accompanying an article by Burton J. Westman titled "The Enigmatic Hope."

On an autumn afternoon shortly after his chief cutter had improved the Diamond's appearance, Harry looked at his appointment book, saw a blissful blank, called up to the sixth floor, and asked to have the Hope brought down to him.

He'd had a busy day; his phone had never stopped ringing. His agent had called from Caracas asking permission to spend $50,000 for a diamond; another called from Brazil with rumors of a 200-carat find; Ari Onassis had called from Athens and the Maharaja of Baroda from his palace in India. By 1958 Harry Winston Inc. was bigger than it had ever been, steadily expanding staff and revenues, rivaling behemoth De Beers in diamond-buying power. "The British royal family owns the world's biggest collection of historic jewels," declared *Life* magazine on March 17, 1952. "The second biggest, however, is owned by a U.S. citizen, Harry Winston," who, when he felt the urge, could roll $12 million worth of gems across his desk—the ultimate cornucopia—feast his eyes, and gloat. Today, however, he wanted only one stone, the storied blue, so he could spend time with it before it moved on to the next chapter in its life.

His idea of what to do with the Hope had come to him several years before in a flash of inspiration, and it was, like the Diamond itself, bril-

liant, for it would bring great fame to Harry Winston the person, to his
jewel business, and to his nation. He wanted to give something back to
the country that had given him, a high-school dropout of humble
Ukrainian background, so very much over the years. Washington's
Smithsonian Institution had only a very modest gem collection,
housed since 1910 in the Museum of Natural History. Harry's secret
ambition was to make America's gemstones rival Britain's in the Tower
of London. He was going to donate the biggest deep blue diamond
known, and certainly the most fabled, to the Smithsonian to serve
as the National Gem Collection's main celebrity and drawing card.
He hoped such a gift would inspire other rich Americans to donate their own magnificent jewels. Harry was a generous man in
many ways, wanting to share his passion for diamonds with everyone he met, wanting to educate the American people to appreci-
ate and understand them. The majority knew nothing about those
miraculous stars burning bright on their fingers or displayed under
their noses.

Donating the Hope would also give Harry, whose taxes had escalated along with his profits, a much-needed tax credit. His accountants
applauded when he told them his plan, but for Harry, a tax break
wasn't his main motivation.

As he sat at his desk, time stopped while Harry held the Hope gently in his left hand and looked into its soul. He could visit it at the
Smithsonian if he felt the need, so this was only *au revoir*, not *adieu*.
He tried to tell himself that he should be glad that some silly, vain,
spoiled woman hadn't bought it. Harry didn't think much of his female
customers; they had "no real feeling" for diamonds, no real reverence
and respect. "I hate to think of that stone going to some of the women
I know," he'd confided to a journalist about one of his big ones.
"Adornment! They'd wear diamonds on their ankles if it was stylish!
They'd wear them in their noses!" Harry liked to think of himself
as the Hope's knight in shining armor; he'd rescued it from such a
banal fate.

He drank in the blue's radiance and gave a mighty sigh. He
thought of the happy spring day nine years earlier in this room when

he'd first held it and entertained such great expectations for it. If he was really being truthful with himself, never mind that this Diamond had advertised Harry Winston Inc. far and wide, or that he'd found it a good home and kept it out of the clutches of some woman, if he was really being truthful he had to admit that the Hope ultimately was one of his failures. First of all, he knew he was the world's best diamond salesman, yet he'd failed to sell it; second, he'd failed—through no fault of his own—to do what he loved doing best: to give such a stone perfect fulfillment of its beauty. The culet recutting was too minor an improvement to do much. The Diamond had come to him lopsided with flawed refraction, and thus it would depart.

Harry put it quickly into his corner safe, where he couldn't see it. The Hope was a stone to cleave a man's heart in two.

Arrangements to donate the Diamond to the Smithsonian went ahead. When an Internal Revenue official phoned to question the substantial amount Harry had written off against it, he replied, "Find me another one like it to compare the price." He also made a point of telling the press that because the gift was being made by his corporation, not by himself as an individual, his tax benefit was much less. For a corporation, he explained, total tax-exempt contributions had to be within 5 percent of the total net income. So if Harry Winston Inc. cleared $1 million a year, the maximum tax credit for contributions would be only $50,000, whereas gifts made by an individual had no limit.

On Friday, November 7, 1958, sitting in his office with a brown paper parcel on his desk, Harry held a press conference, reported in Saturday's newspapers and on page one of the *New York Times*. "The Diamond," wrote Milton Bracker, "will be sent to Washington by mail today as the gift of Harry Winston Inc." "I could have sold it many times for a profit," Harry told the assembled reporters. "But I don't know what its value is." He estimated that while he owned it, the hardworking Hope had covered about 400,000 miles raising money for charity and had "brought him no bad luck."

It had instead brought him fame, new clients, and plenty of free publicity and would go on burnishing his name after it went to the

Smithsonian. But the Diamond had gratified mainly the practical, business side of Harry Winston's dual nature. It had left the dreaming romantic with a hole somewhere inside him, filled with nothing but yearning.

With journalists scribbling in their notebooks, the little drama Harry was staging continued. His fourteen-year-old son Bruce handed the package that contained the Hope to his father, who then passed it to Paul Haase, a former New York policeman who currently worked in Winston's shipping department. The fifty-two-year-old former member of the Midtown Squad had prepared the parcel for the mail on the previous day. First he'd put the Diamond on its Cartier necklace in a rectangular black suede case, then swathed that in tissue. This all went into a white cardboard box, which was wrapped in brown paper and sealed with gummed tape. Winston's label was affixed and the package addressed to "Smithsonian Institution, Washington, D.C. Attention: Dr. Leonard Carmichael, Secretary of the Smithsonian." Then Paul weighed it: three pounds, thirteen ounces, but most of this was packaging, since the Diamond on its own without its companion diamonds weighed just over one-third of an ounce.

After the press conference Friday morning, Paul took the Independent subway from Fifty-third Street and Fifth Avenue to the General Post Office, where the registry clerk Michael Briglia, who'd worked there for twelve years, charged $3.35 to register the package (which included insurance of $10,000, the maximum the postal system provided; since 1949 Harry had insured the Hope with Lloyd's of London for $1 million); $2.44 first-class mail at 4 cents an ounce; plus a surcharge of $139.50 applied to articles of great value, which guaranteed person-to-person handling and guards en route, making a grand total of $145.29. (Early that evening, however, embarrassed post office officials discovered that the surcharge should have been $151.85 and lived in hope that on Monday morning, Mr. Winston would pay his government the $12.35 still owing.) Paul paid $145.29 cash and left, while Michael slapped a metered postage strip on the package and sent the Hope on its way.

By 11:45 A.M. on that gray November Friday, Paul was back at 7 East Fifty-first Street, and the deed was done. The Diamond began retracing its path back to the capital of the great republic in exactly the same democratic way in which it had left nine years before. After thousands upon thousands of miles of jolting, topsy-turvy journeys by train and plane, its traveling days were almost over. Except for three well-chaperoned future escapades, the Hope was going home to Washington for good.

*The Diamond's present home, the Harry Winston Gallery
in the National Museum of Natural History.*

1 0
INSTITUTIONAL CARE

And live to be the show and gaze o' the time.
—WILLIAM SHAKESPEARE, *Macbeth*, act 5, scene 8

On Monday morning, November 10, 1958, the Washington sky was a pale, washed-out gray, and the trees in front of the National Museum of Natural History, situated on the south side of Constitution Avenue through to the mall, had lost most of their leaves. One of six Smithsonian museums and galleries where history was labeled and stored, this building, erected forty-eight years before of cream-colored stone, rising with classical dignity and august pillars to an imposing dome, prepared to welcome its world-famous new resident. At 11:40 A.M., an armored postal truck drew up in front; a blue-clad postman stepped out, clutching a paper parcel containing the Hope, mounted the museum's four broad steps, and carried it inside to begin the final chapter of its life.

Ever since the first human hand had clutched it thousands of years before, the Diamond had been subject to the whim of an individual. Now it was at the service of the American people, all 180 million of them (since grown to 280) and for this particular gem—as we'll see later—there was perhaps no more fitting nation to belong to, given its history, ideals, and myths.

If its new collective owner was the perfect one for the Hope, so was its new domicile. Finding the right retirement home is never easy;

the Diamond could be considered lucky because in the entire Smithsonian complex inanimate objects ruled. The story of humankind's march through time was told not in terms of potentates and kings but in things. In fact, in the Smithsonian, things *were* kings. They were treated with respect and understanding by a large staff who looked after their needs with informed and zealous care and who were genuinely, even obsessively, interested in all their little quirks and eccentricities. And every day was visitors' day. People came for miles, even crossed oceans, to see them and admire. Inmates who were very old and famous with remarkable tales attached garnered most attention, and the Diamond was destined to become, of all the fifty-two thousand items in the Smithsonian (now grown to eighty-one thousand but with only 1 percent on display) the most visited, most revered object of all, king of kings among that vast multitude of things. On that auspicious November morning, as the museum door swung shut behind it, the old blue stone, after an active life of travel and adventure in Asia, Europe, and North America, came, finally and in some, but not all, ways, comfortably to its rest and reward.

The Smithsonian was an apt abode for another reason: it had been founded by an Englishman, James Smithson, who was a contemporary of the man who loved the Diamond best and gave it his name: Philip Hope. If Philip's papers hadn't gone up in flames in 1941, and if James's archive hadn't done the same in 1865, we might well have discovered that these two wealthy, studious, lonely bachelors, both born in continental Europe, both living there much of the time because they were never fully accepted by English society were, in fact, good friends. On the evening of October 23, 1826, while Philip Hope, age fifty-two, was probably sitting alone in his London house in Connaught Place admiring his diamonds, James, age sixty-one, was sitting alone in *his* quarters in Bentinck Street, a little to the east, writing his remarkable will.

"I, James Smithson, son to Hugh, 1st Duke of Northumberland and Elizabeth heiress of the Hungerfords of Studley and niece of Charles the Proud, Duke of Somerset," began James, while his quill pen scratching the paper made the only sound in the room. What he didn't put down for posterity to read was that his mother was mere mistress, not wife, to the duke, so James, born in France in 1765, contended all his life with what was considered a serious handicap, the stain of illegitimacy. Having graduated on May 7, 1782, from Pembroke College, Oxford, with prizes in chemistry and mineralogy, James became a fellow of the Royal Society in 1787, conducted experiments, and wrote many learned papers, twenty-seven of which were published. He invented a better way to brew coffee and once caught a lady's tears in order to discover what they were made of (microcosmic salt and muriate of soda). Since English aristocrats snubbed him, James retreated by turns to Berlin, Rome, Florence, Geneva, and Paris. By 1826 he was frail and ill, which is why he was writing his will. "I bequeath the whole of my property of every nature and kindsoever," continued James. Having made modest bequests to an old servant and to his nephew, he penned a most extraordinary clause, considering that he'd never set foot in that country. He left his entire fortune to "the United States of America, to found at Washington, under the name of the Smithsonian Institution, an establishment for the increase and diffusion of knowledge among men."

James died only three years later, on June 27, 1829, in Genoa, Italy, and was buried in the little English cemetery there.

On the far side of the Atlantic, members of Congress weren't sure they wanted to accept Smithson's generous gift. Fiery Senate member John C. Calhoun ranted that it was "beneath the dignity of the United States to receive presents of this kind from anyone" (most particularly from a British bastard!). However, the wisdom of John Quincy Adams prevailed, and finally in 1838 the clipper ship *Mediator* sailed into New York harbor bearing the bounty: 105 bags of English gold sovereigns, which, shipped to Philadelphia, melted down and recast in American coinage amounted to $508,318.46. On August 10, 1846, President James Polk signed Congress's bill creating the Smithsonian Institution as an independent agency under the patronage of the federal government, and Joseph Henry was named first secretary, the name accorded its director. Under the second secretary, the first museum building, known as "the Castle," raised its Romanesque red sandstone turrets, copied from a twelfth-century Norman stronghold. James Smithson rests now in a marble sarcophagus below, brought from the Genoa cemetery in 1904 by Alexander Graham Bell. In addition to all those gold sovereigns, James had bequeathed his papers and collection of ten thousand minerals to the Smithsonian, but both were destroyed in the Castle's 1865 fire.

The Smithsonian's National Gem Collection began in 1884 when the honorary curator of mineralogy, Frank W. Clarke, spent $2,500 acquiring a thousand stones, one-third of them cut and polished, displayed at the New Orleans and Cincinnati Exhibitions before they came to rest in two flat, plate-glass cases in the Arts and Industries Building, finished in 1881. Gems collected by Dr. Joseph Leidy and Dr. Isaac Lea were added in 1891 and 1894, and in 1910 the modest collection, containing no rare or really valuable stones, was moved to the just-completed National Museum of Natural History, where it was displayed on one row of tables placed down the center of the mineral hall. People tended to lean against the cases, knocking the gems off their pads; the burglar alarm underneath ran on batteries that staff had to test every few weeks to make sure they still functioned. Col. Washington A. Roebling, who built the Brooklyn Bridge, bequeathed his fine collection of both rough and cut gemstones in 1926. But the greatest donation of all was about to be made on that November day in 1958, as the postman James G. Todd quickly climbed the stairs to the second floor, carrying the treasure wrapped in paper that would, with one dramatic leap, catapult the United States National Gem Collection onto the world stage and into the front ranks.

Todd felt a little nervous about what awaited him on the second floor, but he would have felt terrified if he'd known that within a year he who had briefly held a "curse-ridden" object would have his leg crushed by a truck, his head injured in a car crash, and his wife, dog, and house taken from him, the latter burned to the ground. He might well have run screaming from the building, raced down the Mall, and pitched his package as far as he could throw it straight into the Tidal Basin. Instead, he took a firm grip as he reached the Hall of Gems and Minerals, marched through a throng of guards, guests, and onlookers to where Dr. Leonard J. Carmichael, current Smithsonian secretary, Dr.

George S. Switzer, curator of gems and minerals, Postmaster-General Arthur E. Summerfield, and Edna Winston awaited him.

As cameras flashed, James handed the parcel to Dr. Carmichael, a genteel-looking man with a gray mustache and black caterpillar eyebrows, and held out a registry receipt for him to sign. Carmichael snipped strings, removed wrappings, drew out the rectangular suede case within. The group hushed, drew in their breath, held it as he raised the lid, and exhaled in wonder as the Hope Diamond, leaning on a white satin pillow, looked at them with its blue eye and waited for applause. The secretary quickly handed the open box to Edna Winston; Harry had sent her and his seventeen-year-old son, Ron, to represent him, explaining that under the terms of his insurance policy he mustn't be photographed. (Harry, master of publicity, knew that remaining off-camera and mysterious only increased his allure.) With her simple short-sleeved dress and pillbox hat, Edna wore only some quite unremarkable pearls, but her collection of spectacular Winston-designed jewels would eventually grow to fifty pieces (dispersed in a Sotheby's New York auction in October 1992). Edna made a brief speech; "We have hope," she said, making a modest pun, "that this will be the nucleus of a great collection." She handed the Diamond back to Carmichael, who passed it on to Switzer, who disappeared with it behind a screen. Then, with much fidgeting and talking, all the guests, who included Evalyn McLean's former secretary, Nannie Chase, waited until at last the screen was removed to reveal the Hope beaming from inside a glass-fronted safe framed like an art masterpiece. Mrs. Summerfield, Mrs. Polly Guggenheim, and Mrs. Gwen Cafritz, Washington hostesses, quickly clustered around it to be photographed. Gwen, wife of a construction tycoon, had replaced Evalyn McLean and Perle Mesta as Washington's number-one hostess, throwing huge parties and receptions in her mammoth, bunkerlike mansion on Foxhall Road. When she donated an Alexander Calder sculpture to the Smithsonian worth $75,000 and the secretary thanked her for her "handsome gesture," Gwen barked, "Since when has $75,000 been called a gesture?"

After the invited guests straggled out, the public came flooding in at exactly twelve noon, headed by E. H. Walker, student at Maryland University, his camera already pointed, and the Hope began its new existence as "the show and gaze o' the time."

The country's newspapers, which, ever since 1901, had been noting the famous stone's public appearances far more sedulously than the doings of any mere human, described its arrival at the Natural History Museum and, of course, recapped the tired tale of its alleged victims. "As of Monday, if anyone is hexed," commented the *Washington Post*, "it will not be Winston but the staff of the Smithsonian Institution!" A cartoonist drew a battered Uncle Sam wearing the Hope and muttering, "That's all I need!" "The maleficent diamond that has legendarily brought sinister fate to its owners for 300 years last week became the property of everyone in the United States," shuddered *Time* magazine on November 17, while *Life* on November 24 printed two photos of the Diamond's postal trip and one of Dr. Carmichael holding it, plus the usual potted run-through of done-in prey. *Newsweek* had Tavernier not only "torn to pieces by a pack of wild dogs" but dying "penniless and disgraced," as well, and demoted Francis Hope—which he wouldn't have liked—from lord to mere sir.

The Diamond had been in its safe only a few days when the Smithsonian began receiving a daily, ongoing quota of letters from anxious American citizens who over the years would put the blame squarely on the gem for every national misfortune, including President Kennedy's assassination, Vietnam War losses, and every stock-market plunge. Meanwhile, its new custodians examined it under their loupes and took its measure but didn't remove it from the setting that Cartier had designed in 1910.

Every day from 10 A.M. to 5:30 P.M. the Diamond was show stealer and magnet for millions there in the gem hall, a walnut-paneled room completely remodeled one year before by the Smithsonian's exhibits staff under the supervision of Rolland O. Hower. The wall-mounted safe, which was the Hope's tiny home, was at the far end of the room. Visitors entered and passed by all the other gems before they got to the real celebrity. Only two people at a time could peer in through the safe's round glass opening, which bore an unfortunate resemblance to the kind of front-loading washing machines then on the market. The safety glass, made in two layers, was more than one inch thick and slightly tinted; this reduced the Diamond's brilliance by about 25 percent.

In its first three days on display, 9,504 people came to see it, compared with 5,519 visitors to the gem gallery for the same period in the week before it arrived. At the end of a year, between three and four million had come to take a good look at the dark blue Diamond. In the summer months when tourists flocked to Washington, the Hope's fans had to endure long waits and lineups as they filled the gem room and overflowed beyond. It wasn't Lindbergh's brave little plane *The Spirit of St. Louis* or George Washington's venerable camp chest or the dinosaur *diplodocus*, a giant lizard 135 million years old and seventy feet tall that held dominion in "the nation's attic." It was the mineral called Hope, which could hide in a pillbox with room to spare.

In spite of plenty of admirers and a caring staff, the Diamond's days in the gem hall, with two more faces always pressed to the other side of the glass, took on a terrible sameness. Each night a heavy steel door slammed shut and locked over the round glass one; the Hope and all the other objects and preserved creatures in the museum were left to silence, darkness, and echoes of the past. The huge mounted bull elephant thirteen feet tall in the main rotunda would never walk again through damp ferns in the Angolan jungle; the thirteen-foot-long python skeleton in another room would never plump out again and put on its former skin.

And the Hope would hardly ever come in contact with warm, rosy flesh; it was handled rarely by staff, and they always wore white cotton gloves. Every two or three weeks, just before the hordes arrived, it was dusted gently with a soft gem cloth, but apart from that slight variation in routine, one dull day followed another. Sometimes it is hard to be immortal.

At the end of four uneventful years came the Hope's first change of scene since joining America's national "remembrance of things past." The principal jewelry houses in Paris and the South African diamond giant De Beers together sponsored a show at the Louvre called

Dix Siècles de Joaillerie Française (Ten Centuries of French Jewelry). Louvre officials wrote to their counterparts at the Smithsonian asking if the Hope, famed expatriate of France, could return for the May 1962 show. Smithsonian curators said no, reluctant to be deprived of their greatest drawing card for a month during the busy spring tourist season. They were also concerned about the safety of the Diamond; French ruffians had stolen it once before. André Malraux, France's minister of culture, then approached First Lady Jacqueline Kennedy, who loved all things French, and she in turn charmed the mineral curator George Switzer into agreeing to let the Diamond have one last nostalgic trip to Paris. In return, some months later the Louvre graciously lent the United States their greatest treasure: Leonardo da Vinci's *Mona Lisa*. She arrived in New York City on December 20 and went straight into a vault until the public showing at Washington's National Gallery opened on January 8, 1963.

Dr. Switzer decided to carry the Hope to Paris himself, in his pocket. He left Washington by car for Baltimore's Friendship International Airport and felt the first qualm when the plane he boarded there made such a rough landing in Philadelphia that his flight to Paris was canceled. Since he knew that a police escort would be anxiously awaiting him at Paris's Orly airport, he raced to New York, but the only transatlantic flight leaving that night was to Frankfurt, West Germany. He climbed aboard after an hour and a half delay. After another nerve-racking four-hour delay in Frankfurt, during which the Hope, as he tells it, "seemed to burn a hole in my pocket," he finally, nine hours late, reached Paris, where relieved Louvre officials met him; they drove quickly into Paris—and had a minor car accident en route. "Mission accomplished," wired the latest believer in the Hope's wickedness to his colleagues at the Natural History Museum.

In an article he wrote for *National Geographic* magazine in December 1971, Dr. Switzer followed the lead of the Smithsonian secretary, Dr. Leonard Carmichael, who had already referred in a June 1960 article in the same periodical to "sinister legends" attesting that the Hope Diamond's "curse has caused at least a dozen tragic deaths." Dr. Switzer, tongue well in cheek, recounting his harried trip to Paris, wrote that "the glowing gem I held once adorned a statue of the Hindu goddess Sita, wife of Rama. It was stolen by a Brahman priest, and the curse of the angered goddess has been visited upon owners of the diamond ever since." One might well presume that scientists such as Carmichael and Switzer would keep the Hope firmly pinioned to a factual, rational context, but such is the power of imagination, or of the American propensity for public relations hype, that the Smithsonian Institution continued to exploit the Diamond's evil reputation quite as actively as May Yohe, Evalyn McLean, and Harry Winston had.

The gala Paris opening of *Ten Centuries of French Jewelry* took place on May 3, and the former Blue Diamond of the French Crown, considerably shrunken since those days, was reunited in the gallery of Apollo, in the same glass case, with the huge Regent and pear-shaped Sancy diamonds, to whom it hadn't been close for 170 years, ever since that night of terror and burglary in the Garde-meuble, and with the Côte de Bretagne, the red spinel dragon that had pushed against it in Louis XV's Order of the Golden Fleece. All three stones had been recovered by the French government shortly after the robbery; the Regent and the Côte de Bretagne had passed a quiet existence in the Apollo gallery, but the Sancy had been purchased in 1892 by the American William Waldorf Astor for his Virginian-born wife, Nancy, who, in 1919, would become the first woman member of the British House of Commons. It was Nancy who had graciously lent the Sancy to the Louvre for the 1962 show; it would be there permanently after the 4th Lord Astor sold it to the Louvre for $1 million in 1978.

There they were, four famous old Frenchified stones, together for a month, sharing the same glass house and visitors' attention.

After the Hope returned to solitary institutional confinement at the Smithsonian, several more diamonds from its past took up residence in the gem hall. A pair of stunning pear-shaped earrings arrived, which had been given by Louis XVI to Marie Antoinette shortly after he'd begun his reign in 1774 and worn by her constantly until they were seized by revolutionaries after her abortive flight to Varennes. Somehow they passed to the ears of Grand Duchess Tatiana Youssoupoff of Russia and in 1928 into the hands of Pierre Cartier, who sold them that year to the American cereal heiress Marjorie Merriweather Post. She later donated them to the Smithsonian, along with the blue heart diamond that had been with the Hope in Cartier's Paris shop in 1910. After going off to Mrs. Unzue in South America, it had returned to Paris in 1953, spent time with a titled European family, and been bought in 1959 by Harry Winston, who mounted it in a ring with brilliants around it and sold it to Mrs. Post. Harry had done his work well of persuading her and others to give their spectacular jewels to the United States' national collection, well on its way to rivaling Britain's in the Tower of London, Russia's in the Kremlin, and Turkey's in Topkapi Palace. Most of America's family jewels had provenances as shady as the blue Diamond's, full of robberies, recuttings, sudden disappearances, mystery, and murk. All of them could tell a tale or two, although none could match the intrigue of the Hope.

In April 1965 it was off on another plane trip, again traveling in Dr. Switzer's pocket, but this time there were no delays or minor disasters. "Switzer and Baby Doll arrived safely," he cabled back to the museum as soon as they got to Johannesburg, South Africa, where "Baby Doll" would star in the Rand Easter Show (and a copy would stand in for it back in Washington's gem hall). Inside the De Beers Diamond Pavilion, as people trooped by to see it, the blue Diamond sat, like a fat, prey-full spider, at the center of a gold spun web attached to the thorny branches of a golden rosebush.

Senior officials in De Beers Research Laboratory couldn't resist the temptation to examine the rare indigo stone before it returned to America; to them it revealed the first of two long-guarded secrets. Without removing it from its setting, they placed it on a plain background, turned an ultraviolet light full on it in a darkened room, then turned the light off. What they saw next truly astonished them.

Being well-informed mineralogists and diamantaires, they knew that all diamonds are classified as Type 1a or b or Type IIa or b. Type 1a, about 98 percent of all diamonds, contain fairly substantial amounts of nitrogen. Type 1b contain less and are usually yellow. Type IIa, very rare, contain only minute amounts of nitrogen and are colorless. Type IIb, to which the Hope belongs, are blue or gray due to their having one boron atom for every million carbon ones, and they are semiconductors of electricity. If a gemstone continues to emit light after the ultraviolet light source is withdrawn, it is said to phosphoresce. Since all the blue diamonds they had ever tested phosphoresced light blue, that is what the assembled scientists expected the Hope to do. (Phosphorescence, which occurs in a number of different gems, can also be triggered by sunlight, a condition exploited by fortune-tellers to prove a stone's supernatural powers.)

When the ultraviolet light was withdrawn, the Hope indeed phosphoresced, but not light blue. It glowed orange-red, like a fireball, like the sun itself. Not only that, but its intense flame color lasted for thirty to forty seconds, which was a longer period of sustained light than that of other diamonds.

There lay the Hope in that dark room, doing its magic trick for the first time, throwing off generously, weirdly, triumphantly energy in forms beyond mere light. What those forms are and why the stone behaves in this truly singular fashion is not known. The Diamond had revealed its red-hot glow, an astounding physical property, but that was just the skin of its deep secret. Plenty of mystery still pulsed beneath.

Scientists don't like mysteries; they crave rational explanations. They could account for phosphorescence easily enough: ultraviolet rays upset the course of orbiting electrons, which, as they return to normal paths, release pent-up energy in the form of light; therefore, it follows logically that a blue diamond would, of course, phosphoresce in some shade of blue. But *red?* The mineralogists scratched their heads in puzzlement and tried to think of possible causes. Back in Washington, Dr. Switzer, when he heard the astounding news, wondered in the October 2 *Science Newsletter* if perhaps the Diamond's excess energy took the form of heat, which would make a longer wavelength of red light than that of all other Type IIb diamonds, but this was just speculation.

If science can't supply a sure explanation, imagination can. The Hope's scarlet lining, alter ego, secret red alert, retains the molten magma in which billions of years ago, it was created; the searing orb of India's sun; the rivers of blood of the French Revolution; the walls of licking flame at the Tuileries Palace; a fire-breathing dragon crowding it in the Order of the Golden Fleece. There were plenty of traumatic moments in its past when the Diamond was close to red.

For thousands of years humans had wrapped it tightly around with *their* energy: their needs and desires, strong wills and egos. In 1965 the Diamond first revealed that all along it had secretly countered with its own life force: innate, freely flowing, the color of fresh arterial blood. The Hope's energy so abounds that it overflows in all directions, with a natural power, awesome and mysterious, that far outweighs a mere bent for the supernatural. The Diamond is fully, truly alive.

It had been back in its safe at the Natural History Museum for almost exactly a year when the next variation in routine occurred one spring evening, after all visitors had left the building, taking shuffling feet, awed whispers, and nose-flattened faces with them. All was dark and silent in the gem hall, except for the footfalls of a guard far off and a clock ticking somewhere.

All at once five men burst in—was this another robbery? Talking and laughing were two familiars: Dr. Switzer and a museum guard, plus the photographer Lee Boltin with his assistant and the writer Douglas Cooper. He would describe America's family jewels in the December 1966 issue of *Esquire* magazine, while thirty of the most distinguished were photographed for a centerfold spread in what Cooper calls "the most valuable group portrait ever made," since its subjects were worth a cool $10 million. Lifted from its safe by gloved hands, the Hope was placed on a black background on the floor, dwarfed by a 127-carat Portuguese diamond above it and a 157-carat emerald below, bombarded with bright lights for seven hours, and finally, just as dawn was breaking, put back in its vault. The door slammed, locked, everyone left, and the fun was over.

On November 13, 1975, the Hope yielded up another closely guarded secret. On that memorable day Smithsonian staff removed it from its 1910 Cartier setting; the last time it had stood alone, without its sixteen diamond handmaidens, had been seventeen years before, when Harry Winston slightly recut the culet. Excited mineralogists placed it on a sheet of paper and traced round its outline with a pencil just as Françillon had in his London shop on September 19,

1812. They compared their drawing with his and found them to be identical.

Under magnification they examined the Hope for inclusions—its setting could have concealed some—and confirmed Françillon's description of it as "all perfection without specks or flaws." They took a close look at its cut, noting its two extra facets beyond the usual fifty-eight, between the girdle and the top of the pavilion, and the tiny additional girdle facets cut by Cartier. They measured the stone: 12.05 mm deep (about half an inch); 25.60 mm long (about an inch); 21.90 mm wide (about three-quarters of an inch).

Then came the surprise. They weighed the blue stone that, since it surfaced in England in 1812, everyone had described as weighing 44¼ or 44½ carats. Not at all! The Hope weighed an astonishing 45.52 metric carats. It had managed somehow to conceal that extra carat. How had this been possible? First, many descriptions of the Diamond down the years had simply copied an earlier reference without ever verifying it. The Hope had had a bad press in more ways than one. Second, early carat weights weren't standardized, and varied from country to country; metric carat weight (1 carat = 200 milligrams) wasn't proposed in Europe until 1907 or adopted in the U.S. until 1913. Third, when the Diamond was weighed on an inferior set of jeweler's scales, particularly in the nineteenth century, its weight could be off by as much as 3 milligrams.

While it was out of its setting, the museum's gem curator decided that it was a good opportunity to make a slight adjustment to facilitate easier future removals and hired the Washington jeweler Robert Limon to do the work.

Three years later, the second of the men who'd loved the Diamond best died. Harry Winston, at age eighty-two, suffered a fatal heart attack in New York on December 8, 1978. In addition to the Hope, Harry had donated other significant gems to the national collection, including, in the fall of 1962, a pale yellow uncut octahedron with the astonishing weight of 253.70 carats; he'd been given the James Smithson Medal by the Smithsonian the year before he died. If Harry had ever taken time to write "Famous Diamonds I Have Known" he could have described intimately sixty of the world's major stones, all of which had passed through his hands. After Harry's death, Ron assumed his father's mantle as chairman and CEO of Harry Winston Inc., which was then grossing $175 million a year and had moved in 1960 to its present location at 718 Fifth Avenue. Ron had a passion for colored diamonds and liked to point out that no other mineral anywhere in the world came in every color of the rainbow.

It was to Harry Winston Inc. that the Diamond went right after the museum's closing hour on Monday, November 29, 1982. Ron had asked to borrow it for the firm's Fiftieth Anniversary party held that evening in the Engelhard Court of New York's Metropolitan Museum. It was a black-tie affair where the twelve hundred guests, not the resident sculptures, wore most of the clothes, while they listened to string quartets playing medieval music, quaffed Piper Heidsieck champagne, and peered at $300 million worth of gems Harry had once owned and sold, including some of his best-loved babies, with the Hope, as always, stealing the show. The actress Alexis Smith noted with amusement that it was, considering its ill repute, most aptly displayed in a glass case at the foot of Rodin's *Gates of Hell*. "I wouldn't touch it if they let me," shuddered one silk-upholstered matron. "It's so dark for a diamond," complained another. "Diamonds should be *this* color," declared a woman from Monte Carlo, brandishing a ring that occupied half her finger. Albano Bochatay, who ran Winston's Geneva office, explained to a journalist that in Europe, Monte Carlo, Gstaad, and St. Moritz were the only places where people still dared to wear real jewels, and Rita Lackman chimed in to say that she'd stopped wearing hers after four black-hooded gunmen had robbed her of her Mazarin diamond and tied her up in a closet in her Paris apartment.

The Hope's former colleagues at the November party included Cardinal Mazarin's rubies, bequeathed by him to Louis XIV, and the Star of the East, the "carafe stopper" that young Evalyn McLean had bought in Paris from Cartier in 1908 and that Harry had sold first to King Farouk of Egypt and then in 1969 to a private owner. Before ten o'clock the next morning, the Hope was back in its usual spot in

Washington, and none of the fans streaming into the gem hall to see it guessed that it had had a night on the town.

In March 1995 the Hollywood actress Michelle Pfeiffer laid it on her satin skin during a photo shoot held in the gem gallery for *Life* magazine. Jewels always look their best on a beautiful woman, and during its 336 years in the Western world the Diamond had adorned very few: Louisa Hope, Adèle Bichat Hope, probably Henrietta, Duchess of Newcastle, perhaps May Yohe twice only, and a few society women while Winston was lending it to charity balls. Michelle Pfeiffer topped them all.

Science, however, was never far away. The blue brilliant was removed from its setting again in December 1996, when the Gemological Institute of America examined it, describing its color as "an intense fancy, dark grayish blue" and its clarity as VS1 (with very slight inclusions, hard to see without ten times magnification), plus "whitish graining and surface wear marks"—a very old stone's equivalent of wrinkles.

For more than a year, the Diamond had found sanctuary in a temporary setting on the second-floor mezzanine away from construction chaos while its usual home underwent extensive renovations. The gallery reopened with a ceremony for invited guests on September 20, 1997, and a new name: the Janet Annenberg Hooker Hall of Geology, Gems, and Minerals. The philanthropist sister of the publisher Walter Annenberg gave the Smithsonian $5 million of the $13 million collected from private donors for building costs and as well donated an important emerald, a parure of yellow diamonds, and the 330-carat Star of Asia sapphire. The United States' family jewels had now grown to more than ten thousand pieces, with about a thousand on display. The Hope wasn't the rarest diamond in the collection—that honor went to a small scarlet one of 5.03 carats—but the blue Diamond *could* turn red, given the right conditions.

While all the other gems, including its red rival, were bunched together in the same room, the Hope had a most imposing and dignified chamber all to itself, called the Harry Winston Gallery—vaguely modeled on Rome's Pantheon—with circular dome, bronze columns, cherrywood walls, and polished stone floor.

As press and other guests at the opening entered this sanctum, a modesty screen alternating clear and smoked-glass panels heightened suspense by partly hiding the Diamond from view. Ron Winston, who had donated $1 million toward construction, greeted guests, while Harry, in the form of a bronze bust, took it all in from an elevated position just inside the door. "The Hope Diamond," Ron told reporters, is "probably the single most valuable object on earth. It's a very small thing, and it's worth about $200 million." It had come and gone from his Fifth Avenue salon a few days before to be cleaned and readied for its new grandeur.

With fiber-optic lighting making it supremely beautiful, and its known history in printed précis on one wall, the Hope and its necklace rest upon a cylinder and base covered in ultrasuede the exact color of a midsummer sky. This sits in the center of a square, bronze-cornered, glass-sided case with polished stone base and roof, which resembles a modern little temple or mausoleum. One or two security men are always nearby, sentinels on guard.

As the earth turns, so each day turns the Diamond, slowly, there on its motor-driven plinth to fully face each of the four sides of laminate glass, which, unlike the too-thick, tinted glass of its earlier abode, is distortion-free and water clear. At 5:30 P.M., when the sun is either setting or low in the sky, an attendant pushes a button, and the Diamond sinks down behind the rock of its base, to rise again the next morning. The Hope springs eternal, engages, and endures.

The old stone had come full circle. It had been pushed by Tavernier into the grab and greed of Western commerce in 1660; in 1958, almost exactly three hundred years later, it was returned to a place of reverent worship recalling ancient Indian days when it probably served as eye for Siva or some other Hindu god. For the past forty-four years—with no end in sight—it has been daily seen and adored; eight million people a year come now from around the world to pay their respects, but it is Americans who love it best—and not just because it is theirs. Reasons go deeper than that.

When early settlers threw their tea into Boston Harbor, thumbed their noses at Britain, and founded a republic, the whole process was perhaps too sudden and precipitate. With the American Declaration of Independence encapsulating the eighteenth-century ideals of such French *philosophes* as Diderot and Condorcet, Reason marched boldly forward. But Fancy flinched, dragged its feet, looked back, hungered still for gilded coaches, kings in ermine robes, and crowns with great wattages of jewels. In the twentieth century, America was enraptured when Grace Kelly married a prince; when Jackie Kennedy's pillbox hat proclaimed her Queen of Camelot; when Diana, Princess of Wales, danced at the White House with John Travolta. The subconscious wish for kings is as strong as it was in 1776. That is the first reason why Americans flock to see a Diamond that once graced the proud figures of at least three monarchs.

Ever since Thomas Jefferson and the other founding fathers declared that "all men are created equal," his countrymen have been busy creating their own class divisions and hierarchy. "Inequality is as dear to the American heart," realized the novelist William Dean Howells, "as liberty itself." The basis for class status is a simple one. "We have one material which actually constitutes an aristocracy," noted John Adams in 1808; "that material is wealth." Once the United States, after the Civil War, left its rural, agricultural past and rushed into an urban, industrial future, the ranks of the conspicuously wealthy upper class swelled enormously. "The very rich are different from you and me," wrote Scott Fitzgerald. They are, indeed, and how they differ—details of their Porsches and their diamonds as big as the Ritz—fill newspapers, magazines, and television screens. This is the second reason why Americans are drawn to the Hope: it has always belonged to someone very rich.

The third reason why United States citizens really love their blue Diamond is that it symbolizes power, something that's always fascinated them: personal, corporate, political, national, military, every kind. Every American likes to hear that oft-repeated boast that their president is the most powerful man on earth and their country the most powerful nation. Since it went to the Smithsonian in 1958, roughly two hundred million people have flocked to see a tiny blue object that holds two kinds of power and possibly three: the secret of Creation itself, the ability to bring romance and wonder to dull lives, and, perhaps, to cause tragedy and trauma as well.

This latter possible power leads us to the fourth reason why the Diamond excites and enthralls. It gives a harmless focus for very real anxieties and fears. Americans may gravitate to power, but they also feel that most of it dwells somewhere beyond their own person and control, making them mere victims in a deterministic universe. They worry that Chicken Little was right; the sky *is* falling, or at least developing a big hole in its ozone layer that may well end the human race. They fear nuclear holocaust, biological warfare, global plagues, the evil deeds of terrorists, the stock market crashing, their jobs disappearing. Enter the death-dealing Diamond. Fear at one remove, that spine-tingling chill and thrill while one is safe and immune, allows catharsis, feels positively delicious.

If the idea of the Hope's supernatural powers began in the imagination of a roving Parisian reporter in 1909, it was only in America that the myth, unhooded, really soared and plummeted to prey, released by the likes of May Yohe, H. L. Gates, Pierre Cartier, Evalyn Walsh McLean, Harry Winston, legions of journalists, and a few Smithsonian scientists, including at least one secretary and one gem curator.

Along the way a strange thing happened. What began in 1909 Paris as a joke, an embroidery, a tease, a column filler, gained ground and credence. The public began to do what worshiping Hindus did long ago when they looked at Siva's blue omnipotent eye. People in the most modern country in the world began to believe in the supernatural powers of one small blue Diamond. Who knows if the curse is real? Who cares? The story is real enough and substantial enough to stimulate one's imagination and be tossed about there like a hot coal. While one's rational mind proceeds straight ahead on a sidewalk, obeying signals and ignoring dark alleys, imagination skitters like a blown leaf, disappears down rabbit holes with Alice. "At the same time that we are earnest to explore and learn all things," Henry David Thoreau wrote in *Walden*, "we require that all things be mysterious and unexplorable." Our brains aren't programmed for logic; we've mastered it, but we keep slipping out of school straight back into the murk of superstition. Its mystery is the fifth reason why people love the Diamond.

In a culture that worships celebrities the way Indians worshiped Siva, the Hope has become a star in its own right. It has appeared many times on television screens, always with the emphasis on its malevolence. *The Legendary Curse of the Hope Diamond* was presented on national television on March 27, 1975, with Bradford Dillman and Samantha Eggar playing Ned and Evalyn McLean and with Rod Serling as narrator. Americans who learned that Serling, age fifty, died after open-heart surgery less than six months later got an extra chill down the spine. *The Curse of the Hope Diamond*, part of a series called *Ancient Mysteries*, aired on the Arts and Entertainment channel on March 6, 1997, and was followed there by *Treasure! Secrets of the Hope Diamond* on February 1, 1998. When, for the Learning Channel, K and T Productions filmed *Famous Diamonds* and included a clip from George Kleine's 1921 silent movie, the Hope got the lead story. While James Cameron was directing the 1997 feature film *Titanic*, he admitted that in the scene where the heroine, in old age, throws her necklace of one big blue diamond encircled by white ones into the sea, he was inspired by the Hope but increased its sentimental quotient by making it heart shaped, not oval—probably unaware that in doing so, he was merely turning the clock back to 1673, when Pitau had cut it into a heart for Louis XIV.

Some billion years ago, under the Indian plateau, the miracle now bearing the name Hope was born, surfaced, moved through landscape and mindscape with its own ambiguity, both solid and insubstantial, object and wish, matter and myth. Rub one reflecting Diamond against one reflecting mind and magic happens. This gem is able endlessly to reinvent itself: the ultimate chameleon and arcanum, Aladdin's lamp and philosopher's stone.

Jean-Baptiste Tavernier wrenched it from the Indian world of wonder and worship into one where coins counted, quill pens scratched columns of figures, and the concern for net profit was never absent. The Sun King looked for glory in its small blue globe. Louis XV matched it to heroic myth and diminished in comparison. Revolution's blood tide swept it all the way to England, where Philip Hope rescued and adored it. Two later Hopes, Henry Thomas and Lord Francis, demeaned it to the level of farce, while May Yohe led the American rush to superstition with a manufactured curse. Evalyn Walsh McLean kept the Diamond hopping, hoping it would keep her center stage. Harry Winston played Svengali, whip-cracking trainer, and tender lover by turns. Finally, the American people claimed it, by virtue of their national mythology, as irrevocably theirs.

Each morning, the Diamond rises slowly, shines and rotates on its sky-blue surround, descends at dusk. It keeps its own counsel, twinkles mutely, changes dull lives to gold. It is a small object caught fast by science, cataloged and confined. But in the wide world on the other side of the glass, in the million minds it sets alight, its real life goes on.

BIBLIOGRAPHY

1: NATURE

Balfour, Ian. *Famous Diamonds*. London: William Collins, 1987.

Ball, Sydney H. *A Roman Book of Precious Stones*. Los Angeles: Gemological Institute of America, 1950.

Blakey, George G. *The Diamond*. New York: Paddington Press, 1977.

Bruton, Eric. *Diamonds*. Radnor: Chilton Book Company, 1978.

Buchan, James. *Frozen Desire: The Meaning of Money*. New York: Farrar Straus Giroux, 1997.

Cattelle, Wallis Richard. *Precious Stones*. Philadelphia: J. B. Lippincott Company, 1903.

Chopra, Pran. *History of South India*. Vol. III. New Delhi: S. Chand & Company, 1979.

Copeland, Lawrence L. *Diamonds . . . Famous, Notable and Unique*. Santa Monica: Gemological Institute of America, 1966.

Cotterell, Arthur, ed. *The Encyclopedia of Ancient Civilizations*. London: Penguin Books, 1980.

Desautels, Paul E. *Treasures in the Smithsonian: The Gem Collection*. Washington: Smithsonian Institution Press, 1979.

Dickinson, Joan Younger. *The Book of Diamonds: Their History and Romance from Ancient India to Modern Times*. New York: Bonanza Books, 1965.

Dubois, J. A. Abbé. *Hindu Manners, Customs and Ceremonies*. 2 vols. Oxford: Clarendon Press, 1906.

Eck, Diana L. *Darsan: Seeing the Divine Image in India*. New York: Columbia University Press, 1981.

Edwardes, Michael. *Everyday Life in Early India*. London: B. T. Batsford Ltd., 1969.

———. *A History of India from the Earliest Times to the Present Day*. London: Thames and Hudson, 1961.

Emanuel, Harry. *Diamonds and Precious Stones*. New York: G. P. Putnam's Sons, 1873.

Evans, Joan. *Magical Jewels of the Middle Ages and the Renaissance, Particularly in England*. New York: Dover Publications, 1976.

Gaal, Robert A. P., ed. *The Diamond Dictionary*. Santa Monica: Gemological Institute of America, 1977.

Gangoly, O. C. *South Indian Bronzes*. Calcutta: Nababharat Publishers, 1978.

Gaston, Anne-Marie. *Siva in Dance, Myth and Iconography*. Delhi: Oxford University Press, 1982.

Giard, Maurice E. *Les Diamants célèbres*. Besançon: Société d'Éditions Millot et Cie, n.d.

Green, Timothy. *The World of Diamonds*. London: Weidenfeld and Nicolson, 1981.

Hurlbut, Cornelius S. Jr. *Minerals and Man*. New York: Random House, 1970.

Koskoff, David E. *The Diamond World*. New York: Harper & Row, 1981.

Knappert, Jan. *Indian Mythology*. London: Aquarian Press, 1991.

Kramrisch, Stella. *The Presence of Siva*. Princeton: Princeton University Press, 1981.

Kunz, George Frederick. *The Curious Lore of Precious Stones*. New York: Halcyon House, 1938.

Legrand, Jacques. *Diamonds: Myth, Magic and Reality*. New York: Crown Publishers, 1980.

Lenzen, Dr. Godehard. *The History of Diamond Production and the Diamond Trade*. Translated from German by F. Bradley. London: Barrie and Jenkins, 1970.

Mabbett, I. W. *A Short History of India*. Melbourne: Cassell, 1968.

Mawe, J. *A Treatise on Diamonds and Precious Stones*. London: Printed for and sold by the author, 1823.

McCarthy, James Remington. *Fire in the Earth: The Story of Diamonds*. New York: Harper & Brothers, 1942.

Metz, Rudolph. *Precious Stones and Other Crystals*. New York: Viking Press, 1965.

Mitchell, A. G. *Hindu Gods and Goddesses*. London: Her Majesty's Stationery Office, 1982.

Monnickendam, A. *Secrets of the Diamond*. London: Frederick Muller Ltd., 1941.

Narasimhan, Chakravarthi V. *The Mahabharata: An English Version Based on Selected Verses*. New York: Columbia University Press, 1965.

O'Donoghue, Michael. *Gemstones*. New York: Chapman and Hall, 1988.

O'Flaherty, Wendy Doniger. *Asceticism and Eroticism in the Mythology of Siva*. London: Oxford University Press, 1973.

―――. *Siva. The Erotic Ascetic*. Oxford: Oxford University Press, 1973.

Oman, John Campbell. *Cults, Customs and Superstitions of India*. Delhi: Vishal Publishers, 1972.

O'Neil, Paul. *Gemstones*. Alexandria: Time-Life Books, 1983.

Piggott, Stuart. *Prehistoric India to 1000 B.C.* London: Cassell, 1951.

Pillai, M. Arjunan. *Ancient Indian History*. New Delhi: Ashish Publishing House, 1988.

Post, Jeffrey E. *The National Gem Collection. National Museum of Natural History, Smithsonian Institution*. New York: Harry N. Abrams, Inc., 1997.

Randhawa, Mohinder Singh, and Doris Schrier Randhawa. *Indian Sculpture: The Scene, Themes and Legends*. Bombay: Vakils, Feffer & Simons, 1985.

Sastri, Nilakanta K. A. *Foreign Notices of South India*. Madras: University of Madras, 1972.

———. *A History of South India*. Madras: Oxford University Press, 1976.

Schumann, Walter. *Gemstones of the World*. New York: Sterling Publishing Co., n.d.

Shipley, Robert M. *Famous Diamonds of the World*. Los Angeles: Gemological Institute of America, 1955.

Streeter, Edwin W. *Precious Stones and Gems*. London: George Bell and Sons, 5th ed., 1892.

———. *The Great Diamonds of the World*. Ann Arbor: Gryphon Books, 1971.

Twining, Lord [Edward Francis]. *A History of the Crown Jewels of Europe*. London: B. T. Batsford Ltd., 1960.

Voillot, Patrick. *Diamonds and Precious Stones*. London: Thames and Hudson, 1998.

Walker, David E. *Adventure in Diamonds*. London: Evans Brothers, 1962.

Webster, Robert. *Gems: Their Sources, Descriptions and Identification*. Oxford: Butterworth-Heinemann Ltd., 1994.

White, David Gordon. *The Alchemical Body. Siddha Traditions in Medieval India*. Chicago: University of Chicago Press, 1996.

Williams, Gardner F. *The Diamond Mines of South Africa*. New York: Macmillan Company, 1902.

Wilson, A. N. *Diamonds from Birth to Eternity*. Santa Monica: Gemological Institute of America, 1982.

Wodiska, Julius. *A Book of Precious Stones*. New York: G. P. Putnam's Sons, 1909.

Zimmer, Heinrich. *Myths and Symbols in Indian Art and Civilization*. Princeton: Princeton University Press, 1972.

Zucker, Benjamin. *How to Invest in Gems*. New York: Quadrangle, 1976.

2: MONEY

Basham, A. L. *A Cultural History of India*. Oxford: Clarendon Press, 1975.

Bayle, Pierre. *The Dictionary Historical and Critical of Mr. Peter Bayle*. 2d ed. Vol. V. London: Printed for D. Midwinter et al., 1738.

Bernier, Francis. *Travels in the Mogul Empire*. Translated by Irving Brock. London: William Pickering, 1826.

Biographie Universelle. Vol. XLI. Paris: Chez Madame Desplaces, n.d.

Boileau-Déspréaux, Nicolas. *Oeuvres Complètes*. Paris: Editions Gallimard, 1966.

Bonnaffé, Edmond. *Dictionnaire des Amateurs français au XVIIe siècle*. New York: Burt Franklin, 1969.

Brossette, Claude. *Correspondance entre Boileau-Déspréaux et Brossette*. Paris: J. Techener, 1858.

Bussy, Roger de Rabutin, Comte de. *Correspondance de Roger de Rabutin, Comte de Bussy*. Vols. I and II. Paris: Charpentier, 1858.

Chardin, Sir John. *Sir John Chardin's Travels in Persia*. London: The Argonaut Press, 1927.

Forster, E. M. *The Hill of Devi and Other Indian Writings*. London: Edward Arnold, 1983.

Della Valle, Pietro. *The Pilgrim: The Travels of Pietro Della Valle*. George Bull, trans. London: Hutchinson, 1989.

Dwyer, Helen and Barry, ed. *Index Biographique Francais for Archives Biographique* (microfiche). London: K. G. Saur, 1993.

Fryer, John. *A New Account of East India and Persia: Being Nine Years' Travels 1672–1681*. London: Hakluyt Society, 1909–15.

Golant, William. *The Long Afternoon: British India 1601–1947*. New York: St. Martin's Press, 1975.

Haag, Eugène and Émile. *La France Protestante*. Vols. 2 and 4. Paris: Librairie Fischbacher, 1884.

Haig, Lt. Col. Sir Wolseley, ed. *The Cambridge History of India*. Vol. III. Cambridge: Cambridge University Press, 1928.

Hoefer [Johann Christian Ferdinand]. *Nouvelle Biographie générale depuis les temps les plus reculés jusqu'a 1850–60*. Vols. 21 and 43. Copenhagen: Villadsen & Christensen, 1964.

Jal, Auguste. *Dictionnaire critique de biographie et d'histoire*. Vol. II. Geneva: Slatkine Reprints, 1970.

Kincaid, Dennis. *British Social Life in India 1608–1937*. Port Washington: Kennikat Press, 1971.

Linschoten, Jan Huygen Van. *Early Travels in India*. Calcutta: Englishman Press, 1864.

———. *The Voyage of John Huygen Van Linschoten to the East Indies*. New York: Burt Franklin, 1970.

Mason, Philip. *The Men Who Ruled India*. New York: W. W. Norton & Company, 1985.

Meen, V. B., and A. D. Tushingham. *Crown Jewels of Iran*. Toronto: University of Toronto Press, 1968.

Moreland, W. H. *From Akbar to Aurangzeb: A Study in Indian Economic History*. London: Macmillan and Company, 1923.

———. *Peter Floris, His Voyage to the East Indies in the Globe 1611–1615*. London: The Hakluyt Society, 1934.

———. *Relations of Golconda in the Early XVII Century*. London: The Hakluyt Society, 1931.

Moule, A. C., and Paul Pelliot. *Marco Polo: The Description of the World*. London: George Routledge & Sons, 1938.

Patch, Susanne Steinem. *Blue Mystery: The Story of the Hope Diamond*. Washington: Smithsonian Institution, 1976. 2d ed., 1999, in association with Harry N. Abrams, Inc.

Polo Marco, *The Book of Ser Marco Polo*. Sir Henry Yule, ed. 2 vols. London: John Murray, 1903.

Sainte-Beuve, C. A. *Portraits of the Seventeenth Century, Historic and Literary*. New York: Frederick Ungar Publishing, 1964.

Sherwani, H. K., ed. *History of Mediaeval Deccan 1295–1724*. Hyderabad: Government of Andhra Pradesh, 1973.

Tavernier, Jean-Baptiste. *Travels in India*. Translated from the original French edition of 1676 by V. Ball. 2 vols. London: Macmillan and Company, 1889.

———. *Travels in India*. Introduction by W. Crooke, based on Charles Joret's *J-B Tavernier* (1886). 2 vols. Oxford: Oxford University Press, 1925.

Wheeler, J. Talboys. *Early Records of British India: A History of the English Settlements in India*. London: Curzon Press, 1972.

———. *The History of India from the Earliest Ages*. 5 vols. London: N. Trubner & Co., 1869.

3: GLORY

Aldington, Richard, ed. *Letters of Madame de Sévigné*. New York: E. P. Dutton, 1937.

Ashley, Maurice. *Louis XIV and the Greatness of France*. London: English Universities Press, 1966.

Auchincloss, Louis. *False Dawn: Women in the Age of the Sun King*. New York: Anchor Press, 1984.

Barker, Nancy Nichols. *Brother to the Sun King*. Baltimore: Johns Hopkins University Press, 1989.

Bernard, Leon. *The Emerging City: Paris in the Age of Louis XIV*. Durham: Duke University Press, 1970.

Bernier, Olivier. *Louis XIV: A Royal Life*. New York: Doubleday, 1987.

Burke, Peter. *The Fabrication of Louis XIV*. New Haven: Yale University Press, 1992.

Caylus, Madame de. *Souvenirs de Madame de Caylus*. Paris: J. Techener, 1860.

Church, William F. *The Greatness of Louis XIV: Myth or Reality?* Boston: D. C. Heath and Company, 1959.

Cronin, Vincent. *Louis XIV*. London: Collins Harvill, 1964.

Dangeau, Philippe de Courcillon, Marquis de. *Journal de Marquis de Dangeau*. Vols. I, VI and XVI. Paris: Firmin Didot Frères, 1854.

Dumas, Alexandre. *Louis XIV et Son Siècle*. Paris: Chez J. B. Fellens, 1845.

———. *Louise de la Vallière*. Oxford: Oxford University Press, 1995.

Elliott, Charles. *Princesse of Versailles: The Life of Marie Adelaide of Savoy*. New York: Ticknor & Fields, 1992.

Evelyn, John. *The Diary of John Evelyn*. E. S. de Beer, ed. London: Oxford University Press, 1959.

Farmer, James Eugene. *Versailles and the Court Under Louis XIV*. London: Eveleigh Nash, 1906.

Gaxotte, Pierre. *The Age of Louis XIV*. Michael Shaw, trans. New York: The Macmillan Company, 1970.

Grunfeld, Frederic. *The French Kings*. Chicago: Stonehenge Press, 1982.

Haldane, Charlotte. *Madame de Maintenon*. Indianapolis: Bobbs-Merrill Company, 1970.

Hatton, Ragnhild. *Louis XIV and His World*. London: Thames and Hudson, 1972.

Kroll, Maria, ed. and trans. *Letters from Liselotte*. London: Victor Gollancz, 1970.

Lair, Jules. *Louise de la Vallière and the Early Life of Louis XIV*. London: Hutchinson & Co., n.d.

Lewis, W. H. *The Splendid Century*. New York: William Morrow and Company, 1953.

Louis XIV. *A King's Lessons in Statecraft: Louis XIV, Letters to His Heirs*. Herbert Wilson, trans. London: T. Fisher Unwin, 1924.

Mongredien, Georges. *La Vie Privée de Louis XIV*. Paris: Librairie Hachette, 1938.

———. *La Vie Quotidienne Sous Louis XIV*. Paris: Librairie Hachette, 1948.

Motteville, Madame de. *Memoirs of Madame de Motteville on Anne of Austria and Her Court*. Katherine Prescott-Wormley, trans. Boston: Hardy, Pratt & Company, 1902.

Norton, Lucy. *First Lady of Versailles*. London: Hamish Hamilton, 1978.

———. ed. and trans. *Historical Memoirs of the Duc de Saint-Simon*. Vol. I (1691–1709) and II (1710–1715). London: Hamish Hamilton, 1967.

————. *Saint-Simon at Versailles*. London: Hamish Hamilton, 1958.

————. *The Sun King and His Loves*. London: Hamish Hamilton, 1983.

Ogg, David. *Louis XIV*. London: Oxford University Press, 1933.

Prescott-Wormley, Katherine, ed. *The Correspondence of Madame, Princesse Palatine, of Marie-Adélaide de Savoie, Duchesse de Bourgogne and of Madame de Maintenon*. Boston: Hardy, Pratt & Company, 1902.

Prince Michael of Greece. *Louis XIV: The Other Side of the Sun*. London: Orbis Publishing, 1979.

Ranum, Orest and Patricia, ed. *The Century of Louis XIV*. New York: Macmillan, 1972.

Richardson, Joanna. *Louis XIV*. London: Weidenfeld and Nicolson, 1973.

Rubin, David Lee, ed. *Sun King: The Ascendancy of French Culture during the Reign of Louis XIV*. Washington: Folger Books, 1992.

Saint-Germain, Jacques. *Louis XIV. Secret*. Paris: Librairie Hachette, 1970.

Saint-Maurice, Marquis de. *Lettres sur la Cour de Louis XIV, 1667–1670*. Paris: Calmann-Lévy, 1910.

Smith, David L. *Louis XIV*. Cambridge: Cambridge University Press, 1992.

Sourches, Louis François Bouchet, Marquis de. *Mémoires du Marquis de Sourches*. Vol. I. Paris: Librairie Hachette, 1882.

Stevenson, Gertrude Scott, trans. and ed. *The Letters of Madame*. 2 vols. New York: D. Appleton and Company, 1924.

Voltaire [Jean François Marie Arouet de]. *The Age of Louis XIV*. Martyn P. Pollack, trans. London: J. M. Dent & Sons Ltd., 1926.

Wolf, John B., ed. *Louis XIV: A Profile*. New York: Hill and Wang, 1972.

4: SMALL THINGS

Argenson, René-Louis de Voyer, Marquis d'. *Journals and Memoirs of the Marquis d'Argenson*. Katherine Prescott-Wormeley, trans. 2 vols. Boston: Hardy, Pratt & Company, 1902.

Barbier, Edmond Jean François. *Chronique de la Régence et du Règne de Louis XV*. Vols. I and V. Paris: Charpentier, 1857.

————. *Journal d'un Bourgeois de Paris sous le Règne de Louis XV*. Paris: Union Générale d'Éditions, 1963.

Barry, Jeanne Bécu, Comtesse du. *Memoirs of Madame du Barri*. H. T. Riley, trans. 4 vols. London: H. S. Nichols, 1896.

Bernis, Cardinal de. *Memoirs and Letters of Cardinal de Bernis*. Katherine Prescott Wormeley, trans. 2 vols. Boston: Hardy, Pratt & Company, 1902.

Campardon, Émile. *Madame de Pompadour et La Cour de Louis XV*. Paris: Henri Plon, 1867.

Casanova, Jacques de Seingalt. *The Memoirs of Jacques C. de Seingalt*. Arthur Machen, trans. Vols. I to IV. New York: G. P. Putnam's Sons, n.d.

Duclos, Charles Pinot. *Secret Memoirs of the Regency, the Minority of Louis XV*. New York: Sturgis & Walton Company, 1910.

Evans, Joan. *A History of Jewellery, 1100–1870*. Boston: Boston Book and Art, 1970.

Ford, Franklin L. *Robe and Sword*. Cambridge: Harvard University Press, 1962.

Franklyn, Julian, and John Tanner. *An Encyclopaedic Dictionary of Heraldry*. Oxford: Pergamon Press, 1970.

Gaxotte, Pierre. *Louis the Fifteenth and His Times*. J. Lewis May, trans. London: Jonathan Cape, 1934.

Gooch, G. P. *Louis XV. The Monarchy in Decline*. London: Longmans, 1956.

Levron, Jacques. *Pompadour*. London: George Allen and Unwin, 1963.

Lewis, W. S. *Horace Walpole's Correspondence*. Vols. 31–38. New Haven: Yale University Press, 1937–83.

Loche, Renée. *Catalogue Raisonné des Peintures et Pastels de l'École Française XVI, XVII and XVIII Siècles*. Genève: Éditions Slatkine, 1996.

Lough, John. *An Introduction to Eighteenth Century France*. London: Longmans, 1960.

Luynes, Duc de. *Mémoires sur la Cour de Louis XV*. Paris: Firmin Didot Frères, 1862.

Mitford, Nancy. *Madame de Pompadour*. London: Hamish Hamilton, 1954.

Nolhac, Pierre de. *La Vie et l'Oeuvre de Maurice Quentin de La Tour*. Paris: L'Édition d'Art H. Piazza, 1930.

Northumberland, First Duchess of. *The Diaries of a Duchess*. New York: George H. Doran Company, n.d.

Norton, Lucy, ed. and trans. *Historical Memoirs of the Duc de Saint-Simon*. Vol. III (1715–1723). London: Hamish Hamilton, 1972.

Perkins, James Breck. *France Under Louis XV*. 2 vols. Boston: Houghton, Mifflin and Company, 1897.

Stoeckl, Agnes de. *Mistress of Versailles: The Life of Madame du Barry*. London: John Murray, 1966.

Walpole, Horace. *Letters of Horace Walpole*. Charles Duke Yonge, ed. 2 vols. London: T. Fisher Unwin, 1890.

Williams, H. Noel. *Madame de Pompadour*. London: Harper & Brothers, 1902.

5: BURGLARY

Bapst, Germain. *Histoire des Joyaux de la Couronne de France*. (Book VIII, chapters 1–7 have full description of the 1792 robbery of Garde-meuble.) Paris: Librairie Hachette, 1889.

Behrens, C. B. A. *The Ancien Régime*. London: Thames and Hudson, 1967.

Bernier, Olivier. *Secrets of Marie Antoinette*. New York: Doubleday, 1985.

———. *Words of Fire, Deeds of Blood*. Boston: Little Brown, 1989.

Carlyle, Thomas. *The French Revolution*. London: J. M. Dent & Sons, 1933.

Crankshaw, Edward. *Letters from Mercy, and from Marie Antoinette to Empress Maria Theresa*. London: Longmans, 1969.

Cronin, Vincent. *Louis and Antoinette*. London: Collins Harvill, 1989.

Devonshire, Georgiana, Duchess of. *Georgiana*. Earl of Bessborough, ed. London: John Murray, 1955.

Erickson, Carolly. *To the Scaffold: The Life of Marie Antoinette*. New York: William Morrow and Company, 1991.

Favier, Jean, ed. *Chronicle of the French Revolution*. London: Chronicle Communications Ltd., 1989.

Funck-Brentano, Frantz. *The Diamond Necklace*. H. Sutherland Edwards, trans. London: John Macqueen, 1901.

Gaxotte, Pierre. *The French Revolution*. New York: Charles Scribner's Sons, 1932.

Lamballe, Princess. *Secret Memoirs of Princess Lamballe*. Akron: St. Dunstan Society, 1901.

Lewis, Gwynne. *Life in Revolutionary France*. London: B.T. Batsford, 1972.

Loomis, Stanley. *The Fatal Friendship*. New York: Doubleday, 1972.

Lough, John. *France on the Eve of Revolution*. Chicago: Lyceum Books, 1987.

Masters, Brian. *Georgiana, Duchess of Devonshire*. London: Hamish Hamilton, 1981.

Mercy-Argenteau, Comte de. *Correspondance Secrète du Comte de Mercy-Argenteau avec l'Empereur Joseph II et le Prince de Kaunitz*. 2 vols. Paris: Imprimerie Nationale, 1889.

Morel, Bernard. *Les Joyaux de la Couronne de France*. Antwerp: Fonds Mercator, 1988.

Morris, Gouverneur. *A Diary of the French Revolution*. 2 vols. Boston: Houghton Mifflin, 1939.

Palacios, Alvar Gonzalez. *The Age of Louis XVI*. London: Paul Hamlyn, 1969.

Schama, Simon. *Citizens: A Chronicle of the French Revolution*. New York: Random House, Vintage Books, 1990.

Stuart, Dorothy Margaret. *Dearest Bess*. London: Methuen & Co., 1955.

[Twiss, Richard]. *A Trip to Paris in July and August, 1792*. London: Minerva Press, 1793.

Young, Arthur. *Travels in France and Italy During the Years 1787, 1788 and 1789*. London: J. M. Dent & Sons, n.d.

6: BEAUTY

Magazines and Newspapers:
Blackwood's Magazine
Chambers's Edinburgh Journal
Gentleman's Magazine
Illustrated London News
Lapidary Journal
Quarterly Review
Saturday Evening Post

Books:
Alexander, Boyd, trans. and ed. *Life at Fonthill 1807–1822*. London: Rupert Hart-Davis, 1957.

Allen, Thomas. *A New and Complete History of the Counties of Surrey & Sussex*. Vol. II. London: Isaac Hinton, 1829.

Anon., *The Notebooks of a Spinster Lady 1878–1903*. London: Cassell and Company, 1919.

Arbuthnot, Harriet. *The Journal of Mrs. Arbuthnot 1820–1832*. Vol. I. London: Macmillan and Company, 1950.

Ashby, Thomas. "Thomas Jenkins in Rome" in *Papers of the British School at Rome*. London: Macmillan and Company, 1913.

Aspinall, A., ed. *The Correspondence of George, Prince of Wales 1770–1812*. London: Cassell, 1967.

Bahlman, Dudley, ed. *The Diary of Sir Edward Walter Hamilton*. 2 vols. Oxford: Clarendon Press, 1972.

Battiscombe, Georgina. *Mrs. Gladstone, the Portrait of a Marriage.* London: Constable, 1956.

Baumgarten, Sandor. *Le Crépuscule Néo-Classique: Thomas Hope.* Paris: Didier, 1958.

Bence-Jones, Mark. *Burke's Guide to Country Houses.* Vol. I. Ireland. London: Burke's Peerage Ltd., 1978.

Besant, Sir Walter. *London in the Nineteenth Century.* London: Adam & Charles Black, 1909.

Bickley, Francis, ed. *The Diaries of Sylvester Douglas.* London: Constable & Company, 1928.

Blake, Robert. *Disraeli.* London: Eyre & Spottiswoode, 1966.

Boase, Frederic. *Modern English Biography.* Vols. I and II. London: Frank Cass & Co. 1965.

Bradford, Sarah. *Disraeli.* London: Weidenfeld and Nicolson, 1982.

Buist, Marten G. *At Spes Non Fracta, Hope & Co. 1770–1815.* The Hague: Martinus Nijhoff, 1974.

Burke, Sir Bernard. *A Genealogical and Heraldic Dictionary of the Peerage and Baronetage . . .* London: Harrison and Sons, 1904.

Chancellor, E. Beresford. *Life in Regency and Early Victorian Times.* London: B. T. Batsford, n.d.

Clayden, P. W. *The Early Life of Samuel Rogers.* London: Smith, Elder & Co., 1887.

Colvin, Christina, ed. *Maria Edgeworth: Letters from England 1813–1844.* Oxford: Clarendon Press, 1971.

Echard, William E., ed. *Historical Dictionary of the French Second Empire 1852–1870.* Westport: Greenwood Press, 1985.

Edgcumbe, Richard, ed. *The Diary of Frances Lady Shelley 1818–1873.* London: John Murray, 1913.

Fitzmaurice, Lord Edmond. *The Life of Granville George Leveson Gower, Second Earl Granville.* 2 vols. London: Longmans, Green, 1905.

Fothergill, Brian. *Sir William Hamilton, Envoy Extraordinary.* New York: Harcourt, Brace & World, 1969.

Fremantle, A., ed. *The Wynne Diaries.* 2 vols. London: Oxford University Press, 1935.

Fulford, Roger, ed. *Dearest Child: Letters Between Queen Victoria and the Princess Royal.* London: Evans Brothers, 1964.

Garlick, Kenneth, and Angus Macintyre. *The Diary of Joseph Farrington.* 16 vols. New Haven: Yale University Press, 1978.

Gronow, Captain [Rees Howell]. *The Reminiscences and Recollections of Captain Gronow . . . 1810–1860.* London: John C. Nimmo, 1900.

Gunn, J. A. W., John Matthews, Donald M. Schurman, and M. G. Wiebe. *Benjamin Disraeli Letters.* 6 vols. Toronto: University of Toronto Press, 1982.

Hale, J. R., ed. *The Italian Journal of Samuel Rogers.* London: Faber and Faber, 1956.

Hare, Augustus, ed. *The Life and Letters of Maria Edgeworth.* 2 vols. London: Edward Arnold, 1894.

Hewett, Osbert Wyndham. *Strawberry Fair. A Biography of Frances, Countess Waldegrave 1821–1879.* London: John Murray, 1956.

Hibbert, Christopher. *George IV, Prince of Wales.* London: Longman, 1972.

Hope, Thomas. *Anastasius.* 2 vols. London: John Murray, 1836.

Ilchester, Earl of, ed. *Elizabeth, Lady Holland to Her Son 1821–1845*. London: John Murray, 1946.

———. *The Journal of the Hon. Henry Edward Fox 1818–1830*. London: Thornton Butterworth, 1923.

Ireland, Samuel. *A Picturesque Tour through Holland, Brabant and Part of France. Made in the Autumn of 1789*. Vol. I. London: T. and L. Egerton, 1799.

Irving, Pierre M. *The Life and Letters of Washington Irving*. Vol. I. London: H. G. Bohn, 1864.

Kennedy, A. L., ed. *My Dear Duchess: Social and Political Letters to the Duchess of Manchester. 1858–1869*. London: John Murray, 1956.

Law, Henry William and Irene. *The Book of the Beresford Hopes*. London: Heath Cranton Limited, 1925.

Less-Milne, James. *William Beckford*. London: Compton Russell, 1976.

L'Estrange, Rev. A. G. *The Friendships of Mary Russell Mitford*. Vol. II. London: Hurst and Blackett, 1882.

Lewis, Lady Theresa, ed. *Extracts of the Journals and Correspondence of Miss Berry*. London: Longmans, Green, 1865.

Livingstone, Peadar. *The Monaghan Story*. Enniskillen: Clogher Historical Society, 1980.

Marlow, Joyce. *The Oak and the Ivy: An Intimate Biography of William and Catherine Gladstone*. Garden City: Doubleday, 1977.

Masterman, Lucy, ed. *Mary Gladstone (Mrs. Drew), Her Diaries and Letters*. New York: E. P. Dutton, 1930.

Matthew, H. C. G., ed. *The Gladstone Diaries*. Vols. V, IX, X, and XI. Oxford: Clarendon Press, 1978.

Melville, Lewis. *The Life and Letters of William Beckford of Fonthill*. London: William Heinemann, 1910.

Meynell, Wilfrid. *Benjamin Disraeli*. London: Hutchinson & Co., 1903.

Monypenny, William Flavelle. *The Life of Benjamin Disraeli. Earl of Beaconsfield*. Vols. I, II and VI. New York: Macmillan, 1912.

Morris, Anne Cary, ed. *Diary and Letters of Gouverneur Morris*. 2 vols. London: Kegan Paul, 1889.

Mowl, Timothy. *William Beckford*. London: John Murray, 1998.

Munsell, F. Darrell. *The Unfortunate Duke: Henry Pelham, Fifth Duke of Newcastle 1811–1864*. Columbia: University of Missouri Press, 1985.

Newmann, Philipp. *The Diary of Philipp von Neumann 1819–1850*. London: Philip Allan, 1928.

Palmer, Roundell, Earl of Selborne. *Memorials. Part I. Family and Personal. 1766–1865*. 2 vols. London: Macmillan and Company, 1896

Parker, Eric. *Highways and Byways in Surrey*. London: Macmillan and Company, 1921.

Pollock, Sir Frederick, ed. *Macready's Reminiscences, and Selections from His Diaries and Letters*. 2 vols. London: Macmillan and Company, 1875.

Priestley, J. B. *The Prince of Pleasure and His Regency 1811–20*. London: Heinemann, 1969.

Raikes, Thomas. *A Portion of the Journal Kept by Thomas Raikes, Esq. from 1831 to 1847*. London: Longman, Brown, 1858.

Redgrave, Samuel. *A Dictionary of Artists of the English School*. Bath: Kingsmead Reprints, 1970.

Ridley, Jasper. *Napoléon III and Eugénie*. London: Constable, 1979.

Russell, Lord John, ed. *Memoirs, Journals and Correspondence of Thomas Moore*. Vol. VII. London: Longman, Brown, 1853.

Smith, Goldwin. *Reminiscences*. New York: The Macmillan Company, 1910.

Strachey, Lytton, and Roger Fulford, ed. *The Greville Memoirs*. Vol. III. London: Macmillan and Company, 1938.

Surtees, Virginia. *A Beckford Inheritance: The Lady Lincoln Scandal*. London: Michael Russell, 1977.

———. *Charlotte Canning*. London: John Murray, 1975.

Swartz, Helen M. and Marvin, ed. *Disraeli's Reminiscences*. London: Hamish Hamilton, 1975.

Tomes, John. *Blue Guide to Holland*. London: A. & C. Black, 1987.

Vincent, J. R., ed. *Disraeli, Derby and the Conservative Party. Journals and Memoirs of Edward Henry, Lord Stanley*. Hassocks, Sussex: The Harvester Press, 1978.

Waagen, Dr. [Gustav Friedrich]. *Treasures of Art in Great Britain*. Vol. III. London: John Murray, 1854.

Watkin, David. *Thomas Hope and the New-Classical Idea*. London: John Murray, 1968.

Wheatley, Henry B. *London Past and Present*. Vols. I and II. London: John Murray, 1891.

Whibley, Charles. *Lord John Manners and His Friends*. Edinburgh: William Blackwood, 1925.

Young, G. M. *Victorian England*. London: Oxford University Press, 1963.

7: WANING HOPES

Magazines and Newspapers:
London *Times*
New York Times
Publishers Weekly

Books:
Altick, Richard D. *The Shows of London*. Cambridge: Belknap Press of Harvard University Press, 1978.

Archer, Rosemary, and James Fleming, ed. *Lady Anne Blunt. Journals and Correspondence 1878–1917*. Cheltenham: Alexander Heriot, 1986.

Cannadine, David. *The Decline and Fall of the British Aristocracy*. New Haven: Yale University Press, 1990.

Cowles, Virginia. *The Rothschilds: A Family of Fortune*. London: Weidenfeld and Nicolson, 1973.

Davis, Richard. *The English Rothschilds*. London: Collins, 1983.

Gates, H. L. *The Mystery of the Hope Diamond*. New York: International Copyright Bureau, 1921.

Goldschmidt, Arthur Jr. *A Concise History of the Middle East*. New York: Westview Press, 1979.

Haslip, Joan. *The Sultan: The Life of Abdul Hamid*. London: Cassell, 1958.

Horwitz, Rita, and Harriet Harrison. *The George Kleine Collection of Early Motion Pictures in the Library of Congress.* Washington: Library of Congress, 1980.

Hourani, Albert. *The Emergence of the Modern Middle East.* London: Macmillan, 1981.

Lees-Milne, James. *Harold Nicolson: A Biography.* Vol. I. London: Hamish Hamilton, 1987.

Mainwaring, Marion. *Mysteries of Paris: The Quest for Morton Fullerton.* Hanover, New Hampshire: University Press of New England, 2001.

Mander, Raymond, and Joe Mitchenson. *The Theatres of London.* London: Rupert Hart-Davis, 1963.

McCullagh, Francis. *The Fall of Abd-Ul-Hamid.* London: Methuen & Co., 1910.

Nicolson, Harold. *Good Behaviour.* London: Constable & Co., 1955.

Odell, George C. D. *Annals of the New York Stage.* New York: Columbia University Press, 1949.

Paget, Walpurga, Lady. *In My Tower.* London: Hutchinson & Co., n.d.

———. *The Linings of Life.* 2 vols. London: Hurst & Blackett, n.d.

Shaw, Bernard. *Our Theatres in the Nineties: His Weekly Criticisms for Saturday Review.* London: Constable & Co., 1954.

Warwick, Frances, Countess of. *Discretions.* New York: Charles Scribner Sons, 1931.

Wearing, J. P. *The London Stage 1890–1899.* Metuchen, New Jersey: Scarecrow Press, 1976.

Winstone, H. V. F. *The Illicit Adventure.* London: Jonathan Cape, 1982.

Wittlin, Alma. *Abdul Hamid: The Shadow of God.* London: John Lane, 1940.

8: ADDICTION

Manuscript Sources:
Papers of Evalyn Walsh McLean in Manuscript Collection of Library of Congress, Washington, D.C., General Correspondence. Containers Nos. 1 to 5; 15 to 19; 24; 52; 97 to 100; 104; 113 to 116.

Magazines and Newspapers:
Denver Colorado News
London *Times*
New York Times
Time
Vanity Fair
Washington Post
Washington Times-Herald

Books:
Adams, Samuel Hopkins. *Incredible Era: The Life and Times of Warren Gamaliel Harding.* Boston: Houghton Mifflin Company, 1939.

Anon., *The National Cyclopedia of American Biography.* New Jersey: James T. White, 1896.

———. *Who Was Who in America.* Chicago: Marquis Publications, 1966.

Anthony, Carl Sferrazza. *Florence Harding: The First Lady, the Jazz Age and the Death of America's Most Scandalous President.* New York: William Morrow and Company, 1998.

Beebe, Lucius. *The Big Spenders*. New York: Doubleday and Company, 1966.

Butt, Archibald. *Taft and Roosevelt: The Intimate Letters of Archie Butt. Military Aide*. Port Washington: Kennikat Press, 1971.

Cassini, Countess Marguerite. *Never a Dull Moment: The Memoirs of Countess Cassini*. New York: Harper & Brothers, 1956.

Daniels, Jonathan. *Washington Quadrille*. Garden City: Doubleday & Company, 1968.

Ferrell, Robert H. *The Strange Deaths of President Harding*. Columbia: University of Missouri Press, 1996.

Ford, Worthington Chauncey, ed. *Letters of Henry Adams (1892–1918)*. Boston: Houghton Mifflin Company, 1938.

Garraty, John A., and Mark C. Carnes, gen. ed. *American National Biography*. New York: Oxford University Press, 1999.

Green, Constance McLaughlin. *Washington, Capital City, 1879–1950*. Princeton: Princeton University Press, 1963.

Guiles, Fred Lawrence. *Marion Davies*. New York: McGraw-Hill, 1972.

Jacob, Kathryn Allamong. *Capital Elites: High Society in Washington, D.C., after the Civil War*. Washington: Smithsonian Institution Press, 1995.

Longworth, Alice Roosevelt. *Crowded Hours*. New York: Charles Scribner's Sons, 1933.

Lowry, Edward G. *Washington Close-Ups*. Boston: Houghton Mifflin Company, 1921.

McLean, Evalyn Walsh, with Boyden Sparkes. *Father Struck It Rich*. 2d ed. Ouray, Colorado: Bear Creek Publishing Co., 1981.

———. *Queen of Diamonds: The Fabled Legacy of Evalyn Walsh McLean*. An edition of *Father Struck It Rich* with Foreword by Joseph Gregory and Epilogue by Carol Ann Rapp. Franklin, Tennessee: Hillsboro Press, 2000.

Martin, Ralph G. *Cissy: The Extraordinary Life of Eleanor Medill Patterson*. New York: Simon and Schuster, 1979.

Miller, Frederic M., and Howard Gillette Jr. *Washington Seen: A Photographic History, 1875–1965*. Baltimore: the Johns Hopkins University Press, 1995.

Myers, Gustavus. *The History of the Great American Fortunes*. Chicago: Charles H. Kerr, 1911.

Nadelhoffer, Hans. *Cartier: Jewelers Extraordinary*. New York: Harry N. Abrams, 1984.

[Pearson, Drew, and Robert S. Allen]. *Washington Merry-Go-Round*. New York: Horace Liveright Inc., 1931.

Roberts, Chalmers McGeagh. *The Washington Post: The First 100 Years*. Boston: Houghton Mifflin Company, 1977.

Rudoe, Judy. *Cartier: 1900–1939*. New York: Harry N. Abrams and the Metropolitan Museum of Art, 1997.

Russell, Francis. *The Shadow of Blooming Grove*. New York: McGraw-Hill Book Company, 1968.

Simpson, William R. and Florence K., with Charles Samuels. *Hockshop*. New York: Random House, 1954.

Teichmann, Howard. *Alice: The Life and Times of Alice Roosevelt Longworth*. Inglewood Cliffs, New Jersey: Prentice-Hall, 1979.

Wright, William. *The Washington Game*. New York: E. P. Dutton & Co., 1974.

9: WIZARDRY

Magazines and Newspapers:
Lapidary Journal
Life
New York
New Yorker
New York Times
Time
Toronto Globe and Mail

Books:
Arnold, Thurman W. *Fair Fights and Foul: A Dissenting Lawyer's Life*. New York: Harcourt, Brace and World, 1951.

Green, Timothy. *The World of Diamonds*. London: Weidenfeld and Nicolson, 1981.

Gregory, Alexis. *Harry Winston: Rare Jewels of the World*. Paris: Assouline, 1998.

Harlow, George E., ed. *The Nature of Diamonds*. Cambridge: Cambridge University Press, 1998.

Koskoff, David E. *The Diamond World*. New York: Harper & Row, 1981.

Krashes, Laurence S., and Ronald Winston, ed. *Harry Winston: The Ultimate Jeweler*. New York and Santa Monica: Harry Winston and the Gemological Institute of America, 1984.

Wilson, A. N., ed. *International Diamond Annual*. Vol. I, 1971. Johannesburg: Diamond Annual (PTY) Ltd., n.d.

10: INSTITUTIONAL CARE

Magazines and Newspapers:
Esquire
Hobbies
Lapidary Journal
Life
National Geographic
Newsweek
New York Times
Science Newsletter
Smithsonian
Time
W

Books:
Lapham, Lewis H. *The Wish for Kings: Democracy at Bay*. New York: Grove Press, 1993.

Patch, Susanne Steinem. *Blue Mystery: The Story of the Hope Diamond*. Second edition. New York: Harry N. Abrams, Inc., 1999.

Post, Jeffrey E. *The National Gem Collection*. New York: Harry N. Abrams, Inc., 1997.

Robertson, James Oliver. *American Myth, American Reality*. New York: Hill & Wang, 1980.

ACKNOWLEDGMENTS

In the August 1997 issue of *Vanity Fair*, I read Gary Cohen's article on Evalyn Walsh McLean titled "The Lady and the Diamond." Having already written the life story of a famous old house, *Blenheim: Biography of a Palace*, I thought it might be fun to do one of a famous old gem called Hope and so tossed the article into my "Ideas for Books" file. It wasn't until January 1999 that I began research, working in the Robarts Library at the University of Toronto, the Metropolitan Toronto Reference Library, Toronto's Royal Ontario Museum library, and in the Manuscript Reading Room and Motion Picture and Television Reading Room of Washington's Library of Congress. In all these places, librarians were, as always, extremely helpful, ready to search the farthest reaches and go the extra mile. Much of the factual foundation for the Hope's story was laid by Susanne Steinem Patch's excellent little book *Blue Mystery: The Story of the Hope Diamond*. Its ninety pages made the first path through unexplored terrain, and without those clear signposts pointing me in all the right directions, I never could have written this book. I am also grateful for information garnered from Dr. Jeffrey E. Post, the Museum of Natural History's current Curator of the National Gem and Mineral Collection; from Bonnie Selfe of Cartier, New York and Eric Nussbaum of Cartier, Geneva, Director of the Art of Cartier Collection. Ronald Winston, Chairman of Harry

Winston, Inc., and Carrie Niese, Associate Manager of Communications there, responded to my queries efficiently and generously, with information, photographs, slides, and a book I cherish. I have a huge debt to my friend Hugh Brewster, Editorial Director of Madison Press. Hugh not only took time to read and criticize the manuscript; he offered wise counsel concerning publishers, agents, and matters financial, and was at my elbow with champagne when this good advice paid off. My son, Tim, also read the manuscript and vastly improved it. For all seven of my books he has been my best, if severest, critic.

As soon as I announce to friends that I'm starting a new book, they become eagle-eyed for useful material. For this book, Susan Huggard was particularly zealous, supplying a stream of relevant articles and books. Other friends who helped in various ways include Michael Pierson; Gerard Gauci; Professor Peter Clarke, Master of Trinity Hall College, Cambridge, and his wife Dr. Maria Tippett; Kathy and Chris Matthews; Byron Bellows; Inga Tallert; Shirley Mowbrays; and Leslea Macaulay.

Anne Collins, my gifted editor at Random House Canada, worked her magic on my book-in-the-rough, cutting and polishing it with great skill. I am also grateful to Peter Borland at Ballantine, U.S., for seeing the book's potential in its early form and for much help during its fashioning. Thank you to Alison Reid, who brought clarity and care to the task of copyediting. Finally, Jay Mandel, my brilliant agent at the William Morris Agency, worked hard on my behalf, with keen interest, caring support, and unfailing good humor.

PHOTO CREDITS

INDEX

Page numbers in *italics* refer to illustrations.

ABOUT THE AUTHOR

MARIAN FOWLER holds a Ph.D. in English literature from the University of Toronto and is the author of a number of books, including *Blenheim: Biography of a Palace, In a Gilded Cage: American Heiresses Who Married British Aristocrats,* and *The Way She Looks Tonight: Five Women of Style.* She lives in Toronto, Canada.